Sept 1954
TERRAVIEW $8.75
Public School

HEINA — *Emily Carr*

Reproduced by permission of the National Gallery, Ottawa.

SHINING SKIES

CANADIAN READING DEVELOPMENT SERIES

*Oh, what a glory doth this world put on
For him who, with a fervent heart, goes forth
Under the bright and glorious sky . . .*

—HENRY WADSWORTH LONGFELLOW

SHINING SKIES

Fred C. Biehl
J. Ranton McIntosh
Claude E. Lewis

Illustrated by Margaret Salisbury, Mabel Marshall
W. R. Stark and Louis Dobry

The Copp Clark Co. Limited

Toronto   Canada

CANADIAN READING DEVELOPMENT SERIES

General Editor — RANTON McINTOSH
Associate Editor — CLAUDE E. LEWIS

TITLE OF BOOKS IN THE SERIES

UP AND AWAY	— MARIAN D. JAMES
WIDE OPEN WINDOWS	— FRANKLIN L. BARRETT
ALL SAILS SET	— FRED C. BIEHL
HIGH FLIGHT	— F. L. BARRETT, CLAUDE E. LEWIS
SHINING SKIES	— F. C. BIEHL, CLAUDE E. LEWIS

Copyright 1952, by
THE COPP CLARK CO. LIMITED
TORONTO   CANADA

Printed by the Copp Clark Press

TABLE OF CONTENTS

Italicized titles indicate poetry
Asterisk (*) indicates Canadian author or artist

Heina *(colour plate)*   Emily Carr*   ii

Facing Our Problems

A Little Song of Life	Lizette Woodworth Reese	2
Kid Brother	Norman Katkov	2
Leisure	William Henry Davies	18
Double Play	Thelma Knoles	18
The Flood Gate *(colour plate)*	Homer Watson*	25
Rabble-Rouser	Rolland Upton	27
The Athenian Boys' Oath	Anonymous	32
To-Day	Thomas Carlyle	32
Out on a Limb	Louise Baker	33
Split Cherry Tree	Jesse Stuart	42
The Children's Song	Rudyard Kipling	55

Along Nature's Trails

The Unnamed Lake	Frederick George Scott*	58
Dream River	Marjorie L. C. Pickthall*	59
Runaway Bull	Kerry Wood*	60
Stupidity Street	Ralph Hodgson	66
The Snare	James Stephens	66
Black Pirate of the Peaks	Willis G. Craig	67
The Hawk	A. C. Benson	75
Ghost Cat	Roderick L. Haig-Brown*	75
Lone Wolf	Sir Charles G. D. Roberts*	85
The Palomino	Grace Noll Crowell	94
Maple Bloom	J. E. H. MacDonald*	94

Canadian Winter and Spring   *Bruce Hutchison**   95
Heat   *Archibald Lampman**   101

Around the World

Romance	W. J. Turner	104
The Homecoming of the Sheep	Francis Ledwidge	105
The Blue Flower	Josephine Blackstock	106
The Eagle	Alfred, Lord Tennyson	117
Out of Bounds	Theodore Acland Harper	117
Oxen Drinking (*colour plate*)	Horatio Walker*	123
To Iron-Founders and Others	Gordon Bottomley	139
On Strike	Richard Llewellyn	140
Old Grey Squirrel	Alfred Noyes	151
The Ice-Cart	W. W. Gibson	153
Balsa for Kon-Tiki	Thor Heyerdahl	154
The Ferry, Quebec (*colour plate*)	James W. Morrice*	157
The Christ of the Andes	Edwin Markham	173
The Parliament of Man	Alfred, Lord Tennyson	175
These Things Shall Be	John Addington Symonds	176

They Built a Nation

White Water	John Buchan*	178
The Axe Has Cut the Forest Down	Elizabeth Coatsworth	191
The Patriot	Nathaniel A. Benson*	192
Off Rivière du Loup	Duncan Campbell Scott*	213
The Great Days of Canadian Sail	F. C. Biehl*	214
The Flower-Fed Buffaloes	Vachel Lindsay	227
Hunting Trail of the Great Spirit	Elsie Park Gowan*	227
Canadian Achievement	His Royal Highness, the Duke of Edinburgh	234

Sun and Shadow

Nicholas Nye	Walter de la Mare	238
Tiny Tim	Mazo de la Roche*	239

The Song of the Sea Wind	Austin Dobson	249
The Death of the Hired Man	Robert Frost	250
Valley of the Devil River (colour plate)	Maurice G. Cullen*	255
Four Men and a Box	Leslie Gordon Barnard*	258
To a Bull-Dog	J. C. Squire	264
A Petticoat for Linda	Thomas Raddall*	267
At the Cedars	Duncan Campbell Scott*	282
The Listeners	Walter de la Mare	285
The Donkey	G. K. Chesterton	286

Laughing It Off

The Sinking of the *Mariposa Belle*	Stephen Leacock*	288
Village in the Laurentian Mountains (colour plate)	Clarence A. Gagnon*	289
He Was Seldom Surprised by His Horses	Kenneth C. Cragg*	297
The Height of the Ridiculous	Oliver Wendell Holmes	302
Mending the Clock	Sir James Matthew Barrie	304
The Tom-Cat	Don Marquis	310
Jabberwocky	Lewis Carroll	311
Mr. Pickwick on the Ice	Charles Dickens	313
Lucille	Robert Service*	319

Let Us Now Praise Famous Men

Escape	Winston S. Churchill	326
I Love All Beauteous Things	Robert Bridges	337
The Child is Father to the Man	Albert Schweitzer	338
Nancy Hanks	Rosemary Benét	344
How Abe Lincoln Paid for His Stockings	Edward Eggleston	345
"O Captain! My Captain!"	Walt Whitman	362
Sir William Osler	Leonard W. Brockington*	363
The Apology of Socrates	Plato	372

Men at Work

Duellists of the Deep	Edna Staebler*	378
The End of Winter (colour plate)	James Henderson*	387
The Shark	E. J. Pratt*	390
The Long Tradition	Walter Havighurst	391
Train at Night	Arthur S. Bourinot*	402
The Green Key to Sun Power	George H. Waltz, Jr.	403
Grain Elevators	James Sterling Ayars	410
Operation Subway	Alan M. Thomas, Jr.*	410
The Machine	Mary Elizabeth Colman*	416
A Thunderstorm	Archibald Lampman*	417
Forest Fire	Edna Davis Romig	418
The Taming of No. 3	Blair Fraser*	419
Reef and Rainbow (sculpture)	Elizabeth Wyn Wood*	421
On the Grasshopper and Cricket	John Keats	432

Long, Long Ago

Pygmalion and Galatea	Rannie B. Baker	434
Saul and David	The Bible	436
A Dissertation on Roast Pig	Charles Lamb	454
The Ballad of East and West	Rudyard Kipling	458
Gulliver Comes to Giantland	Jonathan Swift	463
Robinson Crusoe Meets His Man Friday	Daniel Defoe	471
How They Brought the Good News from Ghent to Aix	Robert Browning	479
Moses Goes to the Fair	Oliver Goldsmith	481
The Pied Piper of Hamelin	Robert Browning	484
What I Heard in the Apple Barrel	Robert Louis Stevenson	494
The Revenge	Alfred, Lord Tennyson	500

GLOSSARY	505
ACKNOWLEDGMENTS	516

Facing Our Problems

A LITTLE SONG OF LIFE

LIZETTE WOODWORTH REESE

Glad that I live am I,
    That the sky is blue;
Glad for the country lanes,
    And the fall of dew.

After the sun the rain,
    After the rain the sun;
This is the way of life,
    Till the work be done.

All that we need to do,
    Be we low or high,
Is to see that we grow
    Nearer the sky.

KID BROTHER

NORMAN KATKOV

When I came into the kitchen for breakfast, I could see Bobby through the open window, standing on the old porch with his back turned. I could see him standing quiet and absolutely still and waiting. I knew he was waiting, and I looked away to the sketch of the kitchen I'd drawn one day with Mother at the stove. She'd framed it and hung it above the radiator. It was her favourite of everything I'd ever drawn.

I could see the sun on the linoleum. The windows were open and the door was open and it was a good Saturday; it was between football weather and baseball weather, as it should be in September, and nobody was spoiling it for me to-day. Bobby could stand on the porch until to-morrow for all I cared.

The bowl of breakfast food was there on the table. I poured milk over it and started eating fast.

"Ken," Mother said, and I understood the tone.

"No." I looked up. "I'm not taking him, Mother." I knew he could hear me and I wanted him to hear.

"He's your brother, Ken."

I pushed the bowl away. I didn't want cereal and I didn't want eggs. I didn't want any breakfast to-day. I saw him standing there on purpose. I knew him all right, the baby. He'd stand there, and pretty soon he'd turn, looking as if he were going to cry, but this time he wasn't going; and that was final.

This time it was just the club, just the Knights, and no nine-year-old baby was tagging along. We had waited a month for to-day. Boys' House was the biggest in town, even bigger than the Y. Phil Leeds had read that every Saturday groups of kids came from different neighbourhoods and were there all day. We could swim if we wanted, or play table tennis or pool, or be in the gym, or do anything we liked. We each had to bring a dime for lunch. Phil Leeds wrote the letter for the Knights. We waited, and finally Phil got the answer to come this Saturday, to-day. They sent a programme, too, and it said that Sid Glotter, the cartoonist on the *News*, who had the Chuckle-Chuck column, would be there to draw for us. He was marvellous, and from the day Phil got the letter I hadn't gone to sleep without thinking of it. At least twenty times a day I counted the days.

"I know he's my brother," I said, and I was so angry I could have punched him then. "You know something, too," I told her. "You know that when we started the Knights we made a rule that everybody had to be thirteen years old. You know that, Mother."

"Eat your cereal, Ken."

"I don't want any. Maybe I'm late now. Maybe all the Knights are over at the playground waiting. Phil Leeds has a brother, too. Don't forget that; but does his brother always have to tag along?"

"Ken, you know how Bobby is," she said. She sat down next to me. "He's so shy," she said softly, "and he loves you so. Please take him, Ken."

I didn't answer. Take him on hikes, take him to the ball games, take him, take him, take him.

"Please," Mother said. She reached out and pushed my hair back from my eye, and I made up my mind.

"I won't," I said. "Not this time." I got up.

"All right, Ken," she said. I just wanted to get out now. I wanted to be away from there, so I wouldn't have to see Mother.

She had one arm on the table, and she reached over to the centre. I saw two dimes there. She picked up one dime and set it down next to the cereal bowl. "Here is your lunch money, Ken."

I wasn't going to back down now. I picked up the dime. "Thanks, Mother," I said.

She said, "You'd better have a jacket, Ken."

I started across the kitchen to the back door. "I don't need a jacket. It's warm out."

"It may turn cold later to-day," she said.

I stopped at the sink. "I don't want a jacket!" I said, louder than I'd expected to. "I'm not a baby!"

She got up from the chair. "Kenneth," she said; and that was all she said as she walked out of the kitchen toward the bedroom. Behind me I heard Bobby move. All he had to do was to say something. Just let him say anything to me now and he'd wish he wasn't my brother. I was waiting, holding the drainboard with my right hand, when I saw her coming out of the bedroom.

She walked toward me and she had Dad's suede jacket that she had fixed over to fit me after he died. Her face was soft and her eyes were soft and she was smiling. I'd worn it once, to the last assembly in June, when the whole school was there and I got a letter for baseball and Mother was out in front watching me on the stage.

She held the jacket and laid it in my arms as if it were gold.

"A mantle for my Knight," she said, "my gallant protector."

Right there, in the old kitchen, with the dishes piled in the sink, she made a curtsy and held her right hand for me to take and lift her up.

I took her hand and felt it soft in mine. I lifted her hand. She rose, smiling at me, and she was my beautiful mother. I saw her smiling and I had to do it. I didn't want to, and I couldn't stop myself. Holding the jacket, I ran to the table and got the other dime. When I turned to her again, I saw the wet in her eyes.

"Hey, Bobby," I said. He came running into the kitchen. "Get a jacket," I said. "Hurry up. We're late."

Bobby looked at me and he looked at Mother, as though he didn't believe it; as though this were a joke I was playing on him. But Mother nodded, and he dashed past us, into our bedroom. When he came back, he was wearing my blue Knight's jacket. All the club had chipped in to buy a big square of canvas, and I'd cut it up into small circles and on each I'd painted a knight's head with an iron hood that I'd seen in a King Arthur book. I'd painted one for each boy in the club, and each boy's mother had sewn it on the jacket.

"Take it off," I said.

He stood there quiet. I could see his hands, his thin hands with the tiny blue veins showing. I could see his black hair, curly and mussed up, and his black eyes wide as he just watched me, saying nothing at all, until Mother said, "Let him, Ken. He's so proud of you."

I was in it now, I guess. I couldn't say anything now. I'd taken the other dime off the table and I couldn't be mad at her. "Come on," I said to Bobby, and waited while he kissed Mother.

Then I kissed her and she said we could go out the front door to-day.

I crossed Cherokee Street, half running now, with Bobby two steps behind me, trying to keep up. Just so I wasn't late, that's all. Just so they hadn't started without me. Halfway down the block to Sioux Avenue, I saw them standing around home plate on the playground and leaning against the backstop. I slowed down.

Bobby caught up to me then, trotting along beside me to keep even, and I felt his hand in mine. I pulled my hand away, and after a minute I felt it again. I stopped and took his wrist and moved his arm off me.

"Can't you walk without holding someone? Do you have to hold me as if you were crippled or something?"

He didn't answer.

"Don't be holding my hand," I said. "You understand?"

"Yes," he said, and he pushed his hands deep in his pockets, and I heard Phil Leeds.

"Get a move on," he yelled. "We haven't got all day!" Phil Leeds yelled, and I saw him atop the fence. I saw Zami Garlick coming toward the playground from Clinton Avenue off to my right, and then I started running.

All the Knights were there. I got to the fence and turned for Bobby. I got a quick look at Phil, standing with fists pushed against his hips, watching me.

I boosted Bobby over the fence. I got over and saw Zami Garlick coming through the gate beyond left field. I waved at the other Knights and yelled at Zami, and then, there at the backstop, Phil Leeds stopped me.

"What's the idea?" he asked, jerking his thumb at Bobby.

"It's all right, Phil; I've got his dime." I held out the money.

Phil waved at it. "What's money got to do with it?" He was wearing his Knight's jacket, and I looked at the head I'd painted for him. I looked carefully at it — at the nose, the right eye, the left eye, the hood — and Phil, said, "He ain't going."

I saw Bobby watching us, standing alone along the third-base line. I saw him turn, starting to walk toward the gate, and I got Phil's arm. "I promised my Mother, Phil. Please, Phil, I didn't want him to come." Bobby was way beyond third base. "He'll go home to my mother and he'll cry, and then I'll get it. Let him, Phil, and you know what? I've got some canvas left from what we bought and I'll paint a knight on a horse and your mother can sew it on your back for president."

He didn't say anything for a minute, and then he held out his hand.

"Give me the dimes," he said. "And keep him out of our way. We don't want any punks ruining to-day for us."

"Bobby!" I yelled for him, and waved my arms over my head. "Come on!" and saw him running toward us.

He ran funny, almost like a girl, with his arms out wide. Phil Leeds got everybody together, collecting the dimes and knotting the money tight in his handkerchief while I walked out to meet Bobby.

"Now, listen," I said. "You're going. I told Phil Leeds you were coming with us and that's all there is to it. But stay out of our way. Don't be ruining it for us, you hear?"

"Yes," he said, in that soft low voice. He always talked as if he were ashamed of something.

Mush Hanley started singing and we all joined in. Down by the railroad we passed the sausage factory, and Zami Garlick went around to the open doors and came back with six wieners he'd begged. He ran ahead, holding them up in one hand, until Phil Leeds caught him. Phil took them, got out his knife and cut them up, one piece for each.

Everybody was crowded around Phil, and he passed out the pieces. I got mine and waited until there was one piece left. The rest of the fellows were up ahead, starting across the bridge leading to downtown. Bobby was behind me, waiting, and Phil Leeds looked at the piece of wiener in his hand.

"I forgot," he said.

He waited, holding the piece of wiener in his hand, grinning at me, and then he popped it in his mouth and ran up Sioux Avenue to the bridge.

I didn't even look around for Bobby. I began walking, and I knew what I wanted to do to Phil Leeds, all right. I didn't have to guess. Up against the wall and my arm under his chin. My elbow in his neck, and see how he'd like that. Make a fist slow and get my arm back slow, grinning at him. Just let him see the fist and wait for it, and then take my arm from his neck and spit right on his shoes and leave him.

I felt Bobby's hand touching mine.

"Get your hand away!" I said, loudly. "Baby! You're nothing but a baby. Why don't you cry?" But he didn't. "Why don't you run home to mamma and cry to her and tell her how mean I am?" But he stood watching me. "Here," and I held out the piece of wiener. "Take it," I said. "Take it, baby." But he just put his hands behind his back and stood there, and I threw it at him.

Now, all at once, I didn't care what he did; whether he went home or stayed right here the rest of the day. He wasn't ruining it for me, that's all, and I started up the bridge.

But I remembered Mother, saw her in the kitchen holding Dad's jacket for me. And I was responsible. Once, after Dad died, she told me to sit in his chair for supper. She told me that was my new chair and that I was the man for her and Bobby. She told me I had to take care of them, and how could I sit there to-night if I left him here?

I waved my hand for him to hurry. When he reached me, I put him on the old Boy Scout pace — fifty steps running and fifty walking.

We caught up with the Knights at the stop light on Third Street. Phil Leeds made us wait until the light changed to green.

He made us wait on the other side, getting everybody in marching order, two in a row. He picked Zami Garlick to lead with him. I knew that was on purpose, against me.

He put me with Bobby at the very end, and that was on purpose, too, and I decided he'd never get a knight on horseback from me. He could have his club. They could all go jump.

Then we were only two blocks from Boys' House. Phil and Zami started to trot. The cop on Sibley Street stopped traffic for us. We crossed over and went up the marble steps and we were in the lobby.

It was just beautiful. It was just the most wonderful place I ever saw. They had pictures on the wall right in the lobby — signed pictures — Babe Ruth and Gene Tunney and Joe Di Maggio and — everybody. You could name anybody and his picture was on the wall.

I saw the auditorium on the right, and straight ahead, far down the hall from the lobby, I could see the gym, and I guess being here was the best thing a fellow could hope for. I saw Phil Leeds giving the letter he'd got to a man who wore a white sweater.

The man shook hands with Phil and walked around to shake hands with all of us. His name was Mr. Nye. He said he would be with us all afternoon, and how about lunch?

Off to our right was a checkroom, and we all gave the man behind the counter our jackets. Then Mr. Nye took us downstairs, past a big room with tennis tables and pool tables, and into a cafeteria.

It was the best lunch, or even supper, I ever had. There were beans and hot dogs and rolls and potato salad and root beer and pop and cake.

Mr. Nye got a tray for himself and one for Bobby, and they were the first to start down the counter. Bobby couldn't reach above it to get his food, and Mr. Nye just filled his tray until he could hardly carry it.

They were first at the table. I was in line with my tray and I got next to Phil Leeds. I grinned at him and said, "I guess this is the best day the Knights will ever have, huh, Phil?" but he just looked at me and started up the counter. I knew him, all right. He had to be the head of everything, and he'd figured on sitting with Mr. Nye. I got up next to Zami Garlick and we went down the counter together, but when we got to the table, Phil Leeds yelled to Zami and pointed to an empty chair he'd been saving.

All around the cafeteria were other groups of boys, and sitting with each of them a man about as old as Mr. Nye. There must have been more than a hundred kids there.

After lunch everybody wanted to go swimming, but Mr. Nye said we had to wait awhile. We played table tennis, and some of the boys played pool.

It seemed like ten years before Mr. Nye took us down to the pool. We each had a locker and Bobby undressed with me. Nobody wore swimming trunks. Mr. Nye met us in the shower room beside the pool and said everybody had to soap himself down first.

I'll bet that pool was as long as our playgrounds. It was all green marble, and the water looked almost green and almost blue. Mr. Nye came over and said I'd have to watch out for Bobby. I took him down to the shallow end, but he didn't want to go in.

"Don't you want to swim?" I asked.

He shook his head

"You're afraid," I said.

He didn't answer.

"What'd you get undressed for and come out here for?"

He just looked at me.

"Be afraid, then," I said, "but don't bother me. I'm going swimming." I went up to the deep end and dived in. I swam around for a while and then reached out for the gutter that ran under the edge of the pool and held on. Bobby was standing there.

"Come on in," I said. Phil Leeds climbed out of the pool about ten feet from Bobby.

"I'll watch you," I said. "What are you afraid of?"

"Don't want to swim," Bobby said.

I saw Phil coming up, back against the wall, so Bobby couldn't see him.

Phil winked at me. "I'll pull you in," I told Bobby, but he backed away from the edge, his face full of fear. I saw Phil, his finger to his lips, winking at me again. I guess I wanted him to be friends with me more than anything. I said to Bobby, "Come here." He didn't move. "Come here, baby," I said, "I'm not going to hurt you." And he took one step and then another, setting his feet down slowly and carefully as if he were walking across Colorado Street just after the tar truck had gone through.

"Here," I said, smiling, as Phil Leeds jumped out from behind him and grabbed Bobby and shoved hard.

I heard Phil laughing and I heard Bobby scream once, real high and real loud, the most terrible sound I'd ever heard, as he went into the water, falling on his side.

He went down and I didn't see him. He was down for a long time. I couldn't see him and I was afraid and I thought of Mother; and then he came up. I grabbed him and he was choking, his mouth full of water and his face red and his arms moving in the air. But I had him and got him over to the edge and pushed him up on the side.

Mr. Nye was holding Phil with one arm. "Come up here," he said.

I got out of the pool. Bobby was sitting up on the wet marble, and then Mr. Nye said, "We don't think much of tricks like that here, fellows," and he looked at Phil Leeds. He picked him up high and threw him out into the pool. He turned to me. "I could throw you in, too, you know, but it wouldn't help, would it? Bobby told me at lunch that you always took care of him. You take good care of him, don't you?" he said, and he left us there.

I took Bobby back to the locker room. I made him sit on the bench and rest. There was no use trying to save to-day any more. He had ruined to-day for me, all right, but I didn't care any more. It was just as I had expected it to be, with him along. I wanted to get dressed and go home.

"Didn't mean to scream, Ken," Bobby said.

I was pulling on my socks. "It doesn't make any difference," I said.

"You're mad at me," he said.

"I'm not mad."

"Yes, you are," he said. "Didn't mean it."

I had my shoes on. "Can you get dressed?" I asked.

He nodded and reached for his socks.

"Don't have to pay any attention to me, Ken. I'll go home now."

"We're going home now."

He looked up, and I was sure he would cry. "The drawing," he said. "You can't miss the drawing, Ken. The man from Chuckle-Chuck."

"I can miss it."

"That's what you waited for," Bobby said. He was standing in his shoes and socks and shorts. He reached out to touch me, but I pulled away.

"I'm not going to see any drawings, that's all. I'm going home, that's all; and you're going with me — and now. You wanted to come, and now you're going." I reached into the locker for his shirt. "You get dressed." I found it hard to swallow and my eyes were starting to burn. "Hurry up," I said over my shoulder.

The other Knights started to come into the locker room. I went back to Bobby and helped him get his clothes on. We were the first out of there. We got our jackets from the checkroom man. We were passing the trophy case when Mr. Nye stopped us.

"Where are you fellows going?" he asked.

"Home," I said. "We're going home."

"Now, you don't want to do that." He rumpled Bobby's hair. "We've got Sid Glotter, the *News* cartoonist, waiting," and he pointed at the auditorium.

"You, Ken. Bobby told me you're pretty good with a pencil yourself."

Bobby and his big mouth. "Not very good," I said.

"Well, you're staying," Mr. Nye said. He got between us. "Boys' House promised the Knights a full day's show, and you two aren't going to make liars out of us," and he led us into the auditorium. It was marked off in sections with a poster for each group. There was a sign with Knights written on it, and Mr. Nye took us to it. It was halfway back from the auditorium stage, near the windows. He told us to sit down. "Ken, I've got to get the other Knights," he said. "I don't want you to go home." Then he smiled and stuck out his hand. "If you tell me you'll stay, I know you will," and I had to take Mr. Nye's hand, you know that.

He left us and the auditorium started to fill. The other neighbourhoods came in quick, and pretty soon Mush Hanley and Indian Gantman, of the Knights, came. Zami Garlick and Phil Leeds came, and they sat in the row in front of us, right in front of us. Mr. Nye and the other men were walking up and down the aisles. In a few minutes the auditorium was full. Everybody sat down but Mr. Nye, who went up on the stage and behind the curtain.

Then he came out and everybody was quiet. He said we didn't want to see him and he was going to introduce Sid Glotter, and the curtain opened.

I saw the easel and I could feel my heart starting to pound. I saw the big square folio of white paper, and then Sid Glotter came out on the stage. I saw the charcoal pencils in his left hand and I started to clap. Everybody started clapping, and Sid Glotter grinned at us. He was half turned to the easel, and while we were clapping he drew an apple. First an apple with a stem and everything. Then he had his back to us for a minute, and suddenly he stepped away. The apple was gone, but there was a round-faced girl's head, and she wore a tam; the stem was the tip of the tam.

Everybody was clapping and whistling. Sid Glotter smiled and tore the sheet off. He drew a lamp post. Then he turned his back, and when he stepped clear it was a tall, thin, drunken man, such as you see in the comedies. Then he turned his back, and when we saw the easel again the drunk was standing against a new lamp post.

Bobby was laughing. I saw Mush Hanley bent over, he was laughing so hard. I saw Mr. Nye standing in one corner of the stage, his arms folded over his chest, and laughing. I guess I would have given anything to draw like that.

Sid Glotter was drawing again, on a fresh sheet, but all of a sudden I didn't see him at all. All of a sudden I was up there, and it was as if I had my eyes closed and was making a dream. It was as if I saw myself a big painter with famous ladies sitting for me; as if I saw myself in New York and Paris, drawing, and I would come back to town and Mother would have her own house that I bought, and they would ask me to paint the mayor and the Premier . . . and I felt Bobby's elbow in my ribs and heard him. "Listen, Ken, listen," he whispered.

". . . and any of you fellows who want to try it are welcome," Sid Glotter said, as he held out the charcoal pencils.

"Ken," Bobby said, but I grabbed his arm and squeezed it.

"Shut up," I whispered, and my heart was going. "Shut up. Shut up," but Bobby's face was almost white, his eyes big and wide, and he was shaking, he was so excited.

I saw Mr. Nye walk out from the corner of the stage. I prayed he wouldn't say anything or do anything, but he just looked in our direction.

Phil Leeds turned around and watched me, daring me.

"Anybody at all," Sid Glotter said, waiting, and I knew I wouldn't move. I knew I'd sit still, and later — to-night and to-morrow and for a long time — I'd see myself up there, with Sid Glotter standing away from the easel and watching me, and all of them watching me. I knew I'd be sorry, and I wanted to do it more than anything I'd ever wanted in my life, and I felt Bobby pull his arm free.

I felt him moving in the chair, and then he was standing up and his arm was up and my heart was pounding so hard it hurt. I said, "Bobby, don't," but he didn't turn, and I put my head down.

I heard him say, "My brother —"

And I couldn't swallow.

Bobby said, "He's the best—"

And my stomach was sick. I felt myself sick and my chest tight and my heart so loud everybody could hear it, and Mr. Nye was calling for me. Bobby was standing up, looking at me and smiling, and Phil Leeds turned slowly to watch me, and I got up.

I didn't care what happened, he wasn't going to watch me sit there. I wasn't afraid of any Phil Leeds.

Bobby pushed back so I could pass, and next to him Indian Gantman pushed back. I got out of the row and started down the aisle, and I knew—knew I couldn't draw. I knew I'd just stand there paralyzed, but I walked to the stage and up the steps, past Mr. Nye and over to Sid Glotter and the easel.

I'd never had such an easel or seen such an easel or such big squares of paper. Sid Glotter bowed and turned me to the auditorium. I couldn't look out at them. I couldn't. I just couldn't.

But he gave me the pencils. I felt the pencils in my hand as he led me to the easel. Maybe it was the feel of the pencils. Maybe it was the blank white paper. But all of a sudden I took a pencil from the bunch in my left hand.

My heart was pounding and my throat was dry, but now I didn't see anything but the white paper, and I had a trick of my own that nobody had ever seen, not even Mother. I drew a 5. And stepped away to let them see the 5. And stepped back as Sid Glotter had done. I made a wheel of the bottom of the 5 and a seat of the straight top of it. I drew another wheel, working fast and not thinking, but feeling it in my arm and in my hands, and knowing I could do it. In a minute, when I stepped clear, there was a bicycle on the white paper and my brother Bobby riding it.

I heard them clapping. I heard them whistling and stamping their feet. I heard Mr. Nye clapping and Sid Glotter clapping, and above it all, from far back in the auditorium, I heard Bobby yelling my name.

Kid Brother

After that it was easy. After that my heart stopped and my stomach stopped and I could swallow. I drew a baseball pitcher and I drew a halfback carrying the ball, his knees high and his arm out. I drew two fighters in the ring, and Sid Glotter took that one. He told them in the auditorium it was for his column, and my name would be over it.

I guess I would have stayed there all day and all night if they'd let me, but Mr. Nye said Sid Glotter was busy and had to get back to the *News*.

Sid Glotter put his arm around me and we went to the foot of the stage and they clapped for both of us. They clapped all the time we were on the stage. I rolled up all my drawings except the fighters, making a tight tube out of them, and Sid Glotter said for me to go down the steps first, ahead of him.

The Knights grabbed me in the lobby. They slapped my back, and Indian Gantman rubbed my hair. Zami Garlick rolled up his sleeve and asked me to tattoo his arm, and then Phil Leeds was standing in front of me.

He said, "We showed 'em, didn't we, Ken? They know who the Knights are, don't they?"

And I didn't say anything.

Phil Leeds had his knuckles against his hips, and he said, "That one of the halfback carrying the ball, that's the one I want. Right in my room. I'll hang it in my room," and he reached out for the tube, but I stepped away.

I saw Bobby standing alone on the edge of the circle of Knights. He was standing and watching me, and I walked over to him. I shoved the tube under his arm and I turned to Phil.

"You'll have to ask my manager," I told Phil. "These are Bobby's and he's the boss of the drawings," I said, and I took his hand in mine. "Aren't you, Bob?" I asked.

He didn't say anything. He just watched me, smiling and holding my hand tight.

LEISURE

WILLIAM HENRY DAVIES

What is this life if, full of care,
We have no time to stand and stare?

No time to stand beneath the boughs
And stare as long as sheep or cows.

No time to see, when woods we pass,
Where squirrels hide their nuts in grass.

No time to see, in broad daylight,
Streams full of stars, like skies at night.

No time to turn at Beauty's glance,
And watch her feet, how they can dance.

No time to wait till her mouth can
Enrich that smile her eyes began.

A poor life this if, full of care,
We have no time to stand and stare.

DOUBLE PLAY

THELMA KNOLES

The Stars, the girls' softball team of Queen Elizabeth Junior High, completely forgot the crowd filling the bleachers as they went into a huddle before the game.

Olga Hrynchuk, gray eyes dark with excitement, demanded, "Did Gail Clarke really come, Jo?"

"Yes," Jo said importantly. "She had dinner with Dad and

me. She's wonderful. Can you imagine — she's a baseball fan. She's never played herself, but she goes to all the games and knows almost as much about the plays as Coach Thompson himself. You'd never believe she's really a newspaper editor. But she's businesslike, too. She told me she was considering our applications for the job of copy girl."

Olga sighed from her heart. She longed to work on the *Calgary Herald* under Gail Clarke as she had longed for nothing else in her whole fifteen years. But — so did every girl in second year English. Besides, Olga was afraid that because her parents had come from Central Europe, she might not get an equal chance with Toni and Jo.

"Just think," Jo exclaimed, carefully tipping the smart baseball cap over her golden curls, "a copy girl in an editorial office might get to meet *celebrities*."

"Between running errands and filling paste pots," Olga murmured, jamming her own cap over stubby brown pigtails.

But maybe Jo had a right to be confident of getting that job. After all, her father had been a schoolmate of the new editor.

"Don't you think," Toni Taylor asked, "that Miss Clarke might choose a girl with literary talent? I've read that in emergencies copy *boys* used to do some writing, so a copy *girl* might, too."

"After all, Toni," Jo said quickly, "winning a poetry contest doesn't make you exactly an author, you know."

"But it might be a help," Toni insisted.

The other girls looked enviously at Jo and Toni. The choice would rest between them, Olga thought forlornly. She picked up a ball and twirled it, listening to her friends' excited chatter.

She was wishing she had been able to get into her letter of application some part of what a newspaper job, however humble, would mean to her. She had earnestly tried. But it was difficult to put such feeling into words. Why, the very idea of interpreting world events to the public was breath-taking to Olga — recording history in the present — shaping destiny — the power of the press — magic words.

Facing Our Problems

ap out of it, girls!" The coach's harassed voice broke
her dreams. "We have a ball game coming up. Remember?
re's a big crowd out there who've bought tickets and it's up
you to give them a show." His glasses glittered at the girls
in their trim new uniforms. "Those Lethbridge players are out
to win for their school."

"We'll blow those Lethbridge ducks off the diamond,"
declared Patsy Johnson, the Stars' dependable catcher. "Just
the same, I wish Jean had postponed her measles."

So do I, thought Olga grimly, as she and Toni trotted out to
the side lines to warm up. With Jean out of the game, that
left only Toni and Olga as pitchers. And Olga, just promoted
from the sub-team, felt her knees shake at the idea of pitching
a real game. She knew that she was not in the class with Toni
and Jean.

"Dad and Miss Clarke are coming to the game," Jo called
after them. She had saved her big news till the last minute.
"They may be a little late, but they'll be here."

The girls looked at one another with shining eyes. Here was
a chance to impress the lady editor who was also a baseball fan.

The game got under way, with Toni on the mound, Jo
perched gracefully on second base, and Olga warming the
bench. Toni pitched her usual brilliant game, tossing it off so
easily that she hardly disturbed her smooth black hair-do. And
she bettered her already excellent batting record on her first trip
to the plate.

The coach relaxed. Then, in the third inning, several things
happened at once. Just as the Lethbridge batter popped a short
fly toward Toni, Jo, hopping up and down on second, shouted,
"There's Dad!" and waved wildly toward the bleachers.

Toni turned to look, fumbled the fly, and dropped it. The
Lethbridge runner slid safely into first.

"What do you girls think you're playing—" ground out Coach
Thompson in disgust, "pat-a-cake?"

With an arrogant toss of her head, Toni wound up and shot

Double Play

her famous fast ball over the plate. This time the batter smacked it cleanly. The next sent a grounder sizzling down the base line.

"They're on to her," Olga moaned to herself. "She'll have to change."

Patsy signalled to Toni. Her signals were ignored. Toni liked her fast ball. She was out to make an impression on Miss Clarke and she did not intend to give up her speedy, spectacular delivery. Miraculously she pulled herself out of the hole by fanning the next three batters. She walked off the mound to the sound of applause.

Next it was Jo's turn to shine. With two on base, she knocked out a home run. As she crossed home plate she waved triumphantly to her father and the slim, smartly dressed woman beside him.

In the next inning the batters began hitting Toni's fast ball in earnest. Desperately Patsy signalled for a slow ball, a curve — anything. Toni stubbornly ignored her. The coach scowled and muttered savagely under his breath. But he dared not take Toni out, for there was only Olga left to pitch. And Olga was no star.

Finally the second half of the seventh inning arrived, with Lethbridge two runs ahead of the Stars. Jo stepped up to the plate, swinging her bat to the encouraging cheers of the crowd.

"Tie the score!" they yelled.

At the first called strike Jo whirled about to give the umpire an icy stare. Then she turned to the plate again. Swish! Her bat fanned the air. She stepped back, drew a deep breath, and toed the plate.

"Strike three!" the umpire announced. "Batter out."

"Why—" sputtered Jo in a rage, "that was way inside!" She flung down her bat and stalked away, muttering about robbers. Olga was ashamed of her.

The Stars were retired with no further runs. They glumly took their places in the field. Toni wound up and delivered another fast one. The batter sent it up into a high fly between the pitcher's mound and second base.

"It's mine," called Jo, running forward.

"I have it," warned Toni, running backward. The girls collided and went down, and the ball rolled away, to be snatched up by the shortstop and thrown to first for the put-out. Toni got up, clutching her shoulder.

The coach ground his teeth. "You play like a bunch of prima donnas," he barked. "Whatever made me think I could make a ball team out of you!"

He turned to Olga. "Get out there and pitch," he ordered. "Toni's hurt her shoulder."

Toni was led tearfully from the field. "I barely wrenched it," she protested. "I can still play."

Olga moved out to the pitcher's mound in a daze. The bleachers swam before her in a blur of colour. Her knees wobbled and her fingers were so stiff and cold she could hardly grasp the ball. She rubbed her hands briskly together, braced her legs, and closed her eyes for a brief silent plea for help. Then she took a deep breath and stared anxiously at Patsy.

"We'll show them!" Patsy called out encouragingly.

Good, wise old Patsy. You could trust her. She'd know what kind of pitch to call for, and she, Olga, would do her best to deliver it. She had nothing special, like Toni — no beautiful, twisting fast ball; but she could watch signals carefully; and how gladly she would obey them.

She sucked in her breath, wound up, and let go. Then abruptly she wasn't afraid any more. She watched Patsy like a hawk and followed her lead. Patsy was wise to all Lethbridge's little whims about batting. She knew what to call for and when. Lethbridge scored no more runs that inning.

Olga came up to bat in the eighth. There were two on base. How she'd love to knock a home run! She had a feeling she could. Maybe never again in her life, but to-day she could. However, she went into the batter's box with orders to bunt.

A perfect ball came over the plate — just the kind she liked, just the kind she knew she could slam over the fence. Her hand tightened on the bat. Out of the corner of her eye she glimpsed Jo, ready to bat after her.

With an inward sigh Olga tapped out a neat little bunt. It advanced the runner and sent Olga back to the side lines—just another sacrifice in the name of sport. Jo, next up, batted out a three-bagger that tied up the score. Then she actually managed to steal home before the inning was out, to the tune of more wild applause.

Well, thought Olga, taking her place on the mound for the ninth inning, some people are born to star and some to sacrifice. Then she gritted her teeth, took a fresh grip on her confidence, and faced a determined looking Lethbridge batter.

Lethbridge got a runner on base with only one out and it looked bad for the Stars. Toni was pleading violently with the coach to let her go in and finish the game, and Olga could feel the cold sweat breaking out on her back.

She tossed a slow ball and the batter smacked it right back toward her. Her first impulse was to jump high and snare it. But if she let it go, Jo stood a good chance to make a double out of the play. Olga ducked. The bleachers broke into loud cheers as Jo caught the fly and fielded it to retire the crestfallen Lethbridge team.

"Great game, Olga," Patsy congratulated her, as they trotted toward the showers.

"Not by me," replied Olga; "I just followed your orders."

"That's plenty," the catcher replied with feeling.

Jo announced excitedly to the tired girls, "Dad says for us to hurry and change. He's taking us to dinner. Miss Clarke would like to meet the team."

"Oh," breathed Patsy. "Do you suppose she's going to tell us who'll be copy girl?"

"Probably not," Jo declared with decision. "She'll most likely do that confidentially."

Olga whisked out of her uniform, under the showers, and into her T-shirt and skirt. She anxiously patted her funny little pigtails. Why, oh why, hadn't she rolled her hair on curlers and worn her new bandeau. She looked like a cartoon.

After introductions all around, they walked over to McNaughton's, Calgary's famous eating place, and presently Olga found herself a bit behind the others, with Gail Clarke beside her. It was like a dream. Olga was sure Miss Clarke was making a mistake when she smiled at her and said, "I was interested in your game this afternoon, Olga."

Olga never knew what she stammered in reply.

Miss Clarke went on, "And I was very much interested in your letter of application for the copy girl job. You seem to have caught the real significance behind newspaper work."

"I th-think it's wonderful," stammered Olga.

Her grey eyes shone, and her face was so pale that a drift of freckles showed across her cheeks.

"Do you know," Miss Clarke said quietly, "I like to think of the newspaper staff as a team, a team working together for one purpose — to gather and publish the news of the world." Her low voice seemed to throb with Olga's heart. "Anyone new, coming into such work must be the kind who will fit in, who will obey orders, and be willing to sacrifice personal glory if necessary. Many a story has been ruined, Olga, by some reporter selfishly trying to scoop everyone else."

Olga again murmured something.

Miss Clarke said, "Watching you play ball this afternoon, I could see you had the qualities of co-operation that are needed in the newspaper business — even in a copy girl." Olga held her breath to hear every syllable. She could hardly believe the amazing words. "Would you like to see me to-morrow about that job, Olga?"

Would she? Ahead of her, Jo and Toni swished along, talking brightly, bringing out their wittiest conversation for the benefit of the editor. Olga just smiled worshipfully at her new boss.

RABBLE-ROUSER

ROLLAND UPTON

To 40,000 constituents, Mr. Baxter was known as the Honourable James Baxter, M.P., K.C., Minister of the Government of Canada. To Jack Owens, he was Uncle Jim. Jack had always admired his uncle. It was his intention to go into politics as a life work.

"I'm glad you feel that way," his uncle had once said by way of encouragement. "This country needs bright young fellows who will plan a career of public service."

"I'm not only picking my high school courses with that in mind," Jack told the Cabinet Minister, "but I'm also going to get some practical experience in vote-getting next fall."

"Is that so? How?"

"You are looking," boasted Jack, "at the next President of the Brighton High School Student Body."

"Hm," said James Baxter, "you seem pretty confident."

"More than that — positive."

Jack had, indeed, every reason to be sure of victory in the student body election held each autumn.

The high school district included not only the town of Brighton, but several smaller villages and rural settlements as well. And the school population from the outlying districts was somewhat in the majority.

Jack himself was one of those who lived outside of Brighton. "Hicks" was the title often applied to such as he. Jack's idea was simply to organize the "hicks".

Brighton High School had never had a student body president who lived outside of Brighton. This was clearly so unfair that Jack saw an opportunity to make excellent political capital of it. Evan Roberts, his campaign manager, had carefully sown the seeds of discontent.

"Isn't it about time the rural districts got a little recognition in student body affairs?" Evan would say to an audience of rural hearers. "This town bunch has had control of things long enough."

When Jack heard, the day before the election, that his Uncle Jim was home from Ottawa for a short visit while Parliament was in recess, it seemed that his joy was complete. More than anything else, he wanted his distinguished relative to witness his triumph. As soon as school was out, he hurried to Mr. Baxter's favourite retreat when home—his greenhouse.

"Remember what I told you last spring about our student body elections?" he asked.

James Baxter nodded. "Well, rather," he replied; "I'm almost as much interested in your career as you are. Were you elected?"

"Practically."

"Practically?"

"Well, the election isn't until to-morrow but I've more than enough votes promised to win."

"You must have had a good platform to get so many votes!"

"Platform?" asked Jack.

"Yes, plans for your year of administration. What do you propose to do for the student body?"

For the first time in any discussion of his political ambitions Jack was at a loss for words.

"Well, you see," he explained lamely, "I haven't had much time to think about that. I've been pretty busy getting the votes lined up."

Uncle Jim faced his nephew in genuine surprise. "But how did you line up these votes without something to offer in the way of service?"

"Why—why, I didn't need to offer anything. I had a better idea. You see, there are about 300 rural pupils in school and only about 200 who live in Brighton. I just lined up the country against the town."

Uncle Jim looked at Jack intently. "Was that the only issue?"

Jack could not see what his uncle was getting at. "Well — why not? Don't you want me to be elected?"

"Not that way, Jack," replied the federal Minister. "Not by resorting to the world's cheapest political trick."

Jack was stunned. "What trick?"

"Prejudice — setting one class against another for your own selfish ends. Think, Jack. If you should be elected, would you be president of just the rural students or of the whole student body?"

"Why, the whole student body."

"Then, why didn't you appeal to the whole group? Oh, you can win by the method you've chosen. It's been done lots of times. But you admit your ideal isn't to serve your school. The loftiest motive in your whole campaign seems to have been merely to help one side get even with the other."

Jack was silent. He had no defense against his uncle's argument. For the first time he saw his actions as another might see them.

"I was mighty proud of you, Jack, when you chose public service as your life's work," continued his uncle. "You could perhaps be a statesman, not just a — do you know what they call a politician who appeals to prejudice to get votes?"

"No."

"A rabble-rouser."

"But, Uncle Jim, honestly, I'm more than that. After I'm elected I'll be a good president. You admit I have ability."

James Baxter looked at his nephew appraisingly. "Yes," he conceded without enthusiasm, "you have."

Jack walked home slowly. His disappointment was keen. He had gone to his uncle proudly, in a mood to accept congratulations for a clever political stroke. He had met with just the reverse. The joy of victory was gone.

It was the custom at Brighton High School, on the morning before the annual student body election, to give the candidates an opportunity to speak to the assembled students.

Herbert Pennington and Jack received friendly applause. The demonstration was louder and more pronounced when Jack rose to take his bow, but he experienced no thrills of pride. Somehow his uncle's words had taken care of that.

Herbert was speaking: "I wish to outline briefly what I hope to accomplish should I be elected to this office. First of all, I hope to put the school paper on a paying basis."

Herbert had definite ideas as to how this could be done. He spoke convincingly and left little doubt as to his ability to accomplish the aim. He then discussed how the student cooperative book service would be managed. His ideas were good.

Widespread applause greeted the closing words but a few boos and catcalls testified to the bitter feeling Jack and Evan had stirred up among the rural students. Jack could feel no pride in what he had done. He had driven a wedge between two factions in the school.

He heard his name called and a thunderous clamour shook the auditorium. Jack rose to his feet and took his place at the speaker's stand up front.

"Before I start my speech," he said, "I want to thank everybody who has worked for my election. They've worked hard for me without ever asking anything in return and I appreciate it. That's why the thing I have to say now comes pretty hard. It would be a mistake to elect me president."

A shocked silence met the announcement. Evan half-rose in his seat. What was this? If it was some new plan — why hadn't he been informed?

"My whole campaign," continued Jack, "has been based on personal bitterness. I purposely chose the biggest group in school and appealed to their prejudice to elect me and defeat the other candidate. Every vote for me would be a vote for a divided student body. I've just now discovered that I don't want future students in this high school to remember me as the originator of the town-versus-country feud, so please don't vote for me to head the student council."

He swallowed. "As a matter of fact, I'm withdrawing right now from the election. Again I want to thank those who were fooled into working for me."

Amid stunned silence, Jack sat down. For almost half a minute no sound could he heard, and then someone started to applaud. It began as a little ripple somewhere in the balcony and spread throughout the great room. Every student knew the issue at stake, and what it had cost Jack to say what he had. He had done the only thing possible to preserve the unity and fellow-feeling that had always been a part of life at Brighton High.

It was probably the first time in the history of the school that a defeated man received as many congratulations as the victor. Jack was surrounded by fellow-students when the meeting was over. And foremost among them was Herbert Pennington himself.

Defeated? No, the word didn't fit here. Looking down at the audience, catching Evan's eye, Jack thought at first that it did. Evan showed his dismay. But then, amidst the shouts of acclaim and the clamorous applause, Evan's face took on another light. Slowly he came up to Herbert and shook his hand.

"Good luck, Herbert," he said, "you're the man of the day, now."

Herbert grinned and looked in Jack's direction. "The real man of the day," he replied, "is standing over there."

Uncle Jim and his wife, Aunt Ella, were dinner guests at Jack's home that evening. Jack did not mention his day's activities but near the close of the meal the Minister looked across the table at his nephew.

"How did the election turn out?" he asked.

"Herbert Pennington was elected unanimously."

"That's fine," beamed Uncle Jim. "That's great! I knew you'd win."

THE ATHENIAN BOYS' OATH

ANONYMOUS

We will never bring disgrace to this, our city, by any act of dishonesty or cowardice, nor ever desert our suffering comrades in the ranks.

We will fight for the ideals and sacred things of the city, both alone and with many; we will revere and obey the city's laws and do our best to incite a like respect and reverence in those above us who are prone to annul or set them at naught; we will strive unceasingly to quicken the public's sense of civic duty.

Thus in all these ways we will transmit this city not only not less, but greater than it was transmitted to us.

TO-DAY

THOMAS CARLYLE

So here hath been dawning
   Another blue day;
Think wilt thou let it
   Slip useless away?

Out of eternity
   This new day is born,
Into eternity
   At night, will return.

Behold it aforetime
   No eye ever did;
So soon it forever
   From all eyes is hid!

> Here hath been dawning
> Another blue day;
> Think, wilt thou let it
> Slip useless away?

OUT ON A LIMB

LOUISE BAKER

"One of two terrible things will happen," Grandma predicted. "She'll either kill herself, or worse yet, she'll get along fine and end up in vaudeville. We've had six clergymen, a smattering of lawyers and doctors, and a raft of schoolteachers and good honest farmers in this family, but never a show girl!"

"What about Great-great-great-cousin Thaddeus?" Bernice demanded, just to keep things interesting.

"Hah! That was on your mother's side." Grandmother nodded her head with satisfaction. "And even that rascal wasn't a show girl."

"But he was a perfectly marvellous outlaw and shot a man in cold blood," I bragged. "That's just as bad."

"It's not just as bad," Grandma stated with finality.

"Now, listen to me, Mother." On rare occasions Father was bold enough to stand up to Grandma. "We're off the subject. Louise is nine years old, and she wants some roller skates for her birthday. Is there anything so strange in that? Bernice had roller skates when she was nine."

"That's different. Bernice didn't make an unnatural spectacle of herself using them. Everyone will stare and, first thing you know, Louise will become a disgusting little exhibitionist and skate off with a carnival or something, and you'll never see her again. It's a pity she isn't a little lady, content to learn to sew and do water colours and read good literature. I never skated when I was her age, and I had both my limbs."

When Grandmother spoke of her own legs, she called them limbs, as if they were slightly more refined than ordinary appendages.

In reality Grandmother wasn't the sharp-bladed battle-axe she pretended. She was really fond of me, and every new hurdle I wanted to leap seemed twice as hazardous to her as the last one.

But Father bought me the skates. I had already experimented with Barbara Bradley's and knew I could manage. With a skate on my one foot and a crutch on each side, I propelled myself. My balance was exceptional — as is most every uniped's. This is a natural physical compensation that develops quickly — as do strong shoulders and arms. After a few good shoves, I could lift up my crutches and coast along easily on the one skate, pushing with my sticks only when I needed fresh momentum. For a child of nine, supposedly sentenced to a plodding pedestrianism, getting back on wheels was sheer ecstasy.

Of course I fell frequently while developing skill on roller skates. Every child sprawls when learning to skate. I am not convinced that I spread myself out on the sidewalk any more often than a normal child does. But this is the curious fact: my playmates, wise in their childhood, accepted my spills as inevitable to the process of learning — but adults didn't. No army of rescuers advanced double-quick to pick up any other youngster on the block when he came a cropper. But whenever I took a header, for all the turmoil the minor catastrophe created, it might have been a four-car smashup at a busy intersection. All the women in our neighbourhood must have squandered their days with their eyes glued to a crack in the window blind while I learned to roller-skate.

Whenever I fell, out swarmed the women in droves, clucking and fretting like a bunch of bereft mother hens. It was kind of them, and, looking back upon it, I appreciate their solicitude, but at the time I resented and was greatly embarrassed by their interference. It set me apart and emphasized my difference.

"What must her mother think!" was a phrase with which I

Out on a Limb

became very familiar. I know now what my mother thought. Inside our house, she, too, kept her eye on the crack in the blind, and she wrung her hands and took to biting her fingernails while she developed a lot of fortitude. For Mother differed from the other women in only one particular. She never ran out and picked me up. I believe that Father, a normally devoted husband, threatened murder if she did.

Eventually, of course, nobody paid any attention to me. The women abandoned their vigils at windows and went back to more pressing problems — their baking and dishwashing. I rolled up and down the street unheeded and was no longer considered good box office.

However, the roller-skating incident left its mark; consciously or unconsciously, it influenced my future approach to every physical activity. I was by nature energetic and athletic. I wanted to engage in all sorts of "inappropriate" games and sports, but I became overly sensitive to failure — foolishly so. I had a stubborn pride that was wounded by any hint that my handicap was a "handicap". It really wasn't much of one, compared to the frustrating handicaps many less fortunate people carry. Still, my feathers ruffled at the drop of The Word. A wise psychologist friend of mine has since put a name on this attitude of mind. She calls it a tendency to overcompensate.

When I learned to swim, I insisted that Father drive me out to the country to a friend's ranch where, in guarded privacy, I went through my dog-paddling period in a muddy irrigation ditch. I forewent the greater comfort and the companionship of the public swimming pool until I not only swam as well as other eleven-year-olds (the age at which I took to the water), but better. Then, when I made a public appearance, no one even noticed my handicap — I falsely deduced.

My swimming ability, in fact, probably was more conspicuous than utter clumsiness would have been. But blissfully, I never realized it. In the water, my arms and shoulders, disciplined into extra strength by my crutches, compensated in the Australian crawl for my one-cylinder flutter kick. I felt completely anonymous — happy, moron me! Actually, I wasn't the least bit anonymous, although my family encouraged me in this wild surmise. My sister tells me that my red bathing cap, bobbing about in the water, was invariably pointed out to bystanders. "See the little girl in the red cap? Would you believe it, she has only one leg!"

The same was true of tennis, which I learned in semi-secrecy. Father taught me in the early morning hours when the courts were unpopular. My father didn't permit me to feel sorry for myself, but he was sympathetic with my reluctance to display physical clumsiness. Tennis presents more limitations for an amputee than swimming. It is necessary to hold one crutch with just the upper arm, leaving a hand free to manipulate a racket. I heard of a man with a left leg amputation who played tennis with only one crutch. I always used two, since I am both right-handed and right-crutched and could not control, with one arm, both a racket and a completely weight-bearing crutch.

In spite of restrictions as a child, I did fairly well at tennis. I even competed, with average success, in a few junior tournaments. However, this brief period of minor distinction was not the result of exceptional skill. Instead, it was the happy aftermath of earlier and better instruction. My father was an able tennis amateur. He was patient in developing in me a good serve and a strong, deep-court drive to offset my inadequate net game. In playing tennis, I discovered that it is essential to hug the serving line. It is easy to run forward, but not backward, on crutches. I am completely vulnerable at the net or even mid-court where a lob over my head spells defeat. I can't readily retreat to get it on the bounce, and the alternative, a high aerial stroke, invariably makes me drop a crutch.

I once confronted across a net, by conspiracy of some school friends, a boy who was notoriously cocky on the tennis court. The plot was that I must defeat this self-advertising fire-eater so completely that he would never again hold up his arrogant

Out on a Limb 37

head. I had no confidence in my ability to do this, and, frankly, neither did my conspiring boy friends. It was such a superb scheme, however, that they were all willing to co-operate. They concluded that if I won, it would be magnificent irony — a baby stealing candy from a man, for a change.

Two boys were assigned to pound away at my backhand for a week, and spies reported my unsuspecting enemy's weaknesses and strengths. He was definitely not the ball of fire he advertised, but he was better than I, it was mournfully agreed. However, everyone hoped that I could at least give him enough competition to make him feel foolish. I was pledged to outplay myself, even if I collapsed in the process.

I didn't even know Charlie, the victim, but it all seemed solemnly important to me at the time that it happened.

It was contrived that I meet Charlie at the tennis courts, where he was loudly quoting what Bill Tilden said to him and what smart repartee he handed Bill. The game was arranged. We had decided to contract for only one set, as my well-wishers, in their wildest dreams, didn't hope I'd last longer than that.

In analyzing mine and my opponent's weaknesses, one great big one was overlooked. The outcome of that game was not traceable to technique and tenacity and my newly polished backhand, although all these helped, no doubt. The game was won on temper — both mine and Charlie's. To start with, the Cock's first sentence contained fighting words, as far as I was concerned. He said, with a patronizing air, "Sure, I'll take her on if you guys don't want to bother. I don't mind a bit."

I let this go by unchallenged. I merely seethed. Then he suggested that he should be handicapped if he played me. "I'll give you fifteen," he offered pompously. This was red flag to my bull!

"I'll give *you* thirty," I came back. This was red flag to his bull.

We marched out on the court as mad as if we'd just blacked each other's eyes. Temper warms me up, but it completely melted Charlie. He belonged to the racket-throwing type.

I must have been dropped on my head as a baby. I can't imagine any other explanation for squandering energy as extravagantly as I did on that occasion. I wouldn't work that hard to-day if I were promised the Davis Cup for keeps. Somehow, I got the notion embedded in my half-a-mind that there

Out on a Limb

was nothing in the world that mattered so much as beating Charlie.

As soon as Charlie and I spun for serve, all the tennis games in progress on the other courts stopped, and the players became our spectators. They all belonged in my camp and they helped me by none-too-sporting manoeuvres. They worked poor Charlie into fury by catcalls and other impertinences.

When he missed a shot or netted a serve, they'd all yell, "What's s'matter, got a Charlie — *horse?*" This was regarded in our high school circles as over-poweringly witty. Everyone hooted and howled.

"Maybe *you* need some crutches, Charlie!"

"*Fault!*" they'd yell before Charlie's serves even bounced. To ensure a trace of fair play, I had to call all the shots myself.

In spite of the nuisance value of my audience and the demoralizing effect on Charlie of his own temper, I had a desperate time beating him. We ran the set, most of the games long deuce-score ordeals, to twelve-ten before I won.

When it was over, my breath was coming in rattling gasps, and I looked like a dripping hot beet just out of a stewpot. Charlie walked off the court and broke up his racket by bashing it against a steel post. He wasn't a very lofty character.

I rode a brief wave of ecstasy while a crowd of what I regarded as exceedingly smooth boys banged me on my aching back and shouted my praises. Then I staggered home to soak my weary, heroic bones in a hot tub.

Father peered at me over his newspaper as I came in and collapsed on the davenport.

"Good grief!" he gasped. Father was not given to exaggeration so I must have resembled a sister of Grim Death. "What have you been doing?"

"I beat Charlie," I puffed proudly. "Been practising for over a week to do it."

"Well — you look as if *you'd* been beaten — by a bunch of strong-armed thugs. Why was it so important to beat Charlie?"

"Because he's so darned cocky—that's why. Jerry and Frazier and Donald Manker and some other kids thought it up and planned the whole thing."

"Why didn't Frazier beat him?" Father asked with deliberate denseness. "Frazier's the best player in high school."

"Father!" I groaned. "That wouldn't have meant anything. It had to be me."

"Oh—because you're a girl. I see." Father again used his annoying simple-minded ruse. "Why didn't Helen Fitzgerald take on this Charlie? She's twice the tennis player you are. She could have beaten him without getting knocked out."

"Oh, for goodness' sake, Father, are you dumb or something? Can't you see how much worse this dope would feel having *me* be the one to beat him?"

"I get it." Father sighed deeply. "Well, all I can say is that I'm disappointed in you."

"Disappointed! Every single other person in this whole town thinks I'm wonderful, that's all."

"Well, I don't!" Father snapped. "I thought you'd long since decided it wasn't sporting to take advantage of people because of crutches."

"Father—for heaven's sake, what's the matter with you? I didn't take advantage of him. I beat him fair and square. He played just as hard as he could. The score was twelve-ten—that shows you. The gang called a lot of the shots wrong, but I corrected every time in Charlie's favour. And he offered me a fifteen handicap, but I threw it right back in his face."

"You certainly salted his wounds, didn't you?"

I stared, incredulous, at Father.

"You know—" Father paused to frown at me. "You present a very complex moral problem, and I don't have any good precedents to follow in rearing you properly. But of *this* I am convinced: you took greater advantage of that boy to-day than if you'd frankly cheated him. You had a physical and personality advantage over him that must have made his defeat insufferable.

If he'd beaten you twelve-ten, you'd have walked off the court the victor, just the same."

"That's absolutely silly!" I protested, although this was true, and I knew it. We'd counted on just that in our ingenious plot.

"It's complicated, I grant you, but not silly. This isn't complicated, however. I'm glad you can swim and play tennis and ride a horse, but the only reason I'm glad is because these things are fun. That's why you and everyone else are supposed to do them. When you play a game to demonstrate what hot stuff you are on your crutches, it's time you quit and took up china painting, as your grandmother would have you do. Remember Grandma and your first roller skates? She was afraid you'd join a carnival if you learned to skate. Well — for my money, you were too close to the carnival for comfort to-day."

"Honestly, Father, you surprise me!" I protested, even as my mind touched the truth toward which he was leading me. "I suppose you just never want me to win anything."

"Of course, I want you to win — but only the game. Now, beat it! Take a bath and go to bed."

I started to cry as I left the room.

"By the way, you must have played inspired tennis to-day," my father called after me.

"I was hot, all right. I played much better than I am able to play."

"Hum. . . ." Father sighed. "I wouldn't have minded seeing that game."

"You'd have put a stop to it, though, I suppose — you and your ideas!"

"That's right," agreed Father, "I would have."

He was furious enough with me to cheerfully shake out my molars. But at the same time, in spite of himself, he was proud. Being crippled was, I decided, an exceedingly complicated business — but clear enough, nevertheless, so that I never bragged to anyone about beating Charlie.

SPLIT CHERRY TREE

JESSE STUART

"I don't mind staying after school," I says to Professor Herbert, "but I'd rather you'd whip me with a switch and let me go home early. Pa will whip me anyway for getting home two hours late."

"You are too big to whip," says Professor Herbert, "and I have to punish you for climbing up in that cherry tree. You boys knew better than that! The other five boys have paid their dollar each. You have been the only one who has not helped pay for the tree. Can't you borrow a dollar?"

"I can't," I says. "I'll have to take the punishment. I wish it would be quicker punishment. I wouldn't mind."

Professor Herbert stood and looked at me. He was a big man. He wore a grey suit of clothes. The suit matched his grey hair.

"You don't know my father," I says to Professor Herbert. "He might be called a little old-fashioned. He makes us mind him until we're twenty-one years old. He believes: 'If you spare the rod, you spoil the child.' I'll never be able to make him understand about the cherry tree. I'm the first one of my people to go to high school."

"You must take the punishment," says Professor Herbert. "You must stay two hours after school to-day and two hours after school to-morrow. I am allowing you twenty-five cents an hour. That is good money for a high school student. You can sweep the schoolhouse floor, wash the blackboards, and clean windows. I'll pay the dollar for you."

I couldn't ask Professor Herbert to lend me a dollar. He didn't offer to lend it to me. I had to stay and help the janitor and work out my fine at twenty-five cents an hour.

I thought as I swept the floor. "What will Pa do to me? What

Split Cherry Tree

lie can I tell him when I go home? Why did we ever climb that cherry tree and break it down, anyway? Why did we run crazy over the hills away from the crowd? Why did we do all of this? Six of us climbed up in a little cherry tree after one little lizard! Why did the tree split and fall with us? It should have been a stronger tree! Why did Eif Crabtree just happen to be below us plowing and catch us in his cherry tree? Why wasn't he a better man than to charge us six dollars for breaking the tree?"

It was six o'clock when I left the schoolhouse. I had six miles to walk home. It would be after seven when I got home. I had all my work to do when I got home. It took Pa and me both to do the work: seven cows to milk, nineteen head of cattle to feed, four mules, twenty-five hogs, firewood and stovewood to cut, and water to draw from the well. He would be doing it when I got home. He would be mad and wondering what was keeping me!

I hurried home. I ran under the dark, leafless trees. I walked fast uphill. I ran down the hill. The ground was freezing. I had to hurry. I had to run. I reached the long ridge that led to our cow pasture. I ran along this ridge. The wind dried the sweat on my face. I ran across the pasture to the house.

I threw down my books in the chip yard. I didn't take time to change my clean school clothes for my old work clothes. I ran out to the barn. I saw Pa spreading fodder on the ground for the cattle. That was my job. I ran up to the fence. I said, "Leave that for me, Pa; I'll do it. I'm just a little late."

"I see you are," said Pa. He turned to look at me. His eyes danced fire. "What in the world has kept you so? Why have you not been here to help me with this work? Make a gentleman out of one boy in the family and this is what you get! Send you to high school and you get too ornery for the buzzards to smell!"

I didn't say anything. I didn't want to tell why I was late from school. Pa stopped scattering the bundles of fodder. He looked at me. He says, "Why are you gettin' in here this time o' night? You tell me or I'll take a hickory withe to you right here on the spot!"

"I had to stay after school." I couldn't lie to Pa. He'd go to school and find out why I had to stay. If I lied to him, it would be too bad for me.

"Why did you have to stay after school?" says Pa.

I says, "Our biology class went on a field trip to-day. Six of us boys broke down a cherry tree. We had to give a dollar apiece to pay for the tree. I didn't have the dollar. Professor Herbert is making me work out my dollar. I had to stay in this afternoon. I'll have to stay in to-morrow afternoon!"

"Are you telling me the truth?" says Pa.

"I'm telling you the truth," I says. "Go and see for yourself."

"That's just what I'll do in the morning," says Pa. "And just whose cherry tree did you break down?"

"Eif Crabtree's cherry tree!"

"What were you doing clear out at Eif Crabtree's place?" says Pa. "He lives four miles from the county high school. Don't they teach you no books at that high school? Do they just let you get out and gad over the hillsides? If that's all they do, I'll keep you at home, Dave. I've got work here for you to do!"

"Pa," I says, "spring is just getting here. We take a subject in school where we have to have bugs, snakes, flowers, lizards, frogs, and plants. It is biology. It was a pretty day to-day. We went out to find a few of these. Six of us boys at the same time saw a lizard sunning on a cherry tree. We all went up the tree to get it. We broke the tree down. It split at the forks. Eif' Crabtree was plowing down below us. He ran up the hill and got our names. The other boys gave their dollar apiece. I didn't have mine. Professor Herbert put mine in for me. Now I have to work the dollar out at school."

"Poor man's son, huh," says Pa. "I'll attend to that myself in the morning. I'll take care of him. He ain't from this county nohow. I'll go down there in the morning and see him. Letting you leave your books and galavant all over the hills! What kind

Split Cherry Tree

of school is it, anyhow? Didn't do that, my son, when I was a little shaver in school. All fared alike, too."

"Pa, please don't go down there," I says; "just let me have fifty cents and pay the rest of my fine! I don't want you to go down there! I don't want you to start anything with Professor Herbert!"

"Ashamed of your old Pap are you, Dave," says Pa, "after the way I've worked to raise you! Tryin' to send you to school so you can make a better livin' than I've made.

"I'll straighten this thing out myself. I'll take care of Professor Herbert myself! He ain't got no right to keep you in and let the other boys off just because they've got the money! I'm a poor man. A bullet will go in a professor same as it will a poor man. Now you get into this work before I take one o' these switches and cut the shirt off'n your back!"

I thought once I'd run through the woods above the barn just as hard as I could go. I thought I'd leave high school and home forever! Pa could not catch me! I'd get away! I couldn't go back to school with him. He'd have a gun and maybe he would shoot Professor Herbert. Hard to tell just what he would do. I could tell Pa that school had changed in the hills from the way it was when he was a boy, but he wouldn't understand. I could tell him we studied frogs, birds, snakes, lizards, flowers, insects. But Pa wouldn't understand. If I did run away from home, it wouldn't matter to Pa. He would see Professor Herbert anyway. He would think that high school and Professor Herbert had caused me to run away from home. There was no need to run away. I'd just have to stay, finish foddering the cattle, and go to school with Pa the next morning.

I would take a bundle of fodder, remove the hickory-withe band from around it, and scatter it on rocks, clumps of green briers, and brush so the cattle wouldn't tramp it under their feet. I would lean it up against the oak trees and the rocks in the pasture just above our pig-pen on the hill. The fodder was cold and frosty where it had set out in the stacks. I would carry bundles of the fodder from the stack until I had spread out a bundle for each steer. Pa went to the barn to feed the mules and throw corn in the pen to the hogs.

The moon shone bright in the cold March sky. I finished my work by moonlight. Professor Herbert really didn't know how much work I had to do at home. If he had known, he would not have kept me after school. He would have lent me a dollar to pay my part of the cherry tree. He had never lived in the hills. He didn't know the way the hill boys had to work so that they could go to school. Now he was teaching in a country high school where all the boys who attended were from hill farms.

After I'd finished doing my work, I went to the house and ate my supper. Pa and Mom had eaten. My supper was getting cold. I heard Pa and Mom talking in the front room. Pa was telling Mom about me staying in after school.

"I had to do all the milkin' to-night, chop the wood myself. It's too hard on me after I've turned ground all day. I'm going to take a day off to-morrow and see if I can't remedy things a little. I'll go down to that high school to-morrow. I won't be a very good scholar for Professor Herbert. He won't keep me in after school. I'll take a different kind of lesson down there and make him acquainted with it."

"Now, Luster," says Mom, "you just stay away from there. Don't cause a lot of trouble. You can be jailed for a trick like that. You'll get the Law after you. You'll just go down there and show off, and plague your own boy Dave in front of all the scholars!"

"Plague or no plague," says Pa, "he doesn't take into consideration what all I have to do here, does he? I'll show him it isn't right to keep one boy in and let the rest go scot-free. My boy is as good as the rest, isn't he? A bullet will make a hole in a schoolteacher same as it will in anybody else. He can't treat me that way and get by with it; I'll plug him first. I'm going down there bright and early in the morning and get all this straight! I intend to see about bug larnin' and this runnin' all over God's

Split Cherry Tree

creation huntin' snakes, lizards, and frogs. Ransackin' the country and goin' through cherry orchards and breakin' the trees down after lizards! Old Eif Crabtree ought to have poured hot lead into 'em instead o' chargin' six dollars for the tree! He should have got old Herbert, the first one!"

I ate my supper. I slipped upstairs and lit the lamp. I tried to forget the whole thing. I studied plane geometry. Then I studied my biology lesson. I could hardly study for thinking about Pa. "He'll go to school with me in the morning. He'll take a gun for Professor Herbert! What will Professor Herbert think of me! I'll tell him when Pa leaves that I couldn't help it. But Pa might shoot him. I hate to go with Pa. Maybe he'll cool off about it to-night and not go with me in the morning."

Pa got up at four o'clock. He built a fire in the stove. Then he built a fire in the fireplace. He got Mom up to get breakfast. Then he got me up to help feed and milk. By the time we had our work done at the barn, Mom had breakfast ready for us. We ate our breakfast. Daylight came and we could see the bare oak trees covered white with frost. The hills were white with frost. A cold wind was blowing. The sky was clear. The sun would soon come out and melt the frost. The afternoon would be warm with sunshine and the frozen ground would thaw. There would be mud on the hills again. Muddy water would then run down through the little ditches on the hills.

"Now, Dave," says Pa, "let's get ready for school. I intend to go with you this morning and look into bug larnin', frog larnin', lizard and snake larnin', and breakin' down cherry trees! I don't like no sicha foolish way o' larnin' myself!"

Pa hadn't forgot. I'd have to take him to school with me. He would take me to school with him. I was glad we were going early. If Pa pulled a gun on Professor Herbert, there wouldn't be so many of my classmates there to see him.

I knew that Pa wouldn't be at home in the high school. He wore overalls, big boots, a blue shirt, and a sheepskin coat, and a slouched hat gone to seed at the top. He put his gun in its holster. We started trudging toward the high school across the hill.

It was early when we got to the county high school. Professor Herbert had just got there. As we walked up the steps into the schoolhouse, I thought, "Maybe Pa will find out Professor Herbert is a good man. He just doesn't know him. Just like the way I felt toward the Lambert boys across the hill. I didn't like them until I'd seen them and talked to them. After I had gone to school with them and talked to them, I liked them and we were friends. There's a lot in knowing the other fellow."

"You're the Professor here, aren't you?" says Pa.

"Yes," says Professor Herbert, "and I expect that you are Dave's father."

"Yes," says Pa, pulling out his gun and laying it on the seat in Professor Herbert's office. Professor Herbert's eyes got big behind his black-rimmed glasses when he saw Pa's gun. Colour came into his pale cheeks.

"Just a few things about this school I want to know," says Pa. "I'm tryin' to make a scholar out of Dave. He's the only one of eleven youngins I've sent to high school. Here he comes in late and leaves me all the work to do! He said you'd all been out bug hunting yesterday and broke down a cherry tree. He had to stay two hours after school yesterday and work out money to pay for that cherry tree! Is that right?"

"Yes," says Professor Herbert, "I guess it is."

He looked at Pa's gun.

"Well," says Pa, "this is no high school. It's a bug school, a lizard school, a snake school! It ain't no school nohow!"

"Why did you bring that gun?" says Professor Herbert to Pa.

"You see that little hole," says Pa as he picked up the long blue forty-four and put his finger on the end of the barrel; "a bullet can come out of that hole that will kill a schoolteacher just the same as it will kill any other man. It will kill a rich man same as a poor man. But after I came in and saw you, I

Split Cherry Tree   49

knew I wouldn't need it. This maul o' mine could do you in a few minutes."

Pa stood there, big, hard, brown-skinned, and mighty beside Professor Herbert. I didn't know Pa was so much bigger and harder. I had never seen Pa in a schoolhouse before. I'd seen Professor Herbert. He'd looked big before to me. He didn't look big standing beside Pa.

"I was only doing my duty, Mr. Sexton," says Professor Herbert, "and following the course of study the state provided us with."

"Course of study," says Pa, "what study, bug study? Varmint study? Takin' youngins to the woods and their poor old Mas and Pas at home a slavin' to keep 'em in school and give 'em an education! You know that's dangerous, too, puttin' a lot of boys and girls out together like that!"

Students were coming into the schoolhouse now.

Professor Herbert says, "Close the door, Dave, so others won't hear."

I walked over and closed the door. I was shaking like a leaf in the wind. I thought Pa was going to hit Professor Herbert every minute. He was doing all the talking. His face was getting red. The red colour was coming through the brown, weather-beaten skin on Pa's face.

"I was right with these students," says Professor Herbert. "I know what they got into and what they didn't. I didn't send one of the other teachers with them on this field trip. I went myself. Yes, I took the boys and girls together. Why not?"

"It just don't look good to me," says Pa, "a-takin' all this swarm of youngins out to pillage the whole deestrict — breakin' down cherry trees, keepin' boys in after school."

"What else could I have done with Dave, Mr. Sexton?" says Professor Herbert. "The boys didn't have any business at all climbing that cherry tree after one lizard. One boy could have gone up in the tree and got it. The farmer charged us six dollars.

It was a little steep, I think, but we had to pay it. Must I make five boys pay and let your boy off? He said he didn't have the dollar and couldn't get it. So I put it in for him. I'm letting him work it out. He's not working for me. He's working for the school."

"I just don't know what you could have done with him," says Pa, "only a-larruped him with a withe! That's what he needed!"

"He's too big to whip," says Professor Herbert, pointing at me. "He's a man in size."

"He's not too big for me to whip," says Pa. "They're not too big until they're over twenty-one! It just didn't look fair to me! Work one and let the rest out because they got the money. I don't see what bugs has got to do with a high school! It don't look good to me nohow!"

Pa picked up his gun and put it back in its holster. The red colour left Professor Herbert's face. He talked more to Pa. Pa softened a little. It looked funny to see Pa in the high school building. It was the first time he'd ever been there.

"We were not only hunting snakes, toads, flowers, butterflies, lizards," says Professor Herbert, "but, Mr. Sexton, I was hunting dry timothy grass to put in an incubator and raise some protozoa."

"I don't know what this is," says Pa to him. "The incubator is the new-fangled way of cheatin' the hens and raisin' chickens. I'm not so sure about the breed o' chickens you mentioned."

"You've heard of germs, Mr. Sexton, haven't you?" says Professor Herbert.

"Just call me Luster, if you don't mind," says Pa, casual like.

"All right, Luster, you've heard of germs, haven't you?"

"Yes," says Pa, "but I don't believe in germs. I'm sixty-five years old and I haven't seen one yet!"

"You can't see them with your naked eye," says Professor Herbert. "Just keep that gun in the holster and stay with me in the high school to-day. I have a few things I want to show you. That scum on your teeth has germs in it."

Split Cherry Tree 51

"What," says Pa, "you mean to tell me I've got germs on my teeth?"

"Yes," says Professor Herbert, "the same kind as we might be able to find in a living black snake if we dissect it!"

"I don't mean to dispute your word," says Pa, "but I don't believe it. I don't believe I have germs on my teeth!"

"Stay with me to-day and I'll show you. I want to take you through the school anyway! School has changed a lot in the hills since you went to school. I don't guess we had high schools in this country when you went to school."

"No," says Pa, "just readin', writin', and cipherin'. We didn't have all this bug larnin', frog larnin', and finding germs on your teeth and in the middle o' black snakes! The world's changin'."

"It is," says Professor Herbert, "and, we hope, for the better. Boys like your own there are going to help change it. He's your boy. He knows all of what I've told you. You stay with me to-day."

"I'll shore stay with you," says Pa. "I want to see the germs off'n my teeth. I just want to see a germ. I've never seen one in my life. 'Seein' is believin'' Pap allus told me."

Pa walks out of the office with Professor Herbert. I just hoped that he wouldn't decide to have Pa arrested for pulling his gun. Pa's gun has always been a friend to him when he goes to settle disputes.

The bell rang. School took up. I saw the students look at Pa when they marched into the schoolhouse. They would grin and punch each other. Pa just stood and watched them pass in at the schoolhouse door. Two long lines marched into the house. The boys and girls were clean and well-dressed. Pa stood over in the school-yard under a leafless elm, in his sheepskin coat, his big boots laced in front with buckskin, and his heavy socks stuck above his boot tops. Pa's overall legs were baggy and wrinkled between his coat and boot tops. His blue work shirt showed at the collar. His big black hat showed his grey-streaked black hair. His face was hard and weather-tanned to the colour of a ripe fodder blade. His hands were big and gnarled like the roots of the elm tree he stood beside.

When I went to my first class, I saw Pa and Professor Herbert going around over the schoolhouse. I was in my geometry class when Pa and Professor Herbert came into the room. We were explaining our propositions on the blackboard. Professor Herbert and Pa just quietly came in and sat for awhile. I heard Fred Wurts whisper to Glenn Armstrong, "Who is that old man? Gee, he's a rough-looking scamp." Glenn whispered back, "I think he's Dave's pap." The students in geometry looked at Pa. They must have wondered what he was doing in school. Before the class was over, Pa and Professor Herbert got up and went out. I saw them together down on the playground. Professor Herbert was explaining to Pa. I could see the prints of Pa's gun under his coat when he'd walk around.

At noon in the high school cafeteria Pa and Professor Herbert sat together at the little table where Professor Herbert always ate by himself. They ate together. The students watched the way Pa ate. He ate with his knife instead of his fork. A lot of the students felt sorry for me after they found out he was my father. They didn't have to feel sorry for me. I wasn't ashamed of Pa after I found out he wasn't going to shoot Professor Herbert. I was glad they had made friends. I was sure now that he would find out about the high school as I had found out about the Lambert boys across the hill.

In the afternoon when we went to biology, Pa was in class. He was sitting on one of the high stools beside the microscope. We went ahead with our work just as if Pa wasn't in the class. I saw Pa take his knife and scrape tartar from one of his teeth. Professor Herbert put it on the lens and adjusted the microscope for Pa. He adjusted it and worked awhile. Then he says, "Now, Luster, look! Put your eye right down to the light. Squint the other eye!"

Pa put his head down and did as Professor Herbert said. "I see 'im," says Pa. "Who'd a ever thought that? Right on a

Split Cherry Tree 53

body's teeth! Right in a body's mouth. You're right certain they ain't no fake to this, Professor Herbert?"

"No, Luster," says Professor Herbert, "it's there. That's the germ. Germs live in a world we cannot see with the naked eye. We must use the microscope. There are millions of them in our bodies. Some are harmful. Others are helpful."

Pa holds his face down and looks through the microscope. We stop and watch Pa. He sits upon the tall stool. His knees are against the table. His legs are long. His coat slips up behind when he bends over. The handle of his gun shows. Professor Herbert pulls his coat down quickly.

"Oh, yes," says Pa. He gets up and pulls his coat down. Pa's face gets a little red. He knows about his gun and he knows he doesn't have any use for it in high school.

"We have a big black snake over here we caught yesterday," says Professor Herbert. "We'll chloroform him and dissect him and show you he has germs in his body, too."

"Don't do it," says Pa. "I believe you. I just don't want to see you kill the black snake. I never kill one. They are good mousers and a lot of help to us on the farm. I like black snakes. I just hate to see any one kill 'em. I don't allow 'em killed on my place."

The students look at Pa. They seem to like him better after he said that. Pa with a gun in his pocket but a tender heart beneath his ribs for snakes, though not for man! Pa won't whip a mule at home. He won't whip his cattle.

"Man can defend hisself," says Pa, "but cattle and mules can't. We have the drop on 'em. Ain't nothin' to a man that'll beat a good pullin' mule. He ain't got the right kind o' heart!"

Professor Herbert took Pa through the laboratory. He showed him the different kinds of work we were doing. He showed him our equipment. They stood and talked while we worked. They talked louder when they got out in the hall.

When biology class was over, I walked out of the room. It was our last class for the day. I would have to take my broom and sweep two hours to finish paying for the split cherry tree.

I wondered if Pa would want me to stay. He was standing in the hallway watching the students march out. He looked lost among us. He looked like a leaf turned brown on the tree among the treetop filled with growing leaves.

I got my broom and started to sweep. Professor Herbert walked up and says, "I'm going to let you do that some other time. You can go home with your father. He is waiting out there."

I laid my broom down, got my books, and went down the steps.

Pa says, "Haven't you got two hours o' sweepin' yet to do?"

I says, "Professor Herbert said I could do it some other time. He said for me to go home with you."

"No," says Pa, "you are goin' to do as he says. He's a good man. School has changed from my day and time. I'm a dead leaf, Dave. I'm behind. I don't belong here. If he'll let me, I'll get a broom and we'll both sweep one hour. That'll pay your debt. I'll hep you pay it. I'll ask him and see if he won't let me hep you."

"I'm going to cancel the debt," says Professor Herbert. "I just wanted you to understand, Luster."

"I understand," says Pa, "and since I understand, he must pay his debt for the tree, and I'm goin' to hep 'im."

"Don't do that," says Professor Herbert. "It's all on me."

"We don't do things like that," says Pa; "we're just and honest people. We don't want somethin' for nothin'. Professor Herbert, you're wrong now and I'm right. You'll have to listen to me. I've larned a lot from you. My boy must go on. The world has left me. It's changed while I've raised my family and plowed the hills. I'm a just and honest man. I don't skip debts. I haven't taught them to do that. I haven't got much larnin' myself, but I do know right from wrong after I see it."

Professor Herbert went home. Pa and I stayed and swept one hour. It looked funny to see Pa use a broom. He never used one at home. Mom used the broom. Pa used the plow. Pa did hard work. Pa says, "I can't sweep. Durned if I can. Look at

The Children's Song

the streaks o' dirt I leave on the floor! Seems like no work at all for me. Brooms is too light or something. I'll just do the best I can, Dave. I've been wrong about the school."

I says, "Did you know Professor Herbert can get a warrant out for you for bringing your pistol to school and showing it in his office? They can railroad you for that!"

"That's all made right," says Pa. "I've made that right. Professor Herbert is not going to take it to court. He likes me. I like him. We just had to get together. He has the remedies. He showed me. You must go on to school. I am as strong a man as ever come out'n the hills for my years and the hard work I've done. But I'm behind times, Dave. I'm a little man. Your hands will be softer than mine. Your clothes will be better. You'll always look cleaner than your old pap. Just remember, Dave, to be honest and pay your debts. Just be kind to animals and don't bother the snakes. That's all I got agin the school. Puttin' black snakes to sleep and cuttin' 'em open."

It was late when we got home. Stars were in the sky. The moon was up. The ground was frozen. Pa took his time going home. I couldn't run as I did the night before. It was ten o'clock before we got the work finished, and our suppers eaten. Pa sat before the fire and told Mom he was going to take her and show her a germ sometime. Mom hadn't seen one, either. Pa told her about the high school and the fine man Professor Herbert was. He told Mom about the strange school across the hill and how different it was from the school in their day and time.

THE CHILDREN'S SONG

RUDYARD KIPLING

Land of our Birth, we pledge to thee
Our love and toil in the years to be;
When we are grown and take our place,
As men and women with our race.

Father in Heaven, who lovest all,
Oh, help Thy children when they call;
That they may build from age to age,
An undefilèd heritage.

Teach us to bear the yoke in youth
With steadfastness and careful truth;
That, in our time, Thy Grace may give
The Truth whereby the Nations live.

Teach us to rule ourselves alway,
Controlled and cleanly night and day;
That we may bring, if need arise,
No maimed or worthless sacrifice.

Teach us to look in all our ends,
On Thee for judge, and not our friends;
That we, with Thee, may walk uncowed
By fear or favour of the crowd.

Teach us the Strength that cannot seek
By deed or thought, to hurt the weak;
That, under Thee, we may possess
Man's strength to comfort man's distress.

Teach us Delight in simple things,
And Mirth that has no bitter springs,
Forgiveness free of evil done,
And Love to all men 'neath the sun!

Land of our Birth, our faith, our pride,
For whose dear sake our fathers died;
O Motherland, we pledge to thee
Head, heart, and hand through the years to be!

Along Nature's Trails

THE UNNAMED LAKE

FREDERICK GEORGE SCOTT

It sleeps among the thousand hills
  Where no man ever trod,
And only nature's music fills
  The silences of God.

Great mountains tower above its shore,
  Green rushes fringe its brim,
And o'er its breast for evermore
  The wanton breezes skim.

Dark clouds that intercept the sun
  Go there in Spring to weep,
And there, when Autumn days are done,
  White mists lie down to sleep.

Sunrise and sunset crown with gold
  The peaks of ageless stone,
Where winds have thundered from of old
  And storms have set their throne.

No echoes of the world afar
  Disturb it night or day,
But sun and shadow, moon and star
  Pass and repass for aye.

'Twas in the grey of early dawn,
  When first the lake we spied,
And fragments of a cloud were drawn
  Half down the mountain side.

Along the shore a heron flew,
  And from a speck on high,

    That hovered in the deepening blue,
      We heard the fish-hawk's cry.

    Among the cloud-capt solitudes,
      No sound the silence broke,
    Save when, in whispers down the woods,
      The guardian mountains spoke.

    Through tangled brush and dewy brake,
      Returning whence we came,
    We passed in silence, and the lake
      We left without a name.

DREAM RIVER

MARJORIE L. C. PICKTHALL

Wind-silvered willows hedge the stream,
    And all within is hushed and cool.
The water, in an endless dream,
    Goes sliding down from pool to pool.
And every pool a sapphire is,
    From shadowy deep to sunlit edge,
Ribboned around with irises
    And cleft with emerald spears of sedge.

O, every morn the winds are stilled,
    The sunlight falls in amber bars.
O, every night the pools are filled
    With silver brede of shaken stars.
O, every morn the sparrow flings
    His elfin trills athwart the hush,
And here unseen at eve there sings
    One crystal-throated hermit-thrush.

RUNAWAY BULL

KERRY WOOD

The Jersey bull stood on a ledge of rock high on the mountain side, small eyes watching two specks that moved on the valley trail far below. The specks were men, but the tan-coloured bull now viewed all larger creatures as enemies. So he stretched out his black muzzle and sent a challenge trumpeting across the wilds.

Instantly the men reined up their horses.

"That's him!" cried Jordon. "He's alive, Waddy!"

Waddy's binoculars soon focussed upon the animal.

"He's up on that point beyond the break in the timber," he reported, then moved the glasses beyond the bull's position. "I don't see any sign of the cows, Jordon."

"Let's have a look."

"We can hardly expect that they'd live through the winter," Waddy added, handing over the glasses. "Full-blooded Jersey stock is never hardy, and they'd need to be tough to last out a mountain winter spent back here."

Their little herd of registered dairy cattle, led by a proud-stepping, black-maned bull, had somehow climbed the steep walls of a blind canyon at the back of their ranch and crossed over a high pass to get into mountain wilderness. They escaped in the late autumn, and early snows had prevented Jordon and his partner from searching the back country for them. The blood stock made up a large slice of their capital, and Jordon had been unwilling to believe that the winter had killed the runaways. But he and Waddy had been forced to wait until snows melted, before they could get through the high pass to continue their search.

"Looks as if he's on a sort of ledge," Jordon spoke, studying the bull's position through the binoculars. "Maybe there's a

Runaway Bull

little grassy cup or meadow behind him, out of sight from this angle. The cows might be there, behind him."

Waddy smiled and shook his head: "I figure you're asking for too much. Even if we only get the bull back to our ranch, that's worthwhile. After all, he cost us plenty."

"So did the eight cows," Jordon retorted. "Well, let's go. It's going to be a chore to coax our horses away up there."

"I'm not going without my horse," Waddy answered. "I'm not keen on facing that spry bull on foot, after he's run wild so long. I guess we should ha' known better than to turn the dairy herd loose in that blind canyon in the first place."

"No herd ever got out of that pocket before."

"Maybe not, but we never had a bull like this before, either."

They tied their two pack horses to trees, unfastening the strappings on one to reveal a couple of large bundles of oat sheaves. Each man took a fat sheaf under an arm. They turned their saddle horses towards the steep slope of the timbered ravine.

When he saw the men disappear among the spruces, the bull bugled again. He turned to look at his cows as they cropped the sparse grass sprouted around a moss-lined spring. The eight cows were thin, for the winter had been long and food scarce. Grass grew only in the sheltered ravines, where it required hard scraping to pull the deep snows aside and lay bare the wispy fodder. The scarcity of food forced them to move from one ravine to another all winter long. Sometimes, on their travels, the snows were shoulder deep and the danger of being trapped in the white drifts was a constant threat. Often a stranded cow had called despairingly for help, the plucky leader plunging through to break out the trail and urge the straggler to greater effort. When blizzards came, he marshalled his family into the screening evergreens for shelter. Huddled together for warmth, they had to go hungry till the storm slacked off. Only the bull's lion heart had carried his herd alive through the long winter. Now, spring had come again, calving was over, and the cows still dragged weakly along. New grass was not yet plentiful enough to provide rich feeding, but they plucked at it hungrily, now and then raising their heads to glance at the restless leader whose blaring challenge had upset the tranquil afternoon.

While the cows fed, their calves rested or played nearby. Most of the smaller calves were bunched close to the spring, thin legs awkwardly folded under them while they slept. A few older ones frolicked, tails up and tiny hooves kicking out as they pranced happily around. Two of them went some distance above the herd, bounding up the ravine meadow and uttering high-pitched bleats as they raced. Their mothers paid them little heed, heads to the grass and busy with feeding. But the bull was alert to their distance from the band and snorted his warning. The calves froze momentarily, staring wide-eyed down at their protector. When the bull turned away again to watch the quiet valley, the two calves went on with their gambolling.

From the high part of the ravine another pair of eyes watched the calves. As the little fellows strayed farther from the cows and nearer to the narrow neck of the meadow, the watcher's interest warmed, and a pink tongue slavered over the nose that snuffed the warm meat smell. Og-hin-sha-tunga, the giant grizzly bear of the mountains, had been out of his winter lair for only two weeks. At first he had sought medicinal plants to break his long fast, but now his shrivelled stomach craved a gorging meal of hot flesh. In a moment, the ravenous bear had decided to hunt this chance quarry. For all his large heft, the big beast moved like a shadow among the rocks as he stalked his banquet.

The bull, uneasy, wheeled abruptly away from the ledge to join the grazing cows. Again he noted the distance of the two straying calves, and bellowed a short and angry command. The calves jerked their frolic to a stop; their mothers looked up from feeding and seconded the leader's summons with softer appeals. Reluctantly, the two calves edged down the slope towards the herd.

It was at that instant that the huge bear reached the last boulder that could screen his heft from view of the calves. As he saw his quarry turn and go down the ravine, a snarl rumbled in the grizzly's throat. He sprang from his hiding place, charging at full speed. The hindmost calf bleated in sudden terror just before a talon-shod paw axed down and sent him sprawling like an emptied sack on the ground.

The bull was quite as quick. At first sight of the enemy, his urgent bellow marshalled the cows. Calves hustled behind them, and eight mothers aimed a phalanx of horned heads towards the grizzly. The lone calf sprinted down the ravine like a frightened deer, to dodge quivering behind his mother. Then the bull lumbered up the draw, attacking to save his herd.

The bear reared on its haunches, one front paw raised to strike. Straight at his foe the bull charged. As he drew near, his head went down to point his curved horns. Just as those horns came within striking range, the bear's paw stabbed down with terrific force. The blow missed the vital neck target, glancing to one side as the bull's horns jerked up. The humped shoulders of the Jersey were slashed by the curved sabres, and he staggered under the double shock of the blow. His horns had missed his enemy.

Before Og-hin-sha-tunga could deliver another blow, the herd's champion swerved out of reach. Swiftly the bull whirled, one horn raking the grizzly's spine. The huge bear sprang clear, but the horn came away with a crimson stain on it to show that the bull had scored. Loudly the bear squealed, feeling the sudden stab of pain. Then it launched a counter-charge.

But the bull dodged away, sure-footed after spending the winter on the slippery slopes. He had learned caution from that staggering twin-blow suffered in his first blind rush. Now he backed away from his snarling enemy, keeping horns aimed. The grizzly respected those curved weapons, feinting to one side and then the other as it tried for a clear chance to smash at the bull's neck.

Suddenly the bull lunged. Again the bear sprang aside, paws flashing down at terrific speed. The Jersey staggered to his knees, numbed by the blow on his humped shoulder. As he fell, he jerked his head around and the horns raked the bear's ribs. With a nimble twist, he buried the black daggers deep into the other's body. The grizzly screamed, rearing backwards to wrench clear. Then it rushed forward to finish the battle.

By this time, the bull had regained his feet. Once again he levelled his red-stained horns. The bear halted its charge, snarling and wary. The bull kept pivotting, head towards his adversary while the grizzly wheeled around. Jersey nostrils scented the calf that had fallen to the bear's first rush. The herd's champion seemed to forget the fight for a moment, stretching down a questing muzzle to touch the limp calf. The little body failed to respond; the bull had snuffed the cold scent of death. He stepped back from that pathetic body. A bellow erupted from the bottom of his throat.

This time there was no blind charge. The bull inched forward, edging close to the waiting bear. Grizzly's paw poised, ready for the stroke. Then the bull levelled his horns, and instantly the bear dodged aside.

But the Jersey had been watching. Now he lunged with furious acceleration. Full force, the grizzly received the impact of the one-ton body; the sharp horns sank out of sight before their owner wrenched loose his head. A terrible scream tore the air, then Og-hin-sha-tunga fell clear and turned to run. The bull thundered after him. His charge caught the grizzly full on his spine. Bone crackled sickeningly — the fight was ended. The Jersey tossed his massive head, the bear crumpled into a shapeless heap and stayed still.

The victor backed off; he pawed the earth; he challenged once again. This time the bugle was a blare of triumph. The wedge of cows relaxed their vigilance. They bawled in applause as their proud champion stepped briskly down towards them.

At that moment, Jordon and Waddy rode their horses out of the timber and eyed the battlefield.

"I told you there was a fight going on," cried Jordon. "Look — a dead grizzly!"

"Look down there!" shouted Waddy. "All the cows, alive and safe! Seven calves, and all the cows. What a bull!"

The blood-stained leader stopped and turned, staring at the men with hostile eyes. One hoof started to rake the ground, a warning rumbled in his throat. But Jordon rode forward at once, flinging his oat sheaf under his Jersey's lowered head. Nostrils snuffed sweet odours of almost forgotten oats. Now Waddy's bundle tumbled down, doubling the temptation.

The bull heard Jordon talking to him, talking quietly but with remembered authority. Memories swam back into the runaway mind. He recalled alfalfa pastures, warm barns, and herds that were sleek with fat and safe from harm.

The tan throat lowed softly to the waiting cows, inviting them back to domesticity.

STUPIDITY STREET

RALPH HODGSON

I saw with open eyes
    Singing birds sweet
Sold in the shops
    For the people to eat,
Sold in the shops of
    Stupidity Street.

I saw in vision
    The worm in the wheat,
And in the shops nothing
    For people to eat;
Nothing for sale in
    Stupidity Street.

THE SNARE

JAMES STEPHENS

I hear a sudden cry of pain!
    There is a rabbit in a snare:
Now I hear the cry again,
    But I cannot tell from where.

But I cannot tell from where
    He is calling out for aid!
Crying on the frightened air,
    Making everything afraid!

Making everything afraid!
    Wrinkling up his little face!

As he cries again for aid;
— And I cannot find the place!

And I cannot find the place
 Where his paw is in the snare!
Little One! Oh, Little One!
 I am searching everywhere!

BLACK PIRATE OF THE PEAKS

WILLIS G. CRAIG

John Condon plodded steadily up the rough trail that led to the lofty crest of the Coast Range. Suddenly he stopped and scanned the sky. That high keening *kre-e-e, kre-e-e,* which his sharp ears had caught, seemed to come straight from the vault of heaven. Slipping the straps of his pack, he raised the binoculars that hung round his neck. Methodically he quartered the sky. A wheeling mote high overhead leaped into prominence in the powerful glasses. There was no mistaking the long-winged, soaring bird — a duck hawk, *falco peregrinus,* the true peregrine falcon of hawking lore.

Intently Condon studied the bird as it swung in graceful circles above him, shrilling its high-pitched, yelping cry. When he lowered the binoculars he was smiling. Instead of the creamy breast and barred underwings of the typical duck hawk, this swift pirate was almost blue-black!

Two months before, while at San Francisco, he had heard rumours of a black falcon in the mountains above Madrone Canyon, and characteristically he had come to see for himself. He whistled softly under his breath. In all his wanderings, the young naturalist had never seen a black duck hawk. He very much doubted if any of the well-known museums had even a stuffed specimen of this rare black form; and as for a live one, it would be worth its weight in gold. Could he, somehow, secure it?

Pondering a plan which formed in his mind, he shouldered his pack, to the back of which was strapped a willow cage containing a fluttering pigeon. In record time he climbed the last half-mile to a gem-like little meadow nestling in a hollow on a great arc of the mountain.

Long after the westering sun had dropped from sight, the bare upper slopes of the peak reflected its last pink rays. Then they too were gone, and the misty canyons below faded from view. For a time John Condon sat beside his tiny fire and planned his campaign against the black falcon.

In his pack lay a gourd of the most powerful birdlime he had ever seen. He did not know the formula for it, but he had seen it used. Old Dulat Yar, the ancient falconer of Srinagar, had given it to him in the mountains of high Kashmir the year before. Now he was about to put it to another test.

Dawn found him on the mountainside. In one hand he carried the pigeon cage and a thin, light lath about thirty inches in length and shaped like a double paddle. The lath was painted a greyish blue, and at its middle a two-foot length of stout fish line was tied.

When Condon heard the distant cry of the black falcon, he immediately concealed himself in a manzanita thicket. From his pocket he drew the tiny gourd that Dulat Yar had given him, and smeared the hardwood lath with the thick, sticky birdlime.

High up in the first rays of the sun, dots drifted back and forth. So the black pirate had a mate! Condon scowled. That might complicate matters. Perhaps he had better try to locate the eyrie. He balanced the slender lime-smeared lath in his hand. No, he would try Dulat Yar's method first.

At last the soaring pair drew nearer until they were directly overhead. Reaching into the willow cage, Condon took out the pigeon. To its leg he fastened one end of the fish line attached to the lath, but he could not bring himself to blind the pigeon as Dulat Yar had recommended. With a deep breath he tossed the bird upward.

Black Pirate of the Peaks

Once free of the thicket, the big band-tailed pigeon soared aloft on strong wings, the trailing blue-grey lath invisible against the sky. Up and up it rose into the clear mountain air. To Condon, watching with strained eyes from his place of concealment, it seemed that the two hawks would never notice the decoy winging beneath them.

Then a shrill call sounded as the black falcon spied the racing pigeon and launched himself after it. The band-tail, realizing his danger, put on speed, the thin lath trailing a little behind and below him. Swiftly the hawk overtook the pigeon and spiralled for a moment. Then he set his wings and dived like a plummet.

With a lightning wing-over, the pigeon swerved to one side, causing the black thunderbolt to overshoot his mark by inches. Spreading his wings, the pirate zoomed upward with a shrill whistle of wind through stiff pinions.

The band-tail, knowing himself outclassed, turned for safety toward the thick trees below. In that moment he lost, for the female falcon, following her mate's swoop by a matter of seconds, struck the victim like a cannon ball. As the pigeon collapsed in a flurry of feathers under the sledge-hammer blow of the falcon's clenched talons, the bigger bird whirled down and over to make sure of her quarry. Her right wing touched one end of the limed lath and stuck. The other wing, beating wildly, inevitably stuck and adhered to the opposite end of the stick.

The falcon struggled frantically, but the lime was strong and the flexible lath gave with her efforts. She failed to pull free and, together, pigeon and hawk plunged earthward.

Muttering under his breath at the fate that had let the rare black falcon escape at the expense of its mate, John Condon ran from his place of concealment toward the struggling hawk. Overhead the black pirate circled, screaming shrilly as he watched Condon pick up his fighting mate.

Back at his camp once more, Condon carefully loosened the lath from the hawk's wings and sponged the sticky lime from her feathers. He had missed the black pirate, but perhaps he could use its mate as a lure. He was too wise in the ways of hawks to think that he could capture the black falcon in the same manner in which he had snared the female.

For the rest of the morning Condon roamed the mountain, looking for the nest of the duck hawks. Often he heard the harsh *kre-e-e, kre-e-e* of the black pirate calling to its lost mate, but he found no indications of a nest.

At noon he ate a hasty lunch and then, taking a Geological Survey map from his pack, he spread it on the short, flower-strewn grass of the meadow and scanned it closely. On the north side of the mountain he found the brown contour lines of the map crowded closely together near the blue streak that indicated Madrone Creek. In his mind's eye he could visualize the cliff high over the canyon of the Madrone. Painstakingly he counted the massed contour lines. Forty of them! At twenty feet to the contour, that made eight hundred feet. He had a strong hunch that there he would find the nest of the falcons.

Repacking his camping equipment, Condon shouldered his pack, and carrying the black falcon's mate in the willow cage, headed for Madrone Canyon. There, hours later, he threw down his burden beside a backwater of the clear, brawling stream.

Above the poplars and alders in which he camped, the great cliff that he had located on the topographical map soared almost sheer, broken here and there by ledges and dotted with the dark green of sumac, juniper, and scrub oak. Along the crest, almost a thousand feet above, he could see jutting black spires of pines and firs. He did not doubt his ability to climb the cliff, but he knew it would take all his skill.

Propping himself against a sloping alder trunk, he scanned the cliff-face through binoculars. About a hundred feet from the top, under a bulging overhand of rock, he noted a lime-whitened ledge. Carefully he surveyed the spot. Though a logical location for the falcons' nest, it might be the home of a pair of horned

Black Pirate of the Peaks

owls. There was no way to tell until he climbed up to see. Meanwhile, he must feed his captive.

Having cut a three-foot alder club, Condon began searching along the foot of the cliff. At last he saw what he was looking for — a mass of debris that marked the nest of a pack rat. He jumped upon the pile, scuffing the dried sticks with his feet. When the frightened occupant dashed out, Condon dispatched it with a well-aimed blow of his club. Returning to camp, he poked the limp body into the willow cage. Save for the hissing and ruffling of feathers, the captive hawk paid no attention to the offering. Condon grinned. Later, when he was out of sight, the hawk would not be so contemptuous.

Early next morning, carrying a second willow cage and a coarse-meshed net strung over a bowed willow stick, he started to climb to the eyrie. High above him he saw his quarry circling over the mist-filled depths of the canyon. Grimly Condon smiled as he climbed. To-day would tell whether the black hawk was to continue his piratical life above the wild ridges or dwell in a cage in a great zoological park. As he watched the graceful, long-winged bird, he almost hoped that the former would be the case.

Utilizing every bush, crevice, and ledge, Condon worked his way upward. Once an overhanging bulge of rock forced him to retrace his steps, and again a fault zone of loose, fractured rock turned him aside. Then he discovered a chimney which gave him an easy climb of two hundred feet. At last he reached a point about thirty feet below the ledge that he had marked from the canyon floor. There lay the eyrie. He was certain of it now, for the black falcon had swung in from over the canyon and was circling just above his head, screaming angrily.

Condon paused, set the cage down in a stunted juniper and unslung the stout net from his belt. The falcons had chosen their nesting place well. The thirty feet to the ledge was almost vertical and bare of shrubs that would afford a handhold. Carefully Condon checked over the cliff face for a way up. A zigzag fissure cracked the rock, and here and there appeared crevices and projecting knobs. Satisfied that it was scalable, Condon slung the net over his shoulder and started up.

Suspecting that the falcon would attack before he reached the ledge, the naturalist was on the alert to find a place where he could have one hand free to swing the net. Many times he had seen old Dulat Yar in just such a position. He did not fear that the falcon actually would strike him, but he expected that the bird would swoop near him in an attempt to drive him off. In one of those dives he would come too close and the stout net could do its work.

Halfway up to the nest Condon rested. The black falcon circled closer about his head, but try as he might, Condon had found no place where he could free one hand. From the corner of his eye he saw the falcon swing up to a greater height and set his wings. Instinctively he flattened against the rock. With a hissing rush the hawk was upon him. A stunning blow on the side of his head made Condon clutch convulsively at the rough rocks. Contrary to all custom, the hawk, instead of veering off at the last moment, had struck hard with clenched talons.

A warm trickle of blood ran down the angle of Condon's jaw and he shifted position to free his right hand as the hawk zoomed upward. At that movement the jutting rock on which he had braced his foot gave way. Dangling above the depths of the canyon, Condon struggled desperately to find another foothold before the falcon could dive again.

The strain on his arms was terrific, his muscles felt as if they were being torn apart as his feet raked frantically against the cliff face. Six hundred feet of empty space lay beneath.

The speeding falcon was again almost upon the intruder before his groping feet encountered a narrow crevice. Jamming a toe into the crack, Condon threw up a hand to ward off the ebony thunderbolt. Raking pain ran down his arm as the hawk's talons cut into his fingers. Hastily he scrambled down to the safety of the ledge below.

As he rested there, trying to plan out some other way of reaching the nest, a second, broad-winged form drifted up the canyon. The falcon saw it before Condon did, and immediately started to climb in a tight spiral. Fishing his binoculars from their case, Condon trained them on the newcomer. A great golden eagle, majestically winging toward the high country! The climbing falcon was a mere dot in the sky above the leisurely king of birds. Through his glasses Condon watched the pair. On came the eagle until within a few hundred feet of the eyrie — too near to suit its watching owner.

High above, the falcon folded his wings and dived like a black meteor.

"Stop it, you fool! Stop it!" Condon shouted, futilely.

He knew that a hawk was no match for an eagle. Often in the mountains of central Asia, he had watched trained falcons of the Afghans set upon imperial eagles and never had he seen one victorious. Suddenly he felt an almost personal interest in the black falcon, diving to certain destruction.

The huge eagle, warned by the shrill whistle of wind through the hawk's stiff pinions, swung over on his back to receive the falling bird in his powerful steel-like talons. The speed of the falcon was so great that to Condon he seemed merely a black streak. At the last instant, when almost in reach of those deadly claws, the falcon flicked out a wing and swerved to one side, crashing through the stiff flight feathers of the eagle's wing with a crack like the breaking of a board.

The eagle, overbalanced and with his right wing almost broken by the shock of the blow, side-slipped, flapping awkwardly. Before he could recover, the falcon zoomed on extended wings, swerved, and dived again. This time the two met solidly in mid-air. A burst of feathers drifted down the wind as the falcon hit squarely between the eagle's wings. Swiftly the eagle spun over, trying to grasp his smaller, but more agile, opponent in his mighty claws, but the falcon twisted to one side and climbed in tight spirals.

Once more he dived and again the eagle rolled to receive him. Spellbound, Condon watched. That the falcon could avoid a death grip a third time appeared impossible. Then the hawk executed a manoeuvre that left Condon gasping. Within five feet of those deadly claws and at lightning speed, the black pirate flung himself to one side and instantly jibed back at the eagle's head, his hard-clenched talons striking with the force of a bullet.

The broad, powerful wings of the larger bird threshed convulsively and then lay limp, and the great brown body plunged helplessly downward.

Condon expelled his pent-up breath in a mighty sigh, as the black falcon circled out over the canyon, screaming harshly, victoriously. Lifting his hand in silent salute to the sable warrior, he tossed the willow cage far out into the depths, unable to bear the thought of such a gallant winged creature in captivity. He watched the falling cage until it whirled from sight, then started to descend to the canyon bottom far below.

Back at his camp among the alders he went straight to the cage of the female falcon and with his knife cut the withes that bound it. For a moment the hawk crouched in the wreckage, uncertain and confused, then suddenly soared upward on strong wings.

When John Condon shouldered his pack for the homeward trip, he heard again that high keening *kre-e-e, kre-e-e*. Far above the summits of the ridges two dots wheeled joyously. As he strode off down the canyon trail, his lips were pursed in a soundless whistle, a habit of his when he felt contentment in his soul.

THE HAWK

A. C. BENSON

The hawk slipt out of the pine, and rose in the sunlit air;
   Steady and still he poised; his shadow slept on the grass.
And the bird's song sickened and sank; she cowered with furtive stare,
   Dumb, till the quivering dimness should flicker and shift and pass.
Suddenly down he dropped. She heard the hiss of his wing,
   Fled with a scream of terror. Oh, would she had dared to rest!
For the hawk at eve was full, and there was no bird to sing,
   And over the heather drifted the down from a bleeding breast.

GHOST CAT

RODERICK L. HAIG-BROWN

I

North Americans generally rate the cougar as mean, vicious, and cowardly. Dozens of men who have never seen so much as a cougar's track have expressed this view to me most emphatically. Some experienced woodsmen, despite contrary evidence, have said much the same things. Some few men I have known, sound naturalists and thoroughly experienced hunters for the most part, have expressed wholehearted admiration for the cougar's qualities, both as hunter and quarry.

I don't want to claim to be a cougar expert. I have lived in cougar country for some twenty-odd years, have hunted them a good deal, and studied them closely enough to feel justified in writing one book and a few stories about them. The plain fact is that I have found them more fascinating and challenging than any other animal I have known. They are handsome and majestic creatures, superbly powerful, splendidly efficient; they are at once bold and cautious, fearful and fearless, wise and foolish, mysterious and simple.

The cougar is one of the world's medium-sized cats, larger than the bobcat or the lynx, smaller than the lion and the tiger. A well-grown male should weigh in the neighbourhood of one hundred and fifty pounds, a well-grown female around one hundred pounds. However, males of well over two hundred pounds have been recorded, and mature females weighing as little as seventy pounds are not uncommon.

In superficial appearance the cougar is not unlike the African lioness, though slimmer and more graceful and with a much longer and thicker tail. The male has a wider, handsomer head than the female, and gives an impression of great power in the mass of his shoulders and thickness of his forearms. Both are spotted when young and retain handsome black patches on either side of their faces and jaws. When a cougar is treed, looking down at the hunter, these are very noticeable; but the general impression of a cougar travelling on the ground is of slender, tawny-brown grace, made almost clumsy by the high hindquarters and heavy tail, yet beautifully smooth, full of confidence and power.

Cougars have been recorded from within a few miles of the Arctic Circle, clear down to the Straits of Magellan, but I have known them only in the Pacific Northwest, mainly on Vancouver Island. Perhaps the cougar's perfect range is Vancouver Island. Here are deep woods without end, tangled undergrowth, matted swamps, piled windfalls; tall mountains and rough country in abundance; and, above all, deer without number — small Pacific-coast blacktails, weighing from seventy-five to two hundred pounds — prey almost ideally matched to the cougar's strength and hunting skill.

II

Cougars are just as numerous on the Island as these almost perfect conditions suggest, yet they are rarely seen. And this is a strange thing, because they roam widely, the males especially; they seem to have an intense, bold, almost friendly curiosity about human beings and often follow a man through the woods.

Two of the most experienced trappers I have ever known, both men with over thirty years' experience on Vancouver Island, told me when I first knew them that they had never seen a cougar free in the woods. Yet both had trapped many cougars and shot others treed by dogs. And both, within a year or two of telling me that, did see cougars. Carl, who trapped alone far up the Klaanche valley, had the more dramatic experience. It was in the fall, when he was travelling back to his line. He had pitched a small tent and was lying in it half asleep one afternoon. The flaps of the tent were down and quite suddenly Carl's half-closed eyes saw them move. They moved again and Carl, fully awake, but stiffly motionless, found himself looking into the quiet eyes of a cougar, its head and one foreleg well inside the tent. Carl's rifle was down by his feet, practically under the cougar's jaws, and he made no move for it until the head and paw withdrew, as quietly as they had entered.

Carl was not an excitable man and I imagine he waited a little while before moving. Then he reached for his rifle, stepped cautiously out of the tent and saw two cougars standing within fifty feet of him. They made no move to get away but stood watching him with that calm, apparently friendly curiosity that seems so typical of cougars. Carl told me afterward that he was almost ashamed to shoot them.

Jack's cougar was a simpler affair. He saw her from the lake one day as he was passing close to shore in his rowboat — a small female, lying close against a log, watching his boat. He shot her easily, took her down in the boat to his cabin on the other lake, and began to celebrate his triumph.

Quite by chance, three of us who also had trap lines near the lake decided to drop in on old Jack that night. We were all young fellows, and he liked us, and was always very good to us. On that particular night we were doubly welcome because we could celebrate with him. Old Jack was as proud and elated as I had ever seen him. By the time we got to the cabin he made it quite clear to us, not once but many times, that he was celebrating what he felt to be the supreme achievement of a lifetime of woodcraft.

The cougar lay in state on the floor of the cabin; old Jack rested in glory in his bunk; Jim and Alan were draped across the other bunk, and I squatted on the floor beside the cougar to examine her more closely. I picked up a forepaw, pressed the joints to force the claws from their sheaths, looked up at a sudden sharp move from Jack's bunk. Jack was on his feet, his rifle in his hands, pointed straight at me. Jim and Alan jumped for him, forced him back on the bunk and got hold of the rifle. "He don't believe me," Jack said. "He good as called me a liar, picking up that paw to look for the trap mark."

We calmed him at last and were all friends again. But that reaction is the clearest account I can give of the value that an old and thoroughly experienced woodsman set upon the achievement of seeing a cougar free in the woods. I still think that the little dead female on the floor of the cabin was the most dangerous cougar I ever had anything to do with.

III

The cougar's single weakness, the one thing that brings down upon him the contempt of the unknowing, in his readiness to tree for a dog. Most — but by no means all — cougars will tree very readily even for a small dog. In fact, I doubt if the size of the dog has anything to do with it. A yapping keen-hunting fox terrier or cocker spaniol is as likely to tree a cougar as the largest hound or the boldest Airedale if conditions are right — that is, if the dog has been released on a fairly fresh track and the cougar has not grown used to dogs through being hunted before.

It is difficult to account for this readiness to tree. A cougar can kill any dog on which he can lay a paw — some cougars even come down around farms and camps and small settlements to kill dogs. Certainly there is no cowardice in it, for cougars are powerful, and by no means reluctant, fighters. Males fight each other, occasionally to the death, over females; females fight to protect their young; both sexes will fight in defense of a kill and even the black bear, though probably not the grizzly, will give way.

It seems reasonably clear, then, that a cougar does not tree from a small dog because he is afraid of the dog, or even of the man behind the dog. I think rather that he trees from inbred habit, perhaps thousands of years old. Cougars have a very limited lung capacity and can travel at speed only for a short distance. They have always shared their range with wolves, coyotes, and other doglike animals and they must have learned long ago that trees are a safe refuge from the real dangers of big wolves or the minor irritation of yapping coyotes. I am certain that cougars feel safe when treed and I suspect that they are also a little bored — patiently waiting out a passing annoyance.

The fact that most cougars tree readily from dogs does not mean that cougars are necessarily easy to hunt down. At their own speed they are travellers of unlimited endurance and they can keep ahead of slow hounds on a cold scent indefinitely. The good hunter is the man who follows a track by his eyes rather than the noses of his dogs, keeping the dogs silent at his heels until he can release them on a really fresh scent and give them a chance to rush the cougar and quickly to exhaust his lung capacity. This calls for woodcraft of a really high order, and at best there is plenty of room for error — which is precisely what makes cougar hunting at least as fascinating as any other form of large game hunting.

In most large game hunting the immediate personal danger to the hunter from the hunted animal is, I believe, likely to be overrated; and when it does occur it is likely to be the result of unusual circumstances. The latter point is certainly true of cougar hunting. Shooting a cougar in a tree sounds a very simple proposition. Theoretically one catches the dogs, ties them in a safe place, selects a comfortable position to shoot from, aims, fires.

In actual practice innumerable things go wrong. Perhaps one example will be enough to illustrate some of them. The cougar, a big male, had treed just before dusk. The dogs had run on past the tree and it seemed unwise to wait to catch them. The shot would be an easy one and I moved a little way up the hill to get what seemed a clear line on the neck. It was difficult to find the sights in the dim light under the timber and just as I found them and lined them I noticed a single branch, about an inch in diameter, slanting across the cougar's neck. At the same moment I heard the dogs coming back, but I decided to take the shot anyway. It seemed perfect. The cougar's head dropped and his forelegs drew sharply back. I ran for the foot of the tree, to be there ahead of the dogs, and could find no sign of the cougar. Just as the dogs arrived he dropped from the tree, right at my feet and very much alive. I pushed the rifle against the back of his neck and pulled the trigger. But I often wonder what might have happened if he had landed squarely on my back, because the first shot had glanced from the limb and merely nicked the point of his jaw.

IV

But the difficulties of getting your shot at a treed cougar are as nothing to the innumerable factors that can complicate the actual hunting.

Scent can be poor, or hopelessly confused by the passing of other animals; the dogs' feet may be cut or worn raw by crusty snow or rocky ground; the best of dogs will sometimes be drawn off a good scent by coon or bear or — say it softly — deer; tracking can be intensely difficult on dry ground or after a fresh fall of snow; there may be wolves around — sure death to any dog unlucky enough to come upon them. And the cougars have their own ways of complicating things. In steep country, for instance, they will often climb a tree standing close against a tall bluff, then jump from it to the top of the bluff and leave the dogs barking confidently at the foot of the tree.

Some few cougars will run from hounds with all the cunning of the wisest fox. There was a big tom up Brown's River some years ago who seemed to know all the tricks. I hunted him several times with the great Cecil Smith, tracker without peer, but we always ended the day farther behind him than we had been at the beginning. I can remember now the last day we hunted him. We found his fresh track in good snow down in a hollow near the river. We felt certain he had killed recently and would have a full belly to slow him up, and I hadn't a doubt when we turned the dogs loose that they would tree him within a quarter of a mile. They went away in fine style, two big, strong, thoroughly experienced hounds, and we followed in a hurry. Then their voices died and when we found them they were on the far side of the river. We crossed, put them on the track, and within a couple of hundred yards the track took them down to the river again.

Four more times the old tom crossed the river, back and forth, and the dogs were losing their fire, and we were farther behind each time. Then he went for a couple of miles up the left bank of the stream. We blundered after until we found the dogs at fault and hunting aimlessly. The cougar had doubled back, of course, right along his own tracks for a hundred yards or so, then had cut down the slope a little way and passed back downstream within a hundred feet of us. We put the dogs on the new track and they took it keenly—back to the bank of the river again. So it went until it was too dark to hunt. We had left him, we thought, on the far side of the river. But we crossed his track again on the way out, feather-fresh and heading back for where we had found him in the morning. If he hasn't died of old age he's probably still somewhere along Brown's River.

My partners, Ed and Buster Lansdowne, owned a small farm on the Nimpkish River. It was only a few cleared acres and the woods crowded close in on every side of it. Nearly always there was a cougar nearby—if we killed one, another always came to take his place and sooner or later most of them took an interest in the farm. One went right under the house to kill a favourite collie. Another, in broad daylight, trapped Mrs. Lansdowne's cocker spaniel at the edge of the river, held him under the water with one paw until he drowned, then picked him up and carried him away. Mrs. Lansdowne was aboard a small boat anchored twenty or thirty feet out in the river and had to watch the whole thing helplessly—she shouted and threw things at the cougar, but he watched her calmly and completed his deliberate business without a sign of haste.

The boldest and most troublesome cougar of all was one we

met first on a September evening when we came in from hunting. We were hungry and sat down to a great supper in the kitchen. Somewhere, toward the end of it, there was a deal of clucking and clacking in the chicken run. At last we strolled out there. We were inside the run before we saw him — a magnificent male cougar sitting on his haunches between the two chicken houses, a Plymouth Rock hen in his jaws.

It seemed no more than something to do, but I ran back to the house, picked up Ed's rifle and took it out to him. The cougar was still there, still calm, apparently as interested in us as we were in him. Ed took the rifle slowly. "Gosh," he said, "He's beautiful. It seems a shame to kill him."

The rest of it happened quickly and is best forgotten. The cougar moved. Ed's shot was late. The cougar was over the fence and away for the woods, the dog at his heels. He may have treed, but we didn't find him though we searched the woods till dark.

He came back for more chickens that same night, stepping around the traps we had set. I waited on the roof of the chicken house for the next two evenings and undoubtedly he watched me there because he came later, in the dark, and took more chickens. The next evening I waited on the roof of the farmhouse and he came and went through the bracken and I didn't see him.

Eventually, when most of the chickens were gone, he disappeared. A month later he was back. He evaded more traps, killed more chickens, chased the cattle in the pastures at night. We tried to pit-lamp him, but even from a hundred yards away he would only turn his great eyes to the light for a fraction of a second and there was never time to put sights on him. He disappeared again for a while, then suddenly was back again. This time there was snow on the ground. He attacked a young steer in the barn and we heard the disturbance and rushed out with the rifle and a gasoline lamp. As Ed opened the door, the steer burst out of the barn and knocked him over. We thought the cougar had gone out the other way and hunted him there, only to find when we came back that he must have been inside the barn all the time and slipped out when we had gone past.

The next day we hunted him grimly, but not very hopefully, following his tracks in the snow without a dog. They led us a mile or more up river, swung back and seemed very fresh.

Then Ed had his hunch. We knew the travel of cougars on that sidehill, for we had trapped and hunted lesser beasts there. "He's going down by the big spruce," Ed said. "We can cut across and pick up his track there. It'll save time."

So we did that, and by the thousandth chance that sometimes favours hunters, we met him there at the spruce tree, crouched beside the trail to let us pass unseeing. But Ed saw him and yelled, and shot him as he ran.

I haven't hunted a cougar since the war and am not too sure that I want to — there are hunters enough without me, and I hope there will always be cougars on Vancouver Island, lots of them. Around farms and settlements they haven't much place, but in the deep woods and on the mountains they belong. Where deer are hunted intensively cougars must be proportionately controlled. Back beyond the range of deer hunters — and most of Vancouver Island is still beyond their range — the cougar is himself a valuable control. He is also a noble creature, perfectly adapted to the country he ranges, and, if the deer hunters only knew it, a quarry far more challenging to their skill and woodcraft than the little coast blacktails which they hunt.

LONE WOLF

SIR CHARLES G. D. ROBERTS

I

The settlers around the skirts of Lost Mountain were puzzled and indignant. For six weeks their indignation had been growing, and the mystery seemed no nearer a solution. Something was slaughtering their sheep — something that knew its business and slaughtered with dreadful efficiency. Several honest dogs fell under suspicion, not because there was anything whatever against their reputations, but simply because they had the misfortune to be big enough and strong enough to kill a sheep if they wanted to, and the brooding backwoods mind, when troubled, will go far on the flimsiest evidence.

Of all the wrathful settlers the most furious was Brace Timmins. Not only had he lost in those six weeks six sheep, but now his dog, a splendid animal, half deerhound and half collie, had been shot on suspicion by a neighbour, on no better grounds, apparently, than his long legs and long, killing jaws. Still the slaughtering of the flocks went on with undiminished vigour. And a few days later Brace Timmins avenged his favourite by publicly thrashing his too hasty neighbour in front of the crossroads store. The neighbour, pounded into penitence, apologized, and as far as the murdered dog was concerned, the score was wiped clean. But the problem of the sheep killing was no nearer solution. If not Brace Timmins's dog, as everyone made prudent haste to acknowledge, then whose dog was it? The life of every dog in the settlement, if bigger than a woodchuck, hung by a thread, which might, it seemed, at any moment turn into a halter. Brace Timmins loved dogs; and not wishing that others should suffer the unjust fate which had overtaken his own, he set his whole woodcraft to the discovery of the true culprit.

Before he had made any great progress, however, on this trail, a new thing happened, and suspicion was lifted from the heads of all the dogs. Joe Anderson's dog, a powerful beast, part sheep dog and part Newfoundland, with a far-off streak of bull, and the champion fighter of the settlements, was found dead in the middle of Anderson's sheep pasture, his whole throat fairly ripped out. He had died in defense of his charges, and it was plainly no dog's jaws that had done such mangling. What dog indeed could have mastered Anderson's Dan?

"It's a bear, gone mad on mutton," pronounced certain of the wise ones, idling at the crossroads store. "Ye see as how he hain't et the dawg, noways, but jest bit him to teach him not to go interferin' as regards sheep."

"Ye're all off," contradicted Timmins, with authority. "A bear'd hev tore him an' batted him an' mauled him more'n he'd hev bit him. A bear thinks more o' usin' his forepaws than what he does his jaws, if he gits into any kind of onpleasantness. No, boys, our unknown friend up yonder's a wolf, take my word for it."

"A wolf!" Joe Anderson snorted. "Go chase yerself, Brace Timmins. I'd like to see any wolf as could 'a' done up my Dan that way!"

"Well, keep yer hair on, Joe," retorted Timmins, easily. "I'm agoin' after him, an' I'll show him to you in a day or two, as like as not!"

"I reckon, Joe," put in the storekeeper, leaning forward across the counter, "if Brace is right — an' I reckon he be — then it must sure be one of them big timber wolves we read about. You better watch out, Brace. If ye don't git the brute first lick, he'll git you!"

"I'll watch out!" drawled Timmins, confidently; and selecting a strong steel trap chain from a box beside the counter, he sauntered off to put his plans into execution.

These plans were simple enough. He knew that he had a wide-ranging adversary to deal with. But he himself was a wide

Lone Wolf

ranger, and acquainted with every cleft and crevice of Lost Mountain. He would find the great wolf's lair, and set his traps accordingly, one in the runway, to be avoided if the wolf was as clever as he ought to be, and a couple of others a little aside to really do the work. Of course, he would carry his rifle, in case of need, but he wanted to take his enemy alive.

For several arduous but exciting days Timmins searched in vain alike the dark cedar swamps and the high, broken spurs of the mountain. Then, one windless afternoon, far up the steep he found a climbing trail between grey, shelving ledges. Stealthy as a lynx he followed, expecting at the next turn to come upon the lair of the enemy. It was a just expectation, but as luck would have it, that next turn, which would have led him straight to his goal, lay around a shoulder of rock whose foundations had been loosened by the rains. With a kind of low growl, rending and sickening, the rock gave way, and sank beneath Timmins' feet.

Moved by the alert and unerring instinct of the woodsman, Timmins leaped into the air. Both high and wide he sprang, and so escaped being engulfed in the mass which he had dislodged. On the top of the ruin he fell, but he fell far and hard; and for some fifteen or twenty minutes after that fall he lay very still, while the dust and debris settled into silence under the quiet flooding of the sun.

II

At last he opened his eyes. For a moment he made no effort to move, but lay wondering where he was. A weight was on his legs, and glancing downward, he saw that he was half covered with earth and rubbish. Then he remembered. Was he badly hurt? He was half afraid now to make the effort to move, lest he should find himself incapable of it. Still, he felt no serious pain. His head ached, to be sure; and he saw that his left hand was bleeding from a gash at the base of the thumb. That hand still clutched one of the heavy traps which he had been carrying, and it was plainly the trap that had cut him. But where was his rifle? Cautiously turning his head, he peered around for it, but in vain, for during the fall it had flown far aside into the thickets. As he stared anxiously, all at once his dazed and sluggish senses sprang to life again with a scorching throb, which left a chill behind it. There, not ten paces away, sitting up on its haunches and eyeing him contemplatively, was a gigantic wolf, much bigger, it seemed to him, than any wolf had any right to be.

Timmins' first instinct was to spring to his feet, with a yell that would give the dreadful stranger to understand that he was a fellow it would not be well to tamper with. But his woodcraft stayed him. He was not by any means sure that he could spring to his feet. Still less was he sure that such an action would properly impress the great wolf, who, for the moment at least, seemed not actively hostile. Stillness, absolute stillness, was the trump card to be always played in the wilderness when in doubt. So Timmins kept quite still, looking inquiringly at Lone Wolf. And Lone Wolf looked inquiringly at him.

For several minutes this waiting game went on. Then, with easy grace, Lone Wolf lifted one huge hind paw and vigorously scratched his ear. This very simple action was a profound relief to Timmins.

"Sartin," he thought, "the crittur must be in an easy mood, or he'd never think to scratch his ear like that. Or mebbe he thinks I'm so well buried I kin wait, like an old bone!"

Just then Lone Wolf got up, stretched himself, yawned prodigiously, came a couple of steps nearer, and sat down again, with his head cocked to one side, and a polite air of asking, "Do I intrude?"

"Sartin sure, I'll never ketch him in a better humour!" thought Timmins. "I'll try the human voice on him."

"Git out of that!" he commanded in a sharp voice.

Lone Wolf cocked his head to the other side interrogatively. He had been spoken to by Toomey in that voice of authority, but the words were new to him. He felt that he was expected to do something, but he knew not what. He liked the voice—it was something like Toomey's. He liked the smell of Timmins' homespun shirt—it, too, was something like Toomey's. He became suddenly anxious to please this stranger. But what was wanted of him? He half arose to his feet, and glanced around to see if, perchance, the order had been addressed to someone else. As he turned, Timmins saw, half hidden in the heavy fur of the neck, a stout leather collar.

"I swear!" he muttered, "if 'tain't a tame wolf what's got away!" With that he sat up; and pulling his legs, without any very serious hurt, from their covering of earth and sticks, he got stiffly to his feet. For a moment the bright landscape reeled and swam before him, and he had a vague sense of having been hammered all over his body. Then he steadied himself. He saw that the wolf was watching him with the expression of a shy but friendly dog who would like to make acquaintance. As he stood puzzling his wits, he remembered having read about the great fire which had recently done such damage to the Sillaby and Hopkins circus, and he concluded that the stranger was one of the fugitives from that disaster.

"Come here, sir! Come here, big wolf!" said he, holding out a confident hand.

"Wolf" — that was a familiar sound to Lone Wolf's ears! It was at least a part of his name! And the command was one he well understood. Wagging his tail gravely, he came at once and thrust his great head under Timmins' hand for a caress. He had enjoyed his liberty, to be sure, but he was beginning to find it lonely.

Timmins understood animals. His voice, as he talked to the powerful brute beside him, was full of kindness, but at the same time vibrant with authority. His touch was gentle, but very firm and unhesitating. Both touch and voice conveyed clearly to Lone Wolf's disciplined instinct the impression that this man, like Toomey, was a being who had to be obeyed, whose mastery was inevitable and beyond the reach of question. When Timmins told him to lie down, he did so at once, and stayed there obediently while Timmins gathered himself together, shook the dirt out of his hair and boots, recovered his cap, wiped his bleeding hands with leaves, and hunted up his scattered traps and rifle. At last Timmins took two bedraggled but massive pork sandwiches, wrapped in newspaper, from his pocket and offered one to his strange associate. Lone Wolf was not hungry, being full of perfectly good mutton, but, being too polite to refuse, he gulped down the sandwich. Timmins took out the steel chain, snapped it on to Lone Wolf's collar, said, "Come on!" and started homeward. And Lone Wolf, trained to a short leash, followed close at his heels.

Timmins' breast swelled with exultation. What was the loss of one dog and half a dozen no-account sheep to the possession of this magnificent captive and the prestige of such a naked-handed capture? He easily reasoned, of course, that his triumph must be due, in part at least, to some resemblance to the wolf's former master, whose dominance had plainly been supreme. His only anxiety was as to how the great wolf might conduct himself toward settlement society in general. Surely nothing could be more lamblike than the animal's present demeanour, but Timmins remembered the fate of Joe Anderson's powerful dog and had his doubts. He examined Lone Wolf's collar and congratulated himself that both collar and chain were strong.

III

It was getting well along in the afternoon when Timmins and Lone Wolf emerged from the thick woods into the stumpy pastures and rough, burned lands that spread back irregularly from the outlying farms. And here, while crossing a wide pasture known as Smith's Lots, an amazing thing befell. Of course, Timmins was not particularly surprised, because his backwoods philosophizing had long ago led him to the conclusion that when things get started happening, they have a way of keeping it up. Days, weeks, months glide by without event enough to ripple the most sensitive memory. Then the whimsical fates do something different, find it interesting, and proceed to do something else. So, though Timmins had been accustomed all his life to managing bulls, good-tempered and bad-tempered alike, and had never had the ugliest of them presume to turn upon him, he was not astonished now by the sight of Smith's bull. It was a wide-horned, carrot-red, white-faced Hereford, and it came charging down upon him in thunderous fury from behind a poplar thicket. In a flash he remembered that this bull, which was notoriously murderous in temper, had been turned into the pasture to act as guardian to Smith's flocks. There was not a stick big enough for a weapon, and he could not bring himself to shoot so valuable a beast as this fine purebred. "Shucks!" he muttered in deep disgust. "I might 'a' knowed it!" Dropping Lone Wolf's chain, he ran forward, waving his arms and shouting angrily. But that red, onrushing bulk was quite too dull-witted to understand that it ought to obey. It was in the mood to charge an avalanche. Deeply humiliated, Timmins hopped aside, and reluctantly ran for the woods, trusting to elude his pursuer by timely dodging.

Hitherto Lone Wolf had left all cattle severely alone, having got it somehow into his head that they were more peculiarly under man's protection than the sheep. Now, however, he saw his duty, and duty is often a very well-developed concept in the brain of dog and wolf. His ears flattened, his eyes narrowed to flaming green slits, his lips wrinkled back till his long white fangs were clean-bared, and without a sound he hurled himself upon the red bull. Looking back over his shoulder, Timmins saw it all. It was as if all his life Lone Wolf had been killing bulls, so unerring was that terrible chopping snap at the great beast's throat. Far forward, just behind the bull's jaws, the slashing fangs caught. And Timmins was astounded to see the bull, checked in mid-rush, plunge, staggering, forward upon his knees. From this position he abruptly rolled over upon his side, thrown by his own impetus, combined with a dexterous twist of his opponent's body. Then Lone Wolf bounded backward, and stood expectant, ready to repeat the attack if necessary. But it was not necessary. Slowly the great red bull arose to his feet, and stared about him stupidly, the blood gushing from his throat. Then he swayed and collapsed. And Lone Wolf, wagging his tail like a dog, went back to Timmins' side for congratulations.

The woodsman gazed ruefully at his slain foe. Then he patted his defender's head, recovered the chain with a secure grip, and said slowly:

"I reckon, partner, ye did yer dooty as ye seen it, an' mebbe I'm beholden to ye fer a hul' skin, fer that there crittur was sartinly amazin' ugly an' spry on his pins. But ye're goin' to be a responsibility some. Ye ain't no suckin' lamb to hev aroun' the house, I'm thinkin'."

To these remarks, which he judged from their tone to be approving, Lone Wolf wagged assent, and the homeward journey was continued. Timmins went with his head down, buried in thought. Coming to a convenient log, he seated himself and made Lone Wolf lie down at his feet. Then he took out the remaining sandwich — which he himself, still shaken from his fall, had no desire to eat — and contemplatively, in small fragments, he fed it to the wolf's great, blood-stained jaws. At last he spoke, with the finality of one whose mind is quite made up.

"Partner," said he, "there ain't no help for it. Bill Smith's agoin' to hold me responsible for the killin' o' that there crittur o' his'n, an' that means a pretty penny, it bein' a purebred an' imported at that. He ain't never agoin' to believe but what I let you loose on to him apurpose, jest to save my hide! Shucks! Ye may's well realize y'ain't popular 'round these parts; an' first thing, when I wasn't lookin', somebody'd be a-puttin' somethin' onhealthy into your vittles, partner! We've kind o' took to each other, you an' me; an' I reckon we'd git on together fine, me always havin' my own way, of course. But there ain't no help fer it. Ye're too hefty a proposition, by long odds, fer a community like Lost Mountain Settlement. I'm goin' to write right off to Sillaby an' Hopkins, an' let them have ye back, partner. An' I reckon the price they'll pay'll be enough to let me square myself with Bill Smith."

And thus it came about that, within a couple of weeks, Lone Wolf and Toomey were once more entertaining delighted audiences, while the settlement of Lost Mountain, with Timmins' prestige established beyond assault, relapsed into its uneventful quiet.

THE PALOMINO

GRACE NOLL CROWELL

You can see him sometimes on this high wide plain:
   A palomino, golden as the sun,
An aristocrat of horses whose pure strain
   Goes back for centuries — you see him run;
A yellow flame against the azure skies,
   You see him stop as suddenly and still
As all arrested motion, then he flies
   On swift sure feet to climb an emerald hill.

And there he stands — a statue carved in gold,
   His nostrils spread, his mane a misty white,
His tail outspread upon the wind, the old
   Impulse within him urging him to flight.
     He rears, he wheels, then lightning-swift he goes,
    Seeking some far green solitude he knows.

MAPLE BLOOM

J. E. H. MACDONALD

In green lacy bloom
   The old maple tree
Lifts over the pavement
   A fair mystery.

It reaches and swings
   To the rushing of cars,
It glows to the street lamps,
   And fades to the stars.

>   In the harsh traffic
>   Still bringing to birth
>   By pavement and building
>   The sweetness of earth —
>   The hidden, enduring
>   Sweetness of earth.

CANADIAN WINTER AND SPRING

BRUCE HUTCHISON

I

Yesterday the last leaves tugged at the branches, and soon all the branches were bare. The wind was from the north.

They looked up from the stable yard on the prairies, saw the slate-grey sky, and knew that it had come. The cattle wandered dolefully, picking at the dried grass, and the long autumn hair of the horses was ruffled in the wind. The fishermen along the Nova Scotia coast battened down their boats and ran for shore. In the Hope Mountains of British Columbia, Bill Robinson denned up in his cabin, twenty-five miles from other human life, hoping his radio battery would keep going until spring.

To-day it came, the Canadian winter. Snow eddying across the prairies until a woman peering through the windows could not see the neighbour's house and knew she was a prisoner until April. Snow sifting through the streets of Winnipeg and everyone hurrying to get anti-freeze in his radiator, a heater on the windshield; and the vacant lots flooded for the kids' skating rinks. Winter marching eastward over the badlands, placing a puff of snow carefully on every tiny Christmas tree. Winter tiptoeing into an Ontario village by night and all the children awaking with a whoop to get out sleighs and skis and hockey sticks, and the black squirrel in the garden taking one look and disappearing for good.

In Ottawa the Prime Minister and other distinguished statesmen taking their fur caps out of moth balls and coming forth suddenly, like an invasion of Russian Cossacks on the Hill, the policeman at the Senate Entrance sheathed in buffalo coat like an aged bison, members of Parliament hurrying from the Chateau to the Buildings, diving into the warmth of steam heat and never leaving until midnight, rubbers and overshoes piled high in the washroom of the Rideau Club.

In Quebec the big stoves crammed with wood and the habitant out in the back yard with axe and saw, eyeing the wood pile with careful calculation. In the kitchen the pot bubbling with pea soup. In the silent woods, the sleighs brought out with jingle of bells, to carry logs to the river.

In the Maritimes the fisherman hauls up his boat. Snow smudges out the harbour of Halifax and ships move through it vaguely. The liners come into port from the North Atlantic, their shapes distorted with ice, like layers of glass, rigging turned solid, sailors' faces pinched and blue.

Now winter turns westward at his leisure. The valleys of the Rockies can be filled up quickly with snow, and more slides off the hills, carrying trees and rocks with it. Every drip and trickle of water has long since seized up, the rivers drop, and over them grows the winter skin, save where the water breaks it with fierce bubbling and then plunges again under the dumb ice. On the untouched smoothness of the snow there is a single track of moose, or the light touch of weasel or rabbit, or perhaps the smooth path of a ski. Every spruce tree and cedar bears an incredible burden, all the branches borne down, and the snow lies on the bare twigs of tamarack like cotton carefully glued there.

It is time now for Winter to make his annual holiday trip to the Pacific Coast. By December he has settled down in Vancouver, in a cottage by the sea, but he is a changed man. He puffs out a few billows of fog, ties up the traffic for a day or two, forces the coastwise captains to navigate entirely by the echoes of their whistles against the shore and then, after turning on the shower bath, Winter forgets to turn it off. Apart from that, he is a considerate guest. Even the last weary roses escape his touch until January when, as a matter of form, he makes a brief show of anger. Then the Victoria golfers are outraged to miss their eighteen holes even for a day and sadly the gardener cuts down the last frozen chrysanthemum. But the snowdrops are out already, and the first crocus opens its brave cup of gold to show the drop of sunshine inside, the first faint wink of Spring.

II

Spring rides into Canada upon the warm Japan Current. He lands quietly, without public greeting or knowledge, on the southern tip of Vancouver Island, one night early in March; or he may take a notion to come bursting in suddenly at the end of February, in raincoat and galoshes, but wearing violets and daffodils and primroses in his hat. With a wild shout down the western wind, he goes to work.

There are cones to be hung like Christmas candles on the great fir trees of the coast woods, and giant, shaggy sword ferns to be uncurled, and the tender, coiled stalks of maidenhair, like the tight fists of newborn babies. There is the first white lily to be thrust up in a spinster's garden at Cadboro Bay and carried to town in triumph for display in the dingy windows of the *Victoria Daily Colonist*. All the rock gardens require a fast, rough job of painting in quick daubs of purple and yellow. A thousand retired and tweeded British colonels must be roused one morning early and warned that the trout are running the Cowichan. The sea serpent of these parts, genial and obliging Cadborosaurus, must be awakened and reintroduced to the front pages of the local press. Old men must be hustled forth into Stanley Park to shiver a little as they begin their immemorial campaign of outdoor checkers on a board twenty feet square.

Then, with a sigh and a sniff at the first rose, Spring is off for the interior country, following the gold-rush road to Cariboo.

At Ashcroft he stops overnight to warn Joe Wong, the Chinaman, that he had better set out his tomato plants in the warming Dry Belt soil, each with a little paper tent over it. Hastily he sprays the huge, red-barked pines with manly perfume and the sage brush with a clean, burning tang, and next day he sweeps the bare, round hills with a thin water-colour wash of faintest green. And at last he releases a tide of pink apple blossom into the Okanagan Valley, standing by Kalamalka's bank to watch it churn and foam and billow for a hundred miles.

Now eastward again, he toils in to the dark defiles of the Rockies, where the yellow avalanche lilies are waiting for his touch to leap out of bed a foot from the receding snow. That done, he heaves and grunts in many a slide of rock and gravel as he unlocks the winter ice, and presently the Fraser is roaring westward to the sea, fat and oily with its burden of mud, cutting a sharp, dirty line far out into the Gulf of Georgia.

Canadian Winter and Spring

In one leap Spring is on the prairies and racing eastward on the hot breath of a Chinook wind, telling the farmers to test the moisture of the earth, to repair their broken tractors and look to their stores of seed wheat. By the time he has reached the Great Lakes, the first green stalks of grain will be thrusting through the winter crust far behind him, and in Winnipeg the early crop of tin cans and ash heaps will be leaping up suddenly through the snow, and one day, long after he has passed by, Spring will be given a ponderous welcome on the editorial page of the *Free Press*.

Now the Lakes must be freed, the great economic lung of Canada started breathing again, the cigar-shaped grain ships thawed out of their winter's prison, and to the north, in the vast badlands of little trees, a million ponds must be melted, dog sleds must be stored away, canoes repaired, and hibernating settlers left blinking in the doorways of their cabins.

Next (oh, hurry now, for the time grows short!) the hardwood forests of Ontario must be set tardily at the year's work, jagged mountains of ice must be pushed out with a boom from the cold lips of Niagara, the long-growing whisker of icicles shaved off the chin of the canyon and sent hurtling down the St. Lawrence to the ocean.

With one stroke Spring wipes the glistening winter rime from the Gothic towers of Ottawa, sets the heavy carillon bells clanging above the river and, flitting into the dim House of Commons, he whispers into the ears of 245 politicians that it is time to discard winter underwear, to forget votes and divisions and rules of order, and go home. After that Politics, Spring's sworn enemy, can get no more work done.

From Parliament Hill, Spring steals down to the Prime Minister's residence, remembers to release the imprisoned mosquito hordes of Rideau and Chaudiere, and gently wakes the aged senators, who snooze in the Rideau Club.

Now he wades across the river into Quebec, listens for a moment to the first sound of wagon wheels in a melting village street, dawdles for a little among the birches, to try out upon their mottled trunks his new palette of black, white, purple, and faintest pink, and grudgingly goes to work in earnest on the maples, until out of every farmhouse and backwoods shack a small boy comes rushing to shout: "Sap's runnin'!"

After making sure that the holes are bored, the spigots thrust into the oozing sapwood, the sap boiling with sweet smell in every iron syrup pot, Spring sighs a little to leave it all and sets out doggedly, on foot, for the Maritimes. There you may see him entangled in fish nets and lobster pots and brightly painted buoys, or swinging a calking hammer against the hull of a schooner, hard by a field where the new lambs are bawling. And in the evening you will find him in some cozy inn, at the edge of Fundy's Bay, telling some old sea dog that once more the job is done.

HEAT

ARCHIBALD LAMPMAN

From plains that reel to southward, dim,
    The road runs by me white and bare;
Up the steep hill it seems to swim
    Beyond, and melt into the glare.
Upward half-way, or it may be
    Nearer the summit, slowly steals
A hay-cart, moving dustily
    With idly clacking wheels.

By his cart's side the wagoner
    Is slouching slowly at his ease,
Half-hidden in the windless blur
    Of white dust puffing to his knees.
This wagon on the height above,
    From sky to sky on either hand,
Is the sole thing that seems to move
    In all the heat-held land.

Beyond me in the fields the sun
  Soaks in the grass and hath his will;
I count the marguerites one by one;
  Even the buttercups are still.
On the brook yonder not a breath
  Disturbs the spider or the midge.
The water-bugs draw close beneath
  The cool gloom of the bridge.

Where the far elm-tree shadows flood
  Dark patches in the burning grass,
The cows, each with her peaceful cud,
  Lie waiting for the heat to pass.
From somewhere on the slope near by
  Into the pale depth of the noon
A wandering thrush slides leisurely
  His thin revolving tune.

In intervals of dreams I hear
  The cricket from the droughty ground;
The grasshoppers spin into mine ear
  A small innumerable sound.
I lift mine eyes sometimes to gaze:
  The burning sky-line blinds my sight:
The woods far off are blue with haze:
  The hills are drenched in light.

And yet to me not this or that
  Is always sharp or always sweet;
In the sloped shadow of my hat
  I lean at rest, and drain the heat;
Nay, more, I think some blessèd power
  Hath brought me wandering idly here:
In the full furnace of this hour
  My thoughts grow keen and clear.

Around the World

ROMANCE

W. J. TURNER

When I was but thirteen or so
   I went into a golden land,
Chimborazo, Cotopaxi
   Took me by the hand.

My father died, my brother too,
   They passed like fleeting dreams,
I stood where Popocatapetl
   In the sunlight gleams.

I dimly heard the master's voice
   And boys far-off at play,
Chimborazo, Cotopaxi
   Had stolen me away.

I walked in a great golden dream
   To and fro from school —
Shining Popocatapetl
   The dusty streets did rule.

I walked home with a gold dark boy,
   And never a word I'd say,
Chimborazo, Cotopaxi
   Had taken my speech away:

I gazed entranced upon his face
   Fairer than any flower —
O shining Popocatapetl
   It was thy magic hour:

The houses, people, traffic seemed
   Thin fading dreams by day,
Chimborazo, Cotopaxi
   They had stolen my soul away!

THE HOMECOMING OF THE SHEEP

FRANCIS LEDWIDGE

The sheep are coming home in Greece,
Hark the bells on every hill!
Flock by flock, and fleece by fleece,
Wandering wide a little piece
Thro' the evening red and still,
Stopping where the pathways cease,
Cropping with a hurried will.

Thro' the cotton bushes low
Merry boys with shouldered crooks
Close them in a single row,
Shout among them as they go
With one bell-ring o'er the brooks.
Such delight you never know
Reading it from gilded books.

Before the early stars are bright
Cormorants and sea-gulls call,
And the moon comes large and white
Filling with a lovely light
The ferny curtained waterfall.
Then sleep wraps every bell up tight
And the climbing moon grows small.

THE BLUE FLOWER*

JOSEPHINE BLACKSTOCK

I

The knock came at the door. No one moved for a minute. Penelope could hear the rain beating on the roof, and the wind sighing in the mulberry tree; she could distinguish through the window the blacker shadow that the bomb crater made against the other shadows. The little girl wet her dry lips with her tongue; ever since the enemy had taken the village, no one heard a knock at the door without a stir of fear in his heart. Greece belonged to the invaders now, Greece and all its people.

Then Manitza said quietly to Aleko:

"Open the door, my son ... Hush, Paolos! There is nothing to be afraid of."

Penelope watched her brother Aleko cross the stone floor to the door. His face was white; it was as white as the embroidered apron Penelope wore, and his eyes were very still. There was the rusty sound of the old bolt being drawn; the creak of the door opening.

"Jannio!" Penelope heard Aleko say.

And there was the shepherd's son standing there in the fire-lit room. His clothes made a little dripping sound on the floor; he was twisting his old worn fez in his hands. Penelope felt her breath letting out on a little sigh; it was all right; it was not a soldier in an olive-grey uniform. It was only poor simple Jannio who stood there, he who had been away from the village for many months, no one knew where.

"May all your dead become saints!" Penelope's grandmother said. She was making small clucking sounds with her tongue. "Come closer to the fire. It is a long time since we have seen you."

"The good hours be with you," Jannio said, and his mouth

---
*By permission of Alfred A. Knopf Inc., from *Youth Replies, I Can: Stories of Resistance*, edited by May Lamberton Becker, copyright, 1945.

hung open in that silly grin. "God has let loose the goatskins; it rains in torrents."

"Jannio, where have you been? Where have you been, Jannio?" Little Paolos had run and thrown his arms around the big boy. Once Jannio had made him a little boat out of a walnut shell.

"Hush, child," Manitza said quickly.

Penelope saw her grandmother frown; one never asked people a question like that since so many of the men of the village — Father, too — had gone into the mountains to fight the enemy; since that day the bomb had fallen and made the flower garden into nothing but a great gaping hole.

Jannio was fumbling inside his shirt; his black brows were drawn together. He was slowly, carefully, pulling out a small object; he was handing it to Penelope.

"For you," he said, and he began to rub one leg against the other in that way he had that was like a stork.

Penelope was staring at the little wooden doll in her hand; her lips were trembling.

"Where — where did you get it?" she asked in a whisper.

The firelight danced on her long straight blonde hair; on her mouth that curled at the ends.

"Your father — it was your father gave it to me."

It was very still in the room. No one said anything. Father had been away with the Greek guerillas for more than a year, up in those lonely mountain passes. They had had no word from him for many months.

Then Manitza went to the door and listened outside; she drew the bolt and came back, and Penelope said in a whisper: "Jannio, you saw my father?"

"Yes; I saw him; I saw Mr. Vasilios," Jannio said. "I saw him all right."

"Jannio, he was well?"

"His health is good," Jannio said slowly. He stopped, frowning, and bit his lip. Jannio looked just like little Paolos when he was trying to remember the words of his lesson. "I must not tell where he was," Jannio said in a slow, thick voice. "They said the goblins would steal my tongue if I told."

Penelope saw Aleko standing there, with his eyes very black, his hand clenched.

"He still fights the enemy?" Aleko asked.

"Per Bacchus, he is the bravest man in Greece; he is like the hawk, he waits, he watches, he pounces." Jannio looked at Manitza and licked his lips. "That is all right to say, is it not?" he asked in a hoarse voice. "The goblins, they won't—"

Manitza had her arm around Jannio's shoulder. She said in her cracked voice: "No, they won't harm you, lad. You may speak such words, for they are God's truth."

"Yes; God's truth," poor Jannio mumbled, and looked at the floor.

And Aleko said slowly: "Did he send us a message? Did he, Jannio?"

Jannio's eyes went creeping from the window to the door; then they came back to Aleko. He said in a low voice:

"Yes. There were words he said I must speak. The goblins, they won't—"

"Hush," Manitza said. "Stop trembling, Jannio. See; you are safe; you may speak."

"Even the doors and the windows have ears these days," Jannio said. "Come closer to the fire."

"Jannio, Jannio, tell us," Penelope said.

"He said—your father said: 'Give this doll to little Penelope. Tell her I have carved it myself just as I used to.'"

And Manitza's hoarse croaking voice said: "Go on. Go on, lad."

"Yes, Jannio?" Penelope whispered.

"Your father said: 'Tell her to take good care of it. Tell her—'" Jannio's words broke off, and his hand went to his mouth in a clumsy way.

"Jannio, what else did my father say?" Aleko asked.

And again it was very still in the room, except for the noise of the rain on the roof, and Penelope's breathing.

"Yes; there was something else he told me," Jannio said, scowling, trying to remember. "He — he said to say — to say —." Jannio's voice died away.

"Jannio, remember!" Manitza said, and the words were very stern; they sounded like those the Pappas used in church on Sunday.

"It — it was something about seeing that — that the elastic strips had not become loose in the doll's joints."

Manitza was staring at poor Jannio. "There was nothing else?" she asked.

Jannio was rubbing one leg against the other. "No, that was all. I — I would remember if it were not." Then Jannio gave a little start and smiled. "I — I must go now. They told me I could see my mother before — before I went back."

And suddenly Jannio had bolted across the room, had thrown open the door; had disappeared.

After a while, Manitza said: "Child, look at the doll. Aleko, go you and bring in the pitcher of milk, and the heel of cheese; we must celebrate to-night. It is not often we know this joy of hearing from your father. Truly, it is as if the Feast of Easter had come two weeks early."

"No, it is not like Easter," little Paolos said; there were tears in his eyes; "there is no meat, no butter, no eggs; it is just like Lent all the time, Manitza."

"Come, Penelope; I would look at your doll." Manitza was smiling that funny smile that wasn't real, that seemed pasted on her lips. "Your father was ever a great hand with the whittling knife; he has not forgotten his cunning."

"Manitza!" Aleko had made no move to get the pitcher of milk. He was still standing there in the middle of the room. "Jannio, he did not tell us everything. There was something he forgot."

Penelope saw Manitza look at the eikon picture of the Virgin

Mary on the whitewashed wall; Manitza's lips were moving.

"Your father used a poor sick instrument to do his bidding, Aleko; it was no doubt all there was. We must have faith that God guided Jannio's tongue aright to-night."

"But if Father was trying to send a message to us!" Aleko said. "If Jannio forgot it!"

"A message!" Penelope's trembling fingers moved along the smooth brown body of the doll. Its face had tiny features, a smiling, upturned mouth; the eyes were even painted blue like — like her eyes. The legs and arms moved on little joints made of some elastic strips. Where had Father found them? Had he cut pieces from his suspenders?

Penelope said slowly: "Perhaps the message is somewhere on the doll."

Then Aleko said: "Oh, no! What nonsense you talk. How could a doll bear a message? I tell you, Jannio forgot something."

Penelope was not listening. What was it Jannio had said? "See that the elastic has not come loose in the joints." Suddenly Penelope's fingers were pouncing; they were tearing at the little elastic supports in one of the legs; were pulling it free. There was a round hole that ran up inside the doll's body; it seemed larger than the one on the other leg. She put her little finger up the hole; she pushed it up, up. Her finger touched something; something that felt like a scrap of rolled paper. She pulled her finger out; she hit the doll's head sharply; a little piece of paper lay there in her palm. Nobody said anything; they just stood there watching Penelope; she could hear their breaths coming. Penelope straightened out the wad of paper. There was writing on it — Father's writing! She was reading the words; she was reading them out loud:

"Aleko is twelve years old this April; he must fight now for Greece. Tell him to join me. He must take the Kalaba Pass to where the trail turns east near the Great Peak. He must go slowly, with care, for half a mile, watching for a carved cross near a tall ilex. I shall be waiting. Destroy this paper. May God watch over you, my little Penelope, and over all in my house."

Penelope looked up slowly. Aleko was standing there, as if he were frozen. Only his eyes were bright and very still, like the north star over the almond tree.

"I shall start to-night," Aleko said. "God has answered my prayer; now I may fight for Greece!"

II

Next morning Penelope woke very early. It was just beginning to be light. The swallows were stirring in their mud nests in the eaves; she could hear their faint chirpings. She pulled on her little blouse with the wide sleeves that Manitza had embroidered, her full skirt, her apron. She folded up the rug, the blanket, and the mattress that Manitza had filled with maize husks. She hung the bedclothes on the wooden rail to air. She knelt a minute before the eikon under which the little lamp always burnt, as a sign that Christ was the light of the world. Then she pulled open the door.

It was very still outside. There was Manitza's loom, there was the old kneading trough, the hive-shaped oven where Manitza baked bread. There were the thorny plants growing over the fence to keep out the goat and the hens. Everything was the same as usual; everything except that great gaping crater over to the right — over in the place where the beautiful garden once had been. Penelope stood quite still; her clenched fingers bit into her palms; that black hole had swallowed up Father, just as it had the iris and the hyacinths and the yellow roses; now it had swallowed Aleko, too! Aleko was up on that lonely trail now, with its slippery rocks, its twisted roots, where one might fall a hundred feet if one's feet should stumble. He was up in those passes where the enemy soldiers lurked and watched. He was making his way along those black ridges with no food but the little packet of bread and onions and olives that Manitza had packed. He was looking for a cross beside an ilex tree; he was looking for Father and a little band of men who were braving death so that Greece might live.

A little whimpering sound came from Penelope's throat. What would she and Manitza and Paolos do without Aleko? He watched the sheep for old Javaras; with the pennies he earned he bought olives and bread and milk for them; sometimes a bit of cheese and greens. He cut down logs in the forest, and carried them home for firewood. Sometimes he even sang that old song, "Of all the stars of Heaven, But one is like to Thee"; the song that Father sang when she and Paolos danced about the hearth. Well, but Father needed Aleko. No, no; Greece needed Aleko! Greece, the proud and ancient land of Perseus and Ulysses and those other heroes in the legends the Pappas told. Father said that Greece had given the world too many shining and beautiful things even to count. Penelope was looking now at that gaping pit, only partly covered with rude boards. Why, Greece had even given her that garden — Greece and Father. Penelope had always loved flowers better than anything else. They seemed like little bright songs the earth made. Father had taught her about them; he had shown her how to plant the seeds, to water and weed and tend them. Father had set out the row of olive trees, the high, leaning cypress, to keep out the winds. The Pappas had taught her their names. There was a hard knot in Penelope's throat, and she tried to swallow it. She gave her head a half-angry shake. What a coward she was! There were Father and Aleko, the other guerillas up in these mountains, fighting the enemy, and here she was safely at home with Manitza and Paolos. If only there were a single sign to show that Aleko would find that cross where Father was waiting! A sign! Penelope shivered. Had she not heard a hen crow just like a cock this morning? Jannio said that was bad luck. And in the hurry of seeing Aleko off last night, she and Manitza had both forgotten to put a potato in his shirt so that good fortune would go with him. The Pappas would laugh at this as nonsense. What had he said that day when Father left? "When grief comes to you, face it. That way you pull its sting, just as the shepherd draws the fang from the adder, and it can harm no one."

Penelope's steps began to move slowly, hesitatingly, towards the bomb crater. It was her grief; she must go near it; she must face it. Always when she passed the pit, she ran swiftly, with her eyes closed. Ah, but Father and Aleko did not run from grief and danger; they faced it without flinching, without question ... It was very queer, it seemed — it seemed as if these were not her feet that were pulling her slowly over to the pit. They belonged to someone else. They would not stop; they kept straight on. Now she stood at the brink of the crater that Aleko said was fifteen feet deep. She lay flat on the rough ground, and peered down into the blackness there. She shaded her eyes with her hands, but for a minute she could see nothing. There was only darkness and cold and a damp secret smell. Penelope's eyes began to grow used to the blackness; she could see down, down; she could see into the bottom of the pit. Suddenly her breath seemed to stop right there in her throat. *There was something growing down there; something that looked like flowers!* There was a little pulse beating in Penelope's forehead; her lips were moving, but they made no sound. Her fingers were biting into the black soil. She drew herself up. She must go down there; she must find out about those flowers. Now she was running, stumbling over the uneven ground towards the house. She was tugging at the high ladder that Father used to prune the cypress branches. She was dragging it slowly, clumsily, towards the crater. No one saw her; Manitza and Paolos were still asleep. It was just as if there were nothing in the world but that line of rosy sky, the colour of the hedge roses; those strange, secret things at the bottom of the pit; and herself. Panting, her hand bleeding, her dress torn, Penelope pushed the ladder down into the crater. She felt it touch the bottom soil; she moved it until it rested securely against the side of the crater. Penelope began to climb slowly down the rungs.

It was like going down into some queer blue night. Gradually the daylight above grew dimmer and dimmer, as if a candle flickered and went out. Penelope's feet went groping down, feeling for the rungs. Her hands gripped the splintery sides of the ladder. Now it was very dark and very still. Her feet sought another rung; it met instead the soft feel of earth. Penelope knelt down on the soil, and her fingers began to move along the ground. They found something; they closed about the velvet face of a petal, of other petals. She spread out her apron, holding it bunched in one hand; with the other, she dropped in the flowers. She caught the apron ends into her belt, and began to climb the ladder.

For a second, when she reached the top, she sat still, with her eyes closed. The light seemed to blind her; all she could

The Blue Flower

see were pale shapes growing in little clusters in darkness; all she could smell was a delicate, enchanting fragrance. Her sight cleared; she opened her eyes. She spread out her apron. It was full of flowers. They were a clear blue, like the sky up there, and they had golden hearts. They were shaped like stars; their leaves were spiked; they felt like down. What were they? She had never seen nor heard of such flowers before. How had they grown down there in that cold darkness? The Pappas would know. He had those books about flowers on the shelf above the fireplace. She must ask him right away.

When the old priest opened the door at the sound of a knock, his astonished gaze saw a little girl in a torn and dirty dress, her face white, her eyes staring, her apron full of flowers.

"My child," he said, "what brings you here so early?"

"These," said Penelope, and she thrust into his hands a cluster of flowers.

The Pappas stared at them; his mouth hung open a little.

"Where have you found them, child? I have never seen their like."

"At the bottom of the bomb crater. They were growing there."

The Pappas looked at the flowers; one of his fingers touched a velvety petal. His lips moved, but no sound came.

"Pappas, what are they?"

Then the old man said slowly, "How could they grow there in that dark pit?"

"Pappas, Pappas, tell me!"

Suddenly the priest had turned; he was reaching up to a shelf, and pulling down three books. He was opening one. His white head, stooped above the heavy black cassock, bent over the illustrations with their printed text. Penelope sat watching him, hardly breathing. He closed the book, frowned, shook his head, and picked up a second volume. His faded eyes, in their iron-rimmed spectacles, skimmed across the print; his unsteady fingers turned page after page. Then he came to the third book. It was an old and faded volume; its leather cover was cracked, the title almost unreadable. But after the old man had turned the first three pages, Penelope saw his fingers stiffen on the paper; she heard his breath coming like that of someone who had been running a long way.

"Yes, it is here," he said, and he looked at Penelope with queer eyes, and said a long name that she could not understand. His gaze went to the flowers in her apron, and back to an old drawing on the page, and the Pappas spoke:

"This flower grew in Greece more than a hundred years ago. Never has it been seen in bloom since then."

Penelope's mouth was dry; her heart was hammering. She said very low:

"Then — it is a miracle?"

"A miracle, Penelope! Men will say some chemical, some material in the powder of the bomb fertilized that old, old earth, and the flowers bloomed again." The Pappas smiled softly, and said: "But you and I know better; we know it is a sign from Heaven."

A sign from Heaven! Penelope's hands were pulling at the Pappas' black sleeve. "But it is what I was looking for, a sign that Aleko and Father are safe!"

The old clock ticked on rustily; the log in the grate crackled and sputtered. The little dog on the hearth sighed in his sleep. Then the Pappas said: "It is more than a sign, my child. It is a pledge that Greece will flower again, the old Greece of Ulysses and Perseus and Icarus."

"Is it the earth saying so, Pappas?"

"Perhaps, Penelope."

"And — I — I do nothing."

"One does not fight alone with powder and musket; the heart fights, too."

"How can it, Pappas?"

"With courage and with faith, my daughter."

Courage and faith! Penelope smiled; why, those were the words that the blue flowers were saying!

THE EAGLE

ALFRED, LORD TENNYSON

He clasps the crag with crooked hands;
Close to the sun in lonely lands,
Ring'd with the azure world, he stands.

The wrinkled sea beneath him crawls;
He watches from his mountain walls,
And like a thunderbolt he falls.

OUT OF BOUNDS

THEODORE ACLAND HARPER

Rocky Cove was distinctly out of bounds. Mr. Thatcher made that quite clear to all the lads at his New Zealand boarding school. By land, the route to the cove from French Farm School was a perilous climb for all but the most experienced of mountaineers. By sea, frequent and sudden sou'westers churned the Pacific into the cove in a maelstrom of white water.

The headmaster put his boys on their honour not to venture there. Yet Bobby and Fitz felt that they must go. Seventy years ago the collecting of birds' eggs was a consuming interest of young New Zealanders. Both boys were burning to add to their collections. Only this week Abner had told Fitz that the curious sea parrot, the puffin, nested in the crags of Rocky Cove. To all collectors of eggs, the eggs of the puffin were more to be coveted than the Crown Jewels.

Saturday came and, with it, the rumour that Mr. Thatcher would be away on business till late at night. It was now or never. Bobby and Fitz decided to stay out all night, take their chances on evading the Boss's wrath, and each bag one of these precious eggs for his collection.

They met by arrangement on the hillside a quarter of a mile behind the school and compared notes in excited whispers. They each had a blanket, and besides his usual lunch Bobby had managed to annex the remainder of a leg of mutton. Fitz had wheedled a whole loaf of bread from the cook on the plea that there was not enough left in the dining room to go round.

Fitz shouldered his swag. "I know a shorter cut than Tussock Peak! Come on."

They spoke little for the next couple of hours, by which time they had reached the divide at the head of Tekoa Bay. From here they could look down on the whole outside sweep of Banks Peninsula, almost to the Heads. There was a ship a mile or two out on the Pacific.

"See that headland out beyond the patch of bush? Well, from what Abner said, Rocky Cove is on the other side of that, and the puffins nest somewhere between that and the Heads. Gosh! it's a long way. We'll have to work round behind the Cove before we drop down onto the cliffs. How long do you s'pose it will take?"

As far as Bobby could judge it was mostly tussock country, devoid of deep gullies except near the coast line, but he had learned that a bird's-eye view of such an extent of hillside was apt to be deceptive. "It's farther than I thought," he suggested. "We'll never get back to-night."

"Whoever supposed we would?" asked Fitz impatiently. "You needn't come if you're scared."

Bobby let the insult pass. "We'd better know where we're going to sleep before it gets too late." He pointed far out to the southern horizon. "See those clouds? Twice when I've been up on the ridge I've noticed clouds like those and both times there was a sou'wester before night. We're going to get wet if we don't look out."

Fitz scowled, first at the clouds, then at Bobby, and lastly at the headland beyond the patch of bush. He knew more about sou'westers than, just then, he was willing to admit. "You talk an awful lot of rot! Do you suppose that that whaler would be sticking about so close to the headland if a sou'wester was coming along?"

Bobby examined the whaler again. All its sails were set, but it appeared to be motionless. So far there was not a breath of wind. However, he knew too little about the drift of the tide on a lee shore to argue, and he stood silent, frowning a little, wondering about it.

Fitz noted the frown and interpreted it in his own fashion. "What's the matter now? Worrying about Thatcher, and being on our honour, and all that tosh?"

The question was too near the truth to be comfortable, and Bobby sputtered angrily: "Oh, shut up, and quit talking about it! You know jolly well you were too scared to try it alone, so why keep on everlastingly grousing?"

Fitz's one-sided grin admitted the charge. "Darnation! — S'pose there aren't any puffins! . . . And what if Thatcher does get back to-night?"

A large hawk planed by in the quiet air and Bobby watched it until it was out of sight. "I vote we go on," he said. After they had tramped a mile or so he finished the sentence: "And if the Boss does get back before we do, what yarn are we going to spin?"

Fitz tramped steadily along in front. "You bet it'll be nothing about eggs, or he might take them away!" Like Bobby he was some distance nearer the headland before he put the rest of his thought into words. "At that, if you're not a blasted young juggins, you'll leave the talking to me. Anyone can tell when you're trying to lie."

Bobby flushed behind Fitz's back. Trying *not* to lie, rather!

The trouble was that sometimes, when he'd broken rules and Thatcher was decent enough not to ask questions, that mystery called "Family" would start plaguing him; he had visions of his ancestor, the old Lord Chancellor, looking down on him from his gilded frame. And there it was — lies and the old Lord Chancellor simply didn't go. . . .

Fitz's whistle broke into his thoughts. Evidently he wasn't troubled by his ancestors. "Well, I'll be jiggered!" Fitz broke out. "We've come a long way too far down the hill. It's Rocky Cove all right, but we're on the wrong side. Now we'll have to climb up again round that patch of scrub."

Bobby promptly sat down on a rock. "Let's eat something first!"

Fitz was almost too excited to hear him. "Tell you what! Abner knows what he's talking about — the puffins are over there, not more than a mile away after we get across. What I mean is, if we have any luck at finding the eggs we might get back yet before bedtime. S'pose we stick our swags somewhere up there in the scrub so we can get along faster. We can eat while we go along."

They worked their way up the edge of the gulch and crossed the head of it by pushing through thick scrub. When they finally got to the top of the cliff, the high headland cut off their view of the whaler. Not that they observed anything so trivial, for the first uninterrupted sight of thousands of nesting sea birds drove every other thought from their minds.

"Holy smoke!" Fitz spoke reverently, as though he were in church. "Cornish — look! Look! you hopeless blighter — look! Oh, my everlasting hat, why didn't we bring a rope?"

Bobby on his part forgot to breathe. Rookery on rookery, row upon row, wherever there was a ledge or a crevice wide enough for a nest. . . . Cliffs streaked with guano, coloured with the litter of generations. . . . Far below, the sea breaking among the rocks. Birds fishing in the lazy swells; birds alighting delicately on fragile nests without disturbing so much as a feather; birds planing and banking against the sky; diving and banking against the sheer wall of the cliff; the rhythm of their cries swelling and dying and swelling anew, plaintive, staccato, wild, unrestrained.

"Guillemots!" Fitz was pointing with a rigid arm. "Millions

of them! Those long-neck rummies with white fronts. They stand up like penguins, and they only lay one egg apiece — no two alike. It's a good thing they're pear-shaped or more of them would roll off the ledges, because they don't build any kind of nest. Look at the seagulls. They're everywhere. And shags — dirty busters — you can smell them up here. Gannets! . . . at least they look like gannets from here. And mollymawks . . . and terns, away over there, high up near the top. It wouldn't surprise me if there were albatrosses too, but Abner says he never heard of any. *Je-hosh-a-phat!* — I'll bet I can see a million eggs. . . ."

After a long period of absorption Bobby returned to the purpose of the whole adventure. "Which are the puffins?"

Fitz made a hissing noise. "I don't see any. What bad luck! Abner said the other side of Rocky Cove, I'm sure — but you won't find them by staring your eyes out at those cliffs, they nest up here on top among the tussocks, in holes; and when you stick your arm in, if there's a bird inside it jabs its beak into your finger. That is, it will if you give it a chance."

"Why don't we look for holes, then?" Bobby asked.

"Because I don't see any birds flying about," Fitz grumbled. "I expect it means we haven't gone far enough toward the Heads. All the same, keep your eye skinned." He started off at once and began searching along the edge of the cliff.

"Aren't you coming?" he called back.

Bobby had not moved. "Don't we get some of these eggs while we're here?"

"We're hunting puffins, aren't we? . . . I've got all those in my collection."

"I haven't," Bobby answered with determination.

Fitz showed annoyance. "Don't be an ass all your life, Cornish! How d'you suppose you're going to get down there? We'll have to look for some easier place."

The advice seemed reasonable enough, for the altitude of the cliffs fell away steadily for some distance toward the Heads.

Besides, after all their excitement about puffins Bobby was as anxious to find them as Fitz.

He, too, began searching for holes. . . .

II

The hunt lengthened into a couple of hours and carried them a long way from their base. They found mollymawks' eggs— white with brown splotches—on the extreme edge of the cliff; but mollymawks were not puffins, and at last Fitz gave way to discouragement.

"Abner's a liar!" His voice was tragic. "He's been pulling our legs." He threw himself full length on his back.

Bobby was not only discouraged, he was tired as well; and he had pretty well lost faith in the very existence of puffins. But there were still the other eggs he so obstinately desired to possess before Thatcher pronounced his doom, and as Fitz had nothing more to say he left him staring up at the sky and continued along the headland alone.

He came to a place where it broke away precipitously, dropping perhaps two hundred feet to the cliffs, above the open Pacific.

Tussocks and occasional bushes of stunted flax offered a foothold, and after studying the question carefully he determined to risk a descent onto one of the many ledges where the birds had plastered their nests against the face of the rocks. In gingerly fashion he lowered himself.

And now began a breath-taking scramble, most of which he accomplished on his stomach. He had the sensation of inching down a steep roof, depending on the gutter at the bottom to provide safe footing in case of a slip. Half-way down he turned round to look about him. The thought of the two or three hundred feet of perpendicular drop below gave him pause; but a whiff of fresh bird guano sent him scrambling on again.

The next time he stopped to reconnoitre he could see birds nesting against the higher bluffs. A guillemot took note of his sudden appearance and stopped its affairs to observe him, craned its neck sideways, then dropped like a plummet out of sight.

OXEN DRINKING — *Horatio Walker*

Reproduced by permission of the National Gallery, Ottawa.

HORATIO WALKER, R.C.A.
(1858 - 1934)

Horatio Walker was born at Listowel, Ontario, in 1858. Like Homer Watson, he began drawing when he was a very small boy. At twelve years of age he won a prize for a banner he had made for an Orange Lodge parade. Horatio's father recognized the talent which his son displayed and gave him what opportunity he could to enlarge his knowledge. He took Horatio with him to Quebec city whenever he could. At fifteen years of age, Horatio went to Toronto to study art, and remained there for five years.

In 1880 he set off for Quebec which had so thrilled his boyhood days. He walked the distance from Montreal to Quebec and made scores of sketches of the habitant countryside, people, the buildings, and the animals. When he reached Quebec he had sketches enough to work on for a life time. He set to work to make larger canvasses from his sketches. The pictures sold readily, and the prices paid for them grew in amount, for people liked the homely scenes, the careful detail, and the gay, bright colours.

In the year 1882 he travelled in England, Ireland, France, and Spain, but returned again to Quebec. He had already fallen in love with the little hamlet of St. Petronville, on the Isle of Orleans, and now he settled down there. He loved the habitant people and they soon learned to love him. He was soon comfortably well off, and his reputation grew. In 1918 he was elected a member of the Royal Canadian Academy and in 1925 was made its president. He died in 1934.

Oxen Drinking hangs in the National Gallery, Ottawa.

Bobby laughed as he turned over on his stomach again and edged toward the left. He had not gone far when a stone rolled from under his foot, clattered against other stones and dropped into a vacuum of silence which sent his head up listening. He turned round for still another look, and this time his heart missed a beat.

His impression was that it would be necessary only to lean forward in order to look straight down into the breakers, for not much more than ten yards below him the slope ended abruptly. He clutched a handful of tussock and stared into green and white patches of foam as each long swell rolled in from the southwest. Green and white patches of foam with no answering sparkle from the sun.

A corner of his mind warned him of wind — but he paid no attention, for a little farther on, to the left, and only just a little lower down the slope, was what appeared to be a ledge wide enough for him to crawl along. Once again the smell, tantalizingly closer now, urged him to make the final attempt.

He measured the intervening ground. Three, perhaps four, long sliding steps downward to a small flax bush, five or six more to a stunted cabbage tree, and the ledge would be his. He went forward, this time without turning over.

He reached the flax bush, passed above it, used it as a life line to lower himself to the next patch of tussock below, attained the tussock, and shifted one foot over to a rock. Straddled wide between the two and with his back plastered against the slope, he paused to exult, for now he could see beyond doubt that the ledge was three feet wide and that it sloped downward and inward; leading to — what?

He transferred his weight carefully, a pound at a time, to test the stability of the rock. The next inch or so, and he must abandon his last hold on the precious flax bush.

But he did not actually let go, for something as suddenly devastating as an earthquake disintegrated his world. There was a whirring, whirling noise, and the ground between his legs shot up close to his face, or so it seemed. He ducked — overbalancing dangerously — to avoid being struck in the face by something which rose up past him and soared away out into space.

When it was far enough off to get into focus, his eyes took in its details with startled clearness: Plump body; white breast, chunky neck; an enormous parrot's beak, bluish at the base and striped with orange-yellow at the tip.

A puffin!

Puffins were sea parrots — puffins built their nests in holes. Here was one right between his legs!

In his impatience to examine it he turned over without due caution, and his fingers had barely touched the two eggs lying at the bottom of the hole when the ground beneath his feet gave way.

Only the fact that his arm was in the burrow up to the elbow saved him. As it was, the sudden jerk drove his fingers through one of the eggs, and it is fair to say that his next move was made more in the interest of the remaining treasure than for his own safety. Carefully he felt for a new toehold, established it, and brought the unbroken egg to the surface.

It was white and chunky, but he did not stop to examine it in detail. While he stowed it away in the box attached to his belt his mind flew to the probability of other nests within reach; and as soon as it was secure he crawled on down the slope, examining the surface carefully as he went. Before he reached the cabbage tree he had found two more holes.

This time his sense of fair play to the birds prompted him to leave one egg in each nest, which gave him two for himself and one for Fitz. And now — whatever might happen after — their escapade had been a success!

Even so, he was not ready to crawl back to safety, for the ledge which meandered round the face of the bluff was within easy reach, and it would only be necessary to improvise a short length of rope in order to ensure a safe return. He examined the flax bush.

Stunted by many a gale, it was far from being the luxuriantly growing plant with strong green blades eight or ten feet long to which Bobby was accustomed. Yet, once he had clambered precariously back to it he was able to knot together a fairly presentable line. After depositing his puffins' eggs at the base of what remained of the bush, he slid down to the cabbage tree again.

There was need of more patience here to secure the rope; and thereafter all the courage he possessed to trust himself to its strength, but the bluff was not perpendicular, and by using every available crevice he presently found himself on all fours clinging like a fly to the coveted ledge.

His first clear impression was the roar of the sea, breaking far below. His second that of a world populated with birds. Birds perched so close together one could not have stepped among them. Birds hovering gracefully to settle; birds dropping into space with effortless ease, only to spread their wings and plane downward and outward toward the inrolling swells; birds sitting on nests; standing erect to preen their feathers, or quarrelling and buffeting each other with half-open wings.

While he marvelled at the wonder of it, those nearest saw him and sent up a warning cry. In a moment the whole face of the bluff changed colour and texture as they took wing. He straightened up on his knees to watch. It seemed a sheer impossibility that so many winged things could swoop and drop and dart and swoop again, at such incredible speed, without collision. For an interval he was so lost that he forgot his purpose. Then, suddenly, the sou'wester flattened him against the face of the rock.

He was used to the sudden onslaught of the wind; but now the quick change of temperature and the whistle of the gale around his birds' eyrie made it seem like the roar of an enemy, rather than the thing he loved so well. For the first time in his life wind frightened him, and he realized that not only was a sou'wester upon him, but with it drenching rain.

He acted quickly, feeling that he had only moments. An endless array of pear-shaped guillemots' eggs lay within reach. No two were exactly alike. The fact puzzled him, even though Fitz had warned him. He selected five or six, crawled farther on, and annexed several of a different species which he hoped might prove to be gannets'. Tantalizingly close, but out of reach, he saw sea gulls' and shags' eggs, and some that he thought might be terns'.

But a drop of rain warned him to hurry. He still had the problem of safe transportation to solve, for three guillemots' eggs filled his box. He stripped off his coat, and with a spare piece of flax tied the ends of the sleeves, then carefully filled each one with eggs. Not content, he tied each egg into its own little sack, until the sleeves of his coat looked like strings of sausages. The coat itself he tied round his neck.

Now the return journey began. At first the wind baffled him, making his footing seem even more unsafe than before. It robbed him of breath and lashed his hair into his eyes. It produced a giddiness which threatened helplessness. He lifted his head and began to crawl.

Once he had mastered his giddiness the wind helped rather than hindered, for it blew him inward against the face of the bluff. He caught the dangling end of his rope and began to climb; the rain soaked him before he reached the cabbage tree. At the flax bush he stopped to pick up his puffins' eggs.

The tussocks were wet and slippery, and the ground between fast turning into mud; but it is notoriously easier to climb up a steep facing than down, and he made rapid progress.

At the top he encountered an angry and very frightened Fitz, who had long since given him up for lost.

"You blithering, blasted, dashed young idiot! I'll show you —"

Bobby backed out of reach. *"Look out!!* You'd better shut up and listen. I'll swop you one puffin for a shag and a tern — and if you're decent you'll give me a sea gull as well."

Fitz looked at him with profound disgust. "What do you know about puffins, I'd like to ask?"

"Not such a lot," Bobby answered in a voice deliberately calculated to annoy. "Only I happen to have found three! and they aren't addled either. I know, because I broke one."

Reverence entered into Fitz's manner. "Let me see!"

Heads together they settled down in the tussocks, rain and wind alike forgotten.

When the eggs had been examined and stowed away Fitz wiped the moisture out of his eyes. "Well—we'd better leg it back to the hut. We're as wet as shags." He stood up and shook himself like a dog. Then suddenly—in a voice that was stricken by something not unlike terror—he cried:

"Holy smoke!—Look at that ship!"

III

During the calm of the morning and early afternoon the set of the tide had carried the whaler some distance up the coast, and the wind caught her within a mile or so of a lee shore. Now the skipper faced the problem of beating to sea in the teeth of a sou'wester. His chance lay in his ability to clear the headland to the east of Rocky Cove, where the two boys stood silhouetted against the sky.

To Bobby, the ship driving close-hauled into the force of the gale took on an altogether new interest, for without knowing much about seafaring he sensed that he was watching a race.

Fitz put the whole matter into a nutshell. "They'll hit the point if they keep on the same tack for another mile."

"You'd think they'd put on more sail!" Bobby hazarded, not knowing what else to say.

"Too much wind!" Fitz muttered through tight lips. "They're pretty nearly swamped as it is, reefed down close. I wish they'd go about. Oh, I wish they'd go about! . . . There!—look! They're going to clear it yet."

A shift of wind enabled them to point up farther away from the headland, and apparently the skipper decided to use the momentary advantage by going about. He paid off a little to gather way and then attempted to bring his ship up into the wind.

Bobby understood now, and his jaw tightened. He had practised that very manoeuvre in the old school dinghy, rigged up with oddments of sails, and it had not always met with success.

The telltale patch of oily water close under the hull meant leeway, but the ship responded to her helm and came up slowly into the wind. As her sails emptied she straightened to a more even keel, and at the same time took it green over her bow. Even so, inch by inch she swung away toward the other tack, and then a second wave flooded her fore decks.

She came out of it sluggishly, rolled her rails under, hung with all sails flapping — and then paid off slowly again. She had missed stays.

Bobby danced with suspense. In the dinghy, that meant you ran aground unless you promptly got out an oar. He brushed the hair out of his eyes and looked anxiously at Fitz.

"What'll they do now?"

Fitz swallowed. "Try again or get wrecked. There isn't anything else they can do."

There was, however, one other desperate chance. The skipper took it. He tried to wear ship. He had failed to bring her head up into the wind in the usual manner; now he paid her off in an attempt to bring her round by the stern. Under most favourable circumstances such a manoeuvre requires ample sea room, the very thing he lacked; but even so, by prompt handling and a little luck, or by the slightest shift of wind or a moment's lull, he might conceivably miss the rocks.

He came so near success that Fitz began to whistle through his teeth, and then a huge sea struck her amidships, and the foremast went overboard.

Bobby, staring almost straight down onto her decks, did not realize that she had struck until Fitz began to run.

"Quick!" he called back. "We'll get down in the Cove. Somebody might be washed ashore."

It took them half an hour.

On the beach the wind was much less violent, and the rain seemed to have stopped, but the roar of the breakers and the ominous suck of the undertow awed Bobby so that he talked in whispers.

"Is everybody drowned?"

"If they're not, they soon will be." Fitz's voice sounded unnatural, and his slang had deserted him. "The bodies will wash ashore into the Cove. . . . I—I never saw a drowned man."

From the beach the ship looked even closer to land than from above and utterly desolate in a world that seemed to be nothing but motion and noise. A second mast had gone, and seas broke sickeningly over her hull. One could hear them thud as they struck.

Fitz was staring resolutely out to sea. "There's someone coming now!"

Bobby followed the direction of his arm. "Where?—Oh, I see!—But isn't he. . . . Why, Fitz, he's not dead! He's swimming! —He's alive! . . ." The last word was a shout, and his heart beat so fast he felt suffocated.

Now on the crest of a wave . . . now disappearing into the trough . . . coming up again in the smother . . . a black head, driving with incredible speed, came straight toward them.

And then the swimmer was stretched, spreadeagle, on his face—in shallow water—with the undertow sucking him back; and Fitz and Bobby were hurtling themselves to his rescue through surf up to their knees. They tugged at his arm—were knocked down—struggled up in time to tug again, with the added lift of the incoming wave. Then, after a period of confusion, Bobby was lying on the beach with a heavy body that coughed across his legs, and his mouth and ears full of sand and foam.

"Pull, you little beggars—pull! Hand over hand—so. . . ."

The voice was husky — breathless — but alive and in command; and Bobby found himself hauling on a line, one end of which was fastened round the man's waist.

After an interval the light line gave place to a heavier one, the end of which they made fast round a jutting rock. The man leaned against the rock as though he were temporarily spent.

He was a thick-set, heavily breathing man with a stubby black beard, and he wore scarcely any clothing at all. His light brown eyes looked the boys over.

"Here, you — little fellow — climb up the bluff and wave something. Take my shirt." He tore off what remained of it. "Signal the ship — savvy? And you — we need a fire!"

From up on the bluff above the breakers Bobby could distinguish figures clustered under the lee of a deckhouse. They saw his signal almost at once and waved back. Exultant, he hurried down to the beach, impatient to rejoin the man who had brought the lifeline ashore. He found him still leaning against the rock, with Fitz's coat round his shoulders. He was watching the breakers.

"They got your signal? Good! My name is Smith. You two youngsters, whoever you are, turned up just in time to save my life. With luck we'll save the rest now." He held out his hand. Bobby shook it solemnly.

"We're both from Thatcher's school. We were up on the headland when you struck, and we came down."

"Thatcher's school —" The man spoke as though almost he might have heard of it.

"Over in French Farm," Bobby added. He was about to explain how far it was, but the man had ceased to attend.

"Here comes the first one now! Listen — you've got gumption — I'm going into the surf to help that fellow ashore; you stay here and pay out as much line as I need, and if the undertow gets me, take a turn round this rock. Do you understand?"

Out in the surf one of the crew, fastened into a sling which

Out of Bounds

Bobby learned later was called a bosun's chair, was coming hand over hand along the rope. Bobby watched him spellbound.

Before he landed, Fitz appeared with their packs. "Went for matches!" he explained, and he began hurriedly to collect driftwood.

It was exciting to watch each man's battle with the surf as he came ashore, but Bobby realized it was child's play compared to the danger the first man had run. Every few minutes another sailor would come along the rope, and soon strange oaths, and harsh voices, and stamping feet blended with the crackling driftwood fire and the monotonous roar of the breakers. Stronger hands than Bobby's took the line — pushed him aside — told him to keep out of the way.

Bobby looked around him at the fifteen strange faces grouped about the fire. It was said all hands except the skipper were accounted for, and the skipper had been washed overboard when the ship struck. No one watched the lifeline any more. Shoulders shrugged and men spoke quietly under their breath: It was destiny. They crowded closer to the fire, squeezed the water out of their clothes; spat and swore and stamped their feet.

"We ought to be getting along, anyway," said Smith, whose commanding presence marked him as the leader of the group. "It'll be dark after a while, and it's a long tramp to shelter. There's a man called Thatcher over the hill who'll probably fix us up for the night. These two boys will show us the way."

Fitz and Bobby looked at each other. So that was to be the end of their adventure!

IV

Darkness caught them before they got to the divide, but it was open country, and the moon rose as they circled round the upper slopes of Tussock Peak. Bobby was too weary to know where he was. Fitz, stumbling along in front, had not spoken since dark. The man whom they called Smith walked last. He wore

Bobby's blanket round his shoulders and carried the precious eggs slung from his belt.

Every little while he helped Bobby when he stumbled and encouraged him with a laugh. "Buck up, little chap! It's not every day you take part in a wreck."

The lights of the school came into view and then disappeared again, and Bobby wondered vaguely what time it was, and whether Thatcher had come home after all. Not that it would matter now, either way.

The procession stopped in the corner of the playing field. Smith was saying: "Now, then, one of you youngsters, which way?"

Fitz gave Bobby a shove. "You go first!"

He lifted his head and led the way across the field. Lights in the dormitory were out, but a lamp burned in Thatcher's study. He marched up to the door and knocked while the men grouped themselves on the edge of the porch, waiting.

Thatcher himself opened the door. He had either just come in or was on the point of going out, for he had his hat on. For a moment he saw only Bobby.

"Why, Cornish! What's the meaning of this?"

Bobby cleared his throat, but Smith stepped forward and saved him from the necessity of explaining.

"We're very sorry to disturb you, sir, but there's been a wreck."

"Wreck!—Where?" Thatcher went out onto the porch, and a hum of voices followed.

Fitz tugged Bobby's arm. "Now's our time to do a sneak!"

But suddenly Bobby was through with deceit. He pushed Fitz into the study behind the rest, and they stood on the outer fringe, awaiting their turn.

Nearly an hour later Thatcher returned to the study alone. His wife was knitting. He stopped a moment to look down at Bobby, who was sound asleep on the couch.

"Well," he said, "I've got them all fed and fixed up in the schoolroom for the night. Now, about these two boys."

Mrs. Thatcher stopped knitting. "I took them into the kitchen and gave them all the hot milk they could drink, and I did my best to discover how they came to be mixed up in the wreck, but I really haven't found out much. They just looked at each other the way they do when they've agreed not to say anything, and made stupid answers. They were so utterly tired out I didn't press them."

The Boss laid several tin boxes on the table, opened one and looked into it, then held it out to his wife. "There's the answer! Sea-birds' eggs. It was Mason's guess when they didn't show up for supper."

Mrs. Thatcher's eyes snapped. "They laid their plans carefully! —waiting until you were away for the day."

"Naturally!" chuckled Thatcher. "Being boys, they would, and Mason, being another, kept the matter to himself until I got home. As it's turned out, I'm glad he didn't make you needlessly anxious."

"Well, I told them both to go to bed, but Cornish insisted on seeing you first. He's been asleep for half an hour." Her voice softened. "Poor lamb, hadn't we better let him be?"

The Boss's eyes smiled. "As it's Cornish, I think perhaps not. He'll prefer to take his medicine now." He replaced the top of the tin and put the whole lot out of sight, then touched Bobby on the shoulder.

Bobby came out of the depths of a dreamless sleep. It was all in keeping with the confusion of the last few hours. He blinked himself awake to find Thatcher seated beside him on the couch.

"Yes, Cornish. I'm ready to listen now."

Bobby stood up. "Please, sir—please, sir—we were out of bounds. . . . We went to get puffins' eggs."

"I'm glad you told me that."

They looked at each other steadily. "And we knew all the time we were going to be late. We—we were going to stay out all night. We—we—and then the wreck came!"

"Yes, I see. And which of you thought of all this first?"

Bobby's voice held firm. "I don't suppose either of us did. Fitz — Fitzsimmons, I mean — began talking about puffins, but he wouldn't have gone unless I'd wanted to, and we thought —" Here he stuck temporarily. The Boss waited.

"You both collect eggs, is that is? Somebody told you you might find puffins along the cliffs?"

"Yes, sir."

Thatcher seemed to consider. "Who told you?"

Like any other boy, Bobby was sensitive to the smallest change of voice when authority spoke. He noted such a change now, and realized that if he mentioned Abner's name complications would ensue.

"A fellow I met once at Barry's Bay post office told me — I didn't know his name." He salved his conscience with the one little word *didn't* — as a matter of fact, he had not known Abner's name when he first saw him in Barry's Bay.

The Boss went on considering. "H'm! You don't know who told you, and yet you were willing to break bounds on the chance that someone you'd only seen once knew what he was talking about?"

"Oh, yes, sir — you see it was puffins. . . ."

"I see! Well, go to bed now. I'll hear the rest to-morrow, when Fitzsimmons is here."

Accordingly, next morning, an hour after breakfast, the two boys faced Thatcher again. On the table between them the eggs they had gathered were spread out like so many hostile witnesses. Thatcher was unsmiling.

"It is a matter of honour with all you boys not to break bounds. . . . Then this sort of thing happens. . . . I've heard part of the story from Cornish. Now, Fitzsimmons?"

Fitz's mouth climbed earwards. "You see, sir, it was the puffins!"

"So Cornish told me. Are they so very important?"

"Why!" Fitz looked astonished in spite of his embarrassment.

Out of Bounds

"When a fellow has never seen one it's—it's—well, sir, it's pretty hard to miss a chance!"

"Apparently so, in your case, at least. But if you had never seen the birds and Cornish didn't know who it was told him about them, how did you expect to know what to look for?"

This sounded a little like sarcasm, and sarcasm confused Fitz. But to Bobby's surprise all signs of embarrassment fell away.

"Why, sir, of course I knew that!" He launched into a description of puffins which brought them right into the study. "And they're the only sea birds besides mollymawks that nest in burrows. You have to be jolly careful sticking your arm in not to get nipped." He chuckled at the prospect.

Thatcher had watched him narrowly throughout the discussion. "Where did you learn all that?"

"In books. And, of course, I've talked to fishermen, only they don't know much."

"Remarkable, Fitzsimmons! So you have actually read a book without being compelled. I had given up hope."

Fitz's mouth climbed cornerwise again. "I'd think anyone would want to read about birds."

Here Bobby had an inspiration. "Please, sir, he's got over a hundred and thirty-nine sorts. I've only got thirty-seven."

"I'd like to see that collection. Go and fetch it."

For the next twenty minutes all three of them talked freely about eggs—eggs in general, and Fitz's collection in particular. The latter now held the place of honour on the study table. Gradually the Boss came by a pretty accurate knowledge of all that had led up to the expedition to Rocky Cove, as well as all that they knew or conjectured about the wreck.

"Well—now about breaking bounds. . . . Suppose you tell me, one of you, what you think would be fair."

Fitz nudged Bobby.

"Quite so, Fitzsimmons, but since you are the elder, suppose you tell me what *you* think." It was the unsmiling Boss that looked down on them now.

"I think, sir —" Fitz stumbled — "I mean, I expect we ought to be kept in to the end of term."

"And what should be done with these eggs?" Thatcher was looking at Bobby now.

This was the zero hour indeed. Bobby's heart sank into his boots, and yet he recognized the hand of justice holding the scales evenly.

"They ought to be confiscated, sir, especially the puffins." He managed to get it said without his voice trembling.

Thatcher straightened his shoulders. "And perhaps a thrashing in front of the whole school?"

Fitz had experienced that indignity once already. "Yes, sir, I suppose so."

Bobby licked his lips.

Thatcher paced the length of the room and came to a stand in front of them. "That sailor, Smith, tells me that you two boys saved him from drowning in the surf — which means the whole crew, probably. It's the kind of thing I expect from my boys in an emergency. Because you did that I'm not going to keep you in — nor am I going to confiscate your eggs. I'm going to give you something harder to do. From now on you will both set a good example in the school. You, Fitzsimmons, stop bullying boys smaller than yourself. Help them for a change. And, Cornish, this wandering about alone — oh, yes, I know about it — has got to stop. It is a bad example for the whole school. From now on I expect responsibility from both of you. Shall we shake hands on it?"

Fitz was halfway back to the schoolroom before he began his customary humming. Bobby, too, kept silent because his jaw was aching. They went up into the dormitory and sat down on the nearest bed.

Presently Fitz heaved a deep sigh. "I wish my father was like the Boss! That chap understands better than anyone else in New Zealand what a fellow feels like inside."

TO IRON-FOUNDERS AND OTHERS

GORDON BOTTOMLEY

When you destroy a blade of grass,
   You poison England at her roots:
Remember no man's foot can pass
   Where evermore no green life shoots.

You force the birds to wing too high
   Where your unnatural vapours creep:
Surely the living rocks shall die
   When birds no rightful distance keep.

You have brought down the firmament,
   And yet no heaven is more near;
You shape huge deeds without event.
   And half-made men believe and fear.

ON STRIKE

RICHARD LLEWELLYN

Well I remember, though fifty winters have come and gone, the days of the strike in my green Welsh valley. Going home that night we found the streets and the square full of people, men and women, the men black from work, the women dressed for the house and bare-headed, all talking in groups and looking serious.

"What is wrong here, Ellis?" I asked him, while he was putting Mari in the shafts.

"On strike," Ellis said, and in sorrow, and with anxiousness. "I expect our men will be out by the time we are home. Your father and Ianto and Davy and a couple more have gone over to see the owners. God knows what will happen, indeed."

All along the road around the mountain by the river men came running from their houses to have the news from Ellis, who never stopped, but shouted as he slapped the reins on Mari's back, and at his words the men seemed to go dead, and the women were still, or wrung their hands or held their babies tighter.

Round in our village the people were out in the street, and all up the Hill they were out, not talking much, for there was nothing to talk about, but waiting for the men to come back. I jumped off as the people crowded about Ellis, and I heard the low murmur as his words were passed back.

In our house my mother was peeling apples, and Angharad was chopping the peel for jam. Bron was ironing, and Olwen was playing with Gareth in front of the fire.

"Well," said my mother.

"The men are out in the Three Valleys, Mama," I said.

Nobody stopped working, but Bron was crying as I passed her, but so quietly you would never know. All that night I was

On Strike

cleaning Owen's engine, for I had learned to take it to pieces and fit it all back again, and I was taking the grease off my hands when I heard my father's step in the back, and he came in quietly, cap and coat on, and sat down, looking at the candles, wordlessly and with grief, with his moustache like silver.

He cleared his throat as though pain had been his only meal for hours.

"Huw," he said, and still looking at the candles.

"Yes, Dada," I said, and went to him with my hands dripping with grease.

"I am ashamed to go in and face your Mama," he said, and still not looking at me.

"Why?" I said

"O, boy, boy," he said, and if he had had the tears they would surely have come then. "How you and your sons will live, I cannot tell. Come you here, my son."

I went closer, and he put his arms about me, and rested his whiskery cheek against mine.

"I could see you all day to-day," he said, "while they were talking and arguing. You and your sons. What is to happen to you I cannot tell. The ground is cut from under our feet. Nothing to be done. Nothing."

His voice was close to my ear, and heavy with sorrow.

"It is your mother and the other women who will suffer," he said. "They will have the burden. I am ashamed to go in and tell her."

"She is waiting for you, Dada," I said.

He was quiet for a little, and then he put me from him, and got up.

"God bless her," he said, "she always has. Stay you in here for a bit, Huw, my little one."

"Yes, Dada," I said, "there is grease on your coat."

"No matter," he said, and went into the house.

Ianto came in just after he had gone, white and brilliant in the eyes, as a man will look after a fight only half finished.

"Has Dada gone in?" he asked me.
"Yes," I said.
"Good," he said. "I thought we would never get him home."
"Why, then?" I asked him.
"Never mind, boy," he said, with impatience. "How was he?"
"In pain," I said.
Ianto hit his fists softly on the bench.
"Yes," he said, "we are all in pain. And we will stop there, too."
"Are we coming out?" I asked him.
"We are out, now," said Ianto, "since half-past three we have been out."
"Will we win, Ianto?" I asked him.
"As much chance of that as flies in a beer-trap," Ianto said. "No chance. No hopes. Good-night, now."

He went out and listened at the kitchen window for a moment and then went down to Bron's. There seemed nothing that I could do so I climbed up the shed and went through the window to bed.

Next morning I was allowed only two slices of bread, with butter on only one, and no jam. For school, I had a pie and bread and cheese with lettuce, but no tea.

"It will have to be water, Huw, my little one," my mother said. "Your Dada cannot tell when the strike will end, so we must start to have the least of less."

It was strange to go out in the street and find the men out there, on chairs, or sitting on window sills, or just standing in the gutters. There was a feeling of fright in it, too, for the street was always empty at other times. The wind was full of the low rising and falling of their voices, but nobody talking loudly, or laughing.

I looked back at the top of the mountain and saw the Hill; even in the farms, men and women were out in their gardens, standing at the walls, looking down into the Valley, as though they were expecting to see tongues of fire.

On Strike

That was July, and a hot month, when the grass went brown and the river dried, and the rocks so hot that they would almost burn your feet as you crossed them. Meeting after meeting the men held on the mountainside, and it was strange to see them every day going browner and browner with the sun, and it was then I saw how pale they had always been, even my father and brothers, with lack of it.

Nothing was said, not a word at home about the strike. It was never allowed to come past the door. Food got less. Tea we had without sugar and milk, and then no sugar, and after, no tea. Meat came less and less. Bread was spare, thick in the slice, and presently, butter only on Sunday.

August, September.

Still the men held meetings, not only in our Valley, but in the others. My brothers and my father were always tramping over the mountain to meetings. The men wanted more wages. The owners said they were getting less for the coal so wages had to drop. No one would give an inch.

Women were going then, and children were not so ready to play. Men were fighting among themselves for nothing, for they were idle, penniless, and eating little, and their tempers were just under their skins.

At school, nothing was happening, only Mr. Jonas was teaching and I was sitting. Some of the boys and girls stopped coming to school because their shoes were gone and their parents afraid to buy more in case the money was wanted for food. Some stopped coming because they were only eating once a day.

I only noticed it in Shani one morning when she stood next to Edith Moss, of Moss the Butcher's near the school. Edith was a lump of a girl with big red cheeks and black hair, straight, who said she drank blood hot from the carcass when her father slaughtered. Next to her, Shani was a dove to a raven, so small, and thin, and so white in the face.

Her father was in the collieries, too, in the manager's office, but out as well, of course. One dinner time she stayed in class to sew. I went out with my can to the playground, but it was raining, so I went to sit in the cloakroom, and I saw Shani looking through the classroom window. I tapped on the glass and smiled at her, but instead of smiling back, she looked as though she wanted to cry, and jumped down from my sight.

Then she came outside and pretended she was going to have a drink, but when she saw me looking she came closer.

"Just going to have a drink, I was," she said.

"Good," I said, and ready to eat my bread and cheese. "Will I get it for you?"

"No, no," she said, but making no move.

It is a fact that if you are hungry and you see somebody eating something you would like to have your teeth in, too, spit will flood to your mouth and you will swallow to make a noise. That noise Shani made as I watched her. Then I saw her eyes, and they were on my can.

"Why not home for dinner to-day?" I asked her.

"Oh," she said, and going to do something to her hair, "too much trouble to go all that way for old dinner."

"Will you have a bit of this?" I asked her.

"And take from you?" she said. "No, indeed. You have got longer to come."

"No matter," I said. "There is plenty, look. Have to eat, girl."

I held out bread and cheese, crusty bread, and yellow farm cheese, with cress and lettuce from the garden.

She looked at it, and swallowed again, with her hands behind her.

"Come on, girl," I said. "There is slow you are."

So she took them, and bit and bit and bit, until her little mouth was sure to burst, and her eyes had tears, and as she chewed she sobbed. Your throat goes dry and you cannot have your food in peace when somebody is hungry and shows it. So Shani had dinner for two of us that day, and in the afternoon she fell to

On Strike

the floor during history, and Mr. Jonas carried her outside, and she went home with another girl.

I told my mother when I got home but she said nothing, only clicked her tongue and looked tired. There were many in the village just the same. Next morning I went to school with my can packed tight, and more in a brown paper parcel hanging on my coat button. Not a word from my mother, only a little smile.

So Shani and me sat together to have dinner every day in my mother's smile. I never saw her mother or father, and never went home with her, and though I asked her, she never came over in our Valley because they had sold their trap and it was too far for her. And after we had been having dinner for a couple of weeks she stopped coming. It was said that her father had gone to find work in the north, at Middlesbrough.

I will always remember her in something of blue and three lines of yellow braid, and a little bow on top of her hair and her face so pale and looking from the side like the face of the queens on coins of ancient Greece.

July, August, September.

October.

All down the Hill, and along the walls in the village street, a long black mark could be seen where men's shoulders had leaned to rub grease. Up and down in a dim, wavy line, but always at the height of the shoulder. Some of the women had taken a bucket of hot water to scrub it off, but soon it was back, and the line was unbroken again.

The public houses closed except for two days a week, when the farmers came through to sell at the market. The three shops gave credit for a bit, and then closed up. Friendly Societies paid out all they had, then those few shillings stopped. The men in the Union with Ianto and Davy had benefit for weeks and weeks, but then that stopped, too.

Women like my mother, who had sons earning, and had saved and kept a good house, were putting money and food together each week for the babies of women who had just married, or for women with only a husband earning and many children. But as the weeks and months passed by, more and more women had to stop giving, and needed help themselves.

Mr. Gruffydd went time and time again to the Town and came back with food, money, and clothes for the people down in the hovels. But the people of the Hill would never have any of it. He was thinner, and his clothes were loose on him, and my mother said he would have starved if people had not asked him to eat with them, for he was paid by the Chapel, and the money was all gone in food for the hungry ones.

From all the men in idleness he got together a choir, and made Ivor second conductor to him. All over the valleys they walked, singing for funds, and presently men from other valleys were coming over the mountain in dozens and scores to join them.

One night I heard a choir of a thousand voices singing in the darkness, and I thought I heard the voice of God.

Then the children began to die.

The processions over the mountain were long at first, and sometimes two or three a day. Then they grew shorter, and the hymns fewer, for the people had no strength.

July, August, September, October.

November.

The cold was on us, and snow was thick in the very first week. People were burning wood, and some of the men went down to the colliery to get coal and were stopped by the watchmen, but they took no notice and loaded up. Next morning, police came by brake, and went to live in the lamp house. Two men who were caught were taken over the mountain and had six months in jail. So those who had no money for coal went up on the mountain for wood, and since all the people in other valleys were looking for wood, there was soon no wood to be had, except standing trees. But they were green and not to be lit by anything but a fire.

More and more children were dying, and now women were

dying, and men. No more were coffins built by Clydach. A sheet had to do, and did.

Two, three, and four families went into one house to eat and have warmth together. Windows were boarded to keep out cold. Even Mr. Gruffydd had trouble to keep the men from a riot, and going down to the Colliery and killing the police.

One morning in the third week, Ellis the Post stopped Mari outside our house and gave my father a letter.

"Come you in, Ellis," said my mother. "Breakfast is ready."

"No, indeed, Mrs. Morgan, my little one," Ellis said, and pale about the nose with cold. "I will have it when I get home, see."

"You shall have breakfast now," said my mother, "or never come inside this house again."

"Yes, Mrs. Morgan," said Ellis, and off with his cap, and sitting next to me. "But no tea, and no bacon, if you will excuse me."

"Tea you shall have, and bacon, and potatoes," said my mother, and ready to fly at him. "And please to have what you are given."

"Yes, Mrs. Morgan," said Ellis, and hang-dog, with his eyes looking at her upwards and sideways.

"If there shall come a time when you leave this house without a proper something to eat," said my mother, "look for me on the floor."

"Beth," my father said, and passing the letter to Ianto, "the boys and me will go into Town to-day."

My mother looked at him straight, with her fork in the potatoes and one foot on the fender.

"Well?" she said.

"The owners," my father said, with more colour in his face than I had seen for weeks.

"We shall have to give in," Davy said, sipping hot water.

"They have promised a minimum wage," my father said. "That is a straw, at all events."

"And we are the drowners," said Ianto, looking at the letter still.

My father raised his fists and hit the table to make the crockery jump.

"No matter," he shouted, with flames in his eyes. "Let us drown, then. But I will have food in those children's little bellies before the night is out."

"Good, Gwilym," my mother said. "Go you. Angharad, go to Mr. Gruffydd and ask him to breakfast."

"O, Mama," Angharad said, and jumped from the stook, and flew from the house.

We had a lovely breakfast that morning, indeed.

Bacon sliced thick, and potatoes, and toast with butter, and strawberry jelly, and tea, with sugar and milk, too. There is

On Strike

good it is to have good food with taste after a long time without.

"Where have you been hiding all this, Beth my little one?" my father said, eating the breakfast of two and a pleasure to watch.

"You mind your affairs," my mother said, and blushing red and beautiful indeed, "and I will please attend to mine. Have I been living all this time and nothing to show?"

"Beth, my sweet love," my father said, "you were made and the mould was hit with a hammer."

"Go from here," said Mama, tears and laugh together, "before I will give you a good hit with one, too."

The people were crowding round our house, for they knew that Ellis must have brought a letter, and now they began to shout, and their shouting roused everyone, and presently people were running from their houses to fill the street.

"Shall we have a ride to the station, Ellis?" my father said.

"If I will ride on the back of old Mari, you shall, Mr. Morgan," Ellis said, and meant.

My mother went to the box and counted out the money for each, and kissed them, and out they went. As soon as the people saw them in their best, they knew they were off on business, and because of my father's face, they knew they would have good from it.

So they cheered with tears, and my father was crying when Ellis whipped up Mari, and went off down the Hill, with the people running after, all the way down and out of the village.

No school for me that day, but plenty to do, for I made copies of the letter with Ivor and we took them over the mountain for the checkweighmen of other collieries to read out to their men, and asked them over to meet my father coming back next night.

The news the strike was ended came through the telegraph about five o'clock that night, only a few words in pencil, but indeed, people could not have gone crazier if the writing had appeared again upon the wall.

Up and down the street they ran, shouting and dancing with

everybody else, and women looking out of windows and waving, and children playing ring of roses.

When it was dark, about seven o'clock, a big waggon came round the mountain road, and stopped in the middle of the street. People had gone in their houses, for it was cold and starting to snow.

When the driver started to shout they came out one by one, but when he handed out hampers full of groceries, they came running to kill themselves, and he had to ask a couple of the men to make everybody take their turn or he would have been crushed underfoot.

Some said it was a London paper that had asked readers for gifts, and some said it was Old Evans, trying to make peace with the men, and others said it was Mr. Gruffydd again. But Mr. Gruffydd knew nothing about it, and we only found out who it was when my father and the boys came back next night.

Now that was a procession for you.

They came back by train to the end of the line, and then with Thomas the Carrier from there to home. To-night, the men took big torches with them through the snow right to the top of the mountain, where it was so cold that the brass was frozen and the band had to sing instead, and met Thomas as the horses came over the brow. Then they took out the horses and put in pairs of pit ponies from the colliery my father worked in, with all the hauliers dressed up in colours, and lit the torches, and got in lines back and front, and started off for home.

There is pretty to see all those little lights wagging down the mountain and to hear their voice coming nearer and nearer. Hundreds on hundreds were in the procession, more hundreds running to meet them, and hundreds more, with all the women, waiting in the village. So big was the crowd and so much the noise that my poor father could say nothing much himself, for he was tired, but never happier in his life.

"Back to work, boys," he shouted, and the people were cheering to burst the ears. "We will have less, but we have fixed a limit to the less. It has been signed, and it will be made law. Back to work."

"When?" the men were shouting. "When, when?"

"To-morrow," my father shouted back.

"To-morrow," shouted the crowd, and the band struck up for everybody to link arms down the street. The Three Bells opened up to hand out the last of the beer, and then more dancing, until Davy Pryse, who played the big brass horn, had a red ring big as half a crown round his mouth and looking very sore with him, and ice from his breath round the brim of his hat and on his mittens and muffler.

Only the cold, and the torches going out and no more to be had, and nothing much to eat and drink sent the people home.

"For all that has happened, Heavenly Father," my father said when he came in, and went to his knees with my mother beside him, "for the mercies, and the guidance to-day, I do give thanks from my heart. Yesterday I gave thanks, and to-day, thanks again, and to-morrow I will give thanks again, from the heart. In the Name of Jesus the Son."

"Amen," said we all.

OLD GREY SQUIRREL

ALFRED NOYES

A great while ago, there was a school-boy.
    He lived in a cottage by the sea.
And the very first thing he could remember
    Was the rigging of the schooners by the quay.

He could watch them, when he woke, from his window,
    With the tall cranes hoisting out the freight.
And he used to think of shipping as a sea-cook,
    And sailing to the Golden Gate.

For he used to buy the yellow penny-dreadfuls,
   And read them where he fished for conger-eels,
And listened to the lapping of the water,
   The green and oily water round the keels.

There were trawlers with their shark-mouthed flat-fish,
   And red nets hanging out to dry,
And the skate the skipper kept because he liked 'em,
   And landsmen never knew the fish to fry.

There were brigantines with timber out of Norroway,
   Oozing with the syrups of the pine.
There were rusty dusty schooners out of Sunderland,
   And ships of the Blue Cross line.

And to tumble down a hatch into the cabin
   Was better than the best of broken rules;
For the smell of 'em was like a Christmas dinner,
   And the feel of 'em was like a box of tools.

And, before he went to sleep in the evening,
   The very last thing that he could see
Was the sailor men a-dancing in the moonlight
   By the capstan that stood upon the quay.

He is perched upon a high stool in London.
   The Golden Gate is very far away.
They caught him, and they caged him like a squirrel.
   He is totting up accounts, and going grey.

He will never, never, never sail to 'Frisco.
   But the very last thing that he will see
Will be sailor-men a-dancing in the sunrise
   By the capstan that stands upon the quay. . . .

To the tune of an old concertina,
By the capstan that stands upon the quay.

THE ICE-CART

W. W. GIBSON

Perched on my city office-stool
I watched with envy, while a cool
And lucky carter handled ice. . . .
And I was wandering in a trice,
Far from the grey and grimy heat
Of that intolerable street,
O'er sapphire berg and emerald floe,
Beneath the still, cold ruby glow
Of everlasting Polar night,
Bewildered by the queer half-light,
Until I stumbled, unawares,
Upon a creek where big white bears
Plunged headlong down with flourished heels,
And floundered after shining seals
Through shivering seas of blinding blue.
And as I watched them, ere I knew,
I'd stripped, and I was swimming, too,
Among the seal-pack, young and hale,
And thrusting on with threshing tail,
With twist and twirl and sudden leap
Through cracking ice and salty deep —
Diving and doubling with my kind,
Until, at last, we left behind
Those big, white, blundering bulks of death,
And lay, at length, with panting breath
Upon a far untravelled floe,
Beneath a gentle drift of snow —
Snow drifting gently, fine and white,
Out of the endless Polar night,

Falling and falling evermore
Upon that far untravelled shore,
Till I was buried fathoms deep
Beneath that cold white drifting sleep —
Sleep drifting deep,
Deep drifting sleep. . . .

The carter cracked a sudden whip:
I clutched my stool with startled grip,
Awakening to the grimy heat
Of that intolerable street.

BALSA FOR KON-TIKI

THOR HEYERDAHL

Adapted from The Kon-Tiki Expedition

I

The white-haired scientist sat in his dark office on an upper floor of a big museum in New York City. He pushed my unopened manuscript to one side, and looked at me searchingly.

"You're absolutely wrong," he said. "Do you know why? The answer's simple enough. They couldn't get there. They had no boats!"

"They had rafts," I objected hesitatingly. "You know, balsa-wood rafts."

The old man smiled and said quietly: "Well, you try a trip from Peru to the Pacific Islands on a balsa-wood raft!"

That's what made up my mind for me. For the next few days I was busy indeed, squeezing money and supplies from backers in the United States, in England, and from my native Norway for a scheme that everyone called hare-brained.

And that is how I came to send this cable to Erik, Knut, and Torstein — stout friends of mine who had stood side by side with me in the perilous days of the Resistance movement in Norway:

> "AM GOING TO CROSS THE PACIFIC ON A WOODEN RAFT TO SUPPORT A THEORY THAT THE SOUTH SEA ISLANDS WERE PEOPLED FROM PERU. WILL YOU COME? I GUARANTEE NOTHING BUT A FREE TRIP TO PERU AND THE SOUTH SEA ISLANDS AND BACK. REPLY AT ONCE."

Next day came the reply: "COMING, TORSTEIN."

For years I had been sure that the Polynesians came of the same stock as the pre-historic civilizations in Peru. They looked the same, they used the same stone-age implements, their carvings were the same, and they both used the same odd system of writing by tying knots in twisted cord. I wrote a book about it. You have heard how that book was received by distinguished scientists.

Now I was going to prove my theory the hard way — to build a raft of the same wonderful light wood that when dry is lighter than cork, the balsa-wood that grows in Peru and in Ecuador. I was going to cross the Pacific to the islands, using nothing but wind and current, just as I was sure these prehistoric sea-farers had crossed.

The funds raised, the supplies assured, and my friends ready to serve as crew, I bought two plane tickets for South America. The other ticket was for Herman, another friend who had joined me in New York. In Peru we would build our raft, which we had already christened the *Kon-Tiki*, after the old god of the South Sea Islanders.

As the aircraft crossed the equator it began a slanting descent through the milk-white clouds which till then had lain beneath us like a blinding waste of snow in the burning sun. The fleecy vapour clung to the windows till it dissolved and remained hanging over us like clouds, and there appeared the bright green roof of a rolling, billowy jungle. We flew in over the South American republic of Ecuador and landed at the tropical port of Guayaquil.

With yesterday's jackets, waistcoats, and overcoats over our arms, we crawled out into the atmosphere of a hothouse to meet chattering Southerners in tropical kit, and felt our shirts sticking to our backs like wet paper. We were embraced by customs and immigration officials and almost carried shoulder-high to a cab, which took us to the best hotel in the town. Here we quickly found our way to our respective baths and lay down flat under the cold water tap.

We had reached the country where the balsa tree grows, and were to buy timber to build the raft.

The first day we spent in learning the monetary system and enough Spanish to find our way back to the hotel.

On the second day we ventured away from our baths in steadily widening circles, and when Herman had satisfied his childhood's longing to touch a proper palm tree, and when I was a walking bowl of fruit salad, we decided to go and negotiate for balsa.

Unfortunately this was easier said than done. We could certainly buy balsa in quantities, but not in the form of whole logs, as we wanted it. The days when balsa trees were accessible down on the coast were past. The last war had put an end to them; they had been felled in thousands and shipped to the aircraft factories, because the wood was so gaseous and light. We were told that the only place where large balsa trees grew was in the jungle in the interior of the country.

"Then we must go inland and fell them ourselves," we said.

"Impossible," said the authorities. "The rains have just begun, and all the roads into the jungle are impassable because of flood water and deep mud. If you want balsa wood, you must come back to Ecuador in six months; the rains will be over then and the roads up country will have dried."

II

In our extremity we called on Don Gustavo, the balsa king of Ecuador, and Herman unrolled his sketch of the raft with

THE FERRY, QUEBEC — *James W. Morrice*

Reproduced by permission of the National Gallery, Ottawa.

JAMES WILLIAM MORRICE, R.C.A.
(1865 - 1924)

James William Morrice, one of the most significant painters which Canada has produced, was born in Montreal, in 1865. Son of a wealthy textile merchant, he never had to conform to other people's standards so as to support himself, but was able to follow his own genius, which was considerable. He was devoted to the Quebec countryside, and though he lived abroad a good part of his life, he returned again and again to draw the winter landscape of his native province.

Influenced by the French 'impressionists' who painted what they saw, as they saw it, thus creating an "impression", Morrice, with his friend Maurice Cullen, challenged the accepted practice of painting snow white, but began painting it blue, and mauve, and rose. Morrice was a sensitive painter, and capable of subtle colouring. It was he who noticed and recorded the rosy tint in the winter skies of Canadian landscapes.

Morrice's influence upon Canadian art, begun with Cullen, Gagnon, and Robinson, continues to grow as his pictures become more widely known.

The Ferry, Quebec hangs in the National Gallery, Ottawa.

the lengths of timber we required. The skinny little balsa king seized the telephone and set his agents to work searching. They found planks and light boards and separate short blocks in every single saw-mill, but they could not find one single serviceable log. There were two big logs, as dry as tinder, at Don Gustavo's own dump, but they would not take us far. It was clear that the search was useless.

"A brother of mine has a big balsa plantation," said Don Gustavo. "His name is Don Federico and he lives at Quivedo, a little jungle town right up country. He can get you all you want as soon as we can get hold of him after the rains. It's no use now because of the jungle rain up country."

If Don Gustavo said a thing was of no use, all the balsa experts in Ecuador would say it was of no use. So here we were in Guayaquil with no timber for the raft, and with no possibility of going in and felling the trees ourselves until several months later, when it would be too late anyhow.

"Time's short," said Herman.

"And balsa we must have," said I. "The raft must be an exact copy, or we shall have no guarantee of coming through alive."

A little school map we found in the hotel, with green jungle, brown mountains, and inhabited places ringed round in red, told us that the jungle stretched unbroken from the Pacific right to the foot of the towering Andes. I had an idea. It was clearly impracticable now to get from the coastal area through the jungle to the balsa trees at Quivedo, but suppose we could get to the trees from the inland side, by coming straight down into the interior of the jungle from the bare snow mountains of the Andes range? Here was a possibility, the only one we saw.

Out on the airfield was a little cargo plane which was willing to take us up to Quito, high up on the Andes plateau, 9,000 feet above sea level. Jammed in between packing cases and furniture, we caught occasional glimpses of green jungle and shining rivers before we disappeared into the clouds. When we came out again the lowlands were hidden under an endless sea of rolling vapour, but ahead of us dry mountain-sides and bare cliffs rose from the sea of mist right up to a brilliant blue sky.

The aircraft climbed straight up the mountain-side as in an invisible escalator, and although the equator itself was in sight, we began to have shining snowfields alongside us. Then we glided between the mountains and over a rich alpine plateau clad in spring green, on which we landed close to the world's most peculiar capital.

Most of Quito's 150,000 inhabitants are pure or half-breed mountain Indians, for it was their forefathers' own capital long before Columbus and our own race knew America. The city receives its stamp from ancient monasteries containing art treasures of immeasurable value and other magnificent buildings dating from Spanish times, towering over the roofs of low Indian houses built of bricks of sun-dried clay. A labyrinth of alleys winds between the clay walls, and these alleys we found swarming with mountain Indians in red-speckled cloaks and big home-made hats. Some were going to market with pack donkeys, while others sat hunched up along the adobe walls dozing in the hot sun. A few motor-cars containing aristocrats of Spanish origin in tropical kit succeeded, going at half-speed and hooting ceaselessly, in finding a path along the one-way alleys among children and donkeys and bare-legged Indians. The air up here on the high plateau was of such brilliant crystalline clearness that the mountains round us seemed to come into the streets.

Our friend from the cargo plane, Jorge, tried to get us transport over the mountains and down into the jungle to Quivedo. We met in the evening in an old Spanish cafe, and Jorge was full of bad news; we must just put the idea of going to Quivedo out of our heads. Neither men nor vehicle were to be obtained to take us over the mountains, and certainly not down into the jungle where the rains had begun, and where there was danger of attack if one stuck fast in the mud. Only last year a party of ten American oil engineers had been found killed by poisoned arrows in the eastern part of Ecuador, where there were still great numbers of forest Indians who went about in the jungle stark naked and hunted for human heads.

Next day we went up to the American Embassy and were able to see the Military Attaché himself. He was a trim, buoyant young man in khaki and riding-boots, and asked laughingly why we had strayed to the top of the Andes when the local papers said we were to go to sea on a wooden raft.

We explained that the wood was still standing upright in the Quivedo jungle. We were up here on the roof of the continent and could not get at it. We asked the Military Attaché either (a) to lend us a plane and two parachutes or (b) a jeep with a driver who knew the country.

The Military Attaché at first sat speechless at our assurance; then he shook his head despairingly and said with a smile: all right, as we gave him no third choice, he preferred the second!

III

At a quarter past five the next morning a jeep rolled up to the hotel entrance, and an Ecuadorian captain of engineers jumped out and reported himself at our service. His orders were to drive us to Quivedo, mud or no mud. The jeep was packed full of petrol cans, for there were no petrol pumps or wheel-tracks along the route we were to take. Our new friend, Captain Agurto Alexis Alvarez, was armed to the teeth with knives and fire-arms on account of the reports of bandidos. We had come to the country peacefully in jackets and ties to buy timber for ready money down on the coast, and the whole of our equipment on board the jeep consisted of a bag of tinned food, except that we had hurriedly acquired a second-hand camera and a pair of tear-proof khaki breeches for each of us. Further, the Consul-General had pressed upon us his big revolver with an ample supply of ammunition to exterminate everything that crossed our path. The jeep whizzed away through the empty alleys where the moon shone ghostly pale on whitewashed adobe walls, till we came out into the country, and raced at a giddy speed along a good sand road southward through the mountain region.

It was good going all along the range as far as the mountain village of Latakunga, where windowless Indian houses clustered blindly round a whitewashed country church with palms in a square. Here we turned off along a mule track which undulated and twisted westward over hill and valley into the Andes. We came into a world we had never dreamt of. It was the mountain Indians' own world — east of the sun and west of the moon — outside time and beyond space. On the whole drive we saw not a carriage or a wheel. The traffic consisted of bare-legged goat-herds in gaily-coloured ponchos driving forward disorderly herds of stiff-legged dignified llamas, and now and then whole families of Indians came along the road. The husband usually rode ahead on a mule, while his little wife trotted behind with her entire collection of hats on her head and the youngest child in a bag on her back. All the time she ran she spun wool with her fingers. Donkeys and mules jogged behind at leisure, loaded with boughs and rushes and pottery.

The farther we went, the fewer the Indians who spoke Spanish, and soon Agurto's language was as useless as our own. A cluster of huts lay here and there up in the mountains; fewer and fewer were built of clay, while more and more were made of twigs and dry grass. Both the huts and the sun-browned wrinkle-faced people seemed to have grown up out of the earth itself, from the baking effect of the mountain sun on the Andes' rock walls. They belonged to cliff and upland pasture as naturally as the mountain grass itself. Poor in possessions and small in stature, the mountain Indians had the wiry hardiness of wild animals and the child-like alertness of a primitive people, and the less they could talk the more they could laugh. Radiant faces with snow-white teeth shone upon us from all we saw. There was nothing to say that the white man had lost or earned a shilling in these regions. There were no advertisement posters or road-signs here, and if a tin box or a scrap of paper was flung down by the roadside, it would be picked up at once as a useful household article.

We went on up over sun-smitten slopes without a bush or tree and down into valleys of desert sand and cactus, till we climbed right up and reached the topmost crest, with snowfields round the peak and a wind so bitingly cold that we had to slacken speed in order not to freeze to bits as we sat in our shirts longing for jungle heat. For long stretches we had to drive across country between the mountains, over stone slides and grassy ridges, searching for the next bit of road. But when we reached the west wall, where the Andes range falls precipitously to the lowlands, the mule track was cut along shelves in the loose rock, and sheer cliffs and gorges were all about us. We put all our trust in friend Agurto as he sat crouched over the steering-wheel and always swung out when we came to a precipice. Suddenly a violent gust of wind met us; we had reached the outermost crest of the Andes chain, where the mountain fell away sharply in a series of precipices to the jungle far down in a bottomless abyss 12,000 feet beneath us. But we were cheated of the dizzy view over the sea of jungle, for as soon as we reached the edge thick cloudbanks rolled about us like steam from a witch's cauldron. But now our road ran down unhindered into the depths — always down, in steep loops along gorges and bluffs and ridges, while the air grew damper and warmer and ever fuller of the heavy deadening hothouse air which rose from the jungle world below.

Then the rain began. First gently, then it began to pour and beat upon the jeep like drumsticks, and soon the chocolate-coloured water was flowing down the rocks on every side of us. We almost flowed down too, away from the dry mountain plateaus behind us and into another world, where stick and stone and clay slope were soft and lush with moss and turf. Leaves shot up; soon they became giant leaves hanging like green umbrellas and dripping over the hillside. Then came the first feeble advanced posts of the jungle trees, with heavy fringes and beards of moss, and climbing plants, hanging from them. There was a gurgling and splashing everywhere. As the slopes grew gentler, the jungle rolled up swiftly like an army of green giant growths that swallowed up the little jeep as it splashed along the waterlogged clay road. We were in the jungle. The air was moist and warm and heavy with the smell of vegetation.

Darkness had fallen when we reached a cluster of palm-roofed huts on a ridge. Dripping with warm water we left the jeep for a night under a dry roof. The horde of fleas that attacked us in the hut were drowned in next day's rain. With the jeep full of bananas and other southern fruit we went on downhill through the jungle, down and down, though we thought we had reached bottom long ago. The mud grew worse, but it did not stop us, and the robbers kept at an unknown distance.

IV

Not till the road was barred by a broad river of muddy water rolling down through the jungle did the jeep give up. We stood stuck fast, unable to move either up or down along the river bank. In an open clearing stood a hut where a few half-breed Indians were stretching out a jaguar-skin on a sunny wall, while dogs and fowls were splashing about and enjoying themselves on top of some cocoa beans spread out to dry in the sun. When the jeep came bumping along, the place came to life, and people who spoke Spanish declared that this was the river Palenque, and that Quivedo was just on the other side. There was no bridge there, and the river was swift and deep, but they were willing to float us and the jeep over by raft. This queer contraption lay down by the bank. Curved logs as thick as arms and legs were fastened together with vegetable fibres and bamboos to form a flimsy raft, twice the length and breadth of the jeep. With a plank under each wheel and our hearts in our mouths we drove the jeep out on to the logs, and if most of them were submerged under the muddy water, they did bear the jeep and us and four half-naked, chocolate-coloured men who pushed us off with long poles.

Balsa for Kon-Tiki   165

"Balsa?" Herman and I asked in the same breath.

"Balsa," one of the fellows nodded, with a disrespectful kick at the logs.

The current seized us and we whirled down the river, while the men pushed in their poles at the right places and kept the raft on an even diagonal course across the current and into quieter water on the other side. This was our first meeting with the balsa tree and our first trip on a balsa raft. We brought the raft safely to land at the farther bank and motored triumphantly into Quivedo. Two rows of tarred wooden houses with motionless vultures on the palm roofs formed a kind of street, and this was the whole place. The inhabitants dropped whatever they might be carrying, and black and brown, young and old appeared to be swarming out of both doors and windows. They rushed to meet the jeep, a menacing, chattering tide of humanity. They scrambled on to it and under it and around it. We kept a tight hold on our worldly possessions while Agurto attempted desperate manoeuvres at the steering-wheel. Then the jeep had a puncture and went down on one knee. We had arrived at Quivedo and had to endure the embrace of welcome.

Don Federico's plantation lay a bit farther down the river. When the jeep came bumping into the yard along a path between the mango trees with Agurto, Herman and me, the lean old jungle-dweller came to meet us at a trot with his nephew Angelo, a small boy who lived with him out in the wilds. We gave messages from Don Gustavo, and soon the jeep was standing alone in the yard while a fresh tropical shower streamed down over the jungle. There was a festive meal in Don Federico's bungalow; sucking pigs and chickens crackled over an open fire, while we sat round a dish loaded with southern fruit and explained what we had come for. The jungle rain pouring down on the ground outside sent a warm sweet gust of scented blossoms and clay in through the window-netting.

Don Federico had become as brisk as a boy. Why, yes, he had known balsa rafts since he was a child. Fifty years ago, when he lived down by the sea, the Indians from Peru still used to come sailing up along the coast on big balsa rafts to sell fish in Guayaquil. They could bring a couple of tons of dried fish in a bamboo cabin in the middle of the raft, or they might have wives and children and dogs and fowls on board. Such big balsa trees as they had used for their rafts it would be hard to find now in the rains, for flood water and mud had already made it impossible to get to the balsa plantation up in the forest, even on horseback. Anyway Don Federico would

Balsa for Kon-Tiki

do his best; there might still be some single trees growing wild in the forest nearer the bungalow, and we did not need many.

Late in the evening the rain stopped for a time, and we went for a turn under the mango trees round the bungalow. Here Don Federico had every kind of wild orchid in the world hanging down from the branches, with half-cocoanuts as flowerpots. Unlike cultivated orchids, these rare plants gave out a wonderful scent, and Herman was bending down to stick his nose into one of them, when something like a long thin glittering eel emerged from the leaves above him. A lightning blow from Angelo's whip, and a wriggling snake fell to the ground. A second later it was held fast to the earth with a forked stick over its neck, and then its head was crushed.

"Mortal," said Angelo, and exposed two curved poison-fangs to show what he meant.

We thought we saw poisonous snakes lurking in the foliage everywhere, and slipped into the house with Angelo's trophy hanging lifeless across a stick. Herman sat down to skin the green monster, and Don Federico was telling fantastic stories about poisonous snakes and boa constrictors as thick as plates, when we suddenly noticed the shadows of two enormous scorpions on the wall, the size of lobsters. They rushed at one another and engaged in a life and death battle with their pincers, with their hinderparts turned up and the curved poisonous sting at the tail ready for the deathblow. It was a horrible sight, and not till we moved the oil lamp did we see that it had cast a supernaturally gigantic shadow of two quite ordinary scorpions of the size of one's finger, which were fighting on the edge of the bureau.

"Let them be," Don Federico laughed. "One'll kill the other, and we want the survivor in the house to keep the cockroaches away. Just keep your mosquito net tight round the bed and shake your clothes before you put them on, and you'll be all right. I've often been bitten by scorpions and I'm not dead yet."

I slept well, except that I woke up thinking of poisonous creatures every time a lizard or bat squeaked and scrabbled too noisily near my pillow.

V

Next morning we got up early to go and search for balsa trees.

"Better shake our clothes," said Agurto, and as he spoke a scorpion fell out of his shirt-sleeve and shot down into a crack in the floor.

Soon after sunrise Don Federico sent his men out on horseback in all directions to look for accessible balsa trees along the paths. Our own party consisted of Don Federico, Herman and myself, and we soon found our way to an open place where there was a gigantic old tree that Don Federico knew. It towered high above the trees round about, and the trunk was three feet thick. In Polynesian style we christened the tree before we touched it; we gave it the name *Ku*, after a Polynesian deity of American origin. Then we swung the axe and drove it into the balsa trunk till the forest echoed our blows. But cutting a sappy balsa was like cutting cork with a blunt axe; it simply rebounded, and I had not chopped many strokes before Herman had to relieve me. The axe changed hands time after time, while the splinters flew and our sweat trickled in the heat of the jungle.

Late in the day Ku was standing like a cock on one leg, quivering under our blows; soon he tottered and crashed down heavily over the surrounding forest, big branches and small trees being pulled down by the giant's fall. We had torn the branches from the trunk and were beginning to rip off the bark in zigzags in the Indian style when Herman suddenly dropped the axe and leapt into the air as if doing a Polynesian war dance, with his hand pressed to his leg. Out of his trouser leg fell a shining ant as big as a scorpion and with a long sting at its tail. It must have had a skull like a lobster's claw, for it was almost impossible to stamp it under one's heel on the ground.

"A kongo," Don Federico explained with regret. "The little brute's worse than a scorpion, but it isn't dangerous to a healthy man."

Herman was tender and sore for several days, but this did not prevent his galloping with us on horseback along the jungle paths, looking for more giant balsas in the forest. From time to time we heard creaking and crashing and a heavy thud somewhere in the virgin forest. Don Federico nodded with a satisfied air. It meant that his half-bred Indians had felled a new giant balsa for the raft. In a week Ku had been followed by Kane, Kama, Ilo, Mauri, Ra, Rangi, Papa, Taranga, Kura, Kukara and Hiti, twelve mighty balsas, all christened in honour of Polynesian legendary figures whose names had once been borne with Tiki over the sea from Peru. The logs, glistening with sap, were dragged down through the jungle first by horses and for the last bit by Don Federico's tractor, which brought them to the river bank in front of the bungalow.

The logs, full of sap, were far from being as light as corks. They certainly weighed a ton apiece, and we waited with great anxiety to see how they floated in the water. We rolled them out to the edge of the bank one by one; there we made fast a rope of tough climbing plants to the end of the log, that they might not vanish down stream when we let them enter the water. Then we rolled them in turn down the bank and into the river. There was a mighty splash. They swung round and floated, about as much above as below the surface of the water, and if we walked out along them they remained steady. We bound the timbers together with tough lianas that hung down from the tops of the jungle trees, so as to make two temporary rafts, one towing the other. Then we loaded the rafts with all the bamboos and lianas we should need later, and Herman and I went on board with two men of a mysterious mixed race, with whom we had no common language.

VI

When we cut our moorings we were caught by the whirling masses of water and went off downstream at a good pace. The last glimpse we had in the drizzle, as we rounded the first headland, was of our excellent friends standing on the end of the point in front of the bungalow, waving. Then we crept under a little shelter of green banana leaves and left steering problems to the two brown experts who had stationed themselves one in the bows and one astern, each holding a huge oar. They kept the raft in the swiftest current with nonchalant ease, and we danced downstream on a winding course between sunken trees and sandbanks.

The jungle stood like a solid wall along the banks on both sides, and parrots and other bright-coloured birds fluttered out of the dense foliage as we passed. Once or twice an alligator hurled itself into the river and became invisible in the muddy water. But we soon caught sight of a much more remarkable monster. This was an iguana, or giant lizard, as big as a crocodile, but with a large throat and fringed back. It lay dozing on the clay bank as if it had overslept from prehistoric times, and did not move as we glided past. The oarsmen made signs

Balsa for Kon-Tiki

to us not to shoot. Soon afterwards we saw a smaller specimen about three feet long. It was running away along a thick branch which hung out over the raft. It only ran till it was in safety, and then it sat shining in blue and green and stared at us with cold snake's eyes as we passed. Later we passed a fern-clad hillock, and on the top of it lay the biggest iguana of all. It was like the silhouette of a fringed Chinese dragon carved in stone as it stood out motionless against the sky with chest and head raised. It did not so much as turn its head as we curved round it under the hillock and vanished into the jungle.

Farther down we smelt smoke, and passed several huts with straw roofs which lay in clearings along the bank. We on the raft got close attention from sinister-looking individuals on land, an unpleasant mixture of Indian, Negro and Spaniard. Their boats, great dug-out canoes, lay drawn up on to the bank.

At meal-times we relieved our friends at the steering oars while they fried fish and bread-fruit over a little fire regulated with wet clay. Roast chicken, eggs, and southern fruits were also part of the menu on board, while the logs transported themselves and us at a fine speed down through the jungle towards the sea. What did it matter now if the water swept and splashed round us? The more it rained, the swifter the current ran.

When darkness fell over the river an ear-splitting orchestra struck up on the bank. Toads and frogs, crickets and mosquitoes croaked or chirped or hummed in a prolonged chorus of many voices. Now and again the shrill scream of a wild cat rang through the darkness, and soon another, and yet another, from birds scared into flight by the night prowlers of the jungle. Once or twice we saw the gleam of a fire in a native hut, and heard bawling voices and the barking of dogs as we slid past in the night. But for the most part we sat alone with the jungle orchestra under the stars, till drowsiness and rain drove us into the cabin of leaves, where we went to sleep with our pistols loose in their holsters.

The farther down stream we drifted, the thicker became the

huts and native plantations, and soon there were regular villages on the banks. The traffic here consisted of dug-out canoes punted along with long poles, and now and then we saw a little balsa raft loaded with heaps of green bananas.

Where the Palenque joined the Rio Guayas the water had risen so high that the paddle steamer was plying busily between Vinces and Guayaquil down on the coast. To save valuable time Herman and I each got a hammock on board the paddle steamer, and steamed off across the thickly populated flat country to the coast. Our brown friends were to follow, drifting down alone with the timber.

At Guayaquil Herman and I parted. He remained at the mouth of the Guayas to stop the balsa logs as they came drifting down. Thence he was to take them on, as cargo in a coasting steamer, to Peru, where he was to direct the building of the raft and make a faithful copy of the Indians' old-time vessels. I myself took the regular plane southward to Lima, the capital of Peru, to find a suitable place for building the raft.

The aircraft ascended to a great height along the shore of the Pacific, with the desert mountains of Peru on one side and a glittering ocean far below us on the other. It was here we were to put to sea on board the raft. The sea seemed endless when seen from an aircraft high up. Sky and sea melted into one another along an indefinable horizon far, far away to the westward, and I could not rid myself of the thought that even beyond that horizon many hundred similar sea plains curved round a fifth of the earth before there was any more land, in Polynesia. I tried to project my thoughts a few weeks ahead, when we should be drifting on a speck of a raft on that blue expanse below, but quickly dismissed the thought again, for it gave me the same unpleasant feeling inside as sitting in readiness to jump with a parachute.

We had our balsa for *Kon-Tiki* — the great adventure lay ahead.

THE CHRIST OF THE ANDES

EDWIN MARKHAM

After volcanoes hushed with snows,
Up where the white-winged condor goes,
Great Aconcagua, hushed and high,
Sends down the ancient peace of the sky.

So, poised in clean Andean air,
Where bleak with cliffs the grim peaks stare,

Christ, reaching out his sacred hands,
Sheds his brave peace upon the lands.

There once of old wild battles roared
And brother-blood was on the sword;
Now all the fields are rich with grain
And only roses redden the plain.

Torn were the peoples with feuds and hates —
Fear on the mountain-walls, death at the gates;
Then through the clamour of arms was heard
A whisper of the Master's word.

"Fling down your swords; be friends again:
Ye are not wolf-packs: ye are men.
Let brother-counsel be the Law;
Not serpent fang, not tiger claw."

Chile and Argentina heard;
The great hopes in their spirits stirred;
The red swords from their clenched fists fell,
And heaven shone out where once was hell!

They hurled their cannons into flame
And out of the forge the strong Christ came.
'Twas thus they molded in happy fire
The tall Christ of their heart's desire . . .

O Christ of Olivet, you hushed the wars
Under the far Andean stars:
Lift now your strong, nail-wounded hands
Over all peoples, over all lands —

Stretch out those comrade hands to be
A shelter over land and sea!

THE PARLIAMENT OF MAN

ALFRED, LORD TENNYSON

Men, my brothers, men the workers, ever reaping something new;
That which they have done but earnest of the things that they shall do.

For I dipt into the future, far as human eye could see,
Saw the Vision of the world, and all the wonder that would be;

Saw the heavens fill with commerce, argosies of magic sails,
Pilots of the purple twilight, dropping down with costly bales;

Heard the heavens fill with shouting, and there rain'd a ghastly dew
From the nations' airy navies grappling in the central blue;

Far along the world-wide whisper of the south-wind rushing warm,
With the standards of the peoples plunging thro' the thunderstorm;

Till the war-drum throbb'd no longer, and the battle-flags were furl'd
In the Parliament of man, the Federation of the world.

There the common sense of most shall hold a fretful realm in awe,
And the kindly earth shall slumber, lapt in universal law.

THESE THINGS SHALL BE

JOHN ADDINGTON SYMONDS

These things shall be: a loftier race
    Than e'er the world hath known, shall rise,
With flame of freedom in their souls
    And light of knowledge in their eyes.

They shall be gentle, brave, and strong,
    To spill no drop of blood, but dare
All that may plant man's lordship firm
    On earth, and fire, and sea, and air.

Nation with nation, land with land,
    Inarmed shall live as comrades free;
In every heart and brain shall throb
    The pulse of one fraternity.

Man shall love man, with heart as pure
    And fervent as the young-eyed throng
Who chant their heavenly psalms before
    God's face with undiscordant song.

New arts shall bloom of loftier mould,
    And mightier music thrill the skies,
And every life shall be a song,
    When all the earth is paradise.

There shall be no more sin, nor shame,
    Though pain and passion may not die;
For man shall be at one with God
    In bonds of firm necessity.

THEY BUILT A NATION

WHITE WATER

JOHN BUCHAN

A boy stood beside a boat on the grey shingle of a northern island. He looked about sixteen years of age; his freckled face was surmounted by a thatch of hair, bleached almost white by sun and wind; he was tall for his years and had a great breadth of shoulder and length of arm. He wore a fisherman's long knee-boots, and a ragged blue jersey. His companion was an elderly man who had lost an arm and, from his features, must have been a kinsman.

'That's the end of it,' said the boy, 'and thank God for that.'

'It's maybe not the end, Magnus,' said the other. 'Man, it's a queer thing that you should have taken this scunner to the sea when your folk for generations have been fishers and never out of boats. It's not as if you were feared o' other things, for you're a fair deevil to fight. I wonder what gave you this grue of salt water?'

'It's any kind of water,' said the boy sullenly. 'Ay, I'm feared, and that's the plain truth. That's why I'm for Canada, where I'll be a thousand miles from a shore.'

'But there's water other places than the ocean,' said the older man. 'I've heard tell of muckle lakes in Canada and rivers as wide as the Pentland Firth. There was Neil Webster, I mind, him that went from Kittle Bay, and they were saying he was drowned in some river called by a Hieland name. It seems they go about in wee cockles o' boats, and that there's some awfu' rough water.'

The boy shook his head. 'There may be water there, but there's plenty land, too, and I'm going to bide on the land. I'm off next week. I wish I was across that wearifu' Atlantic.'

The old man shook his head. 'Then Orkney will not be

White Water

seeing you again. Unless,' he added with a grin, 'God Almighty dries up the Atlantic as he dried up the Red Sea for Moses, and that's just not very likely.'

Magnus Sinclair, this son of generations of fishermen and sailors had the one fear which could paralyze an otherwise bold spirit. Death, except by drowning, he was ready to face with coolness, but the horror of deep water and wild water had an icy grip on his heart. It was partly a physical shrinking from a special kind of violence, just as another man fears a vicious horse. But the old folks said it was a spell. Magnus's grandfather had seen a mermaid on the skerries and she had laid a curse on him, which was now working on his descendant. The village thought no less of Magnus for this shrinking, for he was bold enough in other things; it was an affliction sent from God, like a deaf ear or a blind eye; and the neighbours heartily approved of his plan of going to Canada when the Hudson's Bay Company had their annual summer recruitment . . .

It was a scared and seasick boy who was decanted at York Factory on the muddy shore of Hudson's Bay. During the 'prentice stage, he learned how to judge the furs that the Indians brought in, and what price in 'made beaver' should be set on the fruits of their trapping and the store goods supplied to them. Presently Magnus went up country and was stationed at Norway House, and there he met his old enemy, water, and the struggle began . . .

He was a good servant to the Company, for he was quick to pick up the Indian tongues, and he could handle discreetly both the Indian trappers and the French voyageurs. With the latter, indeed, he was far the most popular of the 'Arcanis,' as they called the Orkney men. He had a good head for trading, and he was honest as the day, never making up fur packets on his own to spoil the Company's business. Indeed, there was nothing in his job which he did not do well, except travel by water. Now and then he had to make a trip with the fur brigades, up the Saskatchewan or down the Nelson, and once overland to the Churchill and up that river in the long traverse to the Athabasca. When he was only a passenger it was not so bad, for he could avert his eyes from the perils and give all his mind to keeping his nerves still. But sometimes he was in charge of a party, and then it was pure torment, and the boatmen looked anxiously at his distracted eyes, and were puzzled by the tremor in a voice commonly so firm and clear.

He struggled to overcome the fear, but failed lamentably, and lapsed into a mood of sullen resentment against Fate. There came a day when his weakness lost his employers a fine load of beaver skins and imperilled the lives of the crew. He was reprimanded and, miserably conscious of his fault, answered rudely, and was fiercely taken to task. In a fury, which was directed more against himself than against his masters, he flung up the post and joined the rival Nor'-Westers who had long been angling for him.

At first all went well there. His post was far up the Red Deer River in the mountains, and the journeys he had to make were all by land with only inconsiderable hill torrents to ford. But the time came when he was sent north to the Peace River and given charge of all the district between Lake Athabasca and the Rockies. Here most of his movements must be by water, up the Peace, the Smoky, and the Athabasca, or even as far as the great Mackenzie, not to mention an infinity of lakes.

And now things came to a crisis. He had begun to feel the pride of achievement and to enjoy the sense of power. Dreams of great enterprises, which should conquer for his masters the land beyond the mountains, began to hold his mind. But always in the forefront stood the grim barrier of his fear. Until he could vanquish that, there was no hope for him; any day he might shipwreck on it, and the Company would send him packing.

He brooded over the matter until something rose in his heart which was stronger than any fear; anger at himself, anger and bitter contempt. He resolved to conquer his weakness or flee

White Water

from the wilds and hide his self-loathing in some humble trade in a landward town.

First he learned to swim, and that was no easy business. He had to conquer his aversion to deep water, and his first attempts convinced him that he must have company to succeed. Now, few of the Nor'-Westers, or indeed of the Hudson's Bay people could swim. Not an Orkney man, for those islanders, who perished generally by drowning, held that swimming only prolonged the agony. Not the French voyageurs, whose pride it was to handle boats so that swimming would be needless. Not the Indians, who held that devils lived in deep water and seized a man's legs and pulled him down beside them.

But at last he found two men who had mastered the art. One was Lamallice, a Frenchman from the lower St. Lawrence who had learned to swim as a boy among the eel-pots. The other was White Partridge, who, being an Ojibway, came from a country where white water was the rule, and a traveller must learn to ford turbulent streams. In the company of these two Magnus began his course in the backwaters of the Saskatchewan.

He entered the water with a quaking heart, and he was very clumsy while learning from Lamallice the rudiments. But suddenly the whole thing seemed ridiculously easy and familiar. He lost his shrinking from the element, and felt at home in it. Presently, with his broad chest and long arms, he developed remarkable skill. Lamallice showed him how to dive, and in a week he had far outdistanced his master, and for a minute or two at a time could explore the floor of the deepest pools. White Partridge taught him how to breast a current, yielding to it, but always stealing an inch or two, and how to let a strong stream carry him down with no damage to limbs. Soon he had as far outdistanced White Partridge as White Partridge at this special game outshone Lamallice. He began to rejoice in the buffeting of rapids and the clutching arms of whirlpools. A river from a menace became a playmate, and an angry river a friend to be humoured and embraced.

Magnus had mastered the first test — to accustom his body and mind to white water. The next was to learn the art by which a man, while remaining in the upper air, could use white water as his servant. For this purpose a heavy York boat was of no use, for their handling was a corporate effort; he had to acquire a private and personal skill. Here Lamallice was an expert, and under his guidance Magnus learned how to thread acres of foam in a birchbark canoe, and how to pole such a canoe upstream, taking advantage of every patch of shoal water at the edge and every eddy in the main current. He learned how to avoid the deadly peril of a 'cellar', where the river flowed over a sunken rock and dropped into a deep pit with sheer glassy sides and a deadly undertow. He learned when boldness was the path of safety. He learned how, by a turn of the wrist, to shave, with a sixteenth of an inch to spare, a boulder which would have torn out the side of his craft. He learned when a floating log might be a menace, and when a convenient shelter.

His trips with the fur brigades were no longer nightmares but seasons of apprenticeship to which he greatly looked forward. He had Lamallice as his chief attendant, and with him he explored faraway waters. He ran most of the Peace rapids above Hudson's Hope, and one of the three pitches where the Slave River becomes a torrent, and a dozen ugly places on the rough trail from the Churchill to the Athabasca. Once on the Nelson River, at the spot now called the Kettle Rapids, he made an error in judgment, had his canoe stove in, and was washed up a quarter of a mile downstream with two ribs broken and a wrenched ankle. Lamallice, who helped to pull him out, approved the adventure. 'A white-water man,' he said, 'must three times look death in the face. If he still lives, water is no more a peril to him. You have had your first look.'

Then Simon Fraser came upon the scene, and for Magnus the course of life was changed.

Fraser was lean, with a pale skin that no sun or wind could

White Water

tan, and with dark eyes that had leaping fires in them. His speech was the pleasant singsong of the northern Highlands. For months, at Rocky Mountain House on the Peace River where Magnus was stationed, recruits had been drifting in from the East for a great advance across the mountains which was to carry the Company's front to the western sea. Fraser's first visit was brief. He had two officials of the Company with him, Stuart and McDougall. They crossed the passes and ascended the southernmost of the two rivers which met at the forks, that were called the Parsnip, which Alexander Mackenzie had followed a decade earlier. They borrowed Lamallice from Magnus, after they had spent an evening with their pipes, thumbing maps and retailing the gossip of the West.

It was a wonderful time, that dawn of the nineteenth century — the shuttles of the pioneers weaving trails across the ranges, posts installed in the high, wild country beyond the Rockies, big lakes where trout could be taken as big as salmon, Indians of a gentler breed than the Plains tribes, and through it all a great river ravening its way south into the iron hills.

There were sallies from Rocky Mountain House in spring and autumn, and even in deep winter, till there came a morning in May when the hour struck for the last and boldest enterprise. The river across the Rockies was beyond doubt the great Columbia, whose outlet on the Pacific had been known for two generations. Here lay the true road to the West, a water route, it was said, with few portages, which would bring the rich furs of the Coast, the sea otter and the seal, to the Nor'-West depots at Montreal. Nay, more, it would enable the Company to trade its furs across the Pacific to the China markets, and bring back tea and silks and rare porcelains — a second East India Company which needed no Government charter.

Simon Fraser, leaner and more sallow than ever, spoke of this to Magnus.

'We'll make your fortune for you, Magnus, lad,' he said. 'We'll set you up as our wintering partner on the coast, and your commission will soon be like a king's ransom. And we need you. Make your account for that, my dear. This is not a pleasure trip, and nobody knows what kind of country we'll have to go through before we win to the sea. The Carriers — that's the name they have for the Indians in those parts — say it's one dooms-great waterfall, and the folk here tell me you're the best white-water man that ever came out of the North. The thing has been arranged. I've got Duncan McGillivray's instructions for the loan of you in his own hand of write. So it's "Bundle and Go" for you the morn's morn.'

In the pleasant spring weather they crossed the Peace River pass, followed the Parsnip to the height of land, and then struck westward to the big lakes called Macleod and Stewart, where Company posts had been set up. Here there was much delay, for a new fort had to be built, and, since that year the salmon had failed to run, there was something like a famine among the Indians. In the fall, however, the food supply improved, and it was possible to lay down stores of pemmican and dried fish for the next year's venture. At the tail of winter two Company's men, Quesnel and Farris, came through from Rocky Mountain House with trade goods for barter.

Four stout boats were got together — two of them of bark, and two bigger and heavier dugouts of the kind used by the Haidas on the coast. The canoes were odd things to Eastern eyes. Their bark was spruce not birch, and instead of curving bows and sterns they ran out at either end to a point under water. The dugouts were long and narrow, to prevent their being swung about by the river eddies. The party numbered twenty-five all told; Fraser himself, Stuart, Quesnel, and Magnus; nineteen voyageurs, French and half-breeds, with Lamallice among them; and two Carriers as guides, clad modestly in breechcloths and necklets of grizzlies' claws.

They slipped downstream from the lake posts till they reached a strong river coming down from the northeast at a point where it swung to the south. Fraser laughingly took off his hat to it.

White Water

'Hail, Columbia!' he said. 'We're going to give you a mighty fine chance to drown us. You're a braw river, but there's a wanchancy look about you. You're ower fierce for decency.'

Fierce it was, but at the start it was a friendly ferocity which bore the flotilla swiftly, with no need of paddling, from one bivouac to another. The brisk current kept the flies away when camp was made at night on the shore. Food was ample, for the boatmen knocked down many partridges, Magnus's rifle killed a sheep or two and a caribou buck, and the Indians (whom the Frenchmen called Fish-Eaters, that being the name of contempt used by the hunting tribes of the Peace for their kin beyond the mountains) set their lines every evening, and there was broiled trout for breakfast.

'This is fine travelling,' Simon Fraser said, 'but it's ower easy. The morn, or maybe the day after, we'll be battling with some infernal Niagara.'

The change came suddenly. About noon on the third day the mountains seemed to rush under and choke the river into a funnel. At first the pace of the boats was only quickened; the current ran more fiercely but still evenly, with the even unbroken flow of a gigantic mill-race. The spirits of the voyageurs soared, for the river was doing their work for them, and their boatsongs rose above the drone of the water. But Lamallice's brows were drawn. He saw that the channel was beginning to twist, and he knew that at the turns there would be troublesome eddies.

Sure enough there came a patch of wild water, a sharp-angled precipice, and then a broad reach where the river foamed among boulders and sunken rocks. This was the kind of thing familiar to the voyageurs, and they threaded it deftly. But at the next bend the river narrowed into a belt like smooth grey glass. It split at a rock into two streams, each of which dropped in a dizzy glide into a great churning pot. Magnus, who was in the leading canoe, by a lucky instinct took the right-hand stream; if he had taken the other the flotilla must have been cut to pieces on a grid of underwater rock. As it was, they were swirled into the right bank, and managed to make fast to its fringe of alders. There was a slender track along the shore, and Stuart, who had charge of the baggage, made them unload and back-pack it, and line the empty boats out of the maelstrom. This took the last three hours of daylight, and it was a wet and weary company that made camp on a spit of gravel, and watched the river burrowing beyond them into the gloom of a still narrower gorge.

Lamallice spoke. 'The Fish-Eaters say that beyond this it gets worse, and that no man has ever travelled that road. There's still time to go back. There's not much of a shore path, but enough to line the bateaux upstream to where we started.'

Fraser was peering into the dark.

'What say you, Johnnie?' he asked Stuart, without turning round.

Stuart, prim, neat in his dress, always smacking somewhat of the city, had no doubts.

'I'm for back,' he said. 'It was a daft-like gamble from the start. What's to hinder this river from flinging itself over a thousand-foot precipice and taking us with it? It's fair suicide to gang on.'

'The Indians say there's no big waterfall, only rapids,' said Magnus.

'Ay, but they also say that the rapids are ower fearsome for a boat to live in.'

Fraser swung round. 'We're travelling a road no man has travelled before,' he said, 'and I'm not denying there's danger in it. I'll drown no men without his consent, so we'd better take a vote.'

The vote was equal, the Indians being left out — eleven to go on, eleven to turn back.

'It seems we're a divided house,' said Fraser. 'Well, the casting vote falls on me, and I give it for going on. There'll be bad bits, and we'll have to make shift to line the boats past 'em. The

Company's credit is in our hands, and by thunder! it's not going to suffer by me. We're taking no worse risks than Sandy Mackenzie, and he won through to the Pacific. Providence is on the side of mettled folk.'

No one disputed the verdict, for his quiet audacity had laid its spell on the company. That night Magnus slept little, for he knew better than the rest the hazards of the venture. He looked up to the sky, which above the gorge was a thin band of sable, in which the stars burned like hanging lamps with an eerie brilliance. He had faced White Water and conquered it — nay, he had made it his friend. But this was the ultimate challenge. There was a curious excitement in his blood, and a tremor, too, at the pit of his stomach. He had moved far since the days when he had lived in dread of the Orkney seas.

He found one of the Carriers beside him sniffing the night air like a dog on the trail.

'We shall get through,' he said.

'We shall get through,' the Indian repeated, 'but not all.'

Now, when doubt entered even the bravest hearts, it was Fraser's fatalism and Magnus's doggedness which supported the rest. The thunder of the cataracts reverberated between the rock walls, drowning the scream of eagle and fish-hawk, and the songs of the voyageurs.

Magnus and Lamallice, at bow and stern, were in the first canoe. It was their business to prospect, and, if they judged a stretch impossible, to guide the flotilla into the shore and arrange a portage. It was a tricky job, and they made mistakes, avoiding rapids which were reasonably safe and venturing on some which brought them to the edge of disaster. One awful place they encountered on the fifth day, when for nearly two miles the river was constricted to a channel of some thirty yards in which no boat could live for five seconds. On each side the cliffs rose almost sheer, though there was a faint Indian trail among the debris on the right bank. Moreover, they had been warned by the Carriers of unfriendly tribes, and had to post guards on the rock shoulders. The portage was a desperate affair. The boats were lined down, tossing and circling in the whirlpools. The shore trail was widened with spades, and somehow or other the baggage was carried and the canoes lined past the danger point.

A false step would have meant instant destruction. Fraser descended cliffs like a mountain goat, for his Highland boyhood had made him sure-footed. He drove his dagger into the ground and used it as a handhold.

They reached a place where the cliffs fell back a little, and there they found a settlement of Atnah Indians, who were friendly enough, and provided three horses for the next portage. One of the horses slipped and broke its back on the riverside boulders. There, too, one of the Carriers lost his life, falling into a whirlpool which battered in his skull. The body was recovered, and his companion insisted that the funeral must be in accordance with the custom of his tribe, so they had to retrace their steps to the Atnah village. The Atnahs had the same funeral customs as the Carriers, and the body was burnt with strange incantations . . . For the first time in his life Donald knew the sickening smell of roasting human flesh . . .

By this time all the party were ragged and dirty; their nails were half off their fingers, their shoes were in shreds, and their feet and hands were masses of blisters. But Fraser never lost his mastery. He sent scouts ahead to prepare the next batch of Indians for their coming, and when they reached them there was that in his dancing eyes and wild merry face that made them his friends. His cheeks were now so drawn that he seemed to be perpetually grinning.

'I've a better notion of handling savages than Mackenzie,' he told Magnus. 'Sandy couldn't 'gree with the Atnahs, and you saw that they've been eating out of my hand. Sandy was ower much of the dominie.'

They reached the land of the Chilcotins and were well received and well fed, fortunately, for after that they had their worst passage. It was a place where portage was impossible, and

Magnus decided to trust the thread of glassy current which ran between two maelstroms. It was like a stream in a cave, for the cliffs above narrowed to overhangs which showed only a ribbon of sky. Every man held his breath, as for an hour and more they shot down at a giddy speed, with death waiting for them if there was a false paddle-stroke. Below that they landed, and all afternoon the crews slept the heavy sleep of men whose nerves had been stretched too far.

Fraser shook Magnus's hand.

'Man, you're the grand guide,' he said. 'I'm content always to follow your judgment, but for myself I'd have said yon place was naked death.'

'So would I, if it hadn't been for a fish-hawk. The bird kept on steady in front of me, and I got the notion that it was sent for a good omen.'

Fraser laughed.

'Good luck to the bird. But trust your own wits, Magnus, lad. They're safer than omens.'

Presently the river became a chain of cascades which no craft could pass. They stowed their boats on a high scaffold in the jack-pines, and each man humped his eighty pounds' weight of baggage. Then began a heart-breaking portage till they reached a camp of the Lilloets, who welcomed them with much hospitable ceremony. Fraser had made his ragged regiment shave and spruce themselves for the occasion. There they procured two canoes and a supply of dried salmon.

Fraser, who had been conferring with the head man, joined the party with a puckered brow.

'I'm puzzled about this infernal river,' he told Stuart. 'These Indians have drawn me a plan of where it enters the sea, and it's not what I have learned of the Columbia's mouth. Maybe we've hit the wrong water.'

Next day a strong stream came in on their left, and Fraser was more cheerful. He had heard of it, he said, from David Thompson, for whom it had been named, and it was a tributary right enough of the Columbia. His good humour was increased by friendly Indians, who traded him sufficient canoes to embark the whole party. And then came an awful ravine where the canoes had to be abandoned again. The portage was for goats, and not for men. Often the trail became a ladder whose sides were poles fixed between trees and boulders.

It was the last of their tribulations. Beyond it the river settled down in its bed and flowed quietly to the sea. Canoes were obtained again, and on the thirty-fifth day of their journey they were in tidal waters.

Fraser took his bearings and sat for a long time in deep thought. Then he beckoned Magnus.

'We're the better part of three degrees ower far north for the Columbia. You and me, we've found a new river.'

'We're none the worse for that,' was the answer. 'We've got to the coast, and that was our purpose.'

'Ay, but we've found a dooms-rough road. The man's mad that would follow our trail. It's not what the Company want, but all the same it's been a mighty great venture. What'll we call our river?'

'The Fraser,' was the answer. 'There can be but the one name.'

'I'm not so sure. I was the leader in name, but you were the leader in truth. I think it might be called the Magnus. Magnus is Latin for great, and it's a great river . . . And you're a great man. You were born without fear.'

Magnus laughed happily.

'Not me! I was born with the terror of White Water on me. But I faced it and beat it. And now it's my servant.'

Fraser laughed also.

'A very pretty parable,' he said. 'If I were a minister it would be a fine tail to a sermon. If you are afraid of a thing, you respect it; and if you conquer your fear and keep your respect, you learn how to control that thing.'

THE AXE HAS CUT THE FOREST DOWN
ELIZABETH COATSWORTH

The axe has cut the forest down,
The labouring ox has smoothed all clear,
Now apples grow where pine trees stood,
And slow cows graze instead of deer.

Where Indian fires once raised their smoke
The chimneys of a farmhouse stand,
And cocks crow barnyard challenges
To dawns that once saw savage land.

The axe, the plow, the binding wall,
By these the wilderness is tamed,
By these the white man's will is wrought,
The rivers bridged, the new towns named.

THE PATRIOT

NATHANIEL A. BENSON

DRAMATIS PERSONAE

JOHN WATERS	—	pioneer farmer, forty
ANNIE	—	his wife, thirty-two
MICHAEL	—	his son, eleven
MARY	—	his daughter, seven
THE STRANGER	—	William Lyon Mackenzie

Nine o'clock on the night of Saturday, December the ninth, in the year of rebellion, 1837. The main room of a small farmhouse, midway between Hamilton and Stony Creek; to find it a patriot came "through a concession parellel to the Mountain Road above Hamilton, found his way through the Binbrook and Glanford Woods, forded the Twenty-Mile Creek, and rode on for ten miles" which proves that the farmhouse is on no public road nor easy to find. To be candid, only a lost man or a lost patriot would have stumbled upon such an out-of-the-way place.

The room is low-ceilinged, staunch-looking and not overly bright. Entry to this farmhouse living-room of JOHN WATERS, *Hibernian and Orangeman, is by means of a stout and sturdy front door, stout and sturdy as John Waters himself. On either side of the door are two fairly large, small-paned windows which are uncurtained. On their sills the snow is piled high, and outside the December wind howls like a wolf. A door at the back corner of the right-hand wall leads to the kitchen. Two other doors on the left wall lead to bedrooms. An immense fireplace, built of rough-hewn stone, is on the right and in its dim, friendly, red glow the Waters family is clustered. In a huge rocker sits* JOHN, *massive, muscular, strong of arm and feature. He is little over forty and* has a great shock of curly, black hair. On his knee sleeps seven-year-old MARY, in a grey flannel nightgown. ANNIE, *John's wife*, is little over thirty, a dark kindly-eyed colleen, grown a trifle matronly with the bearing of five children. *She is spinning industriously and talking as she does.* MICHAEL, *a lad of eleven with great, dark eyes, sits silent, head on his hands, elbows on his knees, staring into the coals. At intervals the wind blows a gust of sparks down and whines in the chimney.*

JOHN (*taking his great black pipe from his mouth*). Sure, 'tis a good night to be indoors and not out tramplin' in the snow.
ANNIE. It is that, John. You know, in the winter I often get thinkin' that all the cruel spirits in the world are out walkin' the roads in December here. 'Tis not like Ireland in the summer here neither.
JOHN. There's no country like Ireland in the summer, Annie, exceptin' maybe heaven, but here in Canada, a man's land's his own so long as he pays his taxes and votes proper. Sure, you wouldn't find a snugger, warmer bit o' land in all Canada than ours, even though 'tis a bit out o' the way.
ANNIE. You know, I often do be lonesome for a good neighbour until I start workin' so hard I forget. Work's a great thing to make you forget who you are entirely.
JOHN. True, we don't get much time to be rememberin' who we are and thinkin' of our troubles with the toilin' we've had this year past, but we're comin' on slowly. It'll be a rare farm in a year or two, Annie.
ANNIE. Sure, John, we could have worked our whole lives away in Ireland and never been half as well off as we are this day.
JOHN. Oh, aye. We've been very fortunate and cannot be complainin' at all. We're as happy as most in Upper Canada; aye, there's many not so happy at all.
ANNIE. What means all this talk we've been hearin' of rebellion in York that they call Toronto? Is there truth in it?

JOHN. It's a very, very bad business, rebellion is. It gets you nowhere. 'Tis true there's a great deal more power in the hands of a few in Upper Canada than ever should be, but rebellion's no way to right it. From the last word I had of it all, a group o' wild bosthoons were talking of a march on old York and takin' over the whole government.

ANNIE. God save us, an' it's just like Ireland ever since the English put foot in it. Will it be a civil war, John?

JOHN. If those reckless divils once get an idea they'll carry it through, if they can come round the soldiers. I heard they were gatherin' Thursday above York, under that man Mackenzie and Lount and Rolph and the rest.

ANNIE. And what all will they do?

JOHN. There's no tellin' that. From all the talk, they might do a good deal. The crows take them for a parcel of wild, lawless rascals! There no good in rebellion. But then, there's them who say all's not well in the government — and they may be right. There's no reason why six or seven men should run a country, or act like Englishmen in Ireland.

ANNIE. The main thing is this, John — will all this touch the holdin' of our farm? When governments change, 'tis always the poor folk suffer, not havin' time to realize their mistakes in actin' for the old government. Will the farm be safe?

JOHN. Safe as safe can be. The deed protects us from the governin' side and the farm is so out o' the regular way no rebels'll ever come burnin' it.

ANNIE. Oh, God save us if they do!

JOHN. Hush, woman! 'Tis all nonsense we're jabberin'. Whatever rebellin' there'll be will be all away over in York. Divil take that new Indian name if I can say it!

ANNIE. I wish you'd go over and get some real news of it all in the mornin'. No one ever comes by this road to tell us at all.

JOHN. Maybe I will, if you'll hold your whisht. (*He leans forward to poke the fire and sees Michael gazing, rapt, into it.*) Micky,

The Patriot

ye young spalpeen, why do ye sit there, hour after hour, gazin' into the fire as if ye saw something there?

MICKY. Oh, aye, Father, but I do; it's wonderful to look into the fire and see all the grand things that you think of and can't say.

JOHN. An' what do ye see, Mick? Would it be a banshee or a divil's-light or one such?

MICKY. No, it's none of those, da. It's dreams and the like, and fancies, and all the things you want to be, that move in the flames o' the fire.

ANNIE. Sure, Mick, an' what do ye see?

MICKY. Oh, I see everythin' grand. I see you with a carriage and Mary a fine young lady with long curls and da in a great silk hat, makin' laws and such, and I see meself all grown up to be a great soldier—

ANNIE. Soldier is it, ye rascal? Don't speak o' soldierin' to me! 'Tis a farmer ye'll be, like your da there, and keep the farm together. Ye'll do no soldierin' and rebellin' and the like. No son o' me'll join in such wild doin's. Rebels and such!

MICKY. I saw soldiers once. My, but they're fine. I'd like to see a rebel next, a real rebel like Uncle Charlie told me—like Papineau.

ANNIE. The Lord preserve us from all such! Mick, if you don't run off to bed I'll thump your ears for you. (*Mick sits.*)

ANNIE. Mick!

JOHN. Ah, woman, let the young scrimpin' be! I used to see things like that in the fire when I was his age, too — but I kept quiet about them, *(to Mick)* and so do you!

ANNIE. Rebels and the like!

(*Silence.* JOHN *smokes; Annie examines her wheel;* MICKY *stares on into the glow. Another gust of sparks flies down as the wind whistles. Little* MARY *wakes on her father's knee with a start.*)

MARY. Da! (*She clutches her father,*) Da! I hear somethin'.

JOHN. Whisht, child, 'tis only the wind ye hear. Go to sleep and I'll put ye to bed presently.

MARY (*listening intently*). Da! It is somethin' — It is somethin' — Someone's comin' — someone's comin' near us — fast.

(*They start a little, listening uneasily in spite of themselves.*)

JOHN. I hear nothin', child — ye been dreamin'.

MARY (*Her voice rises*). Da! Someone's comin' — ridin', ridin' like the wind. Listen!

(*Thoroughly alarmed,* JOHN *puts her down and springs to the alert.*)

JOHN. I — it *is* someone.

(ANNIE *gathers little* MARY *in her arms and goes to enfold* MICK. *He runs to his father's side and helps him bar the door.* JOHN *picks up an axe standing near the door, and* MICK *a billet of wood. A low thudding sound rises above the wind, the sound of hoofbeats on the hard snow, becoming louder and louder.*)

ANNIE. God save us! who can it be, this time o' night? Don't open the door, John!

(*The hoofs thud near and nearer; the shape of a great, black horse and rider flash past the right-hand window. The snow whirls behind them. A cry is heard as the rider stops his mount and gets off. A knock sounds, peremptory yet not loud.*)

JOHN. Who's there? (*A sharp voice comes.*)

THE VOICE. A traveller — I have lost my road — I am alone.

(JOHN *opens the door a little and, seeing the man's size, admits him.*)

Look carefully at this man, this fugitive who steps across the door-sill of JOHN WATERS' lonely farmhouse, on that bitter night of December the ninth, 1837, for he has written his name largely across the history of Canada. Here he enters, the little patriot who dared to lose all, even his good name, for his country's good. He is forty-two and his face is deeply lined with harsh years that outnumber these. He is a trifle under middle height, slim and wiry. Even the last three days of hard riding and

The Patriot

terrific physical strain have not humbled a spirit that nothing in life could daunt; there is still something of the old, quick, nervous energy, of the spring in his step. His head darts quick glances into the interior. His clothing is tatterdemalion and nondescript, a 'bonnet rouge', a trifle large for him ("wearing the cap of J. Latimer, one of my young men, my hat having been knocked off in a skirmish") a torn homespun, sorry slippers, for his limbs are so swollen that he has had to discard his boots. His beard is unshaven. Seeing ANNIE, his inborn courtesy asserts itself. He bows.)

THE STRANGER. Madam — your ser-rvant.

(His head is massive, high and broad in the frontal region and well rounded. His fine blue eyes are piercing, restless and keen, his chin long and broad, a firm-set mouth with firmly pressed lips which, undulating in a mass, move all that part of his face below the nostrils, keeping time with the motion and twinkle of the clear, eager eyes. Two qualities predominate in that face — courage and unrest.)

THE STRANGER. I am off my way, sir, and ask shelter of you if you will afford me that. I am travelling from Hamilton to Niagara. (He catches sight of the beam of a balance marked "Charles Waters, Maker" hung in a conspicuous place.) Mr. Charles Waters, sir—

JOHN. I'm John Waters, farmer. Charles is my brother in Montreal. (John is hostile, ANNIE not at all, MICKY examines the newcomer from head to foot. Little MARY is slightly frightened.)

THE STRANGER (to MICKY). Well, my lad, (He offers his hand, which MICKY takes, bowing with a "sir". The stranger produces a purse that clinks merrily). Mr. Waters, I would ask you, if you will be so kind as to accommodate me for the nicht, (his Scotch accent creeps in) and see to stabling my horse — my indebtedness would be perhaps two dollars? (He offers them).

ANNIE. Indeed, an' 'tis far too much for our humble style o' livin' and shelter —

THE STRANGER. Madam, in my time I have known far humbler and been well content.

(*This melts* ANNIE *completely, for its sincerity is straight as his lips, comes from his heart, a heart whose nobility is seen by the* WATERS', *even after these few minutes*).

ANNIE. Sit you down, sir, and draw up beside the fire, for 'tis a rare cold night, outside.

THE STRANGER (*Taking off his worn, woollen gloves*). It feels coldest, Mrs. Waters, when one is riding — riding fast.

MARY. (*piping up*). There, 'n I told you, da, the genl'm'n was ridin' fast.

JOHN. Whisht, child.

ANNIE. Sure, sir, 'n she did. Before Mr. Waters or meself ever heard the horse, she waked up from her sleep, sayin' she heard you in the wind. *Seein'*, she is, and a queer one — sensitive.

JOHN. Hold such talk, Annie, 'tis foolish.

THE STRANGER (*Going to* MARY, *smiling and putting his hand on her head*).

"Thou, over whom thy immortality,
Broods like the day, a master o'er a slave,
A presence which is not to be put by . . ."

Ah, Mr. Waters, when we are children, many wonderful things are clearer to us.

ANNIE. Sure, sir, and you talk better than the preacher does. Now, take off your coat, sir, and you'll be after havin' a bit o' supper an' a good cup o' tea.

THE STRANGER. It is long after supper, Mrs. Waters; I'll not trouble you.

ANNIE. Whisht, sir, 'tis no trouble at all.

JOHN. I'll see to your horse and feed him.

MICKY. May I come and help you, da?

JOHN. You can see the beast through the window, Mick (*He goes out, muffled up, and* MICKY *runs to the window*).

The Patriot

(*And now the fallen patriot sits in a great chair before the fire, warming the ardent frame that has felt the evil chills of tyranny and injustice sink deeper than the December frost. The red glow outlines that eager, furrowed, and sensitive face. The mouth twitches. His hands open and close nervously*).

THE STRANGER (*sighs to himself*). Well, what must be, must be. It is God's will.

(MARY *goes up to him timidly*.)

MARY. Would you like to see my doll?

THE STRANGER (*starting a little*). Aye, lassie, I would. What's her name?

MARY. Her name is Charles.

THE STRANGER (*smiles*). Oh, I see.

MARY. After my favourite uncle.

THE STRANGER. Well, well. Would you like to sit on my knee?

MARY. I would, but you look so frightened.

THE STRANGER. I — no — well. (*He lifts her up*.) There, now I'm not frightened any more.

MARY. You look so tired, mister.

THE STRANGER. I am, lassie.

MARY. Well, then, we'll both go to sleep while ma gets supper. Would you like to?

THE STRANGER (*an odd break in his voice*). Aye, lassie, I would.

(*She snuggles up to him. He pretends to sleep and two great tears run down his cheeks.* MICKY *goes over to him*.)

MICKY. Oh mister, that's a grand, big, black horse you have! (*The* STRANGER *motions him to be quiet, for* MARY *has fallen asleep*.) My, I'd love to ride him.

THE STRANGER. Well, then, lad, before I leave in the morning maybe you'll have a wee ride, if you like.

MICKY (*glad to be justified*). Ma, the genl'm'n looks into the fire, too, just like I do.

ANNIE. Ah, such nonsense, boy, indeed! Mick here says he's

always after seein' all manner o' grand things in the fire if he looks long enough. (*She laughs.*)

MICKY (*not very confident*). Can't you see gran' dreams and pictures an' all in the fire, too, mister?

THE STRANGER (*gently*). Aye, lad — once — I could once.

(JOHN *returns, rubbing his hands.*)

JOHN. That's a splendid horse you have there. Not many finer than him in Upper Canada, I'll be bound.

THE STRANGER. Aye, he is, a very noble beast; too good indeed for a born walker like me.

JOHN. Only a good horseman could ride him, mister. You underrate yourself.

MICKY. Da, the genl'm'n says I may ride him in the morning.

JOHN. Can you now, Micky? You know you couldn't ride a cow.

ANNIE. Now, sir, will you come and sit in? The supper's all pipin' hot.

THE STRANGER. Madam, your hospitality is more than a chance wayfarer deserves. (*He sits down.*)

JOHN. Now, Mick, it's high time you an' Mary were in your beds. Off with you! Give Mother and me a kiss and to bed with you.

(MICKY *and* MARY *kiss their father and mother, and* MARY *turns to the* STRANGER.)

MARY. Good-night, mister. (*She waits to be kissed and the* STRANGER *after a moment's hesitation, complies.*)

THE STRANGER. Good-night, my wee lass, may ye never grow to find your dreams less happy than they are now.

(MICKY *holds out his hand.*)

MICKY. An' may I ride your horse in the mornin', sir?

THE STRANGER. Aye, ye may, my boy, and good-night.

(*The children go out, shepherded by* ANNIE.)

This is a rare supper, Mr. Waters, for one who is little favoured by luck.

JOHN. Thank you. (*He is a little curt.*)

The Patriot

ANNIE *(coming back to her spinning-wheel).* Now, mister, if there's anything at all wantin', just call for it. *(She watches him eagerly as he devours the excellent meal before him.)* Have you travelled far this night?

THE STRANGER. I have. Many a weary mile.

JOHN. And why? (JOHN *is more curious than friendly.*)

THE STRANGER. Mr. Waters, I must be at Niagara by the morning.

ANNIE. There's great talk of rebellion in Upper Canada these days, especially those lawless men at York, under Mackenzie. Have you been in York?

THE STRANGER *(turning).* I have — and there's no more rebellion. All the trouble and strife there's been for reform and better government have come to nothing.

ANNIE. And why is that?

THE STRANGER *(almost furiously).* Because a great number of the men who pledged themselves to fight to the last drop of blood in their bodies ran at the first rattle of musket-fire.

ANNIE. And a good thing, too, those lawless bodies left well enough alone.

THE STRANGER. They did not leave well enough alone, madam. They had courage but no bullets with which to fight injustice and tyranny — tyranny as I see it, tyranny and oppression and the long perversion of justice which have lain like a yoke on the neck of Canadian freedom. Freedom of speech and good government are a man's birthright. There is none of either in Upper Canada — and none in Lower. Only a snobbish, aristocratic, small set of rascals in office who even have the power to parcel out the very soil of Canada we tread on, to their friends and relatives.

JOHN. I hold with you there, my friend, but why do you get so upset and wild about it? What is it to you who governs? Askin' your pardon, I feel sure, from your appearance, that you're no man of property whatever.

THE STRANGER *(looks at his ragged clothes).* True, I *am* no man of property — now. I have lost everything, but Canada has lost more than that. She has lost her integrity and character.

JOHN. For a man who has nothing to lose by it, it seems to hit you rarely.

THE STRANGER *(vehemently)*. It does hit me "rarely", as you say, Mr. Waters. It hits me as it should hit every Canadian who wants to see his country lawfully and fairly governed and not by the stupid, cruel, unjust clique of office-holders in power at present. That bellowing bull of a Strachan, and that polished young snob, Robinson, and the rest. Head is a helpless, stupid monkey who dances to their music because he has neither brains nor courage enough to make his own. And the rest — the rare men the Crown sends out — Sir John Colborne and Sir George Arthur, governors of penal settlements, sent as governors of Canada, a country of free men, sent here to cow and brutify a free people.

(*In place of the weary traveller and fugitive there appears now, in the* STRANGER, *the quality and force of "the unpurchasable patriot", the commanding eloquent, vivid, and picturesque leader of the people. He forgets all caution and reveals himself in the character of the gallant, stormy petrel of Upper Canada, the hot-headed idolater of justice with a genius for political agitation.* JOHN *and* ANNIE WATERS *behold, unknown to them, the arch-rebel, the reformer ahead of his time, hearty in his love of public right, passionate in his hatred of public wrong-doers, clever, brave and energetic, the tribune of the Canadian people and fugitive from "justice". His hands open and close restlessly, his features twitch and move, his voice pours out a torrent of words intense as they are sincere.*)

Aye, they give away poor men's lands for their clergy to collect the fees on them. And what do they do with the land? Nothing — nothing — nothing — land that should bear grain and feed cattle, land that should nurture freeman farmers and their children, land that should sustain the Canadians of this country's days to come is portioned off and gobbled up by Strachan and his clique for the greater glory of their church. The church should be like the government, holiest and noblest in its reverent office when it is bringing peace and happiness and safety to its children. Neither church nor government is worthy of the name if its powers are perverted and it turns persecutor of the people whom it exists to serve. The Reform Party asks for principles which, in time, will order the whole British Empire. They're no rebels — if they are, then so are the men who forced the Magna Charta from King John. This rebellion I tell you, is no movement against the British Crown or its authority, but a movement, by patriots, against the abuse and prostitution of that authority by men unworthy of the Queen's confidence!

JOHN *(dogged)*. There's great truth in all you say but there's no need for rebellion and such things. All could be settled without that — there were other ways.

THE STRANGER *(fiercely)*. Aye, Mr. Waters — there *were* other ways. For years, for long, weary years, all of them were tried. Every means of lawful reform was tried — and tyranny and corruption and abuse still triumphed. The right remedies that should have succeeded had all failed. Only one was left — rebellion. No one wanted rebellion but Sir Francis Head; he created it, he prepared for it and, by execution, will get rid of those leaders whom he could not silence by law. The people of Upper Canada wanted justice, not tyranny; peace, not bloodshed. A people never rebel from a mere passion for attack — it is a people's impatience of suffering and that only which lights the fires of rebellion. That is why the patriots marched on Toronto.

ANNIE *(leaning forward, the thread in her hands; less cool than JOHN, she is already part of the Rebellion)*. And did they win? Did they do what they gathered to do?

THE STRANGER *(The fire dies in him)*. They did nothing, madam, nothing. They were ill fitted for fighting, they were frightened, they were but farmers against soldiers.

ANNIE (*indignantly*). And did they not fight to death for this cause you speak so well of?

THE STRANGER. They tried their best — may be that they could not, but had they been fighting for the causes of evil and oppression instead of under the banners of right and justice, they might have had the arms to show more spirit.

ANNIE. And why did their spirit fail them so quickly?

THE STRANGER. There's no clear reason, except that it took so much courage to rise at all in the first place that their courage was all but gone when the time for fighting came. Save for a hundred men, it was a sorry business.

JOHN. I see you've been at York when all this happened. Tell me, was there a battle?

THE STRANGER. Well, one might call it that, but never, in the cause of freedom, was so weak a blow struck. Now toadies and tyrants can label themselves heroes and Loyalists. Loyal — and they who brought the whole rebellion on!

JOHN. But the fight? Where was the fight?

THE STRANGER. Some shots were fired as the rebels lay beside Montgomery's Tavern. The soldiers had some cannon and the balls went through the house, near where the rebels lay. They chose to wait for the soldiers in a wood and fought with spirit. Grape, canister, and broadsides of musketry were poured on them, and they stood firmly for an hour — to stand there longer would have meant massacre. They could do nothing against the military, save stand their ground — and that they did.

JOHN. And their leaders?

THE STRANGER (*bitterly*). The best were taken and the wiser fled. (*All his ardour is gone, sunk in the realization of defeat.*) There's not much glory in dying by a tyrant's rope; it is a kind of noble protest that tyrants never understand. 'Butchered to make a Compact holiday' — the wiser fled, the noble men will perish.

ANNIE. And is the trouble finally over now?

The Patriot

THE STRANGER. In Canada, the cause is finished. (*He gets up and turns to the window, looking out into the driving snow.* JOHN *relights his pipe.* ANNIE *begins to "redd up" the table.*)

ANNIE. I hope you liked the supper, though ye did not eat all I set before ye, mister.

THE STRANGER (*turning*). Madam, 'twas worthier of a better guest. My thanks to you. Let me apologize to you for my whirl of words. I did forget myself.

ANNIE. It was rare news to me. (*She gets the house in order.*) And now, sir, good-night to you. There is your couch — I've spread the blankets on it. (*She fixes a couch to the right of the fireplace.*) Good-night to you.

THE STRANGER. Good-night. (*He bows; she goes to the bedroom left back;* JOHN *fixes the fire.*) It takes no keen eye to see you are unfriendly and ill-disposed to me, Mr. Waters. Before I take the hospitality of your roof you must tell me why that it. I have paid my way and properly, I trust, and am your guest.

JOHN. Rare guest you are — you come this lonely way none ever comes, riding a mighty horse that ill befits your own appearance. Is that not so?

THE STRANGER (*surveying his tattered clothes again*). Aye, that is true.

JOHN. You come by night — from where? Where you are going I'm well assured, out of the country and by secret ways, swift as you can. You toss all this dust of rebellion in our eyes — but you're no rebel — I can tell you that! Would any honest man be glad of such a guest?

THE STRANGER. You speak the truth. Then I will take the road.

JOHN. You need not take the road. I fear you none. I only tell you now what I think. But I'll do this — (*He takes a musket out of the corner.*) I'll keep this by my bedside to be safe and to protect my wife and children too. My ears are good — keep to this side of the room and do not steal away during the night, or I'll shoot after you, and I shoot well.

THE STRANGER. I am your prisoner then?

JOHN. No prisoner are you. But I do not wish you stealin' away in the night with any of my goods. *(He bars the door.)* Goodnight to you. *(Grimly)* Sleep well.

THE STRANGER *(sardonically).* Such hospitality as yours, Mr. Waters, must make my slumbers light.

(JOHN *goes to the bedroom, leaving the door open a little.*)

(*The* STRANGER *looks into the fire for a long moment, sits down on the rough couch and takes off his slippers and rough outer coat. He kneels beside the couch and his head is buried in his hands. His head moves slightly and his prayers, not to be recorded here, are a confused murmur. He gets up and sits in the big rocker, draws it near the fire. He is motionless, staring into the coals. Only his hands twitch a little. The wind blows the panes of the windows. They rattle slightly; sparks fly out from the fire-place, the wind whines uneasily in the chimney, and then everything is still. Out of the near door on the left, the children's bedroom, a little curly head is poked; it is* MICKY'S. *Little by little he appears, in a grey flannel nightgown. He looks furtively at his parents' door and slowly tiptoes over to the fire. The* STRANGER *turns quickly, sees* MICKY, *and his furrowed face breaks into a smile.*)

MICKY *(in a whisper).* I just came out to talk to you, mister.

THE STRANGER *(in another whisper).* Don't talk too loud, my lad. You should be in bed.

MICKY. I know, but we don't have anyone stay with us very often — and nobody like you, ever. Are you a soldier?

THE STRANGER. No, lad.

MICKY. Weren't you ever a soldier?

THE STRANGER. No lad, I never was.

MICKY. Then I know what you are — I knew I did!

THE STRANGER. What am I, then? Tell me.

MICKY. You're a rebel!

THE STRANGER *(starts violently).* A what?

MICKY. Well, aren't you — a rebel?

The Patriot

THE STRANGER *(Who would not lie to a child)*. What made you think I was that?

MICKY. Nothing. I just guessed it. It must be wonderful to be a rebel —

THE STRANGER. Hush, boy!

MICKY. And fight soldiers and ride a big black horse like the wind and ride in the night in dark, lonely places and not be afraid of anyone. Have you a gun? *(Silence)* I say, have you a gun? If you have, I'd like to see it. Where is it?

THE STRANGER. I'll show you it — but you cannot touch it. *(He takes a single-barrel pistol from his homespun. It is one "taken from Captain Duggan during Tuesday's scuffle.")*

MICKY *(Eyes like saucers)*. Oh, isn't it fine? Do you really kill people with it?

THE STRANGER *(smiling in spite of himself)*. Dozens, lad, dozens.

MICKY *(overwhelmed)*. Oooh!

THE STRANGER. Lad, you have no sense at all. You take me for a murdering highwayman, don't you?

MICKY. Well, *aren't* you?

THE STRANGER. No, lad, and, through God's grace I've never knowingly spilled human blood. Rebels aren't pirates, boy, as you think them, at all. They're poor hot-headed bodies trying the last means they know to get justice.

MICKY *(disappointed)*. Oh! And I thought they were like robbers or soldiers, only worse.

THE STRANGER. You're very wrong in that, my lad.

MICKY. No, but everything seems so lovely and excitin' when you first look at it.

THE STRANGER. Aye, it does — it's too bad you ever have to grow up, lad.

MICKY. Oh, but I want to, mister.

THE STRANGER. Well — you'll not always feel that way. I remember when I was little like you, back in Scotland, away over the ocean.

MICKY. Did you sail over the ocean?

THE STRANGER. Yes, a long, long time ago.

MICKY. Tell me about it, please. (*He climbs up on the* STRANGER'S *knee. They get settled and the story begins.*)

THE STRANGER. Well, it was a great, fast, sailing ship she was, the *Psyche*. Longer from bow to stern than this house is, by three times. She was a rare sailer and the waves were as high as the hills, just as high as the blue hills of Scotland, and the foam of the waves was white and they shone in the sun — (*And the story-teller sees that* MICKY *has fallen asleep. He lays his head against the boy's.*)

[*Curtains fall for instant to indicate passage of time*]

(*Morning. It is only a little after six, and the faint, blue light of dawn is cold upon the snow on the window-sills. The glow of the fire is very feeble.* JOHN WATERS' *guest is asleep on the low couch with a rough blanket over him. A tramping is heard from the bedroom and* JOHN *enters, fully clothed, except for his boots, the musket under one arm and his boots under the other. He peers interestedly at the sleeper, yawns, stands the musket in its former corner and sits down to pull on his boots. He throws fresh wood on the fire and puts the kettle on the stove, which he kindles. Rapidly he prepares breakfast of meat, bread, and tea. Then he goes over to the couch.*)

JOHN. It's morning, mister. You'll be wantin' to move soon. Your breakfast's ready.

(*The* STRANGER *gets up quickly and puts on his slippers and coat.*)

THE STRANGER. Thank you, Mr. Waters. That's a very, very comfortable couch, indeed. I slept well.

JOHN. "Well", did ye? The sleep of the just.

THE STRANGER. Whether you believe it or not, Mr. Water, the sleep of the just.

JOHN. Well, there's your breakfast. I'll eat with you if you don't mind.

The Patriot

THE STRANGER. I am honoured. (*He rises as* WATERS *sits **down**.*)
JOHN (*a little embarrassed*). Thank ye. You're a queer one and no mistake. A queer guest.
THE STRANGER. Well, Mr. Waters, as a host, especially a paid one, you have a smack of originality in yourself. (*He smiles.*)
JOHN. The crows speed your compliments!
THE STRANGER. And now, I would ask you, that you may relieve your house of so unwelcome a sojourner, to point me out the way to the Mountain Road opposite Stony Creek. (JOHN *is silent*) Will you put me on the way to that road?
JOHN. And why do you want that road?
THE STRANGER (*evenly*). Because it is the road that I must travel. Will you put me on it?
JOHN (*reluctantly*). Aye, I will.
THE STRANGER (*goes to the window*). Then point it out to me now.
JOHN (*gets up with terrible deliberation and points to the right, the same direction from which his guest has come*). There's your road — through that wood and turn sharp. That is the way.
THE STRANGER. Not to the border.
JOHN (*loudly*). No, but to Mr. McIntyre, the Magistrate! That's the road you're taking and I mean to see that you do.
THE STRANGER. A curious idea, my friend. And why must I go to the magistrate?
JOHN (*angrily*). Because you're a low, sneaking, horse-thief — because you're one of those rascals who have the habit of borrowing honest men's beasts without their leave. Horses have been stolen all over this country and I'm doing my beholden duty by carrying the likes of you to the nearest magistrate — and I mean to do it.
THE STRANGER (*relieved*). Oh, is that all, then?
JOHN. Aye, and 'tis enough to prison you! Mr. McIntyre will see to that.
THE STRANGER. McIntyre? A new magistrate, is he? I've never

heard his name before. (*Slowly*) Would he be a crony of Mr. Allan MacNab of Hamilton?

JOHN. I don't know who he is, but to me he is the law of the land and to him you go. I'm going out now to give your beast a sheaf of oats and some water. Be you ready to leave when I come back. (*He goes, wrapping a scarf about his throat. The* STRANGER *is quiet until* JOHN *goes out. Then he runs over to the corner, unloads the musket and puts the balls in his pocket. He then goes over to his coat, takes out the pistol, sees that it is loaded and stands with his face set, the pistol cocked, and aimed at the door.*)

THE STRANGER. It's the only way. If I tell him the truth he'll turn me over in a minute.

(JOHN *is heard returning — he comes in.*)

JOHN. Now, we'll be gone —

THE STRANGER. Stand your ground, Mr. Waters, and keep your distance — or I shoot you where you stand.

JOHN. You —

THE STRANGER. Or I shoot you where you stand.

JOHN. You wouldn't shoot an unarmed man —

THE STRANGER. You leave me no choice, Mr. Waters — you have come between me and my liberty. To regain my liberty I must do a thing I am sorry for.

JOHN (*his bluster gone*). You mean you'd shoot me down —

THE STRANGER. Will you give me your word of honour neither to interfere with my departure nor to aid in my pursuit?

JOHN. I will not — shoot away — and never mind my children. (*Micky runs out, over to his father, terrified.*)

MICKY. Oh, mister, don't! Don't shoot my father!

THE STRANGER. If I lower this pistol for the sake of your children, will you give me five minute's talk with you? (JOHN *nods — the* STRANGER *lowers the pistol.*) Then, why do you think I am a horse-thief?

JOHN. Because you rode here in great haste, late on a December Saturday night when all honest men are asleep; this is no

The Patriot

public road; you are a lost thief flying from justice; your clothes are torn and ragged, your face scratched and your horse all in a foam. You refuse to say who you are or where you come from. You pay two dollars for the shelter of my humble roof, you're in no hurry to leave and you're riding one of the finest horses in Canada, making for the frontier by lonely roads.

THE STRANGER. I see. But in your house have I done any of the things you would expect a thief to do, Mr. Waters?

JOHN. Your manner is good, but why do you hide your name and your business? If all is right with you, why do you fear a visit to the magistrate's house?

THE STRANGER. I cannot tell you the reasons for all these things, Mr. Waters, but I am an honest man — and no horse-thief as you think. My beast belongs to a great friend of mine.

JOHN (*laughs*). Aye. What's his name?

THE STRANGER. Promise that you will never reveal it.

JOHN (*a little amazed*). I promise you that.

THE STRANGER. The horse belongs to my friend, Mr. Jacob Rymal of Ancaster. Now stand aside.

JOHN. I will not, so help me! I will let no thief pass my door. (*The* STRANGER *raises his pistol again.* JOHN *steps back.*)

THE STRANGER. I am no thief! More things I would ask you and answer quickly. What is your religion?

JOHN. I'm an Irish Orangeman but I'm not very proud of all this tyranny of my church that you spoke of.

THE STRANGER. And what do you think of the Rebellion?

JOHN. A lawless business — there's much cause for it, but it should not have begun.

THE STRANGER. Do you support the Compact and Strachan? (JOHN *hesitates.*) Tell me honestly.

JOHN. I do not. They caused this rebellion and set lawless men like you on the road.

THE STRANGER. Did you ever hear of Mackenzie?

JOHN. From all I hear from my next neighbour, Mr. McCabe, who lived beside him at Queenston some ten years back, he was an honest man and I admire his courage. But why do you ask me all these things?

THE STRANGER. Because I must. I am an old magistrate, but, at present, I am in a situation of some difficulty. If I can satisfy you as to who I am and why I am here, would you desire to gain the price of any man's blood?

JOHN. Sir, you insult me!

THE STRANGER. Bring me the Bible here, lad (MICKY *runs for it*). Swear me now a full and solemn oath, Mr. Waters, that you will not reveal my name. Hold up your right hand.

JOHN (*solemnly, convinced that his visitor is no ordinary person*). I swear that solemnly.

THE STRANGER. I am William Lyon Mackenzie.

JOHN (*thunderstruck*). You — you are Mackenzie?

MACKENZIE. Yes. There is my watch and my seals.

JOHN (*after a long pause; earnestly*). What can I do to help you, Mr. Mackenzie?

MACKENZIE. Keep silent for twenty-four hours.

JOHN. I will not breathe a word to anyone.

MACKENZIE. Show me the main road.

JOHN. I'll not only show you the road, I'll go with you and guide you to the frontier.

MACKENZIE (*shakes his head*). You cannot, my friend. By doing that you would endanger those dependent on you. Show me the road.

JOHN. (*at the door*). Through yon wood and the opposite way to where I said before. You'll not let me come with you?

MACKENZIE (*pulls on his rough coat*). No, I cannot. Good-bye, my friend. Commend me to Mrs. Waters. Good-bye, lad. Some day we'll have that ride. (*He kisses* MICKY).

JOHN. Forgive me all I said, sir.

MACKENZIE. Gladly, my friend. Good-bye. (*He shakes* JOHN'S *hand.* JOHN *takes his in both.* MACKENZIE *goes out. A moment later a clatter of horses' hooves, a shout of farewell and he is bound for the border.*)

Off Rivière du Loup

JOHN *(calling after him).* God speed you, Mr. Mackenzie!
MICKY *(rapt).* Da, who is he?
JOHN. Remember him, lad — a great man and a patriot.

— Curtain —

OFF RIVIERE DU LOUP

DUNCAN CAMPBELL SCOTT

O ship incoming from the sea
   With all your cloudy tower of sail,
Dashing the water to the lee,
   And leaning grandly to the gale;

The sunset pageant in the west
   Has filled your canvas curves with rose,
And jewelled every toppling crest
   That crashes into silver snows!

You know the joy of coming home,
   After long leagues to France or Spain;
You feel the clear Canadian foam
   And the gulf water heave again.

Between these sombre purple hills,
   That cool the sunset's molten bars,
You will go on as the wind wills
   Beneath the river's roof of stars.

You will toss onward toward the lights
   That spangle over the lonely pier,
By hamlets glimmering on the heights,
   By level islands black and clear.

You will go on beyond the tide,
   Through brimming plains of olive sedge,

Through paler shallows, light and wide,
  The rapids piled along the ledge.

At evening off some reedy bay
  You will swing slowly on your chain,
And catch the scent of dewy hay
  Soft blowing from the pleasant plain.

THE GREAT DAYS OF CANADIAN SAIL

F. C. BIEHL

I

Off Tierra del Fuego a hundred years ago! Here the seas have an ill repute as the world's worst, and they are living up to it. The gale has been screaming north from Antarctica with nothing to impede it. It has raised bottle-green mountains of water. In the distance three bare masts seem to walk alone along the crests. Only their maintopsails and jibs are set. Then you see the long lean black hull, the overhanging prow slicing the waves, the sleek copper belly heeled over to windward, the lee deck drowned under green water. Captain and two men are all three muscling the rebellious wheel. The gale slackens off. The lee rail swims awash.

Straightway the master leaves the helm. "All hands make sail!"

"Up and at 'em, boys," roars the mate.

The starboard watch swarm up the rigging and see-saw out on the spars, nothing between their heels and boiling water but a wildly swaying footrope, one hand to hang their life upon, the other hand to fight the crackling canvas. The off watch, wet and frozen under their oilskins, desert what shelter the lee of the deckhouse affords. They haul the halliards and set the braces. Sail after sail wings out over the wet decks.

Soon, with almost an acre of taut canvas trying to pull the masts out of her, the Bluenose clipper is high-tailing it once more

The Great Days of Canadian Sail

for Halifax. The skipper has his heart on another record voyage; the Bluenose crew sing as they reef and trim:

> "For she's the girl to go
> In the passage home in ninety days
> From Cal-i-for-ni-o!"

Those were the great days of Canadian sail, when all the Seven Seas knew the qualities of Maritime men and Maritime ships. Those were the days of wooden ships and iron men, the days that moved a poet to ask, long after the white sea-wings had fled forever:

> "Where are the ships I used to know,
>   That came to port on the Fundy tide
> Half a century ago,
>   In beauty and in stately pride?"

II

In the building of ships Canada got off to a slow start. Samuel de Champlain, the Father of New France, was a naval captain and an expert navigator. But throughout the French régime shipbuilding stayed stagnant. Perhaps it was because the two chief cargoes, fur and fish, required little shipping space; perhaps it was the irritating series of regulations from Paris, like that which required all ships to carry labourers for the colony. Anyway, New France produced little shipping. This may have helped its conquest by the British, for the battle of the Plains of Abraham was really only a result of the naval action which had brought up the British fleet to the very walls of Quebec.

After the conquest it was the British navy which set Canada on its feet as a ship-building country. When Napoleon threatened to shut off most of Europe, Britain turned to Canada for the white pine for its masts and spars. Lumber needed more ships to move it than did fish and fur. Moreover, England's Navigation Acts required all cargo between British ports at home and overseas to be carried in British craft. This gave the ports of the Maritimes and Quebec, with their richly timbered back country, their chance to build and operate ships. By the early 1800's Canadian vessels began to furrow the oceans of the world.

At first it was lack of money that held back Canadian shipbuilders. Even with lumber at one's back door, ships are expensive things to build, and builders had to pay terribly high rates of interest for the money they borrowed. So, if the builders were to escape bankruptcy, the completed vessel had to be sold fast. The result was that, in the years before 1840, Bluenose ships, especially those built at Pictou and Prince Edward Island, had the reputation of being pretty hastily thrown together.

III

They were soon to live this reputation down, for from 1850 to 1875 Canada entered its golden age of building and operating sailing vessels. Our little country of those days rose to become the fourth maritime nation of the world. More than half of the folk of Quebec City depended for their living on ship-building. In one great year, 1864, New Brunswick launched almost 150 ships, and Nova Scotia twice as many. There are interesting reasons for this golden age of Canadian sail.

For one thing, instead of trying desperately to find a buyer for their ships, the men of the Nova Scotia ports began to join together, in a sort of co-operative, to finance the vessels themselves. After the craft was fitted out, men from the same village would frequently man her. The Bluenose was a handyman; he could do many things well. He logged the trees, sawed and adzed the timbers, designed and built the ship, and then worked it. The Fundy and Grand Banks' fisheries made him one of the world's best sailors, and the grudging soil of his coastal farm pushed him out towards the sea. On ship he could do anything. Yankee and British ships carried sail-makers and ships' carpenters; the Maritimer did not need them. The Bluenose could handle needle and chisel as well as he could handle rope and helm.

Frequently the Maritimer, off to 'Frisco or Madras or Cape Town or Valparaiso, would carry one large family party of fathers and sons, of brothers and cousins. Frequently, too, the captain's wife and children would come along — not even shipwreck and six-week voyages in open lifeboats daunted Maritime women.

To show the quality of these down-east sailormen, there is the story of the Moncton firm which built a wooden scow to be delivered in England — a great ugly, empty, helpless box. It would have to be towed across the Atlantic by tug. But ocean tows are fearfully dear, and the thin soil of our Atlantic provinces, like that of old Scotland, has bred economy in the bones of its sons. So a retired ship's captain came forward. Yes, he could save the towing charges, and make something on the cargo besides. Why not load the scow with lumber, for buoyancy, and give her a temporary schooner rig? Even the old salt's ocean-going cronies came to bid him a last farewell before his trip straight down to Davy Jones' locker. When next they heard of him, he had made Liverpool, with such dexterous navigating that the chips of the scow's building still lay along its bulwarks.

Besides the calibre of Bluenose manhood, another thing contributed to the rise of Canadian sail. That was the lumber which was then so easily available. It is strange that this very lumber at first gave trouble. It was tamarack, sometimes called hackmatack, a wood which is strong, straight, and buoyant, but is technically rated as a softwood. But the traditional wood for English ships was oak. Canadian oak rots quicker than English oak. At first, Lloyd's, the English ship insurance men, were prejudiced against Canadian softwood vessels. Therefore their insurance rates on Canadian vessels were high. Too much money is at stake on a ship and its cargo for anyone to risk going without insurance. So the insurance men had to be convinced by experience before they would give Canadian vessels their best rate — A1 — and even then for seven years, as compared with twelve years of A1 rating for oaken ships. Further help towards cheaper rates came in 1852, when Lloyd's sent an expert out to

Quebec. For a fee of twenty-five cents per ton, this expert would inspect a ship for strength during its construction, and then give it a cheaper rate for being built "under special survey". Till the tamarack was exhausted, New Brunswick ports along the Gulf and Northumberland Strait, where this wood grew best, used a large part of this lumber in ship-building. By 1860 there was "not enough tamarack left to build a scow", and ship-building tended to move to the Fundy shores, where the fogs were supposed to grow spruce tougher than anywhere else.

But it was really two things that happened in the United States that brought Canadian shipping into its own. One was the Civil War between North and South from 1861 to 1865. During these years one could see wicked, slinky-looking ships in Halifax Harbour — low-lying and mouse-coloured for invisibility; lean and streamlined for speed. These were the blockade-runners, built to run for their lives from the guns of the Northern naval vessels. If fish and lumber could slip down to Nassau in the Bahamas for transshipment to the South, then gold could slip back to build stone mansions in Halifax, and to help build more ships. This, of course, was temporary, and war's end brought a depression to Halifax.

Another effect of the Civil War was more lasting. Before that war the United States merchant fleet was pressing the British hard all over the world. But the South built sea-raiders, called privateers, whose sole purpose was to sink as many Northern merchant ships as possible. They succeeded so well that at the end of the war the United States had only sixty percent of the ships it had at the beginning. This gave Canadian ships their chance to invade such far-flung markets as the China tea trade, the East Indian spice trade, and, of course, the trade to the West Coast around the Horn.

The second United States event that gave a tremendous spurt to our sailing ships was one which happened in 1849. Gold was discovered in California, and the rush was on. One route for the fortune seekers was overland — across the deserts and the high

The Great Days of Canadian Sail

Sierras with their perils of ugly death by Apaché tomahawk, by thirst, or by frost and starvation in the passes. If a man had money, he chose an easier way — around the Horn by ship. Get-rich-quickers mobbed the east coast shipping offices, brandishing greenbacks and gold pieces, clamouring for passage to San Francisco. Passenger and freight rates went sky-high — a single egg from a hen carried to 'Frisco would sell for a dollar. Eager Yankee, British, Bluenose, and Quebec vessels fought their way around the Horn to share in this bonanza. There was more gold in shipping than there was in the mines.

IV

The immediate result of the California trade was to encourage mightily the building of ships in Canada, as it did all over the world. The second result was to effect great changes in the design of sailing vessels, changes from which arose the most beautiful ship the world has even seen — the clipper.

Before the days of the clipper, the best sailing time passage from New York to San Francisco was 150 days. The clippers whittled this down to 90 days. They could make five return trips to the more conventional ship's three — 67 percent more profit in the same time. The great emphasis in the clipper's design was on speed; before its time emphasis had been on safety and cargo-carrying capacity. After all, ships are really beasts of burden; they can earn only on what they haul. Typical vessels before the time of the clipper have been described as "short, round, and dirty, resembling so many black tubs". In 1845 someone in Baltimore got the idea that more round trips in faster vessels would mean more pay. So they designed the clipper with her long and narrow proportions, her sharp curved prow, her beautifully streamlined hull, and her huge spread of canvas to power her through the waves.

The clippers were beautiful vessels, beautifully kept. Above their lean decks their masts towered to the height of a twenty-storey building. Their sails were custom-tailored to stay taut, so as to squeeze more power from the wind than did the old bellying ones. When they were not needed to work ship, the crews were busied with paint brush retouching the black hull or the white deckhouses, or with a "bear" scouring the immaculate deck with fine white sand, or with polishing rag on the ship's brass — rails and riding lights and binnacles.

Built as they were for speed, they were uncomfortable ships for passengers, in spite of the spruce cabins. Often the decks were wet with waves during the whole voyage. Instead of lying to for a gale, they would plunge through it. The captains had reputations for record voyages to build or maintain. Such masters rode their ships and their crews without mercy, and their bucko mates gave a rough time to slackers. No doubt names of some masters which have come down to us — Bully Bob, Devil Summers, Black Taylor, and Hell-Fire Slocum — were well-earned. Bluenose masters and mates had the reputation of being as hard as any — iron men, indeed, to drive these quivering wooden thoroughbreds. "Sea-lawyers", those contentious sailors who quoted ship's law to avoid work, got short shrift from these Nova Scotians. When, however, you hear some of the more lurid tales of beatings and floggings, you must remember two things. First, Bluenose vessels themselves, as you already know, were manned by Bluenose crews — good men all, often interrelated and from the same village, and all with a common stake in the ship's prosperous voyage. It isn't likely that steel-fisted discipline was either needed or tolerated on such ships. On the other hand, Bluenose masters and mates were much sought after on both Yankee and British ships. Occasionally such ships carried as crew the scum of the earth. Voyages often were months long, and in case of mutiny there were no radios to summon aid. Half a dozen officers had to discipline as many as 150 crew — for the extended rigging of the clipper demanded a great many hands for its working. The officers had to command respect or quit.

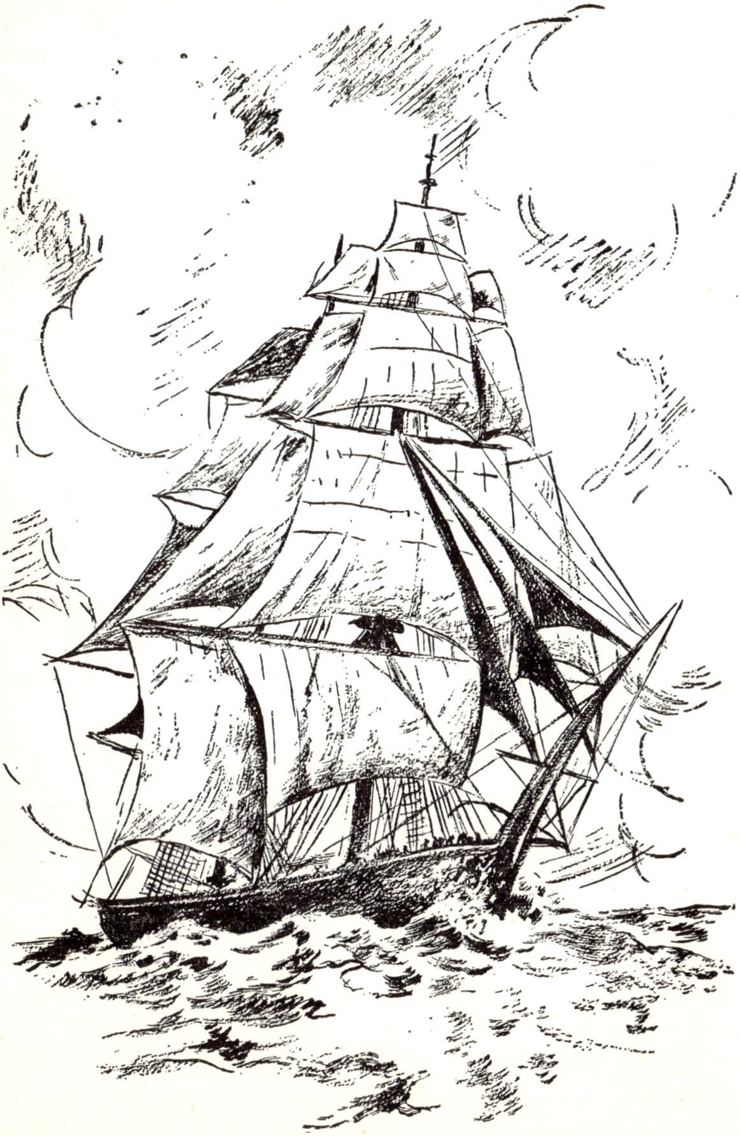

V

The greatest of all the builders of clippers was a Nova Scotian, Donald McKay, born in Shelbourne. When he was barely thirty-three, McKay already had his own shipyard in Boston. Like other creative geniuses, McKay was never satisfied with his finished product. "With all my care," he said once, "I never yet built a ship that came up to my own ideal! I saw something in each ship which I desired to improve." First of his famous clippers was the *Flying Cloud,* who on her maiden voyage from New York to 'Frisco made a record of 89 days. McKay was not content; he wanted something faster and larger than the *Flying Cloud's* 1500 tons. To make a wooden ship larger than that poses many serious engineering difficulties, and no one believed that McKay could do it. No one would advance him the money. "Then I'll build her myself and manage her myself," he said. Within a year he had launched the *Sovereign of the Seas,* of 2421 tons, a ship which could fly over an acre of canvas at one time. With every cent he owned invested in her, and with his own brother as master, McKay's *Sovereign* left New York for 'Frisco in August — the worst time in the year to tackle the worst seas in the world. Off the Horn her rigging tumbled down, but Captain McKay unsnarled and rerigged her in 48 hours, to drive on to 'Frisco for a record winter passage of 105 days. Still unsatisfied, McKay built the *Great Republic,* a ship of three times the tonnage of the *Flying Cloud.* When they were working at her peak, the *Great Republic's* crew see-sawed at the height of a twenty-five storey skyscraper above the deck below. In his latter years, McKay built four lovely clippers for Britain for the Australia trade. One of these, the *Lightning,* made a one-day run of 436 miles — a record which even to-day can be beaten only by the best of the Atlantic liners.

Another Bluenose builder was an artist in ships. He was William Lawrence of Maitland, Nova Scotia. Like McKay, he was driven by the ideal of a larger and faster clipper than had yet been built. Unlike McKay, he stayed at home to build her in his native port. His careful drawings called for a vessel 244 feet long, 48 feet wide, and of 2858 tons. She was to be the largest ever built in Nova Scotia. Other Nova Scotians felt she was too large ever to be launched. He called her the *William D. Lawrence;* they called her "Lawrence's Folly". So a crowd of 4,000 swarmed in to watch her launching. If they had come to witness a failure, they were disappointed; for "she went off like a rowboat". However, two enterprising gentlemen from Truro were certainly disappointed in her launching, for although they had come to watch it, and at the same time to turn an honest penny, they never saw it at all. William Lawrence, who never neglected a detail, had spied them beforehand guarding a barrel of whiskey which they intended to sell to the crowd. He himself showed them the road back to Truro, and off they trudged, trundling their barrel before them in a wheelbarrow.

Lawrence carried on the Bluenose tradition of manning his ship with folk from his own port. He, too, went along for a two-and-a-half-year's voyage around the world: to Liverpool with timber, to Aden with coal, to Callao in ballast, to Havre with guano, and home. His fabulous clipper had accumulated a fabulous host of debts in its building. But Lawrence returned with a fortune in freight charges which his namesake had earned him. It is chronicled that he went around the Halifax waterfront from one ship-fitter's shop to another, with a red bandana handkerchief bulging with golden guineas to pay off his creditors.

VI

Other Canadian ports also turned out the streamlined clippers: Yarmouth, Digby, Liverpool, Lunenberg, Halifax, and Pictou in Nova Scotia; Saint John and Moncton in New Brunswick, as well as the Northumberland Strait and Gulf of St. Lawrence ports; in Quebec City, Pierre Brunelle's famous *Brunelle*, which made a record of fourteen knots, and William Power's *Shooting Star* and *Alfred the Great*.

Let us look at Quebec City in the early summer of 1888, just at the close of the great period of sail. Vessels are lined two-deep along both sides of the river; 300 of them make a forest of masts and spars. Up river lie the one-acre rafts which have floated down from Montreal, where they were made up of logs run down the Ottawa. Tugs scurry like water-bugs across the open water, towing ships up from below the Island of Orleans. Most of the ships are black-hulled three-masted barques, hurrying to make their two return voyages with logs for Bristol before ice locks the river once again. In the crooked narrow streets of Lower Town lumberjacks from the Ottawa valley jostle tars from the Seven Seas. In the taverns crimps ply their nasty trade — they dope drunken sailors and shanghai them to captains who are about to sail short-handed.

Along the harbour the Canadian lumberjacks are working. Logs have been battered by their long ride down from the headwaters of the Ottawa. With one stroke of their broad-axes the jacks trim off a clean quarter inch from log butts, so that they will look fresh for their voyage. Other hob-nailed jacks ride logs out to the ships where they are being loaded. Winter in the forest, spring running logs and rafting, summer in Quebec harbour trimming and loading — this is the life of the jack. With him wherever he goes he takes his work songs — *A la claire fontaine; Oh, Bytown c'est une jolie place,* or *Laissez passer les Raf'man!* — from which he gets his name of *l'homme des chantiers.*

Loading is through the sawn-open bows of the wooden ships. It takes three weeks to load a ship this way, but tradition says that this is the only way to do it; logs require wooden ships. Then, in the year of 1888, a skeptic comes along. He takes an iron steamship, and he loads her from the side with a donkey engine — and does it in one week instead of three. He does not know it, but he has dealt a death-blow to Quebec's timber shipping. Next year the iron steamers will make the passage clear up to Montreal to load logs; steam can penetrate up river

The Great Days of Canadian Sail

channels where sail is powerless. Within three years rafts and wooden sailing ships have deserted Quebec.

VII

This happened at Quebec, and happened suddenly and dramatically. All over Canada's ports the same thing happened more slowly but quite as inevitably. Steam killed sail. And the iron ship did what gales and hurricanes could never do — chased the wooden ship right off the seas.

In 1836, *Rainbow* was launched in England. She was the first ship made of iron. Seamen were dubious. But in 1846 the iron ship *Great Britain* was stranded off the coast of Ireland for eleven months, and she did not break up. Lloyd's were convinced, and they gave iron a preferred rate. As for ship-owners, they came to realize that iron was cheaper in the long run because vessels built of it lasted so much longer. Later, during the American Civil War, two iron ships shot it out, without either being able to sink the other. Henceforth the trend was to iron for ships, in war as well as in peace. Before you can build iron ships, you must invest huge amounts of money in blast furnaces, in rolling mills, and in foundries to shape the metal. There was just not that much money in Lower Canada and the Maritimes. So gradually the Maritime shipyards grew still.

But steam did even more than iron to bring down the flying clouds of sail. It was many years after the first steam vessel before steam could make time across the Atlantic as fast as the trim sail packet ships. Nevertheless, steam was dependable; it did not have to wait upon the weather. And steam made possible that navigation of inland waters which was so necessary to Canada even after the days of the railroads. For only ships can move bulk cargoes economically.

Canada took a hand in killing its own wooden sailing ships. In 1831 a Scots engineer, only 21 years old, built a steam vessel which made two world records. His name was James Goudie. His steamer was the *Royal William,* and she was built at Quebec, close under those cliffs that edge the plain where General Wolfe fell in battle. Other sailing ships with auxiliary steam power had crossed the Atlantic before, but the *Royal William* was the world's first ship to cross under steam all the way. She did this in spite of a gale off the Grand Banks which disabled one of her two engines. She had two paddle-wheel boxes let right into her two sides, as compared with the auxiliary steamers, which had paddle boxes which could be lowered or raised outside the vessel. Each of the seven passengers on the *Royal William's* stormy voyage paid a fare of £20, "not including wines". On that trip it is doubtful whether they ate their £20 worth. The *Royal William* made a second record. Sold in her later years to the Spanish navy, she became the first steam vessel ever to fire shots in battle.

The *Royal William* ran for some years between Quebec and Halifax. When she lay in port in Halifax, a shrewd gentleman used to look her over and question her sailors. His name was Samuel Cunard, and he had made money whaling. Now he was interested in starting a line of steamships across the Atlantic. He did this, and a famous fleet of liners still bears his name. His steamships were destined to take away the Atlantic passenger trade from clippers like the *Lightning*.

And so the great days of the wooden sailing ships came to an end. In the beginning, white pine and tamarack and spruce had grown close to the estuaries. A race of craftsmen had arisen who built the ships. Favourable turns in world history had brought forth the crowning glory of the clipper, "the most beautiful thing that man has ever made". For a while the clippers had "walked the sea like living things". But progress has brought an end to other things of beauty, which had to give place to successors less lovely, but more useful. So it came to pass that the old clippers ended their lives as mastless hulks, hauling gravel and coal and ashes in dingy harbours, while rusty tramp steamers took their places on the Seven Seas.

THE FLOWER-FED BUFFALOES

VACHEL LINDSAY

The flower-fed buffaloes of the spring
In the days of long ago,
Ranged where the locomotives sing
And the prairie flowers lie low: —
The tossing, blooming, perfumed grass
Is swept away by the wheat;
Wheels and wheels and wheels spin by
In the spring that still is sweet.
But the flower-fed buffaloes of the spring
Left us, long ago.
They gore no more, they bellow no more,
They trundle around the hills no more: —
With the Blackfeet, lying low,
With the Pawnees, lying low,
Lying low.

HUNTING TRAIL OF THE GREAT SPIRIT

ELSIE PARK GOWAN

A Radio Play

MUSIC — *prairie theme — softly behind*:

NARRATOR. When the grass bends on the prairie, when the rivers gleam in the sunlight, when the wind blows from the mountains, we listen to John. . . .

MUSIC — *up briefly and fade behind*:

JOHN. I am John McDougall, who did his work on these prairies. But how I came here and why I chose this work, is a story that begins in a log cabin on the western frontier of a hundred years ago. My father was first trapper, settler, trader, sailor, and local preacher at Owen Sound, on Georgian Bay, where I was born. Indian children were my school-fellows. When I was sixteen I went to work in a store at Orillia for my board and five dollars a month, saving my money to go to college next year. Indians from Muskoka traded at that store. One morning as I was taking down the shutters, the storekeeper across the street called out —

HARRIS. Well, there'll be one fewer Injun in town to-day, Johnny!

JOHN. Why, Mr. Harris?

HARRIS. I hear they found somebody froze to death out on the ice in the bay. Bet you a barrel of molasses it's Old Tom Bigwind.

JOHN (*dismayed*). Oh!

HARRIS. Drunk as a lord last night and cold sober this morning, eh?

JOHN (*stern*). Did you sell Tom that whisky, Mr. Harris?

HARRIS (*laughs*). Listen to the preacher's son! Sure I sold him the whisky. (*Ugly*) That's my business.

JOHN. I don't think it's right. Tom's a good man, when he's himself —

HARRIS (*nasty*). Ach, there's no good Injun but a dead Injun. Quicker they're all under the ground the better for the country. (*Smooth*) Oh, good morning, ma'am —

NEIGHBOUR. Mr. Harris, you're wanted at the town hall. They've taken the body there.

HARRIS. Old Tom Bigwind? That old rascal owed me money.

NEIGHBOUR. The drunk man frozen on the lake wasn't Tom, Mr. Harris. He was your son George.

HARRIS (*stunned*). My son . . . my son . . . !

NEIGHBOUR. John, will you come and help me to tell the young man's wife?

HARRIS (*broken*). George . . . my boy . . . (*fading*) my own boy!

JOHN. It began in my mind that winter morning — a hatred of the white man's greed and cruelty to the red. I remembered it two years later. One evening my father came to me with a paper in his hand . . .

GEORGE. Well, John. Marching orders!

JOHN. Orders?

GEORGE. The church conference is sending me to Norway House — at the north end of Lake Winnipeg. Your mother is coming, and the children.

JOHN (*slowly*). I see.

GEORGE. You did well at college last year, John.

JOHN (*eagerly*). It opened the world for me, Father. I want to go back.

GEORGE. I need you, my son.

JOHN. I'm not a preacher.

GEORGE. But you spoke Ojibway before you spoke English. You could teach school for the boys up there, when we're not fishing, hauling logs, running a dog team.

JOHN (*slowly*). How do you get to Norway House?

GEORGE. Well, look at the map. By steamer across the lakes to Milwaukee, overland to the Mississippi, steamboat to St. Paul, stage coach to the Red River, and north on that water way.

JOHN. Plenty of people a lot closer than that need Christianity.

GEORGE (*quickly*). Oh, yes, the battle with evil is everywhere. I choose to fight where I can do the most good. If we don't work for the Indians, John, we leave them to the mercy of selfish, grasping —

JOHN. I know. I saw at Orillia. I'll go with you, Father.

GEORGE (*smiles*). God bless you, John. It's west for both of us then. West, and north, and west . . .

MUSIC — *prairie theme: fade out with:*

JOHN. From that night, the trail was always west. We were two years at Norway House, and in the summer of '62, Father decided to visit the prairies. For the first time I saw the pagan Indians of the plains, hunters and warriors, in buffalo robes, with painted faces and long braids of hair. Some of them wore scalp locks which not many moons before had grown on an enemy's head. In the camp of Maskapetoon, Father spoke to them . . .

GEORGE (*voices fade in*) ... have come to tell you of God's wish that the tribes live together in peace. For one day the buffalo will be gone, and men will grow their food in the earth.

CROWD — *incredulous murmur.*

GEORGE. If God spares my life, after the next snow I will build a lodge near the river, two days travel from Edmonton House. There I will live as one of you, in this country which the Great Spirit has given his children.

MASKAPETOON. My people, the Great Spirit has sent these praying men to teach us His will.

ANTELOPE. Maskapetoon talks like a moulting duck! We do not need these white praying men.

MASKAPETOON. Be silent, Running Antelope.

ANTELOPE. We listen to these strangers only with our ears. Our hearts do not listen.

MASKAPETOON. Perhaps Running Antelope is angry because John ran faster than he in the race this morning.

CROWD — *amused murmur.*

MASKAPETOON. All that my friend has said will come to pass.

ANTELOPE. We do not know that. The white men are few. We can kill them and keep our country as it is.

JOHN. May I speak?

MASKAPETOON. Yes, my grandson.

JOHN. Look, my brothers, at this bunch of grass I hold in my hand. The blades are few and weak. They are the traders and missionaries in this country now. But the white men who will come are more numerous than the grass on the prairie our feet touched this morning. No one can stop the grass from growing nor stop the white man from coming.

MASKAPETOON. Listen to John, my sons. Although he is only a child in years, he is a man in experience. Now go to your tents. Let what my friend has said sink into your hearts.

CROWD — *murmur as they break up.*

MASKAPETOON. You spoke well, John. My young men listen.

Hunting Trail of the Great Spirit

JOHN (*gravely*). I am glad. (*Eager*) Father, could I stay on the prairie this winter?

GEORGE. Stay out here — alone?

JOHN. I'll break some land at the new mission, and put up hay for next spring. I won't be alone. Hardisty, the Hudson Bay fellow, asked me to Edmonton House for Christmas . . .

GEORGE (*with humour*). And what am I to say to your mother?

JOHN (*grins*). Tell her I've been challenged by Running Antelope. And I start training — *now!*

MUSIC — *vigorous, briefly, out with:*

JOHN. Next summer my mother and my little brothers and sisters came up the Saskatchewan in York boats, forty days from Norway House. First a lodge of buffalo skins, then a small log house — we built the mission at Victoria. Soon it became a place of refuge. The sick and the starving came to the door of the white medicine man. We had no food but buffalo meat, and the hunting was my job. War parties camped beside us, too. When the drums beat at night for savage war dances, sometimes I doubted if this people could ever be civilized. Then one day on my way to the buffalo hunt, Maskapetoon rode with me in the ox-cart . . .

SOUND — *heavy cart squealing: establish: hold behind:*

JOHN. A strange looking old Indian came riding towards us . . .

MASKAPETOON. John, I do not want to meet that man.

JOHN. Do you know him?

MASKAPETOON. His name is Black Fox. That man murdered my son.

JOHN (*alarmed*). Your son!

SOUND — *horse trotting: bring up behind:*

MASKAPETOON. Often I have longed to kill him. But I have never seen him until this day.

JOHN. He's riding straight up to us.

SOUND — *horse and wagon stop:*

BLACK FOX. I am glad to see you, young white man. Will you give me your hand.

JOHN. Yes, here is my hand.

BLACK FOX. Your friend turns away his face so that I cannot see who he is. Will he not take my hand?

MASKAPETOON (*slowly*). Look at me, Black Fox. I am Maskapetoon.

BLACK FOX (*terrified*). Maskapetoon . . .

MASKAPETOON. Do not fear me, Black Fox. From these good white men I have heard the teaching of the Great Spirit, who said, "Thou shalt not kill." I have learned the prayer, "Forgive us, as we forgive our enemies." I will take your hand.

BLACK FOX. Maskapetoon, your words put the day into my heart. Let there be peace between us.

MASKAPETOON. Let there be peace.

SOUND — *Horse and cart go on. Fade behind:*

JOHN. We rode on. I thought of those two brown hands clasped together, and I knew the word of God could change lives, could end the cruel bloodshed of generations, if men would listen. As the years passed, the time of leaves following the time of snows, I began more and more to help with my father's work. The path of the rest of my life lay clear before me. I was to live with the Indians in sorrow and joy, in feasting and fasting. We hunted and trapped, held foot races, horse races . . . anything for real sport, and for common brotherhood.

MUSIC — *Up strong: then down for:*

ANNOUNCER. John had chosen his path, the path that for the rest of his seventy-five years he was to follow. The path led him through joys and sorrows, through good hunting and famine, through disease and massacre and rebellion. On it he was to meet whisky-runners and redcoats, voyageurs and fur factors and railway-builders. But John was never to falter along the way.

MUSIC — *Up strong, then down for:*

ANNOUNCER. While the grass bends on the prairie, while the winds blow from the mountains, we remember the name of John McDougall, pathfinder and missionary, who by his life

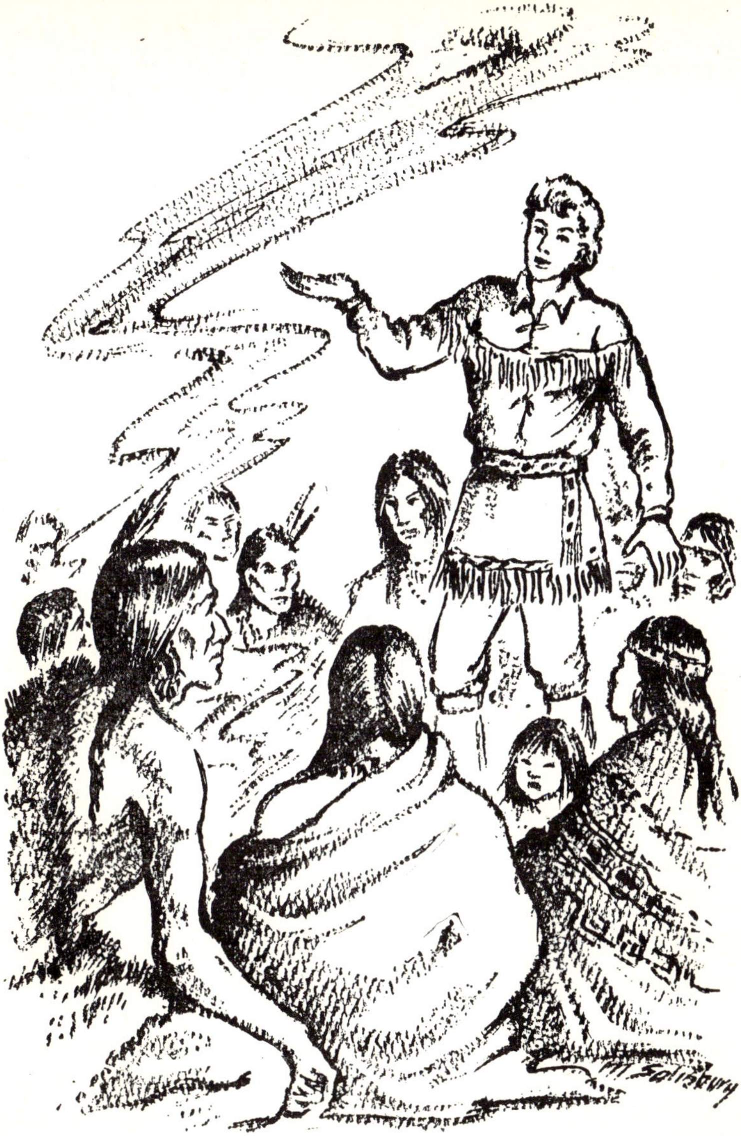

and by his character prepared the way for the settlement of the West. Through the long years, while railways came and cities grew up, John worked for his vision of Canada, and preached the brotherhood of mankind. When he died, six tall chiefs, proud and silent as kings, carried on his last journey "the white man with an Indian heart."
MUSIC — *Up to finish.*

CANADIAN ACHIEVEMENT

HIS ROYAL HIGHNESS, THE DUKE OF EDINBURGH

Address delivered in Toronto, October 13, 1951

Before leaving England I made some enquiries about Commerce and Science in Canada. I was overwhelmed by the helpfulness of the High Commissioner's Office with every sort and kind of information. Reading the material I was struck by the insistence that Canada was a young country full of promise. Meaning no disrespect to the Canadian who wrote this, I would beg to differ.

To me youth means the absence of history or background, a catalogue of untapped resources, and in Culture and Science a reliance upon others for original thought. But coupled with this statement that Canada is a young country was a series of accounts of achievements in every branch of national life which would make many an older country feel proud.

Youth means inexperience, and lack of judgment, and an inability to look after one's own affairs. I do not see how these descriptions can be made to fit a nation that pushed a railway through the Rockies, developed the prairies, and exploited the vast natural resources of timber, oil, and water power, and is steadily pushing the last frontier northward. The Chalk River project alone implies a considerable scientific background which is certainly lacking in many long-established nations. Indeed one

Canadian Achievement

does not have to look very hard for the achievements of Canadian scientists. At the University of Toronto, Professors Banting and Best developed insulin, which means life to diabetics, and at McGill University new hope for those suffering from certain nervous diseases is offered at the Neurological Institute headed by Dr. Penfield.

But perhaps more important than the individual triumphs is the unique and very sensible organization of Science in Canada. From the National and Provincial Research Councils, through the associate Committees, a simple and effective pattern exists for getting problems to the right research worker, and the right answer back to the people who need it. It is also quite evident that the work of the research laboratories, whether they deal with metallurgy, wood-pulp, agricultural machinery, or forestry, is second to none in the world.

To my mind the most important evidence that Canada is no longer a young country, although, I hasten to add, still full of youthful energy, is the publication of the Royal Commission's Report on the National Development in the Arts, Letters, and Sciences. This report is a remarkable attempt to find out exactly what is present and what is lacking in the national culture. It does not try to hide the fact that there is a great deal which is missing, but the fact that this report was written at all implies that it will not be missing for long. It is this consciousness of individuality and determined independence which is the hallmark of a successful nation.

In the old days this independence could only have been won by armed force, but here it has been accomplished by something far stronger and more lasting. It has been accompanied by the living certainty in the minds and hearts of all Canadians that the way of life which you have evolved is full and satisfying and well suited to the conditions under which you live and work. Above all, this has been achieved alongside the parallel development and the powerful influence of the friendly giant at the South Door. It is easy enough to withstand the influence of an unfriendly neighbour, but in your case both countries developed with the same ideals and traditions. That you have maintained your own identity and have not been overwhelmed by kindness is a remarkable achievement.

For all this peace at home, the Armed Forces have built a tradition of courage and determination, not in the emotionally-charged atmosphere of the immediate defence of their homes, but in unselfish service far from home for the freedom of others. In the British Isles the Canadian Army will always be remembered for the security they gave when invasion threatened and the gallantry displayed in the fighting in Italy and North Europe. I can speak from personal experience as I was serving in a destroyer off the beaches at Sicily when the Canadian Division landed there in 1943.

Young men from every part of the Commonwealth, and indeed the world, will remember their period of training in Canada under the British Commonwealth Air Training Plan, which is a monument of what we can do when we get together. The people of Europe have not forgotten the part played by Canadian airmen in bringing them freedom from tyranny.

Naval warfare is seldom spectacular and convoy duty is especially dull, but I can assure you that anti-submarine warfare in the North Atlantic is not for beginners, but that was the cradle of the Royal Canadian Navy.

These martial traditions, the History and Culture, the Scientific and Commercial achievements, prove to me that this is a flourishing nation with a lot to look back on with pride, a present which compares very favourably with any other country, and a future which is a challenge to all that is best in the Canadian character.

SUN AND SHADOW

NICHOLAS NYE

WALTER DE LA MARE

Thistle and darnel and dock grew there,
    And a bush, in the corner, of may,
On the orchard wall I used to sprawl
    In the blazing heat of the day;
Half asleep and half awake,
    While the birds went twittering by,
And nobody there my lone to share
    But Nicholas Nye.

Nicholas Nye was lean and grey,
    Lame of a leg and old,
More than a score of donkey's years
    He had seen since he was foaled;
He munched the thistles, purple and spiked,
    Would sometimes stoop and sigh,
And turn to his head, as if he said,
    "Poor Nicholas Nye!"

Alone with his shadow he'd drowse in the meadow,
    Lazily swinging his tail,
At break of day he used to bray,—
    Not much too hearty and hale;
But wonderful gumption was under his skin,
    And a clear calm light in his eye,
And once in a while, he'd smile—
    Would Nicholas Nye.

Seem to be smiling at me, he would,
    From his bush in the corner, of may—
Bony and ownerless, widowed and worn,
    Knobble-kneed, lonely and grey;

And over the grass would seem to pass
　　'Neath the deep dark blue of the sky,
Something much better than words between me
　　And Nicholas Nye.

But dusk would come in the apple boughs,
　　The green of the glow-worm shine,
The birds in nests would crouch to rest,
　　And home I'd trudge to mine;
And there, in the moonlight, dark with dew,
　　Asking not wherefore nor why,
Would brood like a ghost, and as still as a post,
　　Old Nicholas Nye.

TINY TIM

MAZO DE LA ROCHE

He was quite unaccompanied and he was going out to America as a Christmas present to a young lady. He was nine months old but looked on himself as grown up. His legs were as straight as matches, his body as sensitive, as alive, as tense as a fiddle string, and he had a square muzzle, an hysterical tail, and a black spot over one eye. His pedigree was long as his days were short.

In England he had lived in the house with a young man and an old lady. He had been their darling and their pet. There was not a corner of that house, from attic to basement kitchen, where he was not welcome. The maids in the kitchen let him kiss them or even bite them if he chose. His kisses were swift, moist licks; his bites mumbling, gnawing, long-drawn-out worryings that left a good deal of slobber on the part bitten, but no pain.

Of course, that is not the way he bit boots or rubber balls, or the way he would have bitten cats if he could have caught them. His favourite dream was the way he would have bitten cats, if he could have caught them. He would wake from this dream gnashing his small teeth, twitching all over. With one electric movement he would spring to his feet and stare about him.

"Cats, is it?" the old lady would inquire, and she would hobble to the door and let him out into the garden. He would rage up and down it, screaming of his desire to catch a cat in it.

The old lady had been a most untidy old body. Three tidy maids and a tidy grown-up grandson could not keep the house from looking as though it had been stirred up with a spoon. It was an exquisitely happy home for Tiny Tim, because, no matter what he did in it, he could never do wrong.

So the first nine months of his life passed, and then the untidy old lady died. Tim missed her a good deal. She had made a delightful cushion to lie on when he was tired from play, and she had always been ready to hobble to the door to let him in or out.

But what he perhaps missed most was her untidiness. Now if he worried the corner of a rug, it was soon laid back in place. Old shoes, old bones, which he had loved to keep handy on the drawing-room rug, were taken quite away where he could not find them. There had always been at least four dishes of food and drink on the floor of the room where he and she sat. Every time he barked at the sugar basin she had given him a lump. He always had the jam spoon to lick. It was useless for her grandson to tell the old lady that Tim would die if she kept on like this. She knew better. She knew that it was she herself who was most likely to die.

So when she died and the young man was given a post in the East, he decided to send Tim as a Christmas present to a young lady in America. And Tim was to carry all the young man's love with him. Some day, it was hoped, those three would live together.

Tiny Tim

When Tim found himself in a small cage in a small room on board ship, he felt more curious than alarmed. His only companion was an immense Irish wolfhound whose name was Oona, and who was accompanied by a very grim and silent master. Oona utterly ignored Tim. When they were let out of their cages for exercise, he tried to make up to her at once.

She looked straight through him with a sombre gaze.

He brought his ball and his rubber bone to show her. He got directly in her way, looking up in her face with an ingratiating grin. But she turned her head away from ball and from bone, and when he stood in her path she simply stepped over him.

She was so large and he was so small. He was exquisitely clean and dainty. She was unkempt, strong-smelling. She had an immense attraction for him. He would sit gazing at her by the hour, nervous shivers running down his spine and through his legs.

It was a bad voyage. From the first day out they encountered fog, rough seas, then gales and rougher seas. Oona became more and more melancholy. She began by being very sick, and after that, she refused all food but a mouthful or two of dry biscuit.

No sort of weather affected Tim's stomach. He crunched his biscuit with his square little muzzle turned up to the face of Grierson, his keeper. He swept the dish clean of his soft meal in three gulps that almost lifted him off his feet.

Oona's master was as unfriendly as Oona herself. Twice daily he took her for a walk. They stalked out, stalked around the deck, and stalked back again without looking in the direction of any one else.

When Tim saw Oona's lead being snapped to her collar, he was wild with excitement, wild to go with her to the deck. He danced about on his toes and filled the air with his pleadings. But he might not have existed as far as Oona and her master were concerned.

But on the third morning something quite different happened.

A young man and a young lady, having nothing better to do, came to look at the dogs, and decided to take Tim for a walk on deck.

He bounced in an ecstasy of hope. Surely now he might find his own house, his own garden, his own old lady.

But he found none of them. The young couple, whose names were Jean and John, held him so closely on his lead that he became quite tired and ceased to strain. He walked sedately with wistful looks into the faces of all he met. Everyone was so kind to him. It became the thing for Jean and John to take him for frequent walks. Everyone knew him by name, and bits of cake and sweets constantly came his way.

Jean usually led him because he was so becoming to her, and she held his lead so short that he always felt as though he were about to choke. They often passed Oona and her master looking gloomier and more aloof as the days went on.

In this new world of Tim's there were only two dogs, himself and Oona, and Oona would not look at him, would not exchange sniff for sniff or lick for lick. The more he saw of John and Jean, the less he liked them. He grew thinner and thinner. At night he dug into the straw of his cage and tried to dig through the floor itself. He lay curled up in a little shivering heap. He longed to obliterate himself.

Then on his rocking horizon appeared a new old lady. She was even more solid, more impressive, more comfortable than his own old lady.

She came up the steps from the Tourist Class, hanging on firmly to the brass rail, and promenaded solidly around the deck leaning on her ebony stick and peering through windows and doors with an air of dignified curiosity.

One of the deck stewards came up to her apologetically.

"I'm very sorry, madame," he said, "but this deck is reserved for the Cabin passengers."

She stared at him.

"Can't I walk about and look at it?" she asked.

Tiny Tim   243

"I'm afraid not," he returned still more apologetically.

"Well, well, I'm sorry I have come where I shouldn't, but when one is on one's first sea voyage one likes to look about."

"Of course." The steward spoke deferentially. "It's quite natural, and I'm very sorry indeed—"

"It's your duty," she interrupted and turned back toward the stairs.

The steward assisted her down them and, returning, met John and Tim on the lead. They were waiting for Jean.

"Did you see that old lady?" asked the steward.

"Yes," answered John, without interest.

"Well, she's one of the Mount-Dyce-Mounts."

"One of the Mount-Dyce-Mounts!" echoed John unbelievingly.

"Yes, and it's her first trip. She's going out to see a daughter-in-law in British Columbia. Travelling alone. I hated terribly to turn her back off this deck. But I couldn't help it. She's a lovely old lady, she is indeed."

"And a Mount-Dyce-Mount!" exclaimed John, and forgetting all about Jean, he hurried down the steps, dragging Tim after him, and went up to where the old lady had settled herself in her chair.

John introduced himself with a charming air to old Mrs. Mount-Dyce-Mount, and begged her to let him know if he could be of the slightest service to her.

She thanked him kindly and was interested in Tim. She patted her lap and he sprang onto it. His nostrils quivered over the stuff of her dress. Then he looked long and earnestly into her face. He swiftly touched her cheek with his tongue. He gave a joyous bark. It seemed too good to be true. He had found another old lady!

He saw a good deal of her, though not half as much as he desired. John took him to the Tourist deck to call on her twice every day. If John went without him she asked at once for the little dog.

When John, knowing that Jean was waiting impatiently for

him to play tennis with her, dragged Tim away to the kennels, Tim dug his nails into the deck, made his small body rigid, and turned up his hazel eyes full of pleading and hate for John.

Once the old lady said, "Do let him stay!" And Tim curled up on her lap for an hour of supremest content. When John came to fetch him, Tim snapped at him, and when they were alone together, John hit him with the end of the lead.

There was a fog off Newfoundland. The ship lay motionless in the sullen, ice-cold water while all night long the warning whistle sounded. Tim lay curled up tightly, shivering through all his tender being. That day John and Jean had become engaged, and each lay awake planning the future. Old Mrs. Mount-Dyce-Mount lay awake, too, thinking of the past and dreading the long rail journey to British Columbia and wondering if her daughter-in-law really wanted her.

Toward morning the engines started, the rhythm of their pulsing ran through the ship. All the passengers who were awake gave sighs of relief and thought, "Thank goodness, we're off."

The ship moved through the sullen water very quietly, as though feeling her way. But an iceberg submerged in the depths collided with her in a shock so terrible that those who slept were soon awake, wild with fear. A heavy sea was rolling.

The attendant let Tim and Oona out of their cages. Already Tim had been startled by the sharp blasts on the whistle and the shriek of the siren. Oona was unmoved by the excitement about her, but when her master appeared she went at once to him with a slow wag of the tail and a sombre light in her eyes.

Tim capered over the deck, a new hope possessing him. Perhaps this strange world of the ship was about to disappear and he would find his way back to his own house and garden. He liked the peculiar listing of the deck which the humans found so terrifying. He dug in his little nails, cocked his ears, and investigated places where John and Jean had never permitted him to go.

Presently he saw them rushing frantically hand in hand, Jean's silk pyjamas fluttering in the icy wind. He flew after them, barking.

It was not one of those shipwrecks in which people behave with fortitude, though heroic deeds were afterwards recounted in the newspapers.

Perhaps there were too many on board like John and Jean, who fought their way hysterically to the best places, not giving a second thought to old Mrs. Mount-Dyce-Mount.

Tim loved the sight of these pyjamaed legs. He had always longed to bite them, and now he darted after them, nipping first one and then the other. Jean shrieked terribly.

"Oh, oh," she screamed, "he's gone mad!"

John screamed too as Tim's pointed teeth caught him.

Tim circled round and round them, growing more exhilarated with each nip. At last John was quick enough to give him a sharp kick, screaming again as he did so:

"Somebody kill this brute! He's bitten us!"

Women screamed in a new terror and a man unexpectedly whipped out an automatic from his pocket and fired at Tim. The boat listed still more. There was pandemonium aboard.

Tim had not liked the revolver shot at all. He skulked down a stairway and trotted, one ear pricked and the other lopping, along a deserted passage. Even he began to think the slant of the floor extraordinary.

He sat down and licked the spot where John had kicked him. He could feel a tender lump there. Then he humped himself and began a wrinkled-nosed search for fleas, of which Oona had given him quite a number. He scratched, and the thumping of his elbow on the floor sounded like an imperative knocking.

"Go away!" A harsh old voice came from within.

It was the voice of the old lady. Tim was galvanized by it into joyous activity. He tore at the door and it swung open.

Mrs. Mount-Dyce-Mount was revealed sunk on a seat beneath the closed porthole which showed nothing beyond but gray-green water. The luggage in the cabin had slid to one side. The toilet articles were on the floor.

Tim saw nothing of this. He saw only his dear old lady, and he leaped into her lap and began ecstatically to lick her face, whimpering with joy as he did so.

"Timmie, Timmie, oh, you naughty little boy!" she murmured, and for a moment she hugged him to her. Then she said, "But you should not have done this! You should not have done this!"

But Tim thought he should. He was immensely pleased with himself. He leaped from her lap and began to investigate the cabin. He became even more worked up, for he smelled Oona in it. Yes, there was the unmistakable smell of Oona. He leaped back into his old friend's lap and informed her with hysterical barkings that Oona had been there.

"But you should not have done it," she repeated. "Poor little Tim, you should not have done it. Perhaps if you go up on deck some one will save you. Go away, now! Naughty boy! Oh, dear, I wish you would go!"

Her voice broke and she began to cry.

Tim curled up in a tight ball and began to shiver from head to tail. But almost instantly he uncurled and stood tense on the slanting floor, listening. He heard Oona and her master coming. They were creeping cautiously along the passage, which was becoming more and more difficult to negotiate.

When Oona's master opened the door he gave a start of astonishment.

"Why — why — " he stammered. "I thought this was my cabin."

"I dare say it is," returned Mrs. Mount-Dyce-Mount. "I'm just staying in it for the time being."

"But, — don't you know we're going down?"

"Of course I do," she returned irritably. "That's why I said for the time being."

"But you can't stay here! You'll drown! Don't you realize that? Where is your life preserver?"

Tiny Tim

"I couldn't get it on. I'm not the right shape. I just couldn't get it on. Then everybody was jostling so, I got my ankle turned, and some young people almost knocked me over, and I was frightened and I came in here. But — this dear little dog — I wish you could save him!"

Oona's master took her by the arm and lifted her to her feet.

"You must come at once!" he said sternly.

The old lady clung to his shoulder and began to cry a little. He quickly opened a drawer and took out a packet he had come back for.

"Would you mind," he asked, "sending this to the address written on it — if you have the opportunity?"

"Certainly I shall," she answered, and put the packet into her hand bag.

Tim paid no heed to these proceedings. He was occupied by Oona's sudden condescension toward him. She who had never given him so much as a glance was now delicately sniffing him all over. Her strong tail was wagging approval of him. When she thrust her muzzle under his chest she lifted him clear off his feet. She uttered a low whine of pleasure in him.

As her master half carried Mrs. Mount-Dyce-Mount along the passage, the old lady asked:

"What about your dog?"

"I don't want to be saved without her," he returned. "I'm not even sure that I want to be saved with her."

The captain and his officers had been able to quiet the hysterical passengers. The second last of the lifeboats was about to be lowered into a sun-gilded sea. A dozen hands reached out to help Mrs. Mount-Dyce-Mount.

The vessel was sinking fast. There was not a moment to spare. Oona's master picked up Tim and dropped him into the old lady's lap.

He perched on her knees, alert in every nerve.

Still he could see John and Jean clinging together in a boat quite near, and he began to bark at them loudly, vindictively, with a kind of gulping snarl between each explosion. John called out:

"Mrs. Mount! Throw that dog out! He's mad! It's not safe for you to hold him!"

"Yes, he's quite mad!" cried Jean. "He'll bite you!"

Tiny Tim barked louder, and Mrs. Mount-Dyce-Mount held him close.

The last lifeboat was lowered. The captain, some sailors, a stoker, and Oona and her master were in it. He had refused to leave her, and they found room for her in the boat.

A sudden squall broke, and the ship, shaken as though by a great convulsion, rolled over and sank. A driving storm of sleet and snow blurred the vision.

Tim stood—tiny, shivering, indomitable—on Mrs. Mount-Dyce-Mount's lap. With his bright eyes he strove to pierce the blurring icy flakes. His instinct was directed toward Oona and all his eager senses sought to search her out.

When a bitter wave slashed across the lap where he was braced, he lifted a paw and stood shivering on three legs.

The squall passed like the wing of a bird of prey. The face of the sun was suddenly clear and it rose on the horizon ruddy and beautiful for Christmas morning. The ship had disappeared and two of the lifeboats had been swamped. The waves were romping with wreckage and with the bodies of those who clung to it.

Tim soon discovered John and Jean clinging together in the sea, more dead than alive. He showed his little teeth in a grin of rage at their nearness and gave out such a volley of barks as almost threw him overboard.

Then he saw Oona and his barking ceased. She was swimming round and round as though searching for something.

The SOS had been heard and another steamer was already coming to the rescue. The wind fell, the sun rose, and some one had the courage to call out, "Merry Christmas!"

John and Jean were the first to be picked up. The captain, the sailors, the stoker, all those who had been in the last lifeboat were saved — all but Oona and her master. And she might have been saved, but when they tried to reach her, she swam out of their way, her gaunt head raised, her sombre eyes searching the waves.

THE SONG OF THE SEA WIND

AUSTIN DOBSON

How it sings, sings, sings,
Blowing sharply from the sea-line,
With an edge of salt that stings;
How it laughs aloud, and passes,
As it cuts the close cliff-grasses:
How it sings again, and whistles
As it shakes the stout sea-thistles —
How it sings!

How it shrieks, shrieks, shrieks,
In the crannies of the headland,
In the gashes of the creeks;
How it shrieks once more, and catches
Up the yellow foam in patches;
How it hurls it out and over
To the corn-field and the clover —
How it shrieks!

How it roars, roars, roars,
In the iron under-caverns,
In the hollows of the shores;
How it roars anew, and thunders,
As the strong hull splits and sunders:
And the spent ship, tempest-driven,
On the reef lies rent and riven —
How it roars!

How it wails, wails, wails,
In the tangle of the wreckage,
In the flapping of the sails;
How it sobs away, subsiding,
Like a tired child after chiding;
And across the ground-swell rolling
You can hear the bell-buoy tolling —
How it wails.

THE DEATH OF THE HIRED MAN

ROBERT FROST

Mary sat musing on the lamp-flame at the table
Waiting for Warren. When she heard his step,
She ran on tip-toe down the darkened passage
To met him in the doorway with the news
And put him on his guard. "Silas is back."
She pushed him outward with her through the door
And shut it after her. "Be kind," she said.
She took the market things from Warren's arms
And set them on the porch, then drew him down
To sit beside her on the wooden steps.

"When was I ever anything but kind to him?
But I'll not have the fellow back," he said.
"I told him so last haying, didn't I?
'If he left then,' I said, 'that ended it.'
What good is he? Who else will harbour him
At his age for the little he can do?
What help he is there's no depending on,
Off he goes always when I need him most.
'He thinks he ought to earn a little pay,
Enough at least to buy tobacco with,

The Death of the Hired Man

So he won't have to beg and be beholden.'
'All right,' I say, 'I can't afford to pay
Any fixed wages, though I wish I could.'
'Someone else can.' 'Then someone else will have to.'
I shouldn't mind his bettering himself
If that was what it was. You can be certain,
When he begins like that, there's someone at him
Trying to coax him off with pocket-money,—
In haying time, when any help is scarce.
In winter he comes back to us. I'm done."

"Sh! not so loud: he'll hear you," Mary said.

"I want him to: he'll have to soon or late."

"He's worn out. He's asleep beside the stove.
When I came up from Rowe's I found him here.
Huddled against the barn-door fast asleep,
A miserable sight, and frightening, too—
You needn't smile—I didn't recognize him—
I wasn't looking for him—and he's changed.
Wait till you see."
                   "Where did you say he'd been?"

"He didn't say. I dragged him to the house,
And gave him tea and tried to make him smoke.
I tried to make him talk about his travels.
Nothing would do: he just kept nodding off."

"What did he say? Did he say anything?"

"But little."
              "Anything? Mary confess
He said he'd come to ditch the meadow for me."

"Warren!"

"But did he? I just want to know."

"Of course he did. What would you have him say?
Surely you wouldn't grudge the poor old man
Some humble way to save his self-respect.
He added, if you really care to know,
He meant to clear the upper pasture, too.
That sounds like something you have heard before?
Warren, I wish you could have heard the way
He jumbled everything. I stopped to look
Two or three times — he made me feel so queer —
To see if he was talking in his sleep,
He ran on Harold Wilson — you remember —
The boy you had in haying four years since.
He's finished school, and teaching in his college.
Silas declares you'll have to get him back.
He says they two will make a team for work:
Between them they will lay this farm as smooth!
The way he mixed that in with other things.
He thinks young Wilson a likely lad, though daft
On education — you know how they fought
All through July under the blazing sun,
Silas up on the cart to build the load,
Harold along beside to pitch it on."

"Yes, I took care to keep well out of earshot."

"Well, those days trouble Silas like a dream.
You wouldn't think they would. How some things linger!
Harold's young college boy's assurance piqued him.
After so many years he still keeps finding
Good arguments he sees he might have used.
I sympathize. I know just how it feels
To think of the right thing to say too late.

The Death of the Hired Man

Harold's associated in his mind with Latin.
He asked me what I thought of Harold's saying
He studied Latin, like the violin,
Because he liked it—that an argument!
He said he couldn't make the boy believe
He could find water with a hazel prong—
Which showed how much good school had ever done him.
He wanted to go over that. But most of all
He thinks if he could have another chance
To teach him how to build a load of hay—"

"I know, that's Silas' one accomplishment.
He bundles every forkful in its place,
And tags and numbers it for future reference,
So he can find and easily dislodge it
In the unloading. Silas does that well.
He takes it out in bunches like big birds' nests.
You never see him standing on the hay
He's trying to lift, straining to lift himself."

"He thinks if he could teach him that, he'd be
Some good perhaps to someone in the world.
He hates to see a boy the fool of books.
Poor Silas, so concerned for other folk.
And nothing to look backward to with pride,
And nothing to look forward to with hope,
So now and never any different."

Part of a moon was falling down the west,
Dragging the whole sky with it to the hills.
Its light poured softly in her lap. She saw
And spread her apron to it. She put out her hand
Among the harp-like morning-glory strings,
Taut with the dew from garden bed to eaves,
As if she played unheard the tenderness

That wrought on him beside her in the night.
"Warren," she said, "he has come home to die;
You needn't be afraid he'll leave you this time,"

"Home," he mocked gently.

"Yes, what else but home?
It all depends on what you mean by home.
Of course he's nothing to us, any more
Than was the hound that came a stranger to us
Out of the woods, worn out upon the trail."

"Home is the place where, when you have to go there,
They have to take you in."

"I should have called it
Something you somehow haven't to deserve."

Warren leaned out and took a step or two,
Picked up a little stick, and brought it back
And broke it in his hand and tossed it by.
"Silas has better claim on us you think
Than on his brother? Thirteen little miles,
As the road winds, would bring him to his door.
Silas has walked that far no doubt to-day.
Why didn't he go there? His brother's rich,
A somebody — director in the bank."

"He never told us that."

"We know it though."

"I think his brother ought to help, of course.
I'll see to that if there is need. He ought of right
To take him in, and might be willing to —

VALLEY OF THE DEVIL RIVER — *Maurice G. Cullen*
Reproduced by permission of the National Gallery, Ottawa.

MAURICE G. CULLEN, R.C.A.
(1866 - 1934)

Maurice G. Cullen, born in Newfoundland, in 1866, came as a child to Montreal, where he lived all his life except for the six years spent at art school in Paris. There he met Morrice, and they became friends. They often travelled together and painted together, but their ways were sure to part for Cullen had to consider popular taste to make a living. Fortunately, he painted with fidelity the Quebec scene; he loved to paint the streets of Montreal, the gusty drifting of snow, or vapour rising from the river; he painted the Laurentian hills and the glitter of the sun on winter snow. With Morrice he established the blue, pink, and mauve colours seen in the snow. He and Morrice, with Gagnon, Suzor-Coté, and A. H. Robinson portrayed for the Canadian people the beauty of the cultivated Quebec countryside.

Valley of the Devil River is in the National Gallery, Ottawa.

The Death of the Hired Man

He may be better than appearances.
But have some pity on Silas. Do you think
If he'd had any pride in claiming kin
Or anything he looked for from his brother,
He'd keep so still about him all this time?"

"I wonder what's between them."

"I can tell you.
Silas is what he is — we wouldn't mind him —
But just the kind that kinsfolk can't abide.
He never did a thing so very bad.
He don't know why he isn't quite as good
As anyone. He won't be made ashamed
To please his brother, worthless though he is."

"I can't think Si ever hurt anyone."

"No, but he hurt my heart the way he lay
And rolled his old head on that sharp-edged chair-back.
He wouldn't let me put him on the lounge.
You must go in and see what you can do.
I made the bed up for him there to-night.
You'll be surprised at him — how much he's broken.
His working days are done; I'm sure of it."

"I'd not be in a hurry to say that."

"I haven't been. Go look, see for yourself,
But, Warren, please remember how it is:
He's come to help you ditch the meadow.
He has a plan. You mustn't laugh at him.
He may not speak of it, and then he may.
I'll sit and see if that small sailing cloud
Will hit or miss the moon."

It hit the moon.
Then there were three there, making a dim row,
The moon, the little silver cloud, and she.
Warren returned — too soon, it seemed to her,
Slipped to her side, caught up her hand and waited.

"Warren," she questioned.
"Dead," was all he answered.

FOUR MEN AND A BOX

LESLIE GORDON BARNARD

They came from the primordial jungle, four gaunt specimens of the human race, walking as men might walk in their sleep, or before a taskmaster whose lash drives them on to the limit of endurance. Their beards were matted, their skin full of sores, and the leeches had sucked their blood day and night.

They hated each other with the hatred of men bound by a duty, a hatred that had increased with every torturing mile through the green-walled labyrinth of the jungle. They hated still more, as time went on, the thing they carried; but they bore it as if it were an ark of the covenant and their God was a jealous God.

"We got to get Markgraff's stuff through," they said. "He was a good guy. We promised him."

Of the reward at the journey's end they said nothing; but each man mumbled of it in his own mind, in his own way.

They had gone with Markgraff into this doubtful adventure because he paid them well in advance. Now he was dead and they were living. Death had struck him down — some swift tropical disease had ended this geologic madness of his.

They would have understood the whole thing better if his quest had been for gold. But Markgraff had said, smiling:

"There are substances which science has found to be more precious than gold." At the end they thought Markgraff had failed, that all he'd found in the jungle was Death. But it seemed otherwise; the box he gave them to take back was heavy. He'd made it himself, roughly hewn, and with the secrecy of the scientist, he'd packed and sealed it when he knew that he, himself, was doomed.

"It will take four of you to tote it — two at a time," Markgraff had told them.

"There are four of us," said Barry, the student.

"You'll have to spell each other," Markgraff directed. "I want every man to promise me that he'll stick with it until it's safely delivered. You'll find the address on top. What you have there, if you deliver it to my friend Professor MacDonald at the coast, is more precious than gold. You won't fail? I can assure you that you'll be rewarded."

They promised him, because he was a dying man and they respected him. His personality had held them together when, a score of times, with the jungle's vast monotony eating into them, they might have quarrelled fatally.

Then Markgraff had smiled at them, and died. He did it quietly, as he did all things — this elderly scientist, this man who had bound them to him by ties of intangible strength. They buried him in the heart of the jungle, baring their heads, while Barry, the student, spoke brief, remembered words of committal. Even as the clods fell, the jungle loomed larger, more menacing. Each man felt a shrinking of his own stature, a terrible aloneness, a doubt of his fellows, a suspicion that, with Markgraff gone, it would be every man for himself.

They were a curious assortment: Barry, the spectacled student; McCready, the big Irish cook; Johnson, the down-and-out, the bum Markgraff had enticed out of a water-front tavern to follow him; and Jim Sykes, the sailor, who talked a lot about home but never went there.

Sykes had the compass and map, which, when they stopped to rest, he would get out and study. He put a stubby finger on it and said, "There's where we've got to get to." It looked easy — on the map.

The jungle deepened about them. They missed Markgraff, who no longer could encourage them with an optimism that was usually justified, who could find in an almost impenetrable tangle some logic for going forward. At first they talked with each other, the sound of their voices important to them, only to discover that the weight they carried, toting this box of Markgraff's, discouraged any waste of breath. Then silence fell on them, and something worse than silence.

Longing for his water-front tavern as a parched soul in Inferno might yearn for water, Johnson began to find that sudden ways opened to him, on the right hand or the left, tempting him. McCready's face grew sullen and dark; he kept repeating, "I'm goin' my own way. I'm not travelling with this outfit any more.

I guess I've got the grit to make it." And he would cast a brooding, speculative eye on the map to which Sykes, the sailor, clung.

As for Sykes, he developed a horror of this jungle, this high-walled man-trap. He wanted the sea. He demanded horizons. He mumbled about it in his sleep, and by day cursed the upreaching forest that could so easily shut off the sky and deny the clean wind. He spoke of his home, and how for years he'd meant to get back to the missus and kids — and now never would.

Barry, the student, said little, but there was a girl of whom he was thinking. He'd lie sleepless, tormented by insects, haunted by a face that at times, like the faces of those dear to us, refused at this distance any clear definition. To think of her was to think of a campus, green with spring and russet with autumn; of a sports field, and classrooms, and a library; of dances and moonlit walks, and a sweet, tearing moment of good-bye.

Sometimes one or another of them would pray, would call out in a way that the insensitive might think was cursing: He had made this fierce jungle, these incredible trees, these exotic flowers, and on a scale so large they seemed to reduce man to a pigmy. When the mind failed to cope with Nature successfully it turned on its own kind.

There had been bickerings and quarrels even when Markgraff was with them, but his personality, and his cause — which was their cause — had muted the quarrels. Now, there was only Markgraff's box, growing heavier as their strength grew less. It was real when everything else had become a mental haze. It held their bodies when their minds rebelled. It chained them when they would have split apart. Turn and turn about — this routine held them; two men alone would long since have abandoned the precious thing.

They hated it as a prisoner hates his chains, but they carried it as they had promised Markgraff they would.

They watched each other, covertly, lest any come near the sacred thing except to lift and bear it another torturing mile.

Then came a day when suddenly — as by a miracle — the walls of the forest opened.

"Glory!" Sykes cried. "We made it." He took out the map, and, putting his cracked lips to it, he kissed it.

"Yes," Johnson breathed, his eyes queer, and no quarrel now on his lips. He even slapped McCready, the cook, on the back, and they laughed with strange hysterical laughter.

When they lifted their load again, it seemed lighter, but only for a while. They were weak now, because safety was in sight and their job nearly done. Eventually the four of them, staggering with exhaustion, bore Markgraff's box up a street, while natives and a few whites stared at them.

All they asked was to deliver it, and have done.

And yet, when they asked for a Professor MacDonald and found him to be a withered man in a greasy white suit, there was a triumph in them, for a moment rising above their personal emotions, the glory of a thing shared.

When they had rested, Professor MacDonald gave them food, and they told him of Markgraff, of his death, and of their promise to him.

It was Johnson who, running his tongue thirstily across his lips, spoke of the reward.

The old man spread his hands in a gesture of inadequacy. "I have nothing," he said, "not a thing to reward you with except my thanks. Markgraff was my friend. He was a clever man. He was more than clever, he was a good man. You have kept faith with what he asked. I can only thank you."

Derisively, Johnson stared at him. "In the box," he said hoarsely. "In the box."

"The box," repeated Sykes eagerly.

"Now you're talking," McCready said.

"Open it," they demanded. They put their joint strength to it, prying off layer after layer. McCready began to curse. "All that weight, all that everlasting carrying," he complained, and Johnson said, "Wood and more wood. What kind of joke is that?"

Four Men and a Box

But Sykes said, "Something is there. I heard it rattle. I heard it when we walked. Look, you're through to it." They all drew close, their minds leaping, remembering the substances which science had unearthed and harnessed, beyond money and beyond price; they stared at the old man when he took the loose bits of rock in his hands, and let them drop. "Worthless," he said, puzzled, trying to feel his way into Markgraff's mind.

"Worthless?" Sykes was unbelieving.

Then McCready, the cook, exploded. "I always thought that guy was nuts. Telling us what was in the box was worth more'n gold."

"No," Barry said quickly. "I remember his exact words. What he told us was: 'What you have there, if you deliver it to my friend Professor MacDonald at the coast, is more precious than gold.'"

"So what?" shouted McCready, angry disappointment in his eye.

"Yeah, so what?" echoed Jim Sykes, the sailor. "Maybe I couldn't do with some gold for the missus and kids, and myself!"

Johnson just ran his tongue thirstily along his dry lips.

Barry looked at them all: at McCready, the big Irish cook; at Sykes, the sailor, who might some day go home to his missus and kids; at Johnson, the water-front bum.

Then he thought of a campus green with spring, and a girl who waited; he thought of the jungle from which they had come—in which many a man, wandering alone, was now a heap of whitened bones; and he thought of the dogged resolution which had made four men fight through together to keep a promise, four men held together only by a common cause. This had been Markgraff's gift to them.

"He said we'd be rewarded," Johnson whined. "I heard him say it, myself. Now what do we get out of it?"

Barry turned on him, quickly. "Our lives," he said. "That's what we get, our lives—for what they're worth."

TO A BULL-DOG

J. C. SQUIRE

The following poem was written in memory of Sir John C. Squire's son William, a Captain (Acting Major) in the Royal Field Artillery, who was killed in action April 12, 1917. Mamie had been William's pet and inseparable companion.

We shan't see Willy any more, Mamie,
   He won't be coming any more:
He came back once and again and again,
   But he won't get leave any more.

We looked from the window and there was his cab,
   And we ran downstairs like a streak,
And he said "Hullo, you bad dog," and you crouched to the floor,
   Paralyzed to hear him speak,

And then let fly at his face and his chest
   Till I had to hold you down,
While he took off his cap and his gloves and his coat.
   And his bag and his thonged Sam Browne.

We went upstairs to the studio,
   The three of us, just as of old,
And you lay down and I sat and talked to him
   As round the room he strolled.

Here in this room where, years ago
   Before the old life stopped,
He worked all day with his slippers and his pipe.
   He would pick up the threads he'd dropped.

To a Bull-Dog

Fondling all the drawings he had left behind,
   Glad to find them all still the same,
And opening the cupboards to look at his belongings
   . . . Every time he came.

But now I know what a dog doesn't know,
   Though you'll thrust your head on my knee,
And try to draw me from the absent-mindedness
   That you find so dull in me.

And all your life you will never know
   What I wouldn't tell you even if I could,
That the last time we waved him away
   Willy went for good.

But sometimes as you lie on the hearthrug
   Sleeping in the warmth of the stove,
Even through your muddled old canine brain
   Shapes from the past may rove.

You'll scarcely remember, even in a dream,
   How we brought home a silly little pup,
With a big square head and little crooked legs
   That could scarcely bear him up;

But your tail will tap at the memory
   Of a man whose friend you were,
Who was always kind, though he called you a naughty dog
   When he found you on his chair;

Who'd make you face a reproving finger
   And solemly lecture you
Till your head hung downwards and you looked very sheepish!
   And you'll dream of your triumphs too,

Of summer evening chases in the garden
    When you dodged us all about with a bone:
We were three boys, and you were the cleverest,
    But now we're two alone.

When summer comes again,
    And the long sunsets fade,
We shall have to go on playing the feeble game for two
    That since the war we've played.

And though you run expectant as you always do
    To the uniforms we meet,
You'll never find Willy among all the soldiers
    In even the longest street,

Nor in any crowd; yet, strange and bitter thought,
    Even now were the old words said,
If I tried the old trick and said, "Where's Willy?"
    You would quiver and lift your head,

And your brown eyes would look to ask if I were serious,
    And wait for the word to spring.
Sleep undisturbed: I shan't say *that* again,
    You innocent old thing.

I must sit, not speaking, on the sofa,
    While you lie asleep on the floor;
For he's suffered a thing that dogs couldn't dream of,
    And he won't be coming here any more.

A PETTICOAT FOR LINDA

THOMAS RADDALL

It puts me in mind, (says my Uncle Hugh MacAra, yarnin' away one night in the little old Bluenose port of Pictou) o' the little old *Linda M. Smardon*, brigantine out o' this very town. Back in the 80's and 90's there was quite a few brigantines sailin' out o' home in the West India and South American trade; two hundred tonners, mostly, just a handy size for the out-ports o' the island where the big ships didn't go. Ours was a shipbuilding town and when Ned Smardon got money enough to buy a vessel for himself 'twas only natural to get her built at home.

Ned was a good rough-and-ready sailor but one o' those easy-goin' fellers that needs a woman with a sharp tongue at their helm, and Amanda Smardon was just the woman for it. She went to sea with him, like many a Bluenose captain's wife in those times, and ran the vessel the way she ran Ned. She kept charge o' the medicine chest, so the men had to come to her with their symptoms, and the way she'd look 'em up in the doctor book and feed 'em pills was a caution. She wrote all the captain's letters and did most o' the talkin' with agents and charterers, for she'd a crackajack head for figgers while Ned couldn't add two two's and make four. That's why she worked up his noon reckonin's for him, I s'pose. More'n once I've seen her out on the deck with Ned's sextant, takin' the sun, and checkin' with the mate. Oh, she was a terror, I tell ye, a li'l, plump, bright-eyed terror with a smile as sweet as sugar.

They had one child, a girl named Linda, born somewhere in the Doldrums aboard the barquentine *Pandora*, and when the new brigantine was finished in Spooner's yard — over there where the undertaker's parlour is now — Amanda Smardon smacked a bottle o' lime juice (blue ribbon, Amanda was) over the bow and named her *Linda M. Smardon.* Young Linda was nine then, a li'l carrot-topped thing, all brown eyes and legs and long red pigtails.

The old sailors and longshoremen puckered up their lips when they seen the lime juice, and said the vessel would prove sour. Well, she begun sour enough. When they'd split out the keel blocks and sawed through the launchin' ways and packin' spewin' out from under her like straws, she run her stern smack on the packet-steamer wharf and bust her rudder. Then she swung with the river current and outgoin' tide and shoved her bowsprit into Johnny Durfee's sail loft.

That's the way she began. Well, they got her rigged and went off to Demerara with a load o' deals, with Captain Ned and Amanda and l'il Linda in the cabin aft. Spooner always said he'd never build another vessel for the Smardon's on account o' Amanda interferin' all the time. I guess it begun with the plans; Amanda wantin' this changed, and that. She'd been goin' to sea with Ned ever since she was a young bride and knew more about a vessel than he did, or thought so anyway. And after the plans, she interfered in the buildin', time and again, till she had Spooner and his carpenters half crazy.

I came to know what sort o' craft Amanda Smardon had concocted, for I shipped in the *Linda M. Smardon* afore the mast, along about 1879. She was full about the bows and had a poor run — a great lump o' wood under the quarter, so when she was goin' about six knots the water boiled up under her stern with a sound like the Ridge Brook in a spring thaw; and she left a wake as broad as a street. With any wind it took two men to the wheel, and they had a job to hold her within four points o' the course. She had a nasty trick o' sneakin' up into the wind and catchin' her foreyards aback, and you had to watch her like a hawk, for no matter how you trimmed her canvas you had to be usin' the wheel the whole time, comin' up and fallin' off and comin' up again. But she was a good sea-boat, I'll say that for her, and with just a rag on her would lie-to very nice in a

A Petticoat for Linda

gale. And she carried a surprisin' cargo for her size and proved a money-maker, like those awkward vessels often did. But us sailors called her *The Workhouse* on account of her tricks.

Young Linda was a favourite with all hands. There was no fear in her. She'd run about the riggin' like a monkey, wearin' a li'l pair o' duck trousers and a shirt, and her feet bare. When she was fourteen they put her ashore with her Aunt Jane, for to get her schoolin' and grow into a lady. And some years went by.

Captain Ned was a good sailor and Amanda was chock full o' business; they begun buyin' fish and lumber and takin' it south to sell on their own account, and they made money hand over fist. And I stayed in the brigantine with 'em, I dunno why. I guess 'twas because the *Linda M.* was like home. Amanda had fixed up the after cabin with hooked rugs, pine needles in the settee cushions, "God Bless Our Home" in the crewel work on one o' the maple panels, and "The Highlanders at the Alma" on another, and a li'l foot-tread organ in a corner.

Sunday evenin's at sea we'd get around that organ and sing hymns and old songs like we was back home in the parlour after church. The grub was good, too, for those times. And in a home vessel you were pretty sure o' seein' the old town two or three times a year. Anyhow I stayed by the *Linda M.* and got to be second mate.

Then — it must ha' been the spring o' '91 — Linda Smardon came aboard, in New York. We'd been a long time in the southern trade out o' New York, and Linda had finished her education and grown into a young woman in the time gone by. So she was a surprise to the rest of us when she walked aboard in the East River docks. I can see her now, wearin' a green rig that went nice with that chestnut hair, and a li'l fore-and-aft hat and a parasol. New York was full o' pretty women, those days; but they weren't a patch on Linda.

We'd shipped a new mate in Trinidad the trip before, young Bob Laurie, lookin' for a passage home to Nova Scotia. He'd been owner-skipper of a li'l old tern schooner in the salt fish trade, and lost her somewhere along the Spanish Main in a norther, with everything he had. Bob was one o' those black-haired blue-eyed fellers from Pictou way, a li'l old timber-drogher at fifty dollars a month. A qualified shipmaster, I mean. But he'd shipped north with us, and Ned and Amanda was tryin' to persuade him to stay.

Truth was, they figgered to go home for good pretty soon, and build a couple more ships and go into the southern trade the way they knew how, and they wanted a captain with a smart head on him to leave in charge o' the *Linda M*. Bob wasn't a bit interested. He was still pretty down in the mouth and figgered to pay off afore the brigantine sailed south again.

I was standin' beside him on the half-deck when Linda stepped aboard, and he gave a kind o' gasp.

"Who's that?" he says.

"The skipper's daughter," I says. "Twenty-three and fancy free."

Linda was tall as Bob, and taut and springy like a new topmast just set up, but moulded very nice. She had one o' those complexions you only find in our part o' the world, barrin' the Isles o' Scotland, and when she smiled, her skin seemed to glow. She had her father's eyes, big and brown and laughin'.

Bob Laurie was bowled end for end. Linda was takin' a trip south. He gave up his cabin without askin', for her to use, and took the spare bunk in mine; and he signed for another voyage so eager his hand shook in the shippin' office. Well, boys, there was all the makin's of a very fine romance; for Bob Laurie was as fine a man as ever walked a deck, and Linda was — well, Linda.

It didn't take her long to get back into shipboard ways again. 'Course she didn't go shinnin' up the riggin' any more. But she was on deck in all kinds o' weather — especially if t'was the mate's watch — and she'd walk up and down with him, talkin' about the sea, and how he came to be there, and everything like that. She'd sit on the main hatch, warm evenin's in the Trades, and get the darkie cook, who was our chanty-man,

A Petticoat for Linda

singin' ballad songs; and sometimes she'd sing herself, with Ned and Amanda sittin' in their rattan chairs on the half-deck, and the watch below comin' out quiet just to listen, and Bob Laurie leanin' ag'in the spokerailin' with a seegar 'tween his fingers, never takin' his eyes off her face.

Oh, she had him on his beam ends, I tell ye, and she knew it, and he knew it. 'Twas good as a play to watch 'em. I dunno how long it took Captain Ned to catch on, but Amanda knew, right off. I'd seen her watchin' 'em with those bright li'l grey eyes behind the spectacles.

We got into San Fernando, Trinidad, which is a kind o' sheltered bay. Ye run in till your vessel takes ground in the soft mud off-shore, get your anchors over, and discharge right into the water, makin' the lumber into rafts for the black men to warp ashore. As the cargo comes out, the vessel rises free o' the mud and rides to her anchors. 'Twas a busy time for the mate. Every now and agin the darkies 'ud get a notion to pole one o' the rafts ashore, and there'd come a bit o' wind and they'd be in trouble. I dunno how many times Bob put off in a boat with a warp and kedge and then helped the black fellers heave her in. Bob was a strong feller, not afraid to put his hand to the work in a pinch, and he'd a good quick eye that could see trouble a mile off. I noticed Amanda sizin' him up and noddin' to herself and Ned.

After that we went up the coast a ways to load molasses in puncheons that come off-shore in lighters. There was nothin' ashore but a few plantation houses and a sugar mill, but Amanda insisted on Linda and Bob goin' off each afternoon and evenin' for to see the country.

"A bit of a holiday won't do you any harm," she says to Bob, and smiles at him the way I've seen her smile at a bill o' ladin' when she fixed up a good charter. So Bob and Linda went ashore. The planters gave 'em a good time, a carriage to drive about in, just the two of 'em, with a darkie on the box, and music and dancin' in the evenin's. On board, they couldn't hide it from anybody, the way they'd be lookin' in each other's eyes, on deck, at the table, everywhere they went, and Captain Ned winkin' to me, and Amanda smilin' her fat li'l smile.

When we got home, Captain Ned and Amanda gave the town a double sensation, announcin' they was comin' ashore for good, and that Bob Laurie was goin' to skipper both Lindas, with his chest stowed in the captain's cabin and a fine weddin' in the Methodist church come Tuesday. The whole town turned out for that weddin', I tell ye. A reg'lar old-fashioned splice it was, too, the bridegroom lookin' worried to death and the rest o' the men grinnin'; the bride lookin' sunny as a May mornin' and the rest o' the women weepin'; and everybody chuckin' rice and old shoes.

Men and girls didn't go trapesin' about the province on a honeymoon, those times. Bob and Linda spent their honeymoon takin' the brigantine to Madeira with a load of pine boards. I was promoted mate and Charlie Stockwell brought his chest aft to be second mate, and we was a happy ship all round. We had a right nice passage out, and Madeira's a fine place for a young man to show his bride around. We chucked the lumber overboard and the Portuguese swum it in through the surf, a sight to watch. Then we took in beach gravel for ballast, out o' lighters, and made sail for the West Indies. We come down the trades to Barbados, twenty-one days without clewin' so much as a royal, a sea-goin' picnic.

Linda sat in a cane chair they'd bought in Funchal, under the awnin' on the half-deck, watchin' Bob with that warm glow in her eyes. And Bob was in a sailor's heaven — a ship to command, a girl to love, and always fair weather. 'Twas a treat to look at 'em. Just after we'd made out the land Linda calls out, carelesslike, "Isn't it time you got a range of chain over the windlass and your anchors overside?"

"Plenty of time," Bob says, busy with his telescope.

"There's nothing like being ready," says Linda, and sung out to me, for'ard, "Mister McAra, don't you think you'd better get

A Petticoat for Linda

the anchors ready to let go?" Well, I looked over to Bob, instinctive-like, but he didn't say a word. She'd put it the way Amanda used to put her orders — "Mister, hadn't you better do so-and-so?" So I called up a couple o' hands and got the anchors ready. And that was that.

At Barbados we got orders for Gonaives in the island o' Haiti, to load logwood. On the way, Linda came on deck one mornin' and threw a glance aloft like the born sailor she was.

"Charlie," she says to the second mate, "I think your tops'l yard's up too sharp, don't you?"

Bob was comin' up the companion behind her. He stuck his head out.

"I don't think so, Linda."

"Oh, but it is, Bob. Only look! Charlie, do slack up your lee tops'l brace and check in the weather brace a bit." Charlie looked at Bob. There was a little flush on Bob's face but he said nothin'. Charlie called a hand and they checked the braces like she wanted.

That was the way it began, just a li'l order here and there. Nobody minded — Linda could ha' wiped her shoes on any man aboard, from Bob Laurie down; but in the back o' my mind was an uneasy feelin' that Linda was goin' to be her mother all over again if this went on. Well, it went on. I s'pose Linda was just kind o' bored with sittin' around. Anyway, she begun to take more of a hand in the command o' the vessel — all in a very nice way, y' understand.

At Gonaives we lay off-shore again, with the log-wood comin' off in lighters and Linda puttin' in a word here and there. The wood came down the mountain junked in short len'ths, aboard donkeys loaded so ye couldn't see a thing but their head and tail. Linda went right aboard the agent, tellin' him 'twas cruel on the donkeys, and how he could do it cheaper. Comin' north to Boston t'was the same; over-ridin' Bob's objections with that lovely warm smile o' hers and tellin' the men to go ahead and do what she said. 'Twas gettin' on Bob's nerves, and sometimes he'd object when he knew she was right, and o' course that made her all the more sure he needed her advice.

There was a li'l rat in the fo'c'sle, name of Lumley, that we'd picked off the beach at Berbice a trip or two before. One mornin' Linda sent him aloft to put some new rovin's on the t'gallants'l, which had been slattin' a bit in the night. He came for'ard to get the spunyarn, swearin'. I happened to be standin' by the fore hatch and asked him the trouble.

"I ain't used to petticoat rule," he says.

"Bob Laurie's the master o' this vessel," I says.

"He's on'y the captain's mate," says Lumley with his li'l ratty grin. I swivelled my weather eye towards the half-deck where Linda was, but the foreyard was pretty nigh square and she couldn't see us for the sail. So I let him have it. I could hit pretty hard, those times, bein' what the books call nowadays a bucko Bluenose mate, and Lumley didn't come to for an hour, with lame Sammy sloshin' buckets o' water over him. Linda seen Sammy bailin' up the Gulf Stream with his rope bucket and came for'ard to see what was up. One look was enough. Up came her head with a snap, and the gold specks burnin' in her brown eyes like sparks.

"Mister MacAra," — you'd ha' swore 'twas Amanda talkin' — "there's never been any need of bruisin' aboard this vessel, and there's none now. Kindly keep your hands to yourself."

What could I do but swaller me quid and me feelin's together — and keep me hands to meself?

We discharged our log-wood in Boston and made sail for Nova Scotia, with all hands busy paintin' and polishin' to get the *Linda M.* lookin' her best. We got in to the river late of a Saturday afternoon, and Captain Bob took the crew up to the li'l old shippin' office, in the corner o' Murphy's bakehouse, and paid 'em off. Him and Linda went ashore after supper and spent the night with Ned and Amanda in their new house back o' the tannery. And o' course, Sunday mornin' they all went

A Petticoat for Linda

to church, and had a big old-fashioned dinner afterwards to celebrate their first voyage and the homecomin'.

Now, in those times lots o' people had buggies and some o' the ship-owners and merchants had fine horses and spankin turn-outs in the carriage and surrey line; but once ye reached the town limits the roads ran off through the woods and were tarnation rough. So the chief amusement of a fine Sunday afternoon was to stroll along the waterfront lookin' at the vessels.

Well, boys, that Sunday afternoon was as fine as silk and there was a big crowd along the docks. All the carpenters and caulkers from the shipyards were there with their wives and families, and the lawyers and the ministers, and the merchants and clerks and Tom, Dick, and Harry. Such a flock o' bustles and parasols, and hard hats and watch-chains as you never saw in your young lives.

Along about three o'clock down comes the Smardons and Bob and Linda — Linda in a swell new get-up she'd bought in Boston. There was a reg'lar mob on the wharf by our brigantine, and the Smardons and Lauries were proud fit to bust, knowin' how smart the *Linda M.* was always kept. Then they noticed the people laughin' and nudgin' each other, and pointin' aloft to the main topmast. And there, plain for the whole town to see, was a red flannel petticoat flyin' from the mast-head.

Linda was the last to see it. She was twirlin' her parasol over her shoulder and hangin' on Bob's arm, proud as sin, when she followed Bob's eyes aloft and saw that thing at the mast-head. Her face turned the colour o' the petticoat. She could feel Bob's big muscles stiffenin' under the sleeves o' his Sunday jacket, and she hung on to him hard. All the people stopped laughin' when they saw the look on Bob's face.

"Whose work is that?" says Bob, quiet and dangerous. Not a word out o' anybody. Truth was, nobody knew; though everybody knew what it meant. Truth was, Lumley had borrowed it off one o' the girls at Shanahan's, and shinned up the mast in the night to hang it there for Sunday. There was no sign o' Lumley, o' course. He'd lit out.

"Some of those young devils of boys," snaps old Ned.

"You'd better get it down, Robert," says Amanda.

But the crew'd been paid off and there was nobody aboard but Sammy, the black cook, who'd a club foot and couldn't ha' got higher'n the topmast cross-trees. Bob was itchin' to tear it down but he wouldn't give the crowd the pleasure o' seein' him do it; so the Smardons and Lauries marched off up the wharf with their heads in the air and the petticoat still flyin'. I came down to the vessel in the evenin', saw it there, whipped aloft in a hurry and dropped it in the river.

Well, we loaded white pine boards for Martinique. Ned Smardon had bought the shipment from a mill up the river. On deck we stowed an extra special lot — 100,000 feet o' clear white pine such as ye couldn't find to-day if ye searched the whole Dominion. Ned came down and watched every stick put aboard. 'Twas a sample lot, see? Ned and Amanda had high hopes o' some good business with Martinique on the stren'th of it.

We got the stores aboard, shipped a crew, and begun to fasten the deck-load secure for sea. Now the way we always fastened a lumber deck-load was this: first we laid what's called lashin'-planks acrost the deck-load from side to side. The ends o' these planks was cleated to hold the lashin's in place. The lashin's was three-inch hemp, rove through eye-bolts in the rail and around the ends o' the lashin'-planks, and the whole thing frapped to set it up tight. We done it with dry rope, o' course, so that the first rain, or the first sea over the side, would set it up tighter'n ever.

Linda came along the wharf with her father just as we was gettin' started with the lashin'-planks.

"Wait a minute, Hugh," she says to me. "I don't like those old-fashioned fastenings, do you? They were all right before wire was invented."

"What's your idea?" asks Captain Bob pleasant.

A Petticoat for Linda

"Use wire," says Linda, quick and eager — just like her mother. "One wire to each eye-bolt. Bring the ends together on top of the deck-load and set them up tight with a lanyard."

"There's quite a weight to hold, in a seaway," objects Bob.

"But wire cable?" she says. "Oh come, Bob, you men are too set in your ways. No sea could break a good wire cable."

"She's right," chirps old Ned, pleased as punch with his daughter's brains.

Bob looked like he wanted to say somethin' more, but Linda called out to me to go up to the riggin' loft and get some good stout wire cable and some eyes. So that was that. We lashed the deck-load with Linda's cables and set 'em up tight with lanyards, like she said. And we sailed, with Ned and Amanda down to see us off, and bawlin' instructions after Bob as far as their tongues could reach.

We had a soldier's passage till we got south o' Bermuda. Then we run into a storm and had to lay-to hours under a storm trysail and a small main staysail. Finally the wind shifted and there was a big cross sea. The vessel shipped a couple o' green ones just afore dark, and Captain Bob called me on deck. He didn't say a word. He just pointed to those deck-load lashin's. I stared at 'em a minute while the vessel rolled, and then my eyes begun to pop. That wire cable couldn't break, maybe, but it could bend. Linda's patent lashin's was givin' to leeward and takin' up the slack from windward; the whole deck-load was creepin' down leeward inch by inch, and there wasn't a dog-gone thing we could do about it.

The further it went, the more the *Linda M*, listed, and the further she listed, the more purchase the wind got on her windward side. The sensible thing was to cut loose the lashin's and chuck Ned's fancy lumber overboard. But just then Linda came on deck in oilskins, the way she liked to do in heavy weather, and I could read Bob's mind like a book. Linda's notions had got us into this mess, and it was up to Linda to give the word.

But she didn't notice the lashin's! I guess she thought 'twas the wind alone that pressed the vessel over so. She stood near the wheel, which was lashed, with a hand standin' by. I was at the for'ard end o' the half-deck, and Bob was on the deck cargo near the foremast. I heard someone yell "Look out!" and I crouched down and grabbed a ring-bolt just as a big sea came over the whole len'th of her. Bob jumped for the foremast riggin' and began to run up the under side o' the ratlines; but that sea was higher than he could climb in the time he had.

The sea pitched him off the riggin', flung him slap through the main staysail, and took him overboard on the lee side in one tremenjus rush o' water. It took the storm trysail clean. It smashed to kindlin' the small boat on the fore hatch. It busted the fo'c'sle slide and poured a stream inside the full size o' the door; a fine mess, sea chests washin' and smashin' about, the cook's kitten drowned in its basket in his bunk; and a bar'l o' sauer kraut, that we'd no room for in the lazareete, spewin scraps o' salt cabbage over everything.

I'll never forget Linda's scream. Ye could hear it above the noise o' the water and the wind. I came to me feet yelling, "Man overboard!" The deck-load was slanted like the pitch of a roof now. I slid down to loo'ard. I could see Bob swimmin' hard in the smother sixty or seventy yards off the port quarter. I knew he couldn't hold up long in his seaboots and oilskins. All the lee runnin' riggin' was covered on its pins by the deck cargo, which had slid down hard ag'in the standin' riggin; so there wasn't a rope-end to throw.

The sea had staggered the brigantine and took her way off; she was driftin' to loo'ard the same as Bob. Then I noticed the rags o' the staysail — the one Bob went through — blowin' out to loo'ard like streamers. Me and the helmsman caught hold of 'em and let 'em down into the sea so Bob could catch a hold. He got a good grip on 'em, and we pretty nigh had him in reach when we heard Linda scream again and saw another big green wall comin' over the starboard side.

The helmsman and me grabbed the fore t'gallant and fore

A Petticoat for Linda

royal backstays while that sea went thunderin' over us. It pretty nigh took our arm out o' the sockets and it knocked the breath out of us, but we hung on. The sea tore Bob loose of his hold on the rags o' the sail. We saw him to loo'ard ag'in, but not so far off, and swimmin' like a good 'un. Once again we worked the strips o' canvas down to him, then worked him alongside. We got out on the fore chains and each slipped a hand under his armpits and swung him aboard. And like a flash there was Linda flingin' her arms about him, laughin' and cryin' and sayin' "Darling, darling, darling", like that. I'd a job to get 'em both out o' harm's way aft.

Soon as he got his breath, Bob says: "We've got to put the ol' hooker before it, somehow." All our storm canvas was gone. The men was coming out o' the fo'c'sle now like wet rats. Bob sent a couple aloft to goose-wing the lower topsail. That squared her off before the wind, and the *Linda M.* begun to move again, all hunched over to port. Then came a lull. The wind died, flat, and the brigantine rolled and pitched in the big greasy seas. 'Twas hot. We were all gaspin' for air that didn't seem to be there. The glass had dropped like a stone. Then it came to me what was in Bob's mind, back home, when Linda sprung her notion about the lashin's. 'Twas the hurricane season. And we'd walked straight into a West Indy buster.

There wasn't time now to sling the deck-load overside — a slow job with a small crew, board by board. There was other things to do. We got another storm trysail bent and stowed on the boom. We put the helm down hard and lashed it there. We battened the fo'c'sle hatch with boards and canvas, and all hands came aft. Bob sent Linda below, promisin' to come down every hour or so after the wind begun to blow again, so she could see he was all right. Finally we rigged a life-line acrost the half-deck and stood there, waitin' for the big blow.

It was a long time comin', but then it came in a rush, first a hard squall, then the main wind. What went before was nothin'. This was the real thing. The sound it made would frighten ye out o' your boots. It beat that big lumpy sea down flat — flat as a floor — in ten minutes, tearin' off the tops and whippin' the water away in spray. 'Twas like a nor'east blizzard back home, only blowin' three times as hard, and spray flyin' thick instead o' snow. Ye couldn't see for-ard from aft. The brigantine lay over to it, further and further, till the fore yard-arms were in the water and we thought it was all up with us.

Bob opened the companion and yelled for Linda to come on deck. Up she came, white, but clear grit for all that, a real Bluenose girl. He put a lashin' on the binnacle and slipped the loop over her shoulders. She had an oilcoat on but no hat, and her long chestnut hair blew out o' the combs and streamed out like a banner. She didn't take her eyes off Bob. He yelled in my ear, "Get a couple of axes. We'll cut the deck-load away!" So I fetched up a sharp axe for each of us. Bob wouldn't trust the job to anyone else — and Linda cried out "No, Bob! No!" when she saw what we were goin' to do. He thought she was worryin' about the old man's prize lumber, but Bob was the only thing in her mind, then or after. He gave his head an angry shake.

Ye couldn't stand up in that wind without support, and ye couldn't swing an axe, for the wind would ha' taken it out o' your hands. We had to crawl on our bellies, hangin' on any way we could, till we got to the rope lanyards that bound the wire end together. We begun amidships; Bob was to cut for'ard and I was to cut aft. That 'ud give us a chance to jump clear afore the boards begun to go. It took a long time, sawin' the axe blades back and forth acrost the lanyards till they let go. When my last lashin' was cut I jumped for the life-line on the half-deck, and saw Bob crouchin' ag'in the fo'c'sle, watchin' the boards go.

That was a sight! The wind lifted 'em in tiers of ten or twelve, the way ye'd flip a few cards off a pack, and they went sailin' over the lee forebraces, high in the air, and vanished in the smother to loo'ard. The lower tiers didn't go so fast, for the vessel was comin' up as the weight went off her port side; but

A Petticoat for Linda

in less'n fifteen minutes not a board was left o' that fine pine lumber for Martinique. The *Linda M.* righted herself as far as she could with that wind blowin'. We set the storm trysail — that's a story in itself — and rode out the hurricane handsome.

A big sea came up when the wind begun to slack, but we didn't care for a sea any more, not after what we'd come through. Altogether the storm lasted thirty-six hours on end, and when we got a chance to drop we lay around the deck like dead men.

When we got into Martinique the place was rim-racked, all the palm trees down and the clay huts o' the black people blown into the gullies o' the hillside. But the queerest sight was a barque, dismasted and capsized, high and dry on the beach with her keel to the sky. To a seafarin' man there was somethin' awful about that. I saw Linda starin' at it with her brown eyes very wide, and not saying a word.

Well, we sailed for home with rum and molasses and had a good passage north. Bob made a fine landfall — Black Point, just thirty mile from home. 'Twas a Saturday and all hands were pleased to be gettin' home for Sunday, but it come up thick in the night and Bob held her off the river mouth till mornin'.

Him and Linda came on deck together as we squared the brigantine away for the river bar. He saw all hands grinnin' and looked aloft. There was a pair of his own white duck trousers flying from the main top. They was nailed there. Bob jumped round on us, fightin' mad, liftin' those big fists o' his.

"Who did that?" he snaps.

"I did," Linda says. "Last night in the fog. I still know how to climb rigging."

"What's the idea?" snorts Bob.

"A number o' things," Linda says, gettin' pink and lookin' past his shoulders somewheres. "For one thing I want to give those sniggering dockside loafers something to open their eyes. For another thing," Linda says, still dodgin' his eyes, "it means I'm goin' to live ashore after this and make a home for you and the boys."

"Boys!" he says.

"Boys," she says, and gives him a look. "There's to be no more sea-farin' women in this family. Just you keep that in mind, Bob Laurie." And away she runs below afore he can catch and kiss her.

"Shall I send a hand aloft to tear those things down?" I asks, solemn.

Bob looks aloft, then he looks over towards the town, towards the Smardon house on the Argyle road, and his eyes narrow a bit.

"No," he says, slow, "leave 'em stay till they rot and blow away." And he grins at me. "It ain't a bad house-flag, that, for a family o' boys."

AT THE CEDARS

DUNCAN CAMPBELL SCOTT

You had two girls — Baptiste —
One is Virginie —
Hold hard — Baptiste!
Listen to me.

The whole drive was jammed
In that bend at the Cedars;
The rapids were dammed
With the logs tight rammed
And crammed; you might know
The Devil had clinched them below.

We worked three days — not a budge,
"She's as tight as a wedge, on the ledge,"

At the Cedars

Says our foreman;
"Mon Dieu! boys, look here,
We must get this thing clear."

He cursed at the men
And we went for it then;
With our cant-dogs arow,
We just gave he-yo-ho;
When she gave a big shove
From above.

The gang yelled and tore
For the shore,
The logs gave a grind
Like a wolf's jaws behind,
And as quick as a flash,
With a shove and a crash,
They were down in a mash,
But I and ten more,
All but Isaac Dufour,
Were ashore.

He leaped on a log in the front of the rush,
And shot out from the bind
While the jam roared behind;
As he floated along
He balanced his pole
And tossed us a song.
But just as we cheered,
Up darted a log from the bottom,
Leaped thirty feet square and fair,
And came down on his own.

He went up like a block
With the shock,
And when he was there

In the air,
Kissed his hand to the land;
When he dropped
My heart stopped,
For the first logs had caught him
And crushed him;
When he rose in his place
There was blood on his face.

There were some girls, Baptiste,
Picking berries on the hillside,
Where the river curls, Baptiste,
You know — on the still side.
One was down by the water,
She saw Isaac
Fall back.

She did not scream, Baptiste,
She launched her canoe;
It did seem, Baptiste,
That she wanted to die too,
For before you could think
The birch cracked like a shell
In that rush of hell,
And I saw them both sink —

Baptiste! —
He had two girls,
One is Virginie,
What God calls the other
Is not known to me.

THE LISTENERS

WALTER DE LA MARE

"Is there anybody there?" said the Traveller,
   Knocking on the moonlit door;
And his horse in the silence champed the grasses
   Of the forest's ferny floor;
And a bird flew up out of the turret,
   Above the Traveller's head:
And he smote upon the door again a second time;
   "Is there anybody there?" he said.
But no one descended to the Traveller;
   No head from the leaf-fringed sill
Leaned over and looked into his grey eyes,
   Where he stood perplexed and still.
But only a host of phantom listeners
   That dwelt in the lone house then
Stood listening in the quiet of the moonlight
   To that voice from the world of men:
Stood thronging the faint moonbeams on the dark stair,
   That goes down to the empty hall,
Harkening in an air stirred and shaken
   By the lonely Traveller's call.
And he felt in his heart their strangeness,
   Their stillness answering his cry,
While his horse moved, cropping the dark turf,
   'Neath the starred and leafy sky;
For he suddenly smote on the door, even
   Louder, and lifted his head: —
"Tell them I came, and no one answered,
   That I kept my word," he said.
Never the least stir made the listeners,

Though every word he spake
Fell echoing through the shadowiness of the still house
   From the one man left awake:
Ay, they heard his foot upon the stirrup,
   And the sound of iron on stone,
And how the silence surged softly backward,
   When the plunging hoofs were gone.

THE DONKEY

G. K. CHESTERTON

When fishes flew and forests walked
   And figs grew upon thorn,
Some moment when the moon was blood
   Then surely I was born;

With monstrous head and sickening cry
   And ears like errant wings,
The devil's walking parody
   On all four-footed things.

The tattered outlaw of the earth,
   Of ancient crooked will;
Starve, scourge, deride me: I am dumb,
   I keep my secret still.

Fools! For I also had my hour;
   One far fierce hour and sweet:
There was a shout about my ears,
   And palms before my feet.

Laughing it off

THE SINKING OF THE *MARIPOSA BELLE*

STEPHEN LEACOCK

Stephen Leacock was a great Canadian with a bubbling sense of humour. He was a professor of economics, but his funny bone kept showing even in his writing on this dry and sober science. When he came to write on what he loved best — the summer resort country around Orillia, Ontario — then he really let himself go. For years he summered beside Lake Simcoe, lounging around in old clothes, raising vegetables, and gossiping with people. In the story that follows you will see how Leacock's imagination worked upon what his shrewd eyes saw during these long gossipy summers. The story is taken from *Sunshine Sketches of a Little Town*.

Down the lake, mile by mile over the calm waters, steamed the *Mariposa Belle*. Early that Dominion Day morning, the little excursion steamer had left for the other end of Lake Wissanotti, with half of the town of Mariposa on board, and the other half standing on the dock to see her off. Now in the long July evening she was headed back for the town, twenty miles away.

I suppose you have often noticed the contrast there is between an excursion on its way out in the morning and what it looks like on the way home.

In the morning everybody is so restless and animated and moves to and fro all over the boat and asks questions. But coming home, as the afternoon gets later and later and the sun sinks beyond the hills, all the people seem to get so still and quiet and drowsy.

So it was with the people on the *Mariposa Belle*. They sat there on the benches and the deck chairs in little clusters, and listened to the regular beat of the propeller and almost dozed off asleep as they sat. Then when the sun set and the dusk drew on, it grew almost dark on the deck and so still that you could hardly tell there was anyone on board.

VILLAGE IN THE LAURENTIAN MOUNTAINS — *Clarence A. Gagnon*

Reproduced by permission of the National Gallery, Ottawa.

CLARENCE GAGNON, R.C.A.
(1881 - 1942)

Clarence Gagnon was born in Montreal, in 1881. Even as a small boy he was interested in drawing; but he received no encouragement from his father. Fortunately he was given assistance by his aunt who sent him to art school. At the end of his first year, his teacher, William Brymner, saw such promise in the boy that he saw that he got scholarships to continue his studies for two years more. By this time he had attracted the attention of a wealthy patron, Mr. James Morgan, who sent him to Paris to study. Here he studied etching and won praise for his work, but his chief interest reverted to painting. In 1909 he returned to Canada. He soon found himself immersed in the life of the Charlesvoix district at Baie St. Paul, and many of his paintings were done in this district. He loved the Quebec villages and the habitant people, and painted them with sympathetic insight.

Never long content in one place, he moved back and forth between Paris and Baie St. Paul. One of his most famous achievements was a series of illustrations he made for a French publishing house, which desired to bring out a special edition of Louis Hemon's book *Maria Chapdelaine*. This job particularly pleased Gagnon for it enabled him to paint his beloved Quebec habitant for the benefit of his friends in Paris. So successful was his work that the drawings became nearly as famous as the book.

In 1921 he was elected member of the Royal Canadian Academy, but in 1924 he returned to Paris. He remained in Europe for twelve years. On his return to Canada, he tried to institute a 'folk museum' such as he had found so successful in Sweden, but at his death in 1942 he had not succeeded.

Village in the Laurentian Mountains is in the National Gallery, Ottawa.

And if you had looked at the steamer from the shore or from one of the islands, you'd have seen the row of lights from the cabin windows shining on the water and the red glare of the burning hemlock from the funnel, and you'd have heard the soft thud of the propeller miles away over the lake.

Now and then, too, you could have heard them singing on the steamer,—the voices of the girls and the men, blended into unison by the distance, rising and falling in long-drawn melody: "O—Can-a-da O—Can-a-da."

You may talk as you will about the intoning choirs of your European cathedrals, but the sound of *"O Can-a-da"*, borne across the waters of a silent lake at evening is good enough for those of us who know Mariposa.

I think that it was just as they were singing like this: *"O—Can-a-da"*, that word went round that the boat was sinking.

If you have ever been in any sudden emergency on the water, you will understand the strange psychology of it,—the way in which what is happening seems to become known all in a moment without a word being said. The news is transmitted from one to the other by some mysterious process.

At any rate, first one then the other on the *Mariposa Belle* heard that the steamer was sinking. Somebody finally came to Judge Pepperleigh and woke him up and said there was six inches of water in the steamer and that she was sinking. And Pepperleigh said it was a perfect scandal and passed the news on to his wife and she said that they had no business to allow it, and that if the steamer sank, that was the last excursion she'd go on.

So the news went all round the boat, and everywhere the people gathered in groups and talked about it in the angry and excited way that people have when a steamer is sinking on one of the lakes like Lake Wissanotti.

Dean Drone, of course, and some of the others were quieter about it, and said that one must make allowances and that naturally there were two sides to everything. But most of them wouldn't listen to reason at all. I think, perhaps, that some of them were frightened. You see the last time but one that the steamer had sunk, there had been a man drowned and it made them nervous.

What? Hadn't I explained about the depth of Lake Wissanotti? I had taken it for granted that you knew; and in any case parts of it are deep enough, though I don't suppose in this stretch of it from the big reed beds up to within a mile of the town wharf, you could find six feet of water in it if you tried. Oh, pshaw! I was not talking about a steamer sinking in the ocean and carrying down its screaming crowd of people into the hideous depths of green water. Oh, dear me, no! That kind of thing never happens on Lake Wissanotti.

But what does happen is that the *Mariposa Belle* sinks every now and then, and sticks there on the bottom till they get things straightened up.

On the lakes round Mariposa, if a person arrives late anywhere and explains that the steamer sank, everybody understands the situation.

You see when Harland and Wolff built the *Mariposa Belle,* they left some cracks in between the timbers that you fill up with cotton waste every Sunday. If this is not attended to, the boat sinks. In fact, it is part of the law of the province that all steamers like the *Mariposa Belle* must be properly corked, — I think that is the word, — every season.

So you can imagine, now that I've explained it a little straighter, the indignation of the people when they knew that the boat had come uncorked and that they might be stuck out there on a shoal or a mudbank half the night.

Safe! I'm not sure now that I come to think of it that it isn't worse than sinking in the Atlantic. After all, in the Atlantic there is wireless telegraphy, and a lot of trained sailors and stewards. But out on Lake Wissanotti, — far out, so that you can only just see the lights of the town away off to the south, — when the propeller comes to a stop, — and you can hear the hiss of steam as they start to rake out the engine fires to prevent an

The Sinking of the Mariposa Belle

explosion — and when you turn from the red glare that comes from the furnace doors as they open them, to the black dark that is gathering over the lake — and there's a night wind beginning to run among the rushes — and you see the men going forward to the roof of the pilot house to send up the rockets to rouse the town — safe? Safe yourself, if you like; as for me, let me once get back into Mariposa again, under the night shadow of the maple trees, and this shall be the last, last time I'll go on Lake Wissanotti.

Safe! Oh, yes! Isn't it strange how safe other people's adventures seem after they happen? But you'd have been scared, too, if you'd been there just before the steamer sank, and seen them bringing up all the women on to the top deck.

I don't see how some of the people took it so calmly; how Mr. Smith, for instance, could have gone on smoking and telling how he'd had a steamer "sink on him" on Lake Nipissing and a still bigger one, a side-wheeler, sink on him in Lake Abitibi.

Then, quite suddenly, with a quiver, down she went. You could feel the boat sink, sink — down, down — would it never get to the bottom? The water came flush up to the lower deck, and then — thank heaven — the sinking stopped and there was the *Mariposa Belle* safe and tight on a reed bank.

Really, it made one positively laugh! It seemed so queer and, anyway, if a man has a sort of natural courage, danger makes him laugh. Danger? Pshaw! Fiddlesticks! Everybody scouted the idea. Why, it is just the little things like this that give zest to a day on the water.

Within half a minute they are all running round looking for sandwiches and cracking jokes and talking of making coffee over the remains of the engine fires.

* * * *

I don't need to tell at length how it all happened after that. I suppose the people on the *Mariposa Belle* would have had to settle down there all night or till help came from the town, but some of the men who had gone forward and were peering out into the dark said that it couldn't be more than a mile across the water to Miller's Point. You could almost see it over there to the left—some of them, I think said "off on the port bow", because you know when you get mixed up in these marine disasters, you soon catch the atmosphere of the thing.

So pretty soon they had the davits swung out over the side and were lowering the old lifeboat from the top deck into the water.

There were men leaning out over the rail of the *Mariposa Belle* with lanterns that threw the light as they let her down, and the glare fell on the water and the reeds. But when they got the boat lowered, it looked such a frail, clumsy thing as one saw it from the rail above, that the cry was raised: "Women and children first!" For what was the sense, if it should turn out that the boat wouldn't even hold women and children, of trying to jam a lot of heavy men into it?

So they put in mostly women and children and the boat pushed out into the darkness so freighted down it would hardly float.

In the bow of it was the Presbyterian student who was relieving the minister, and he called out that they were in the hands of Providence. But he was crouched and ready to spring out of them at the first moment.

So the boat went and was lost in the darkness except for the lantern in the bow that you could see bobbing on the water. Then presently it came back and they sent another load, till pretty soon the decks began to thin out and everybody got impatient to be gone.

It was about the time the third boat-load put off that Mr. Smith took a bet with Mullins for twenty-five dollars, that he'd be home in Mariposa before the people in the boats had walked round the shore.

No one knew just what he meant, but pretty soon they saw Mr. Smith disappear down below into the lowest part of the

The Sinking of the Mariposa Belle

steamer with a mallet in one hand and a big bundle of marline in the other.

They might have wondered more about it, but it was just at this time they heard the shouts from the rescue boat — the big Mackinaw lifeboat — that had put out from the town with fourteen men at the sweeps when they saw the first rockets go up.

I suppose there is always something inspiring about a rescue at sea, or on the water.

After all, the bravery of the lifeboat man is the true bravery, — expended to save life, not to destroy it.

Certainly they told for months after of how the rescue boat came out to the *Mariposa Belle*.

I suppose that when they put her in the water the lifeboat touched it for the first time since the old Macdonald Government placed her on Lake Wissanotti.

Anyway, the water poured in at every seam. But not for a moment — even with two miles of water between them and the steamer — did the rowers pause for that.

By the time they were half-way there, the water was almost up to the thwarts, but they drove her on. Panting and exhausted (for mind you, if you haven't been in a fool boat like that for years, rowing takes it out of you) the rowers stuck to their task. They threw the ballast over and chucked into the water the heavy cork jackets and lifebelts that encumbered their movements. There was no thought of turning back. They were nearer to the steamer than to the shore.

"Hang to it, boys," called the crowd, from the steamer's deck, and hang they did.

They were almost exhausted when they got them; men leaning from the steamer threw them ropes and one by one every man was hauled aboard just as the lifeboat sank under their feet.

Saved! By heaven! saved, by one of the smartest pieces of rescue work ever seen on the lake.

There's no use describing it; you need to see rescue work of this kind by lifeboats to understand it.

Nor were the lifeboat crew the only ones that distinguished themselves.

Boat after boat and canoe after canoe had put out from Mariposa to the help of the steamer. They got them all.

Pupkin, the other bank teller, with a face like a horse, who hadn't gone on the excursion — as soon as he knew that the boat was signalling for help and that his beloved Miss Lawson was sending up rockets — rushed for a row boat, grabbed an oar (two would have hampered him), and paddled madly out into the lake. He struck right out into the dark with the crazy skiff almost sinking beneath his feet. But they got him. They rescued him. They watched him, almost dead with exhaustion, make his way to the steamer, where he was hauled up with ropes. Saved! Saved!

* * * *

They might have gone on that way half the night, picking up the rescuers, only, at the very moment when the tenth load of people left for the shore — just as suddenly and saucily as you please, up came the *Mariposa Belle* from the mud bottom and floated.

FLOATED?

Why, of course she did. If you take a hundred and fifty people off a steamer that has sunk, and if you get a man as shrewd as Mr. Smith to plug the timber seams with mallet and marline, and if you turn ten bandsmen of the Mariposa band on to your hand pump on the bow of the lower deck — float? Why, what else can she do?

Then, if you stuff in hemlock into the embers of the fire that you were raking out, till it hums and crackles under the boiler, it won't be long before you hear the propeller thud-thudding at the stern again, and before the long roar of the steam whistle echoes over to the town.

And so the *Mariposa Belle,* with all steam up again and with the long train of sparks careering from the funnel, is heading for the town.

But no Christie Johnson at the wheel in the pilot house this time.

"Smith! Get Smith!" is the cry.

Can he take her in? Well, now! Ask a man who has had steamers sink under him in half the lakes from Temiskaming to the Bay, if he can take her in? Ask a man who has run a York boat down the rapids of the Moose when the ice is moving, if he can grip the steering wheel of the *Mariposa Belle?* So there she steams safe and sound to the town wharf!

Look at the lights and the crowd! If only the federal census taker could count us now! Hear them calling and shouting back and forward from the deck to the shore! Listen! There is the rattle of the shore ropes as they get them ready, and there's the Mariposa band, — actually forming in a circle on the upper deck just as she docks, and the leader with his baton — one — two — ready now —

"O CAN-A-DA!"

HE WAS SELDOM SURPRISED BY HIS HORSES

KENNETH C. CRAGG

Father always said there was more twaddle written about the horse than about any one other living thing.

There were, he claimed, few things more belittling to a man's pride than to be left standing in the middle of a ten-acre pasture, looking silly and rattling oats in a tin pail, while the horses he wanted cavorted around, kicking their heels and making vulgar noises.

According to horse-lovers — the man's-best-friend school of thinking — when a farmer wanted his horses for cutting hay or drawing in, all he needed to do was go to the pasture bars, whistle, and the ever-loving horses would trot right up and beg for the bridles, their croupers, and the other more or less uncomfortable pieces of harness.

His horses were stupid enough, "big, blamed, awkward things," but not that stupid, claimed Father. At least they were smart enough not to like work, which was an exasperation but seemed more natural than the way horse-lovers had it.

"Remember," suggested Father, when well warmed up to the subject, "the story of the brave horse which not only stayed by the side of his master, who had fallen and broken his leg, but helped him back in the saddle as well?"

"It was a touching story," Father agreed, "but what about the other side of it? How did the man break his leg? Why," said Father, "it was the horse that threw the man so that he broke his leg. And the story was wrong anyway. The horse ran off to join a band of wild mustangs and the man would have died from thirst except that a kind rattlesnake took pity on him and bit him."

So far as Father ever learned, no man has ever devised a surefire method of catching a horse, although he once came very close to it. He did it by fixing a device on the oat pail that would hold the halter in such a way that once the horse put his nose in the pail, the halter could be slipped on over the horse's head and you had him.

This differed from the standard method only in that it was supposed to be easier to get the nose of the horse inside the halter. But it was by no means foolproof and Father gave it up after one time when, by some fluke, the halter went over his own head and Maude, the big bay mare, ran away with the oats.

"It was downright humiliating," Father, in deep disgust, said later, and for the rest of the early part of the summer he kept the horses which were used the most, in the stable. Before the first hay went into the barn he cut grass out of the orchard for them with the scythe and trundled it to them in the wheelbarrow. In the long run it was easier, and besides it was dignified.

Never having any illusions about the horse, Father was seldom surprised at anything his horses did. Most of them had individual characteristics, few of them endearing to man, but as long as their little foibles were remembered and played up to, the farm work proceeded quietly and without untoward incident.

One rather remarkable beast—we had her until Father traded her off on three calves and a quantity of seed oats—every time she was harnessed took a big, deep breath just as soon as Father or the man reached for the belly band.

In time, no one thought anything about it, but simply jabbed her in the soft part of the belly with the thumb of the right hand and quickly drew up the belly band before she got a fresh breath. In addition, because of another whimsy, she couldn't bear to be touched when on the lead. Slap her and she was apt to walk over whoever was leading her. It was surprising because she was such an old tired-looking horse.

Lionel, the Englishman, who had a slow gait and a tendency to know it all, had been warned about this. Perhaps that day he was brooding overmuch because few people in Canada did things the way they were done "over 'ome" or even cared. In any event, while leading the mare to water, he slapped her in the flank with the end of the rope.

In an instant she had crowded Lionel into the water trough. He went in full length. Father saw it from the cowstable door and swore she put out one foot and held Lionel under for a spell, but this was believed by others to be exaggeration.

The oldest horse on the place and the one that came nearest to a sentimental description of a faithful servant was half-blind Maude. She was the one who dumped Father out of the cutter and down the steep side of a snow-bank because the edge of the bank was on her blind side.

She had had a lot of steam in her youth and in those days would as soon bite a person as not, sooner, in fact. But her affliction worked a slow change and finally the other eye dimmed and it was kind of pitiful to see the one-time wicked and vicious Maude befuddled in the field or lost in the little thicket in the barn-side pasture where branches swished at her face every time she moved.

She would stand still and whinny for help until some one came. Her ears would prick up when she heard footsteps and she would make little sounds of welcome. You could always lead her out with a light touch on her forelock. In the old days she would have taken an arm off, but now with a hand pressing on top of her head she would duck, without hesitation, to go under a branch or a low beam.

Maude, by the time she was nearly blind, was as intelligent as horses are supposed to be. She got her exercise by drawing the milk a half-mile away to the cheese factory, and through odd jobs like hauling people on errands round the farm in the milk cart or on a stoneboat.

She came within an ace of getting the tanning of her life the day she ran away with Father and the turnip seeder. The field had been nicely worked and ridged in long straight rows. The seeder has been taken from the stone-boat and the container filled with the seed like fine bird shot. Maude, unlike herself, seemed agitated the moment she put her foot in the field.

She was hollered at and hitched and, all of a sudden, she snorted and ran, Father hanging to the handles of the seeder, bawling, and taking great long steps as they clattered across the rows. He fell on his face half-way down the field and was not in a pranksome mood when he caught up to old Maude down at the fence.

What saved her was her trembling. Father couldn't make it out. It wasn't just the fear of getting the lines wrapped forcibly around her behind. She kept on trembling until she was unhitched and taken out of the field. Mother guessed the cause — artificial fertilizer made from blood and slaughterhouse waste, used on the farm for the first time.

"Old fool," said Father, who was still picking little stones out of his face, "probably had a glimpse of the horse's hereafter."

Horses seemed bent on galling Father, who was a patient man. Walter, who worked for us sometimes and could pin the ears of a horse back with a few well-chosen words, always claimed they took advantage of his patience.

It was a sorrowful thing to see him plowing the stony field. The plow would hit a stone and bounce out. Father would haul it back for a fresh start and fairly plead with the team to back up so as to give him enough slack.

Then, when the plow was back far enough and he had lifted the handles up high so the plowshare would dig in fast, he had to plead and coax them to go ahead.

"Blamed dirty —," Father would holler at them, almost dancing up and down and still holding the plow handles high up in the air.

Finally they would get their ponderous Clydesdale feet going, and all would be well until the plow hit another stone and the whole thing would be repeated. Father used to get weary plowing the stony field.

Then he bought a riding plow, which was quite an event. There was no reason why he shouldn't have had a riding plow years before. Most of the fields had long turns and he always had plenty of horses. But he belonged to the generation that fancied the straight and beautifully turned furrow and would have been shocked by more recent claims that smooth plowing could be bad plowing.

In addition to this pride in his work, a little streak in him considered it wrong to do things the easy way if a harder could be found. In a subconscious way he felt that it was necessary and good to mortify the flesh.

But with a riding-plow new horizons were opened. He found he could sit in well-bundled comfort, look after three adjusting levers, work a foot trip and still have enough free hand to carry a long lashed whip. After a day or two of that, he no longer pleaded with the horses and got results without Walter's verbal attacks. He didn't even always have to carry the whip.

Another victory was soon to be his, the first time he was run away with on a riding-plow. He was moving back the lane to the far twenty acres, and had just climbed back to the plow seat after driving the three horses through the barn gap, when the offside horse put her tail over the line and clamped it tight. Father naturally hollered at her, and all three started to run, with the plow, a mere featherweight to the big horses, clattering behind.

Father couldn't control the horses because the mare still held the line, as in a vise, under her tail. It was then he showed what a thinking brain can do in a moment of crisis. In a trice he had his levers up and the plow down, and the share bit into the earth and the dirt washed up over him like the bow wave of a fast motorboat.

Big Clydes don't accelerate fast, but they're like heavy trains, they have a lot of momentum. But the drag of the plow soon took the ginger out of them and they stopped.

"Well," said Father, spitting dirt out of his mouth and wiping his ears, "that'll learn them."

THE HEIGHT OF THE RIDICULOUS

OLIVER WENDELL HOLMES

I wrote some lines once on a time
  In wondrous merry mood,
And thought, as usual, men would say
  They were exceeding good.

They were so queer, so very queer,
  I laughed as I would die;
Albeit, in the general way,
  A sober man am I.

I called my servant and he came;
  How kind it was of him
To mind a slender man like me,
  He of the mighty limb.

The Height of the Ridiculous

"These to the printer," I exclaimed
   And, in my humorous way,
I added (as a trifling jest),
   "There'll be the devil to pay."

He took the paper and I watched
   And saw him peep within;
At the first line he read, his face
   Was all upon the grin.

He read the next; the grin grew broad
   And shot from ear to ear;
He read the third; a chuckling noise
   I now began to hear.

The fourth, he broke into a roar;
   The fifth, his waistband split;
The sixth, he burst five buttons off
   And tumbled in a fit.

Ten days and nights, with sleepless eye,
   I watched that wretched man,
And since, I never dare to write
   As funny as I can.

MENDING THE CLOCK

SIR JAMES MATTHEW BARRIE

It is a little American clock, which I got as a present about two years ago on my coming of age. The donor told me it cost half a guinea, but on inquiry at the shop where it was bought (this is what I always do when I get a present), I learned that the real price was four-and-sixpence. Up to this time I had been hesitating about buying a stand for it, but after that I determined not to do so. Since I got it, it has stood on my study mantelpiece, except once or twice at first, when its loud tick compelled me to wrap it up in flannel and bury it in the bottom of a drawer. Until a fortnight ago my clock went beautifully, and I have a feeling that had we treated it a little less hardly it would have continued to go well.

One night a fortnight ago it stopped, as if under the impression that I had forgotten to wind it up. I wound it up as far as was possible, but after going for an hour it stopped again. Then I shook it, and it went for five minutes. I strode into another room to ask who had been meddling with my clock, but no one had touched it. When I came back, it was going again, but as soon as I sat down it stopped. I shook my fist at it, which terrified it into going for half a minute, and then it went *creak, creak,* like a clock in pain. The last thing it did before stopping finally was to strike nineteen and alarm the neighbourhood for two and a half minutes.

For two days I left my clock serenely alone, nor would I ever have annoyed myself with the thing had it not been for my visitors. I have a soul above mechanics, but when these visitors saw that my clock had stopped they expressed surprise at my not mending it. How different I must be, they said, from my brother, who had a passion for making himself generally useful. If the clock had been his, he would have had it to pieces and

Mending the Clock

put it right within the hour. Then the donor of the ill-fated clock called for the first time since he had smilingly presented me with the gift, and murmured some incoherent words about ingratitude and hardness of heart. I pointed out that my mind was so full of weightier matters that I could not descend to clocks, but they had not the brains to see that what prevented my mending the clock was not incapacity but want of desire to do so. This has ever been the worry of my life, that, because I don't do certain things, people take it for granted that I can't do them. I took no prizes at school or college, but you entirely misunderstand me if you think that was because I could not take them. The fact is, that I had always a contempt for prizes and prizemen, and I have ever been one of the men who gather statistics to prove that it is the boy who sat at the foot of the class that makes his name in after life. I was that boy, and though I have not made my mark in life as yet, I could have done it, had I wanted to do so, as easily as I could mend a clock. My visitors, judging me by themselves, could not follow this argument, though I have given expression to it in their presence many times, and they were so ridiculous as to say it was a pity that my brother did not happen to be at home.

"Why, what do I need him for?" I asked irritably.

"To mend the clock," they replied, and all the answer I made them was that if I wanted the clock mended I would mend it myself.

"But you don't know the way," they said.

"Do you really think," I asked them, "that I am the kind of man to be beaten by a little American clock?"

They replied that that was their belief, at which I coldly changed the subject.

"Are you really going to attempt it?" they asked, as they departed.

"Not I," I said. "I have other things to do."

Nevertheless, the way they flung my brother at me annoyed me, and I returned straight from the door to the study to mend the clock. It amused me to picture their chagrin when they dropped in the next night and found my clock going beautifully. "Who mended it?" I fancied them asking, and I could not help practising the careless reply, "Oh, I did it myself." Then I took the clock in my hands and sat down to examine it.

The annoying thing, to begin with, was that there seemed to be no way in. The clock was practically hermetically sealed, for, though the back shook a little when I thumped it on my knee, I could see quite well that the back would not come off unless I broke the mainspring. I examined the clock carefully round and round, but to open the thing was as impossible as to get into an egg without chipping the shell. I twisted and twirled it, but nothing would move. Then I raged at the idiots who made clocks that would not open. My mother came in about that time to ask how I was getting on.

"Getting on with what?" I asked.

"With the clock," she said.

"The clock," I growled, "is nothing to me," for it irritated me to hear her insinuating that I had been foiled.

"But I thought you were trying to mend it," she said.

"Not at all," I replied; "I have something else to do."

"What a pity," she said, "that Andrew is not here." Andrew is the brother they are always flinging at me.

"He could have done nothing," I retorted, "for the fools made this clock not to open."

"I'm sure it opens," my mother said.

"Why should you be sure?" I asked fiercely.

"Because," she explained, "I never saw or heard of a clock that doesn't open."

"Then," I snarled, "you can both see and hear of it now"—and I pointed contemptuously at my clock.

She shook her head as she went out, and as soon as the door shut I hit the clock with my clenched fist (stunning my fourth finger). I had a presentiment that my mother was right about the clock's opening, and I feared that she still laboured under

Mending the Clock

the delusion that I had been trying to mend the exasperating thing.

On the following day we had a visit from my friend Summer, and he had scarcely sat down in my study when he jumped up exclaiming:

"Hullo, is that the right time?"

I said to him that the clock had stopped, and he immediately took it on his knees. I looked at him sideways and saw at once that he was the kind of man who knows about clocks. After shaking it, he asked me what was wrong.

"It needs cleaning," I said at a venture, for if I had told him the whole story, he might have thought that I did not know how to mend a clock.

"Then you have opened it and examined the works?" he asked, and not to disappoint him, I said yes.

"If it needs cleaning, why did you not clean it?" was his next question.

I hate inquisitiveness in a man, but I replied that I had not had time to clean it. He turned it round in his hands, and I knew what he was looking for before he said: "I have never taken an American clock to pieces. Does it open in the ordinary way?"

This took me somewhat aback, but Summer, being my guest, had to be answered.

"Well," I said cautiously, "it does, and it doesn't."

He looked at it again, and then held it out to me, saying:

"You had better open it yourself, seeing that you know the way."

There was a clock in the next room, and such a silence was there in my study after that remark that I could distinctly hear it ticking.

"Curiously unsettled weather," I said.

"Very," he answered. "But let me see how you get at the works of the clock."

"The fact is," I said, "that I don't want this clock mended; it ticks so loud that it disturbs me."

"Never mind," Summer said, "about that. I should like to have a look at its internals, and then we can stop it if you want to do so."

Summer talked in a light way, and I was by no means certain whether, once it was set agoing, the clock could be stopped so easily as he thought, but he was evidently determined to get inside.

"It is a curious little clock," I said to him; "a sort of puzzle, indeed, and it took me ten minutes to discover how to open it myself. Suppose you try to find out the way?"

"All right," Summer said, and then he tried to remove the glass.

"The glass doesn't come off, does it?" he asked.

"I'm not going to tell you," I replied.

"Stop a bit," said Summer, speaking to himself. "It is the feet that screw out?"

It had never struck me to try the feet; but I said: "Find out for yourself."

I sat watching with more interest than he gave me credit for, and very soon he had both the feet out; then he unscrewed the ring at the top, and then the clock came to pieces.

"I've done it," said Summer.

"Yes," I said, "but you have been a long time about it."

He examined the clock with a practised eye, and then —

"It doesn't seem to me," he said, "to require cleaning."

A less cautious man than myself would have weakly yielded to the confidence of this assertion, and so have shown that he did not know about clocks.

"Oh, yes it does," I said in a decisive tone.

"Well," he said, "we had better clean it."

"I can't be bothered cleaning it," I replied, "but, if you like, you can clean it."

"Are they cleaned in the ordinary way, those American clocks?" he asked.

Mending the Clock

"Well," I said, "they are, and they aren't."

"How should I clean it, then?" he asked.

"Oh, in the ordinary way," I replied.

Summer proceeded to clean it by blowing at the wheels, and after a time he said, "We'll try it now."

He put it together again, and then wound it up, but it would not go.

"There is something else wrong with it," he said.

"We have not cleaned it properly," I explained.

"Clean it yourself," he replied and flung out of the house.

After he had gone I took up the clock to see how he had opened it, and to my surprise it began to go. I laid it down triumphantly. At last I had mended it. When Summer came in an hour afterward, he exclaimed:

"Hullo, it's going."

"Yes," I said, "I put it to rights after you went out."

"How did you do it?" he asked.

"I cleaned it properly," I replied.

As I spoke I was leaning against the mantelpiece, and I heard the clock beginning to make curious sounds. I gave the mantelpiece a shove with my elbow, and the clock went all right again. Summer had not noticed. He remained in the room for half an hour, and all that time I dared not sit down. Had I not gone on shaking the mantelpiece, the clock would have stopped at any moment. When he went at last, I fell thankfully in a chair, and the clock had stopped before he was halfway down the stairs. I shook it, and it went for five minutes, and then stopped. I shook it again, and it went for two minutes. I shook it, and it went for half a minute. I shook it, and it did not go at all.

The day was fine, and my study window stood open. In a passion I seized hold of that clock and flung it fiercely out into the garden. It struck against the trunk of a tree and fell into a flower bed. Summer must have wound up the alarm when he was dickering with the thing, for a wild *tr-r-ring* suddenly cleft the noontide stillness. An old tabby leaped on the garden wall, made a spinal curve for a second, and then vanished. I stood at the window sneering at the clock, when suddenly I started. I have mentioned that it has a very loud tick. Surely I heard it ticking! I ran into the garden. The clock was going again! Concealing it beneath my coat, I brought it back to the study, and since then it has gone beautifully. Everybody is delighted except Summer, who is naturally a little annoyed.

THE TOM-CAT

DON MARQUIS

At midnight in the alley
    Tom-cat comes to wail,
And he chants the hate of a million years
    As he swings his snaky tail.

Malevolent, bony, brindled,
    Tiger and devil and bard,
His eyes are coals from the middle of hell
    And his heart is black and hard.

He twists and crouches and capers
    And bares his curved sharp claws,
And he sings to the stars of the jungle nights
    Ere cities were, or laws.

Beast from a world primeval,
    He and his leaping clan,
When the blotched red moon leers over the roofs,
    Give voice to their scorn of man.

He will lie on a rug to-morrow
    And lick his silky fur,
And veil the brute in his yellow eyes
    And play he's tame, and purr.

> But at midnight in the alley
> He will crouch again and wail,
> And beat the time for his demon's song
> With the swing of his demon's tail.

JABBERWOCKY

LEWIS CARROLL

"Jabberwocky" has been called the greatest nonsense poem in the English language, a bit of riotous fun, a composition of meaningless but unforgettable music. Though it cannot be explained, Lewis Carroll has teasingly "explained" parts of it. The odd, unfamiliar words he called portmanteau words — that is, two or three words run together. For instance, if you try to say "fretful" and "fuming" and "furious" all at once, you are sure to come up with "frumious." Similarly, when he says that the hero comes "galloping" back in "triumph" after slaying the Jabberwock, he naturally comes "galumphing" back.

In *Through the Looking Glass,* Humpty Dumpty tries to explain some of the words to Alice. "Brillig," he says, "means four o'clock in the afternoon — the time when you begin broiling things for dinner."

"That'll do very well," said Alice: "and 'slithy'?"

"Well, 'slithy' means 'lithe and slimy'. 'Lithe' is the same as 'active'. You see it's like a portmanteau — there are two meanings packed up into one word."

"I see it now," Alice remarked thoughtfully: "and what are 'toves'?"

"Well, 'toves' are something like badgers — they're something like lizards — and they're something like corkscrews."

"They must be very curious-looking creatures."

"They are that," said Humpty Dumpty: "also they make their nests under sun-dials — also they live on cheese."

"And what's to 'gyre' and to 'gimble'?"

"To 'gyre' is to go round and round like a gyroscope. To 'gimble' is to make holes like a gimlet."

"And 'the wabe' is the grass-plot around a sun-dial, I suppose?" said Alice, surprised at her own ingenuity.

"Of course it is. It's called 'wabe', because it goes a long way before it, and a long way behind it —"

"And a long way beyond it on each side," Alice added.

"Exactly so. Well, then, 'mimsy' is 'flimsy' and 'miserable' (there's another portmanteau for you). And a 'borogove' is a thin shabby-looking bird with its feathers sticking out all round — something like a live mop."

"And then 'mome raths'?" said Alice. "I'm afraid I'm giving you a great deal of trouble."

"Well, a 'rath' is a sort of green pig: but 'mome' I'm not certain about. I think it's short for 'from home' — meaning that they'd lost their way, you know."

>'Twas brillig, and the slithy toves
>   Did gyre and gimble in the wabe;
>All mimsy were the borogoves,
>   And the mome raths outgrabe.
>
>"Beware the Jabberwock, my son!
>   The Jaws that bite, the claws that catch!
>Beware the Jubjub bird, and shun
>   The frumious Bandersnatch!"
>
>He took his vorpal sword in hand:
>   Long time the manxome foe he sought —
>So rested he by the Tumtum tree,
>   And stood awhile in thought.
>
>And as in uffish thought he stood,
>   The Jabberwock, with eyes of flame,
>Came whiffling through the tulgey wood,
>   And burbled as it came!
>
>One, two! One, two! And through and through
>   The vorpal blade went snicker-snack!
>He left it dead, and with its head
>   He went galumphing back.
>
>"And hast thou slain the Jabberwock?
>   Come to my arms, my beamish boy!
>O frabjous day! Callooh! Callay!"
>   He chortled in his joy.

'Twas brillig, and the slithy toves
  Did gyre and gimble in the wabe;
All mimsy were the borogoves,
  And the mome raths outgrabe.

MR. PICKWICK ON THE ICE

CHARLES DICKENS

On Christmas morning Mr. Wardle invited Mr. Pickwick, Mr. Snodgrass, Mr. Tupman, Mr. Winkle, and his other guests to go down to the pond.

"You skate, of course, Winkle?" said Mr. Wardle.

"Ye — s; oh yes!" replied Mr. Winkle. "I — I — am *rather* out of practice."

"Oh, *do* skate, Mr. Winkle," said Arabella. "I like to see it so much."

"Oh it is so graceful," said another young lady.

A third young lady said it was "elegant", and a fourth expressed her opinion that it was "swanlike".

"I should be very happy, I am sure," said Mr. Winkle, reddening, "but I have no skates."

This objection was at once overruled. Trundle had a couple of pairs, and the fat boy announced that there were half a dozen more downstairs; whereat Mr. Winkle expressed exquisite delight, and looked exquisitely uncomfortable.

Mr. Wardle led the way to a pretty large sheet of ice; and the fat boy and Mr. Weller having shovelled and swept away the snow which had fallen on it during the night, Mr. Bob Sawyer adjusted his skates with a dexterity which to Mr. Winkle was perfectly marvellous, and described circles with his left leg, and cut figures of eight, and inscribed upon the ice, without once stopping for breath, a great many other pleasant and astonishing devices, — to the excessive satisfaction of Mr. Pickwick, Mr.

Tupman, and the ladies, — which reached a pitch of positive enthusiasm when Mr. Wardle and Benjamin Allen, assisted by Bob Sawyer, performed some mystic evolutions which they called a reel.

All this time Mr. Winkle, with his face and hands blue with the cold, had been forcing a gimlet into the soles of his shoes, and putting his skates on, with the points behind, and getting the straps into a very complicated state, with the assistance of Mr. Snodgrass, who knew rather less about skates than a Hindoo. At length, however, with the assistance of Mr. Weller, the unfortunate skates were firmly screwed and buckled on, and Mr. Winkle was raised to his feet.

"Now, then, sir," said Sam, in an encouraging tone, "off with you, and show them how to do it."

"Stop, Sam, stop!" said Mr. Winkle, trembling violently, and clutching hold of Sam's arms with the grasp of a drowning man. "How slippery it is, Sam!"

"Not an uncommon thing upon ice, sir," replied Mr. Weller. "Hold up, sir!"

This last observation of Mr. Weller's bore reference to a demonstration Mr. Winkle made at the instant of a frantic desire to throw his feet in the air, and dash the back of his head on the ice.

"These — these — are very awkward skates; aren't they, Sam?" inquired Mr. Winkle, staggering.

"I'm afraid there's an awkward gentleman in 'em, sir," replied Sam.

"Now, Winkle," cried Mr. Pickwick, quite unconscious that there was anything the matter. "Come; the ladies are all anxiety."

"Yes, yes," replied Mr. Winkle, with a ghastly smile. "I'm coming."

"Just going to begin," said Sam, endeavouring to disengage himself. "Now, sir, start off!"

"Stop an instant, Sam," gasped Mr. Winkle, clinging most

Mr. Pickwick on the Ice

affectionately to Mr. Weller. "I find I've got a couple of coats at home that I don't want, Sam. You may have them, Sam."

"Thank 'ee, sir," replied Mr. Weller.

"Never mind touching your hat, Sam," said Mr. Winkle, hastily. "You needn't take your hand away to do that. I meant to have given you five shillings this morning for a Christmas-box, Sam. I'll give it to you this afternoon, Sam."

"You're wery good, sir," replied Mr. Weller.

"Just hold me at first, Sam, will you?" said Mr. Winkle. "There — that's right. I shall soon get in the way of it, Sam. Not too fast, Sam; not too fast."

Mr. Winkle, stooping forward, with his body half doubled up, was being assisted over the ice by Mr. Weller, in a very singular and unswanlike manner, when Mr. Pickwick most innocently shouted from the bank, "Sam!"

"Sir?"

"Here. I want you."

"Let go, sir," said Sam. "Don't you hear the governor calling? Let go, sir."

With a violent effort, Mr. Weller disengaged himself from the grasp of the agonized Pickwickian, and in so doing, administered a considerable impetus to the unhappy Mr. Winkle. With an accuracy which no degree of dexterity or practice could have insured, that unfortunate gentleman bore swiftly down into the centre of the reel, at the very moment when Mr. Bob Sawyer was performing a flourish of unparalleled beauty. Mr. Winkle struck wildly against him, and with a loud crash they both fell heavily. Mr. Pickwick ran to the spot. Bob Sawyer had risen to his feet, but Mr. Winkle was far too wise to do anything of the kind on skates. He was seated on the ice, making spasmodic efforts to smile; but anguish was depicted on every lineament of his face.

"Are you hurt?" inquired Mr. Benjamin Allen, with great anxiety.

"Not much," said Mr. Winkle, rubbing his back very hard.

Mr. Pickwick was excited and indignant. He beckoned to Mr. Weller, and said in a stern voice, "Take his skates off."

"No; but really I had scarcely begun," remonstrated Mr. Winkle.

"Take his skates off," repeated Mr. Pickwick, firmly.

The command was not to be resisted. Mr. Winkle allowed Sam to obey in silence.

"Lift him up," said Mr. Pickwick. Sam assisted him to rise.

Mr. Pickwick retired a few paces apart from the bystanders; and beckoning his friend to approach, fixed a searching look upon him, and uttered in a low but distinct and emphatic tone, these remarkable words, "You're a humbug, sir."

"A what?" said Mr. Winkle, starting.

"A humbug, sir. I shall speak plainer, if you wish it. An impostor, sir."

With those words, Mr. Pickwick turned slowly on his heel, and rejoined his friends.

While Mr. Pickwick was delivering himself of the sentiment just recorded, Mr. Weller and the fat boy, having by their joint endeavours cut out a slide, were exercising themselves thereupon in a very masterly and brilliant manner. Sam Weller, in particular, was displaying that beautiful feat of fancy sliding which is currently called "knocking at the cobbler's door," and which is achieved by skimming over the ice on one foot, and occasionally giving a postman's knock upon it with the other. It was a good, long slide, and there was something in the motion which Mr. Pickwick, who was very cold with standing still, could not help envying.

"It looks like a nice warm exercise that, doesn't it?" he inquired of Mr. Wardle.

"Ah, it does indeed," replied Wardle. "Do you slide?"

"I used to do so on the gutters, when I was a boy," replied Mr. Pickwick.

"Try it now," said Wardle.

"Oh, do, please, Mr. Pickwick!" cried all the ladies.

Mr. Pickwick on the Ice

"I should be very happy to afford you any amusement," replied Mr. Pickwick, "but I haven't done such a thing these thirty years."

"Pooh, pooh! Nonsense!" said Wardle, dragging off his skates with the impetuosity which characterized all his proceedings. "Here, I'll keep you company; come along!" And away went the good-tempered old fellow down the slide, with a rapidity which came very close upon Mr. Weller, and beat the fat boy all to nothing.

Mr. Pickwick paused, considered, pulled off his gloves and put them in his hat, took two or three short runs, stopped as often, and at last took another run and went slowly and gravely down the slide, with his feet about a yard and a quarter apart, amidst the gratified shouts of all the spectators.

"Keep the pot a-boiling, sir," said Sam; and down went Wardle again, and then Mr. Pickwick, and then Sam, and then Mr. Winkle, and then Mr. Bob Sawyer, and then the fat boy, and then Mr. Snodgrass, following closely upon each other's heels, and running after each other with as much eagerness as if all their future prospects in life depended on their expedition.

It was the most intensely interesting thing to observe the manner in which Mr. Pickwick performed his share in the ceremony; to watch the torture of anxiety with which he viewed the person behind gaining upon him at the imminent hazard of tripping him up; to see him gradually expend the painful force he had put on at first, and turn slowly round on the slide, with his face towards the point from which he had started; to contemplate the playful smile which mantled his face when he had accomplished the distance, and the eagerness with which he turned round when he had done so and ran after his predecessor; his black gaiters tripping pleasantly through the snow, and his eyes beaming cheerfulness and gladness through his spectacles; and when he was knocked down (which happened on the average of every third round), it was the most invigorating sight that can possibly be imagined to behold him gather up his hat, gloves, and handkerchief, with a glowing countenance, and resume his station in the rank with an ardour and enthusiasm that nothing could abate.

The sport was at its height, the sliding was at the quickest, the laughter was at the loudest, when a sharp, smart crack was heard. There was a quick rush towards the bank, a wild scream from the ladies, and a shout from Mr. Tupman. A large mass of ice disappeared; the water bubbled up over it; Mr. Pickwick's hat, gloves, and handkerchief were floating on the surface, and this was all of Mr. Pickwick that anybody could see.

Dismay and anguish were depicted on every countenance; the men turned pale, and the women fainted; Mr. Snodgrass and Mr. Winkle grasped each other by the hand, and gazed with frenzied eagerness at the spot where their leader had gone down; while Mr. Tupman, by way of rendering the promptest assistance, ran off across the country at his utmost speed, screaming "Fire!" with all his might.

It was at this moment, when Mr. Wardle and Sam Weller were approaching the hole with cautious steps, that a face, head, and shoulders emerged from beneath the water, and disclosed the features and spectacles of Mr. Pickwick.

"Keep yourself up for an instant — for only one instant!" bawled Mr. Snodgrass.

"Yes, do, let me implore you — for my sake!" roared Mr. Winkle, deeply affected.

"Do you feel the bottom, old fellow?" said Wardle.

"Yes, certainly," replied Mr. Pickwick, wringing the water from his head and face, and gasping for breath. "I fell upon my back. I couldn't get on my feet at first."

The clay upon so much of Mr. Pickwick's coat as was yet visible bore testimony to the truth of this statement; and as the fears of the spectators were still further relieved by the fat boy's suddenly recollecting that the water was nowhere more than five feet deep, prodigies of valour were performed to get him out. After a vast quantity of splashing, and cracking, and struggling,

Mr. Pickwick was at length fairly extricated from his unpleasant position, and once more stood on dry land.

"Oh, he'll catch his death of cold," said Emily.

"Let me wrap this shawl round you," said Arabella.

"Ah, that's the best thing you can do," said Wardle; "and when you've got it on, run home as fast as your legs can carry you, and jump into bed directly."

A dozen shawls were offered on the instant. Three or four of the thickest having been selected, Mr. Pickwick was wrapped up, and started off, under the guidance of Mr. Weller, presenting the singular appearance of an elderly gentleman, dripping wet, and without a hat, with his arms bound down to his sides, skimming over the ground, without any clearly defined purpose, at the rate of six good English miles an hour.

But Mr. Pickwick cared not for appearances in such an extreme case, and urged on by Mr. Weller, he kept at the very top of his speed until he reached the door of Manor Farm, where he paused not an instant till he was snug in bed.

LUCILLE

ROBERT SERVICE

Of course you've heard of the *Nancy Lee,* and how she sailed away
On her famous quest of the Arctic flea, to the wilds of Hudson's Bay?
For it was a foreign Prince's whim to collect this tiny cuss,
And a golden quid was no more to him than a copper to coves like us.
So we sailed away and our hearts were gay as we gazed on the gorgeous scene;
And we laughed with glee as we caught the flea of the wolf and the wolverine;

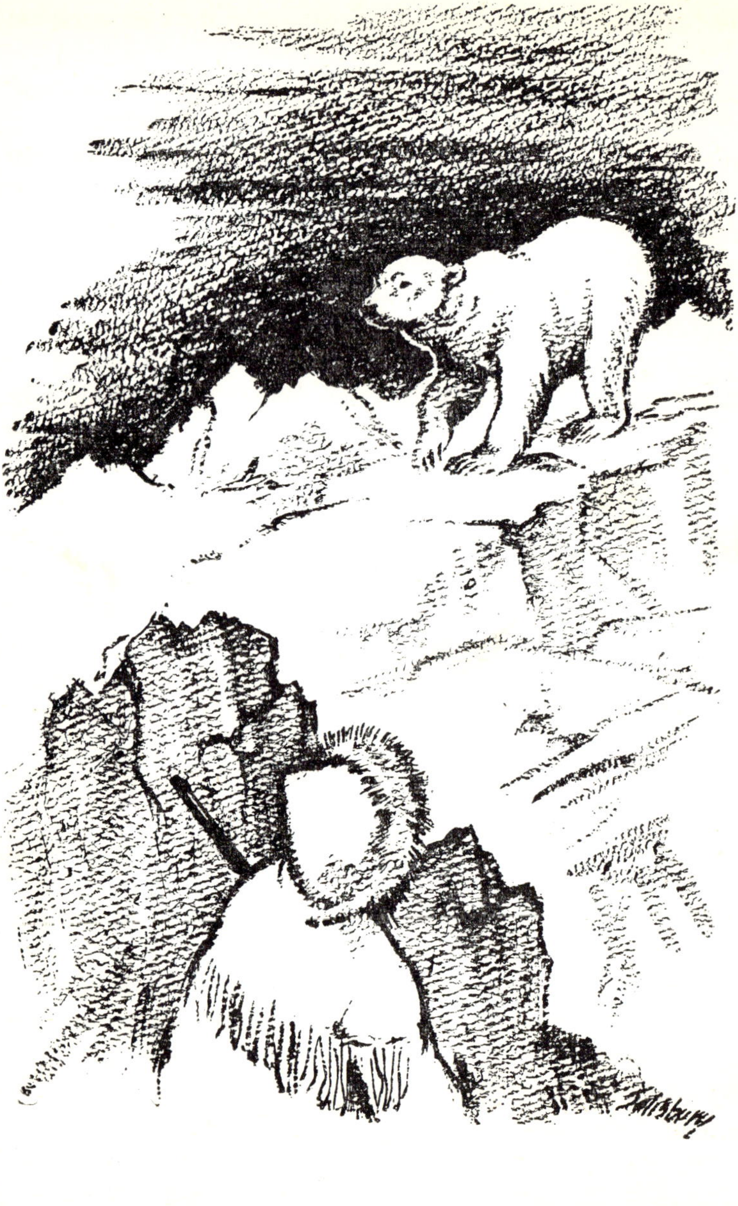

Lucille

Yea, our hearts were light as the parasite of the ermine rat we slew,
And the great musk ox, and the silver fox, and the moose and the caribou.
And we laughed with zest as the insect pest of the marmot crowned our zeal,
And the wary mink and the wily "link," and the walrus and the seal.
And with eyes aglow on the scornful snow we danced a rigadoon,
Round the lonesome lair of the Arctic hare, by the light of the silver moon.
But the time was nigh to homeward hie, when, imagine our despair!
For the best of the lot we hadn't got — the flea of the polar bear.

Oh, his face was long and his breath was strong, as the Skipper he says to me:
"I wants you to linger 'ere, my lad, by the shores of the H'artic Sea;
I wants you to 'unt the polar bear the perishin' winter through,
And if flea ye find of its breed and kind, there's a 'undred quid for you."
But I shook my head: "No, Cap," I said; "it's yourself I'd like to please,
But I tells ye flat I wouldn't do that if ye went on yer bended knees."
Then the Captain spat in the seething brine, and he says: "Good luck to you,
If it can't be did for a 'undred quid, supposin' we call it two?"
So that was why they said good-bye, and they sailed and left me there—
Alone, alone in the Arctic Zone to hunt for the polar bear.
Oh, the days were slow and packed with woe, till I thought they would never end;

And I used to sit when the fire was lit, with my pipe for my
    only friend.
And I tried to sing some rollicky thing, but my song broke off
    in a prayer,
And I'd browse and dream by the driftwood gleam: I'd dream of
    a polar bear;
I'd dream of a cloudlike polar bear that blotted the stars on high,
With ravenous jaws and flenzing claws, and the flames of hell
    in his eye.

And I'd trap around on the frozen ground, as proper hunter
    ought,
And beasts I'd find of every kind, but never the one I sought.
Never a track in the white ice-pack that humped and heaved
    and flawed,
Till I came to think: "Why, strike me pink! if the creature ain't
    a fraud."
And then one night in the waning light, as I hurried home to
    sup,
I hears a roar by the cabin door, and a great white hulk heaves
    up.
So my rifle flashed, and a bullet crashed; dead, dead as a stone
    fell he,
And I gave a cheer, for there in his ear — Gosh ding me! — a
    tiny flea.

At last, at last! Oh, I clutched it fast, and I gazed on it with pride;
And I thrust it into a biscuit-tin, and I shut it safe inside;
With a lid of glass for the light to pass, and space to leap and
    play;
Oh, it kept alive; yea, seemed to thrive, as I watched it night
    and day.
And I used to sit and sing to it, and I shielded it from harm,
And many a hearty feed it had on the heft of my hairy arm.

For you'll never know in that land of snow how lonesome a
        man can feel;
So I made a fuss of the little cuss, and I christened it "LUCILLE."
But the longest winter has its end, and the ice went out to sea,
And I saw one day a ship in the bay, and there was the *Nancy
        Lee*.
So a boat was lowered and I went aboard, and they opened wide
        their eyes —
Yes, they gave a cheer when the truth was clear, and they saw
        my precious prize.
And then it was all like a giddy dream; but to cut my story short,
We sailed away on the fifth of May to the foreign Prince's
        court;
To a palmy land and a palace grand, and the little Prince was
        there,
And a fat Princess in a satin dress with a crown of gold on her
        hair.
And they showed me into a shiny room, just him and her and me,
And the Prince he was pleased and friendly-like, and he calls
        for drinks for three.
And I shows them my battered biscuit-tin, and I makes my
        modest spiel,
And they laughed, they did, when I opened the lid, and out
        there popped LUCILLE.

Oh, the Prince was glad, I could soon see that, and the Princess
        she was too,
And LUCILLE waltzed round on the tablecloth as she often used
        to do.
And the Prince pulled out a purse of gold, and he put it in my
        hand;
And then he turned with a sudden cry, and he clutched at his
        royal beard;
And the Princess screamed, and well she might — for LUCILLE
        had disappeared.

"She must be here," said his Noble Nibbs, so we hunted all around;
Oh, we searched that place, but never a trace of the little beast we found.
So I shook my head, and I glumly said: "Gol darn the saucy cuss!
It's mighty queer, but she isn't here; so . . . she must be on one of us.
You'll pardon me if I make so free, but — there's just one thing to do:
If you'll kindly go for a half a mo', I'll search me garments through."
Then all alone on the shiny throne I stripped from head to heel;
In vain, in vain; it was very plain that I hadn't got LUCILLE.
So I garbed again, and I told the Prince, and he scratched his august head;
"I suppose if she hasn't selected you, it must be me," he said.
So he retired; but he soon came back, and his features showed distress:
"Oh, it isn't you and it isn't me" . . . Then we looked at the Princess.
So she retired; and we heard a scream, and she opened wide the door;
And her fingers twain were pinched to pain, but a radiant smile she wore:
"It's here," she cries, "our precious prize. Oh, I found it right away . . ."
Then I ran to her with a shout of joy, but I choked with a wild dismay.
I clutched the back of the golden throne, and the room began to reel . . .
What she held to was, ah, yes! a flea, but . . . it wasn't my LUCILLE.

LET US NOW PRAISE FAMOUS MEN

ESCAPE*

WINSTON S. CHURCHILL

Winston Churchill is best known to most of us as the war time Prime Minister of Great Britain. His service to his country has been long and distinguished. He has been Chancellor of the Exchequer, Home Secretary, First Lord of the Admiralty; in 1951 he was re-elected Prime Minister. He fought as a young man in many parts of the world. He is an artist of merit and a writer of distinction.

The story which follows is part of his own account of an experience he had as a war correspondent in South Africa many years ago. He had been taken prisoner by General Botha. After a month's imprisonment he escaped. The Boers were very anxious to recapture him because he was an important person.

There was nothing for it but to plod on across the veldt — but in an increasingly purposeless and hopeless manner. I felt very miserable when I looked around and saw here and there the lights of houses and thought of the warmth and comfort within them, but knew that they meant only danger to me. Far off in the moonlit horizon there presently began to shine a row of six or eight big lights which marked either Witbank or Middleburg station. Out in the darkness to my left gleamed two or three fires. I was sure they were not the lights of houses, but how far off they were, or what they were, I could not be certain. The idea formed in my mind that they were the fires of a Kaffir kraal. Then I began to think that the best use I could make of my remaining strength would be to go to these Kaffirs. I had heard that they hated the Boers and were friendly to the British. At any rate, they would probably not arrest me. They might give me food and a dry corner to sleep in. Although I could not speak a word of their language, yet I thought perhaps they might understand the value of a British banknote. They might even

*Abridged from *My Early Life* by Winston S. Churchill

be induced to help me. A guide, a pony — but above all, rest, warmth, and food. Such were the promptings which dominated my mind. So I set out towards the fires. I must have walked a mile or so in this resolve before a realization of its weakness and imprudence took possession of me. Then I turned back again to the railway line and retraced my steps perhaps half the distance. Then I stopped and sat down completely baffled, destitute of any idea what to do or where to turn. Suddenly, without the slightest reason, all my doubt disappeared. It was certainly by no process of logic that they were dispelled. I just felt quite clear that I would go to the Kaffir kraal. I had sometimes in former years held a "Planchette" pencil and written while others had touched my wrist or hand. I acted in exactly the same unconscious or subconscious manner now.

I walked on rapidly towards the fires, which I had in the first instance thought were not more than a couple of miles from the railway line. I soon found they were much farther away than that. After about an hour or an hour and a half they still seemed almost as far off as ever. But I persevered, and presently between two and three o'clock in the morning I perceived that they were not the fires of a Kaffir kraal. The angular outline of buildings began to draw out against them, and soon I saw that I was approaching a group of houses around the mouth of a coal-mine. The wheel which worked the winding gear was plainly visible, and I could see that the fires which had led me so far were from the furnaces of the engines. Hard by, surrounded by one or two slighter structures, stood a small but substantial stone house two storeys high.

I halted in the wilderness to survey this scene and to resolve my action. It was still possible to turn back. But in that direction I saw nothing but the prospect of further futile wanderings terminated by hunger, fever, discovery, or surrender. On the other hand, here in front, was a chance. The odds were heavy against me, and it was with faltering and reluctant steps that I walked out of the shimmering gloom of the veldt into the light of the furnace fires, advanced towards the silent house, and struck with my fist upon the door.

There was a pause. Then I knocked again. And almost immediately a light sprang up above and an upper window opened.

"*Wer ist da?*" cried a man's voice.

I felt a shock of disappointment and consternation to my fingers.

"I want help; I have had an accident," I replied.

Some muttering followed. Then I heard steps descending the stairs, the bolt of the door was drawn, the lock was turned. It was opened abruptly, and in the darkness of the passage a tall man hastily attired, with a pale face and dark moustache, stood before me.

"What do you want?" he said, this time in English.

I had now to think of something to say. I wanted above all to get into parley with this man, to get matters in such a state that instead of raising an alarm and summoning others he would discuss things quietly.

"I am a burgher," I began. "I have had an accident. I was going to join my commando at Komati Poort. I have fallen off the train. We were skylarking. I have been unconscious for hours. I think I have dislocated my shoulder."

It is astonishing how one thinks of these things. This story leapt out as if I had learnt it by heart. Yet I had not the slightest idea of what I was going to say or what the next sentence would be.

The stranger regarded me intently, and after some hesitation said at length, "Well, come in." He retreated a little into the darkness of the passage, threw open a door on one side of it, and pointed with his left hand into a dark room. I walked past him and entered, wondering if it was to be my prison. He followed, struck a light, lit a lamp, and set it on the table at the far side of which I stood. I was in a small room, evidently a dining-room and office in one. I noticed besides the large table, a roll desk, and two or three chairs. On his end of the table my host had laid a revolver, which he had hitherto presumably been holding in his right hand.

"I think I'd like to know a little more about this railway accident of yours," he said, after a considerable pause.

"I think," I replied, "I had better tell you the truth."

"I think you had," he said, slowly.

So I took the plunge and threw all I had upon the board.

"I am Winston Churchill, War Correspondent of the *Morning Post*. I escaped last night from Pretoria. I am making my way to the frontier." (Making my way!) "I have plenty of money. Will you help me?"

There was another long pause. My companion rose from the table slowly and locked the door. After this act, which struck me as unpromising, and was certainly ambiguous, he advanced upon me and suddenly held out his hand.

"Thank God you have come here! It is the only house for twenty miles where you would not have been handed over. But we are all British here, and we will see you through."

It is easier to recall across the gulf of years the spasm of relief which swept over me than it is to describe it. A moment before, I had thought myself trapped; and now friends, food, resources, aid, were all at my disposal. I felt like a drowning man pulled out of water and informed he has won the Derby.

My host now introduced himself as Mr. John Howard, manager of the Transvaal Collieries. He had with him at the mine-head, besides his secretary, who was British, an engine-man from Lancashire and two Scottish miners. All these four were British subjects and had been allowed to remain only upon giving their parole to observe strict neutrality. He himself as burgher of the Transvaal Republic would be guilty of treason in harbouring me, and liable to be shot if caught at the time or found out later on.

"Never mind," he said, "we will fix it up somehow," and added, "the Field Cornet was round here this afternoon asking about you. They have got the hue and cry out all along the line and all over the district."

I said that I did not wish to compromise him.

Let him give me food, a pistol, a guide, and if possible a pony, and I would make my own way to the sea, marching by night across the country far away from the railway line or any habitation.

He would not hear of it. He would fix up something. But he enjoined the utmost caution. Spies were everywhere. He had two Dutch servant-maids actually sleeping in the house. There were many Kaffirs employed about the mine premises and on the pumping-machinery of the mine. Surveying these dangers, he became very thoughtful.

Then: "But you are famishing."

I did not contradict him. In a moment he had bustled off into the kitchen. He returned after an interval with the best part of a cold leg of mutton and various other delectable commodities and, leaving me to do full justice to these, quitted the room and let himself out of the house by a back door.

Nearly an hour passed before Mr. Howard returned. "It's all right," he said. "I have seen the men, and they are all for it. We must put you down the pit to-night, and there you will stay till we can see how to get you out of the country. One difficulty," he said, "will be the skoff (food). The Dutch girl sees every mouthful I eat. The cook will want to know what has happened to her leg of mutton. I shall have to think it all out during the night. You must get down the pit at once. We'll make you comfortable enough."

Accordingly, just as the dawn was breaking, I followed my host across a little yard into the enclosure in which stood the winding-wheel of the mine. Here a stout man, introduced as Mr. Dewsnap, of Oldham, locked my hand in a grip of crushing vigour.

A door was opened and I entered the cage. Down we shot into the bowels of the earth. At the bottom of the mine were the two Scottish miners with lanterns and a big bundle which afterwards proved to be a mattress and blankets. We walked for some time through the pitchy labyrinth, with frequent turns, twists, and alterations of level, and finally stopped in a sort of chamber where the air was cool and fresh. Here my guide set down his bundle, and Mr. Howard handed me a couple of candles.

"Now we must plan how to feed you to-morrow," he said. "Don't you move from here, whatever happens," was the parting injunction. There will be Kaffirs about the mine after daylight, but we shall be on the look-out that none of them wanders this way. None of them has seen anything so far."

My four friends trooped off with their lanterns, and I was left alone. Viewed from the velvety darkness of the pit, life seemed bathed in rosy light. After the perplexity and even despair through which I had passed I counted upon freedom as certain. In this comfortable mood, and speeded by intense fatigue, I soon slept the sleep of the weary — but of the triumphant.

I do not know how many hours I slept, but the following afternoon must have been far advanced when I found myself thoroughly awake. I put out my hand for the candle, but could feel it nowhere. I did not know what pitfalls these mining galleries might contain, so I thought it better to lie quiet on my mattress and await developments. Several hours passed before the faint gleam of a lantern showed that someone was coming. It proved to be Mr. Howard himself, armed with a chicken and other good things. He also brought several books. He asked me why I had not lighted my candle. I said I couldn't find it.

"Didn't you put it under the mattress?" he asked.

"No."

"Then the rats must have got it."

He told me that he had been to the house of an English doctor twenty miles away to get the chicken. He was worried at the attitude of the two Dutch servants, who were very inquisitive about the depredations upon the leg of mutton for which I was responsible. If he could not get another chicken cooked for the next day, he would have to take double helpings on his own plate and slip the surplus into a parcel for me while the servant was out of the room. He said that inquiries were being made for me all over the district by the Boers, and that the Pretoria Government was making a tremendous fuss about my escape. The fact that there were a number of English remaining in the Middleburg mining region indicated it as a likely place for me to have turned to, and all persons of English origin were more or less suspect.

I again expressed my willingness to go on alone with a Kaffir guide and a pony, but this he utterly refused to entertain. It would take a lot of planning, he said, to get me out of the country, and I might have to stay in the mine for quite a long time.

He stayed with me while I dined, and then departed, leaving me, among other things, half-a-dozen candles, which, duly warned, I tucked under my pillow and mattress.

I slept again for a long time, and woke suddenly with a feeling of movement about me. Something seemed to be pulling at my pillow. I put out my hand quickly. There was a perfect scurry. The rats were at the candles. I rescued the candles in time, and lighted one. Luckily for me, I have no horror of rats as such, and being reassured by their evident timidity, I was not particularly uneasy. All the same, the three days I passed in the mine were not among the most pleasant which my memory re-illumines.

On the 15th Mr. Howard announced that the hue and cry seemed to be dying away. No trace of the fugitive had been discovered throughout the mining district. The talk among the Boer officials was now that I must be hiding at the house of some British sympathiser in Pretoria. They did not believe it was possible I could have got out of the town. In these circumstances he thought that I might come up and have a walk on the veldt that night, and that if all was quiet the next morning I might shift my quarters to the back room of the office. On the one hand he seemed reassured, and on the other increasingly excited by the adventure. Accordingly, I had a fine stroll in the glorious fresh air and moonlight, and thereafter, anticipating slightly our programme, I took up my quarters behind packing-cases in the inner room of the office. Here I remained for three more days, walking each night on the endless plain with Mr. Howard or his assistant.

On the 16th, the fifth day of escape, Mr. Howard informed me he had made a plan to get me out of the country. The mine was connected with the railway by a branch line. In the neighbourhood of the mine there lived a Dutchman, Burgener by name, who was sending a consignment of wool to Delagoa Bay on the 19th. This gentleman was well disposed to the British. He had been approached by Mr. Howard, had been made a party to our secret, and was willing to assist. Mr. Burgener's wool was packed in great bales and would fill two or three large trucks (freight cars). These trucks were to be loaded at the mine's siding. The bales could be so packed as to leave a small place in the centre of the truck in which I could be concealed. A tarpaulin would be fastened over each truck after it had been loaded, and it was very unlikely indeed that, if the fastenings were found intact, it would be removed at the frontier. Did I agree to take this chance?

I was more worried about this than almost anything that had happened to me so far in my adventure. However, in the end I accepted the proposal of my generous rescuer, and arrangements were made accordingly.

The afternoon of the 18th dragged slowly away. I remember that I spent the greater part of it reading Stevenson's *Kidnapped*. I was startled by the sound of rifle-shots close at hand, one after another at irregular intervals. A sinister explanation flashed through my mind. The Boers had come! Howard and his handful of Englishmen were in open rebellion in the heart of the enemy's country. I had been strictly enjoined upon no account to leave my hiding-place behind the packing-cases in any circumstances whatever, and I accordingly remained there in great anxiety. Presently it became clear that the worst had not happened. The sounds of voices and presently of laughter came from the office. Evidently a conversation, amicable, sociable in its character, was in progress. At last the voices died away, and then after an interval my door was opened and Mr. Howard's pale, sombre face appeared suffused by a broad grin. He relocked the door behind him and walked delicately towards me, evidently in high glee.

"The Field Cornet has been here," he said. "No, he was not looking for you. He says they caught you at Waterval Boven yesterday. But I didn't want him messing about, so I challenged him to a rifle match at bottles. He won two pounds off me and has gone away delighted."

"It is all fixed up for to-night," he added.

"What do I do?" I asked.

"Nothing. You simply follow me when I come for you."

At two o'clock on the morning of the 19th I awaited, fully dressed, the signal. The door opened. My host appeared. He beckoned. Not a word was spoken on either side. He led the way through the front office to the siding where three large bogie trucks stood. Three figures, evidently Dewsnap and the miners, were strolling about in different directions in the moonlight. A gang of Kaffirs were busy lifting an enormous bale into the rearmost truck. Howard strolled along to the first truck and walked across the line past the end of it. As he did so he pointed with his left hand. I nipped on to the buffers and saw before me a hole between the wool bales and the end of the truck, just wide enough to squeeze into. From this there led a narrow tunnel formed of wool bales into the centre of the truck. Here was a space wide enough to lie in, high enough to sit up in. In this I took up my abode.

Three or four hours later, when gleams of daylight had reached me through the interstices of my shelter, and through chinks in the boards of the flooring of the truck, the noise of an approaching engine was heard. Then came the bumping and banging of coupling-up. And again, after a further pause, we started rumbling off on our journey into the unknown.

I now took stock of my new abode and of the resources in munitions and supplies with which it was furnished. First there was a revolver. This was a moral support, though it was not easy to see in what way it could helpfully be applied to any problem I was likely to have to solve. Secondly, there were two roast chickens, some slices of meat, a loaf of bread, a melon, and three bottles of cold tea. The journey to the sea was not expected to take more than sixteen hours, but no one could tell what delay might occur to ordinary commercial traffic in time of war.

There was plenty of light now in the recess in which I was confined. There were many crevices in the boards composing the sides and floor of the truck, and through these the light found its way between the wool bales. Working along the tunnel to the end of the truck, I found a chink which must have been nearly an eighth of an inch in width, and through which it was possible to gain a partial view of the outer world. To check the progress of the journey I had learnt by heart beforehand the names of all the stations on the route. I can remember many of them to-day: Witbank, Middleburg, Bergendal, Belfast, Dalmanutha, Machadodorp, Waterval Boven, Waterval Onder, Elands, Nooidgedacht, and so on to Komati Poort. We had by now reached the first of these. At this point the branch line from the mine joined the railway. Here, after two or three hours' delay and shunting, we were evidently coupled up to a regular train, and soon started off at a superior and very satisfactory pace.

All day long we travelled eastward through the Transvaal; when darkness fell we were laid up the night at a station which, according to my reckoning, was Waterval Boven. We had accomplished nearly half of our journey. But how long should we wait on this siding? It might be for days; it would certainly be until the next morning. During all the dragging hours of the day I had lain on the floor of the truck occupying my mind as best as I could, painting bright pictures of the pleasures of freedom, of the excitement of rejoining the army, of the triumph of a successful escape — but haunted also perpetually by anxieties about the search at the frontier, an ordeal inevitable and constantly approaching. Now another apprehension laid hold upon me. I wanted to go to sleep. Indeed, I did not think I could possibly keep awake. But if I slept I might snore! And if I snored while the train was at rest in the silent siding, I might be heard. And if I were heard! I decided in principle that it was only prudent to abstain from sleep, and shortly afterwards fell into a blissful slumber from which I was awakened the next morning by the banging and jerking of the train as the engine was again coupled to it.

All this day, too, we rattled through the enemy's country, and late in the afternoon we reached the dreaded Komati Poort. Peeping through my chink, I could see this was a considerable place, with numerous tracks of rails and several trains standing on them. Numbers of people were moving about. There were many voices and much shouting and whistling. After a preliminary inspection of the scene I retreated, as the train pulled up, into the very centre of my fastness, and covering myself with a piece of sacking lay flat on the floor of the truck and awaited developments with a beating heart.

Three or four hours passed and again I wondered about the dangers of snoring. But in the end I slept without mishap.

We were still stationary when I awoke. Perhaps they were searching the train so thoroughly that there was consequently a great delay! Alternatively, perhaps we were forgotten on the siding and would be left there for days or weeks. I was greatly tempted to peer out, but I resisted. At last, at eleven o'clock, we were coupled up, and almost immediately started. If I had been right in thinking that the station in which we had passed the night was Komati Poort, I was already in Portuguese territory. But perhaps I had made a mistake. Perhaps I had miscounted. Perhaps there was still another station before the frontier. Perhaps the search still impended. But all these doubts were dispelled when the train arrived at the next station. I peered through my chink and saw the uniform caps of the Portuguese officials on the platform and the name Resana Garcia painted on a board. I restrained all expressions of my joy until we moved on again. Then, as we rumbled and banged along, I pushed my head out of the tarpaulin and sang and shouted and crowed at the top of my voice. Indeed, I was so carried away with thankfulness and delight that I fired my revolver two or three times in the air as a *feu de joie*. None of these follies led to any evil results.

I LOVE ALL BEAUTEOUS THINGS

ROBERT BRIDGES

I love all beauteous things,
I seek and adore them;
God hath no better praise,
And man in his hasty days
Is honoured for them.

I too will something make
And joy in the making;
Altho' to-morrow it seem
Like the empty words of a dream
Remembered on waking.

THE CHILD IS FATHER TO THE MAN

ALBERT SCHWEITZER

In 1950 — half-way through our twentieth century — many magazines and periodicals searched diligently among the experts to find an answer to this question: "Who have been the greatest men of our half-century?" Most of the answers to this question contained the name of one man — a man living in the steaming tropical jungle of Lambarene, French Equatorial Africa. His name was Albert Schweitzer.

In 1905, at the age of thirty, Albert Schweitzer had a glittering career ahead of him. Already his name was known to scholars throughout the world for his "Life of Jesus". He was head of the Faculty of Theology of the University of Strasbourg. He was a magnificent organist; the noble instruments of the cathedrals of Europe were open to him wherever he chose to play. And wherever he played musicians thronged to hear him.

But at the age of thirty Schweitzer renounced this life of fame in three fields. He renounced it as he had planned to do nine years before. He renounced it to exchange his honoured position as head of a university for six grinding years as a humble medical student in the same university. When he graduated as a physician, he went to "the white man's graveyard" of west Africa, there to devote the rest of his life to healing the humblest of God's people. At the age of 21, Albert had decided that since much had been given him, it was his duty by the time he reached thirty to repay his debt to mankind.

"The Child is Father to the Man." Here are three incidents of Albert Schweitzer's boyhood in the little mountain village of Gunsbach in Alsace, as he has told them himself, to a Swiss friend, in a wait between trains on one of his hurried trips back to Europe. Perhaps we can see in little Albert the seeds of what grew into the "Greatest Man of the Half-Century."

I

I never looked for trouble by being aggressive, but I liked measuring my bodily strength with that of others in a friendly tussle. One day on the way home from school I had a wrestle with George Nitschelm — he is now underground — who was bigger than I, and was supposed to be stronger, but I got him down. While he was lying under me, he jerked out, "Yes, if I got broth to eat twice a week, as you do, I should be as strong as you are!"

I staggered home, overcome by this finish to our play. George Nitschelm had, with cruel plainness, declared what I had already been obliged to feel on other occasions: the village boys did not accept me as one of themselves. I was to them one who was better off than they were, the parson's son, a sprig of the gentry. The certainty of this caused me much suffering, for I wanted to be exactly like them, and not a bit better off. The broth became nauseous to me; whenever I saw it steaming on the table I could hear George Nitschelm's voice.

So I now watched most carefully to see that I did not make myself in any way different from the others. For winter wear I had been given an overcoat made out of an old one of my father's. But no village-boy wore an overcoat, and when the tailor was fitting it on he said, "By Jove, Albert, now you're a regular gentleman!" It cost me a big effort to keep back the tears. The day I was to wear it for the first time — it was for church on a Sunday morning — I refused point-blank, and there was an unpleasant scene. My father gave me a box on the ear, but that did no good. They had to take me to church without the overcoat, and everytime I was expected to wear it, it was the same tale over again. What a number of times I got the stick over this new garment! But I stood firm.

That same winter my mother took me to Strassburg to visit an elderly relative, and she wished to use the visit as an opportunity for buying me a cap. In a fine big shop they tried several on me, and at last my mother and the shopwoman agreed on a handsome sailor's cap which I was to take for my own. But they had reckoned without their host. The cap displeased me altogether, because no village boy wore a sailor's cap. When they went on pressing me to take this one or that one from among all those they had tried on me, I got into such a passion that everybody in the shop ran up to us.

"Well, what sort of cap do you want, you stupid lad?" the shopwoman shouted at me. "I won't have one of your new-fashioned ones; I'll have one like what the village boys wear." So a shop-girl was sent out, and she brought me from the unsaleable stock a brown cap that one could pull down over one's ears. Beaming with joy, I put it on, while my poor mother had to put up with some cutting remarks and some contemptuous glances on account of her young duffer. It hurt me that she had been put to shame before the townspeople on my account, but she did not scold me; it seemed as if she suspected that there was some real reason behind it all.

This stern contest lasted all the time I was at the village school, and poisoned not only my life but that of my father, too. I would only wear fingerless gloves, because the village boys wore no others, and on weekdays I would go out only in wooden clogs, because the village boys wore their leather boots only on Sundays. Every time a visitor came the contest was started afresh, for it was my duty to present myself dressed "suitably to my station in life". Indoors, indeed, I yielded in every way, but when it was a case of going out to pay a visit dressed as a "sprig of the gentry", I was again the intolerable creature who provoked his father and the courageous hero who put up with boxes on the ear and let himself be shut up in the cellar. And it was a real grief to me to be so perverse with my parents. My sister Louise, who was a year older than I, had some understanding of what my ideas really were, and she was quite sympathetic.

The village boys never knew what I went through on their account; they accepted without emotion all my efforts not to be

The Child is Father to the Man

in any way different from them, and then, whenever the slightest dispute arose between us, they stabbed me with the dreadful word, "sprig of the gentry".

II

It was quite incomprehensible to me — this was before I began going to school — why in my evening prayers I should pray for human beings only. So when my mother had prayed with me and had kissed me good-night, I used to add silently a prayer that I had composed myself for all living creatures. It ran thus: "O, heavenly Father, protect and bless all things that have breath; guard them from all evil, and let them sleep in peace."

A deep impression was made on me by something which happened during my seventh or eighth year. Henry Brasch and I had with strips of india-rubber made ourselves catapults, with which we could shoot small stones. It was spring and the end of Lent, when one morning Henry said to me, "Come along, let's go on to the Rebberg and shoot some birds." This was to me a terrible proposal, but I did not venture to refuse for fear he should laugh at me. We got close to a tree which was still without any leaves, and on which the birds were singing beautifully to greet the morning, without showing the least fear of us. Then stooping like a Red Indian hunted, my companion put a bullet in the leather of his catapult and took aim. In obedience to his nod of command, I did the same, though with terrible twinges of conscience, vowing to myself that I would shoot directly he did. At that very moment the church bells began to ring, mingling their music with the songs of the birds and the sunshine. It was the warning-bell, which began half an hour before the regular peal-ringing, and for me it was a voice from heaven. I shooed the birds away, so that they flew where they were safe from my companion's catapult, and then I fled home. And ever since then, when the Passiontide bells ring out to the leafless trees and the sunshine, I reflect with a rush of grateful emotion how on that day their music drove deep into my heart the commandment: "Thou shalt not kill."

From that day onward I took courage to emancipate myself from the fear of men, and whenever my inner convictions were at stake I let other people's opinions weigh less with me than they had done previously. I tried also to unlearn my former dread of being laughed at by my school-fellows. This early influence upon me of the commandment not to kill or to torture other creatures is the great experience of my childhood and youth. By the side of that all others are insignificant.

While I was still going to the village school we had a dog with a light brown coat named Phylax. Like many others of his kind, he could not endure a uniform, and always went for the postman. I was, therefore, commissioned to keep him in order whenever the postman came, for he was inclined to bite, and had already been guilty of the crime of attacking a policeman. I therefore used to take a switch and drive him into a corner of the yard, and kept him there till the postman had gone. What a feeling of pride it gave to me to stand, like a wild beast tamer, before him while he barked and showed his teeth, and to control him with blows of the switch whenever he tried to break out of the corner! But this feeling of pride did not last. When, later in the day, we sat side by side as friends, I blamed myself for having struck him; I knew that I could keep him back from the postman if I held him by his collar and stroked him. But when the fatal hour came round again I yielded once more to the pleasurable intoxication of being a wild beast tamer!

During the holidays I was allowed to act as driver for our next door neighbour. His chestnut horse was old and asthmatic, and was not allowed to trot much, but in my pride of drivership I let myself again and again be seduced into whipping him into a trot, even though I knew and felt that he was tired. The pride of sitting behind a trotting horse infatuated me, and the man let me go on in order not to spoil my pleasure. But what was the end of the pleasure? When we got home and I noticed during the unharnessing what I had not looked at in the same way when I was in the cart, *viz.* how the poor animal's flanks were working, what good was it to me to look into his tired eyes and silently ask him to forgive me?

On another occasion — it was while I was at the Gymnasium, our high school, and at home for Christmas holidays — I was driving a sledge when neighbour Loscher's dog, which was known to be vicious, ran yelping out of the house and sprang at the horse's head. I thought I was fully justified in trying to sting him up well with the whip, although it was evident that he only ran at the sledge in play. But my aim was too good; the lash caught him in the eye, and he rolled howling in the snow. His cries of pain haunted me; I could not get them out of my ears for weeks.

III

A Jew from a neighbouring village, Mausche by name, who dealt in land and cattle, used to come occasionally through Gunsbach with his donkey-cart. As there was at that time no Jew living in the village, this was always something of an event for the boys; they used to run after him and jeer at him. One day, in order to announce to the world that I was beginning to feel myself grown up, I could not help joining them, although I did not really understand what it all meant, so I ran along with the rest behind him and his donkey-cart, shouting: "Mausche, Mausche!" The most daring of them used to fold the corner of their shirt or jacket to look like a pig's ear, and spring with that as close to him as they could. In this way we followed him out of the village as far as the bridge, but Mausche, with his freckles and his grey beard, drove on as unperturbed as his donkey, except that he several times turned round and looked at us with an embarrassed but good-natured smile. This smile overpowered me. From Mausche it was that I first learnt what it means to keep silent under persecution, and he thus gave me a most valuable lesson. From that day forward I used to greet him politely, and later, when I was in the Gymnasium, I made it my practice to shake hands and walk a little way along with him, though he never learnt what he really was to me. To me he has always been "Mausche" with the tolerant smile, the smile which even to-day compels me to be patient when I should like to rage and storm.

NANCY HANKS

ROSEMARY BENÉT

If Nancy Hanks
Came back as a ghost,
Seeking news
Of what she loved most,
She'd ask first,
"Where's my son?
What's happened to Abe?
What's he done?

"Poor little Abe,
Left all alone
Except for Tom,
Who's a rolling stone;
He was only nine
The year I died.
I remember still
How hard he cried.

"Scraping along
In a little shack,
With hardly a shirt
To cover his back,
And a prairie wind
To blow him down,

Or pinching times
If he went to town.

"You wouldn't know
About my son?
Did he grow tall?
Did he have fun?
Did he learn to read?
Did he get to town?
Do you know his name?
Did he get on?"

HOW ABE LINCOLN PAID FOR HIS STOCKINGS

EDWARD EGGLESTON

To the City Hotel in the little village of Moscow, Illinois, there came, on the first day after Tom's arrest, one of those solitary horsemen who gave life to nearly every landscape and mystery to nearly every novel of that generation. This horseman, after the fashion of the times, carried his luggage in a pair of saddlebags, which kept time to his horse's trot by rapping against the flaps of his saddle.

"Howdy, Cap'n Biggs," said the traveller to the landlord, who was leaning stolidly against the doorjamb and showing no sign of life, except by slowly and intermittently working his jaws in the manner of a ruminating cow.

"Howdy, Abe," was the answer. The rider alighted and stretched the kinks out of his long, lank limbs, the horse meanwhile putting his head halfway to the ground and moving farther into the cool shade. Then the horseman proceeded to disengage his saddlebags from the stirrup straps, now on one side of the horse and then on the other.

"Have yer hoss fed some corn?" In asking this question, Captain Biggs with some difficulty succeeded in detaching himself from the doorpost, bringing his weight perpendicularly upon his legs; this accomplished, he sluggishly descended the three doorsteps to the ground and took hold of the bridle.

"What's this I hear about Tom Grayson, Cap'n?" said the newcomer, as he tried to pull and wriggle his trouser legs down to their normal place.

"Oh, he's gone 'n' shot Lockwood, like the blasted fool he is. He wuz blowin' about it afore he lef' town las' month, but nobody reckoned it wuz anything but blow. Some trouble about a purty gal. I s'pose Tom's got to swing fer it, 'nless you kin kinder bewilder the jury like, an' git him off. Ole Mis' Grayson's in the settin' room now awaitin' to see you about it."

Captain Biggs lifted his face, on which was a week's growth of stubby beard, to see how his guest would take this information. The tall, awkward young lawyer only drew his brow to a frown and said nothing; but turned and went into the tavern with his saddlebags on his arm, and walking stiffly from being so long cramped in riding. Passing through the cool barroom with its moist odours of mixed drinks, he crossed the hall into the rag-carpeted sitting room beyond.

"Oh, Abra'm, I'm that glad to see you!" But here the old lady's feelings overcame her, and she could not go on.

"Howdy, Mrs. Grayson. It's too bad about Tom. How did he come to do it?"

"Lawsy, honey, he didn't do it."

"You think he didn't?"

"I know he didn't. He says so himself. I've been a-waitin' here all the mornin' to see you an' git you to defend him."

The lawyer sat down on the wooden settee by Mrs. Grayson, and after a little time of silence, said:

"You'd better get some older man, like Blackman."

"Tom won't have Blackman; he won't have nobody but Abe Lincoln, he says."

"But — they say the evidence is all against him; and if that's the case, an inexperienced man like me couldn't do any good."

Mrs. Grayson looked at him piteously as she detected his reluctance.

"Abra'm, he's all the boy I've got left. Ef you'll defend him, I'll give you my farm an' make out the deed before you begin. An' that's all I got."

"Farm be hanged!" said Lincoln. "Do you think I don't remember your goodness to me when I was a little wretch with my toes sticking out of my ragged shoes! I wouldn't take a copper from you. But you're Tom's mother, and of course you think he didn't do it. Now what if the evidence proves that he did?"

Barbara had been sitting in one corner of the room, and Lincoln had not observed her in the obscurity produced by the shade of the green slat curtains. She got up and came forward. "Abra'm, do you remember me?"

"Is this little Barby?" he said, scanning her face. "You're a young woman now, I declare."

There was a simple tenderness in his voice that showed how deeply he felt the trouble that had befallen the Graysons.

"Well, I want to say, Abra'm," Barbara went on, "that after talking to Tom, we believe that he doesn't know anything about the shooting. Now you'd better go and see him for yourself."

"Well, I'll tell you what, Aunt Marthy," he said, relapsing into the familiar form of address he had been accustomed to use toward Mrs. Grayson in his boyhood; "I'll go over and see Tom, and if he is innocent, as you and Barby think, we'll manage to save him or know the reason why. But I must see him alone, and he musn't know about my talk with you."

Lincoln got up and, laying his saddlebags down in one corner of the room, went out immediately. First, he went to inquire of Sheriff Plunkett what was the nature of the evidence likely to be brought against Tom. Then he got the sheriff to let him into the jail and leave him alone with his client. Tom had been allowed to remain in the lightest of the cells, since there was no fear of his escape on this day, when all the town was agog about the murder, and people were continually coming to peer into the jail to get a glimpse of the monster who, in the darkness, had shot down one who had helped him out of a gambling scrape.

Lincoln sat down on the only stool there was in the room, while Tom sat on a bench.

"Now, Tom," said the lawyer, fixing his penetrating gaze on the young man's face, "you want to remember that I'm your friend and your counsel. However proper it may be to keep your own secret in such a situation as you are, you must tell me the whole truth, or else I cannot do you any good. How did you come to shoot Lockwood?"

"I didn't shoot Lockwood," said Tom brusquely; "and if you don't believe that, it's no use to go on."

"Well, say I believe it then, and let's proceed. Tell me all that happened between you and that young man."

Tom began and told all about the gambling in Wooden & Snyder's store, and how he was led into it, and about his visit to Hubbard Township to get money to pay Lockwood. Then he told of his anger and his threats, his uncle's break with him, and his talk with Barbara the evening before the murder; and finally he gave a detailed account of all that happened to him on the campground, and of his flight and arrest.

"But," said Lincoln, who had looked closely and sometimes incredulously at Tom's face while he spoke, "why did you take a pistol with you to the camp meeting?"

"I did not. I hadn't had a pistol in my hand for a week before the shooting."

"But Plunkett says that there's a man ready to swear that he saw you do the shooting. They've got a pistol out of one of your drawers, and this witness will swear that you used just such an old-fashioned weapon as that."

"Good Heavens, Abe! Who would tell such an infernal lie on a fellow in my fix? That makes my situation bad." Tom got up and walked the stone-paved floor in excitement. "But the bullet will show that I didn't do it. Get hold of the bullet, and if it fits the bore of that old-fashioned pistol I won't ask you to defend me."

"But there wasn't any bullet." Lincoln was now watching Tom's countenance with the closest scrutiny.

"No bullet! How in creation did they kill him, then?"

"Can't you think?" He was still studying Tom's face.

"I don't know any way of killing a fellow with a pistol that's got no bullets unless you beat his brains out with the butt of it, and I thought they said George was shot."

"So he was."

"But how was he killed?" demanded Tom.

"With buckshot."

Tom stood and mused a minute.

"Now tell me who says I did the shooting."

"I never heard of him before. Sovine, I believe his name is."

"Dave Sovine? W'y he's the son of old Bill Sovine; he's the boy that ran off four years ago, don't you remember? He's the swindler who won all my money. What does he want to get me hanged for? I paid him all I owed him."

Lincoln hardly appeared to hear what Tom was saying. He sat now with his eyes fixed on the grating, lost in thought.

"Tom, I've made up my mind that you're innocent, but it's going to be dreadful hard to prove it," he said at last. "Who was the strapping, big, knockdown fellow that used to be about your place — hunter, fisherman, fist fighter, and all that?"

"Do you mean Bob McCord?"

"That must be the man. Big Bob, they called him. He's friendly to you isn't he?"

"Oh, yes!"

"Well, you have Big Bob come to see me next Tuesday at the tavern, as I go back. I'll be there to dinner. And if you are called to the inquest, you have only to tell the truth. We won't make any fight before the coroner. You'll be bound over anyhow, and it's not best to show our hand too soon."

With that Abe took his leave. When he got out of the prison, he found Mrs. Grayson and Barbara waiting to see him.

"Well, Aunt Marthy," he said, "it doesn't seem to me that your boy killed that fellow. It's going to be hard to clear him, but he didn't do it. I'll do my best. You must get all Tom's relations to come to the trial. And have Big Bob McCord come to see me next Tuesday."

The coroner's inquest was held in a barn where the corpse was taken and where the people of the whole countryside gathered.

Dave Sovine swore that he saw Tom Grayson shoot and kill George Lockwood. This testimony so angered the crowd that, had the officers not taken Tom away in secret, he would have suffered death at the hands of the unreasonable mob. Tom Grayson was bound over to the circuit court.

On the date set for the trial in court, the people gathered in large numbers, and those who had seats in the courtroom were, for the most part, too wise to vacate them during the noon recess. In the afternoon Judge Watkins' austere face assumed a yet more severe expression; for though pity never interfered with justice in his nature, it often rendered the old man unhappy, and therefore more than usually ill-tempered.

There was a painful pause after the judge had taken his seat and ordered the prisoner brought in. It was like a wait before a funeral service, but rendered ten times more distressing by the element of suspense. The judge's quill pen could be heard scratching on the paper as he noted points for his charge to the jury.

The spectators who sympathized with Tom Grayson watched Lincoln as he took his seat in moody silence. Why had the lawyer not done anything to help Tom? Any other lawyer with a desperate case would have had a stack of law books in front of him, as a sort of dam against the flood. But Lincoln had neither law books nor so much as a scrap of paper.

The prosecuting attorney, with a taste for climaxes, reserved

How Abe Lincoln Paid for His Stockings

his chief witness to the last. Even now he was not ready to call Sovine. He would add one more stone to the pyramid of evidence before he capped it all with certainty. A witness was therefore put up to identify the old pistol which he had found in Tom's room. Lincoln again did not cross-examine the witness. The lawyer Blackman felt certain that he himself could have done better. He mentally constructed the questions that should have been put to the deputy sheriff. Was the pistol hot when you found it? Did it smell of powder? Did the family make any objection to your search? — Even if the judge had ruled out such questions the jury would have heard the questions, and a question often has weight in spite of rulings from the bench.

The prosecuting attorney began to feel sure of his own case; he had come to his last witness and his great stroke.

"Call David Sovine," he said, wiping his brow and looking triumphant.

"David Sovine! David Sovine! David Sovine!" cried the sheriff in due and ancient form, though David sat almost within whispering distance of him.

The witness stood up.

"Hold up your right hand," said the clerk.

Then, when Dave's right hand was up, Magill rattled off the form of oath in the most approved and clerkly style, only adding to its effect by the mild brogue of his pronunciation.

"Do sol'm swear't yu'll tell th' truth, th' ole truth, en nuthin' b' th' truth, s' yilpye God?" said the clerk, without once pausing for breath.

Sovine ducked his head and dropped his hand, and the solemnity was over.

Dave, who was evidently not accustomed to stand before such a crowd, appeared embarrassed. He had deteriorated in appearance lately. His patent-leather shoes were bright as ever, his trousers were trimly held down by straps, his hair was well kept in place by bear's oil or what was sold for bear's oil, but there was a nervousness in his expression and carriage that gave him the air of a man who had been drinking to excess. Tom looked at him defiantly, but Dave was standing at the right of the judge, while the prisoner's dock was on the left. The witness did not look at Tom at all. He told his story with clarity, although something of the bold assurance which he displayed at the inquest was lacking. His coarse face twitched and quivered, and this seemed to annoy him. He sought to hide it by an air of indifference, as he rested his weight now on one foot and now on the other.

"Do you know the prisoner?" asked the prosecutor with a motion of his head toward the dock.

"Yes, well enough;" in saying this Dave did not look toward Tom, but out of the window.

"You've played cards with him, haven't you?"

"Yes."

"Tell his Honour and the jury when and where you played with him."

"We played one night last July, in Wooden & Snyder's store."

"Who proposed to Tom to play with you?"

"George Lockwood. He hollered up the stovepipe for Tom to come down an' take a game or two with me."

"What did you win that night from Tom?"

"Thirteen dollars, an' his hat an' coat an' boots, an' his han'ke'chi'f, an' knife."

"Who, if anybody, lent him money to get back his things which you had won?"

"George Lockwood."

Here the counsel paused a moment, laid down a memorandum he had been using, and looked about his table until he found another; and then resumed his question.

"'Tell the jury whether you were at the Timber Creek camp meeting on the ninth of August."

"Yes; I was."

"What did you see there? Tell about the shooting."

Dave told the story, with a little prompting in the way of questions from the lawyer, substantially as he told it at the

How Abe Lincoln Paid for His Stockings

coroner's inquest. He related his parting from Lockwood, Tom's appearance on the scene, Tom's threatening speech, Lockwood's entreaty to Tom not to shoot him, and then Tom's shooting. In making these statements Dave looked at the stairway in the corner of the courtroom with an air of entire indifference, and he even made one or two efforts to yawn, as though the case was a rather dull affair to him.

"How far away from Grayson and Lockwood were you when the shooting took place?" asked the prosecutor.

"Twenty foot or more."

"What did Tom shoot with?"

"A pistol."

"What kind of pistol?"

"One of the ole-fashion' sort — flintlock, with a ruther long barrel."

The prosecuting lawyer now beckoned to the sheriff, who handed down to him, from off his high desk, Tom's pistol.

"Tell the jury whether this looks like the pistol."

"'Twas just such a one as that. I can't say it was that, but it was hung to the stock like that, an' about as long in the barrel."

"What did Grayson do when he had shot George, and what did you do?"

"Tom ran off as fast as his feet could carry him, an' I went up towards George, who'd fell over. He was dead afore I could get there. Then purty soon the crowd come a-runnin' up to see what the fracas was."

After bringing out some further details, the prosecuting attorney turned to his opponent with an air of confidence and said:

"You can have the witness, Mr. Lincoln."

There was a brief pause, during which the jurymen changed their positions on the hard seats, making a little rustle as they took their right legs from off their left and hung their left legs over their right knees, or vice versa. In making these changes they looked inquiringly at one another, and it was clear that their minds were so well made up that even a judge's charge in favour of the prisoner, if such a thing had been conceivable, would have gone for nothing. Lincoln at length rose slowly from his chair, and stood awhile in silence, regarding Sovine, who seemed excited and nervous, and who visibly paled a little as his eyes sought to escape from the lawyer's gaze.

"You said you were with Lockwood just before the shooting?" the counsel asked.

"Yes." Dave was all alert and answered promptly.

"Were you not pretty close to him when he was shot?"

"No, I wasn't," said Dave, his suspicions excited by this mode of attack. It appeared that the lawyer, for some reason, wanted to make him confess to having been nearer to the scene and perhaps implicated, and he therefore resolved to fight off.

"Are you sure you were as much as ten feet away?"

"I was more than twenty," said Dave huskily.

"What had you and George Lockwood been doing together?"

"We'd been — talking." Obviously Dave took fresh alarm at this line of questioning.

"Oh, you had?"

"Yes."

"In a friendly way?"

"Yes, t'be shore; we never had any fuss."

"You parted from him as a friend?"

"Yes, of course."

"By the time Tom came up you'd got — how far away? Be careful now."

"I've told you twicet. More than twenty feet."

"You might have been mistaken about its being Tom, then?"

"No, I wasn't."

"Did you know it was Tom before he fired?"

"T'be shore, I did."

"What time of night was it?"

"Long towards ten, I sh'd think."

"It might have been eleven?"

How Abe Lincoln Paid for His Stockings

"No, 'twustn't later'n about ten." This was said doggedly.

"Nor before nine?"

"No, 'twas nigh onto ten, I said." And the witness showed some irritation and spoke louder than before.

"How far away were you from the pulpit and meeting place?"

"Twixt a half a mile an' a mile."

"Not over a mile?"

"No, it's nigh onto a mile. I didn't measure it, but it's a mighty big three-quarters."

The witness answered combatively, and in this mood he made a better impression than he did on his direct examination. The prosecuting attorney looked relieved. Tom listened with an attention painful to see, his eyes moving anxiously from Lincoln to Dave as he wondered what point in Dave's armour the lawyer could be driving at. He saw plainly that his salvation was staked on some last throw.

"You didn't have any candle in your hand, did you, at any time during the evening?"

"No!" said Dave positively. For some reason this questioning disconcerted him and awakened his suspicion. "What should we have a candle for?" he added.

"Did either George Lockwood or Tom have a candle?"

"No, of course not! What'd they have candles for?"

"Where were the lights on the campground?"

"Close't by the preacher's tent."

"More than three-quarters of a mile away from the place where the murder took place?"

"Anyway as much as three-quarters," said Dave, who began to wish that he could modify his previous statement of the distance.

"How far away were you from Lockwood when the murder took place?"

"Twenty feet."

"You said 'or more' awhile ago."

"Well, 'twusn't no less, p'r'aps," said Dave, showing signs of worry. "You don't think I measured it, do yeh?"

"There were no lights nearer than three-quarters of a mile?"

"No," said the witness, the cold perspiration beading on his face as he saw Lincoln's trap opening to receive him.

"You don't mean to say that the platform torches up by the preacher's tent gave any light three-quarters of a mile away and in the woods?"

"No, of course not."

"How could you see Tom and know that it was he that fired, when the only light was nearly a mile away, and inside a circle of tents?"

"Saw by moonlight," said Sovine snappishly, disposed to dash at any gap that offered a possible way of escape.

"What sort of trees were there on the ground?"

"Beech."

"Beech leaves are pretty thick in August?" asked Lincoln.

"Ye-es, ruther," gasped the witness, seeing a new pitfall yawning just ahead of him.

"And yet light enough from the moon came through these thick beech trees to let you know Tom Grayson?"

"Yes."

"And you full twenty feet away?"

"Well, about that; nearly twenty, anyhow." Dave shifted his weight to his right foot.

"And you pretend to say to this court that by the moonlight that you got through the beech trees in August you could even see that it was a pistol that Tom had?" This was said with a little laugh, very exasperating to the witness.

"Yes, I could," answered Dave with dogged resolution not to be faced down.

"And just how the barrel was hung to the stock?" There was a positive sneer in Lincoln's voice now.

"Yes." This was spoken feebly.

"And you twenty feet or more away?"

"I've got awful good eyes, an' I know what I see," whined the witness apologetically.

Here Lincoln paused and looked at Sovine, whose extreme distress was only made the more apparent by his feeble endeavour to conceal his agitation. The counsel, after regarding his uneasy victim for a quarter of a minute, thrust his hand into the tail pocket of his blue coat, and after a little needless fumbling drew forth a small pamphlet in green covers. He turned the leaves of this with extreme deliberation, while the courtroom was utterly silent. The members of the bar had, as by general consent, put their chairs down on all fours and were intently watching the struggle between the counsel and the witness. The sallow-faced judge had stopped the scratching of his quill and had lowered his spectacles on his nose, that he might study the distressed face of the tormented Sovine. Mrs. Grayson's hands were on her lap, palms downward; her eyes were fixed on Abra'm, and her mouth was half open, as though she were going to speak.

Barbara found it hard to keep her seat, she was so eager for Lincoln to go on; and Tom was leaning forward breathlessly in the dock; his throat felt dry, and he choked when he tried to swallow. It seemed to him that he would smother with the beating of his heart.

Lincoln appeared to be the only perfectly deliberate person in the room. He seemed disposed to protract the situation as long as possible. He held his victim on the rack and he let him suffer. He would turn a leaf or two in his pamphlet and then look up at the demoralized witness, as though to fathom the depth of his torture and to measure the result. At last he fixed his thumb firmly at a certain place on a page and turned his eyes to the judge.

"Now, your Honour," he said to the Court, "this witness," with a half-contemptuous gesture of his awkward left hand toward Sovine, "has sworn over and over that he recognized the accused as the person who shot George Lockwood, near the Union camp meeting on the night of the ninth of August, and that he, the witness, was standing at the time twenty feet or more away, while the scene of the shooting was nearly a mile distant from the torches inside the circle of tents. So remarkably sharp are this witness's eyes that he even saw what kind of pistol the prisoner held in his hands, and how the barrel was hung to the stock, and he is able to identify this pistol of Grayson's as precisely like and probably the identical weapon." Here Lincoln paused and scrutinized Sovine. "All these details he saw and observed in the brief space of time preceding the fatal shot — saw and observed them at ten o'clock at night, by means of moonlight shining through the trees — beech trees in full leaf. That is a pretty hard story. How much light does even a full moon shed in a beech woods like that on the Union campground? Not enough to see your way by, as everybody knows who has had to stumble through such woods."

Lincoln paused here, that the words he had spoken might have time to produce their due effect on the judge, and especially on the slower wits of some of the jury. Meanwhile, he turned the leaves of his pamphlet. Then he began once more:

"But, may it please the Court, before proceeding with the witness I would like to have the jury look at the almanac which I hold in my hand. They will here see that on the night of the ninth of last August, when this extraordinary witness" — with a sneer at Dave, who had sunk down in a chair in exhaustion — "saw the shape of a pistol at twenty feet away, at ten o'clock by moonlight, the moon did not rise until half past one in the morning."

Sovine had been gasping like a fish newly taken from the water while Lincoln uttered these words, and he now began to mutter something.

"You may have a chance to explain when the jury get done looking at the almanac," said the lawyer to him. "For the present you'd better keep silent."

There was a rustle of excitement in the courtroom, but at a

How Abe Lincoln Paid for His Stockings

word from the judge the sheriff's gavel fell and all was still. Lincoln walked slowly toward the jury box and gave the almanac to the foreman, an intelligent farmer. Countrymen in that day were used to consulting almanacs, and one group after another of the jurymen satisfied themselves that on the night of the ninth, that is, on the morning of the tenth, the moon came up at half past one o'clock. When all had examined the page, the counsel recovered his little book.

"Will you let me look at it?" asked the judge.

"Certainly, your Honour;" and the little book was handed up to the judge, who with habitual caution looked it all over, outside and in, even examining the title page to make sure that the book was genuine and belonged to the current year. Then he took note on a slip of paper of the moon's rising on the night of August ninth and tenth and handed back the almanac to Lincoln, who slowly laid it face down on the table in front of him, open at the place of its testimony. The audience in the courtroom was utterly silent and expectant. The prosecuting attorney got halfway to his feet to object to Lincoln's course, but he thought better of it and sat down again.

"Now, may it please the Court," Lincoln went on, "I wish at this point to make a motion. I think the Court will not regard it as out of order, as the case is very exceptional — a matter of life and death. This witness has solemnly sworn to a story that has obviously not one word of truth in it. It is one unbroken falsehood. In order to take away the life of an innocent man he has invented this atrocious web of lies, to the falsity of which the very heavens above bear witness, as this almanac shows you. Now why does David Sovine go to all this trouble to perjure himself? Why does he wish to swear away the life of that young man who never did him any harm?" Lincoln stood still a moment and looked at the witness, who had grown ghastly pale about the lips. Then he went on, very slowly. "Because that witness shot and killed George Lockwood himself. I move, your Honour, that David Sovine be arrested at once for murder."

These words, spoken with extreme deliberation and careful emphasis shook the audience like an explosion.

The prosecutor got to his feet, probably to suggest that the motion was not in order, since he had yet a right to a redirect examination of Sovine, but, as the attorney for the State, his duty was now a divided one as between two men charged with the same crime. So he waved his hand hesitantly, stammered inarticulately, and sat down.

"This is at least a case of extraordinary perjury," said the judge. "Sheriff, arrest David Sovine! This matter will have to be looked into."

The sheriff came down from his seat and went up to the now stunned and bewildered Sovine.

"I arrest you," he said, taking him by the arm.

The day-and-night fear of detection in which Dave had lived for all these weeks had wrecked his self-control at last.

He muttered, dropping his head with a sort of shudder.

"Tain't any use keepin' it back any longer. I — didn't mean to shoot him, an' I wouldn't a' come here ag'inst Tom if I could 'a' got away."

The words appeared to be wrung from him by some internal agony too strong for him to master. They were the involuntary result of the breaking down of his forces under prolonged suffering and terror, culminating in the slow torture inflicted by his cross-examination. A minute later, when his spasm of weakness had passed off, he would have retracted his confession if he could. But the sheriff's deputy, with the assistance of a constable, was already leading him through the swaying crowd in the aisle, while many people got up and stood on the benches to watch the exit of the new prisoner.

When at length Sovine had disappeared out of the door, the spectators turned and looked at Tom, sitting yet in the dock, but with the certainty of speedy release before him. The whole result of Lincoln's masterful stroke was now for the first time realized, and the excitement bade fair to break over bounds. McCord

How Abe Lincoln Paid for His Stockings

doubled himself up once or twice in an effort to repress his feelings out of respect for the Court, but his emotions were too much for him; his big fist, grasping his ragged hat, appeared above his head.

"Hooray!" he burst out with a loud voice, stamping his foot as he waved his hat.

At this the whole courtroomful of people burst into cheers, laughter, cries, and waving of hats and handkerchiefs, in spite of the sheriff's sharp rapping and shouts of "Order in court!"

The lawyers presently congratulated Lincoln, Barbara tried to thank him, and Judge Watkins felt that Impartial Justice herself, as represented in his own person, could afford to praise the young man for his conduct of the case.

"Abr'am," said Mrs. Grayson, "d'yeh know I kind uv lost confidence in you when you sot there so long without doin' anything." Then, after a moment of pause: "Abr'am, I'm thinkin' I'd ort to deed you my farm. You've earned it, my son; the good Lord A'mighty knows you have."

"I'll never take one cent, Aunt Marthy — not a single red cent," and the lawyer turned away to grasp Tom's hand. But the poor fellow who had so recently felt the halter about his neck could not speak his gratitude. "Tom here," said Lincoln, "will be a help in your old days, Aunt Marthy, and then I'll be paid a hundred times. You see it'll tickle me to think that when you talk about this you'll say: 'That's the same Abe Lincoln that I used to knit stockings for when he was a poor little fellow with his toes sticking out of ragged shoes in the snow.' No — I wouldn't take a copper — not a copper."

"O CAPTAIN! MY CAPTAIN!"
(Abraham Lincoln, 1809-1865)

WALT WHITMAN

O Captain! my Captain! our fearful trip is done,
The ship has weathered every rack, the prize we sought is won,
The port is near, the bells I hear, the people all exulting,
While follow eyes the steady keel, the vessel grim and daring;
  But O heart! heart! heart!
   O the bleeding drops of red,
  Where on the deck my Captain lies,
   Fallen cold and dead.

O Captain! my Captain! rise up and hear the bells;
Rise up — for you the flag is flung — for you the bugle trills,
For you bouquets and ribboned wreaths — for you the shores
  a-crowding,
For you they call, the swaying mass, their eager faces turning;
  Here Captain! dear father!
   This arm beneath your head!
  It is some dream that on the deck
   You've fallen cold and dead.

My Captain does not answer, his lips are pale and still,
My father does not feel my arm, he has no pulse nor will,
The ship is anchored safe and sound, its voyage closed and done,
From fearful trip the victor ship comes in with object won;
  Exult O shores, and ring O bells!
   But I with mournful tread,
  Walk the deck my Captain lies,
   Fallen cold and dead.

SIR WILLIAM OSLER

LEONARD W. BROCKINGTON

The following is part of an address given by Mr. Brockington in the Chapel of Trinity College School, Port Hope, Ontario, on Sunday, October 2nd, 1949, at a service commemorating the centenary of the birth of William Osler. The address was broadcast over CBC and later published by Trinity College School.

I have been asked to praise a famous man. His praise is recorded far more eloquently than I can speak it, in the life which he lived, in the lessons which he taught, and above all, in the things he did. It is, however, fitting that praise should be given in this place and at this time. For Sir William Osler, or Dr. Osler as a grateful world knew him best, was born one hundred years ago and came as a boy to Trinity College School in 1866. He was, you will remember, a Prefect and your first Head Boy. If you had known him when he was a famous man, I think you would have felt that even *then* he was your schoolfellow. For wherever he went and whatever he did, he never let his heart and mind grow old, or his hopes grow dim. He carried his Ontario boyhood with him into all the world. And I like to think that in a real sense he is still your schoolfellow and that the memory of his goodness and greatness is now, and will be for ever, a blessing to this place.

No Canadian who ever lived had a clearer title to greatness, or a richer life than Sir William Osler, or touched the world of men at more points and with greater distinction. He studied at Toronto, McGill, and in Europe. He became the most famous professor of his day in the Medical Schools of McGill, Pennsylvania, Johns Hopkins, and Oxford. He was the author of the greatest medical book of his time, and one of the greatest of all times, *The Principles and Practice of Medicine*. He reintroduced and developed the system of teaching medicine by the bedside of the patient, and nearly every Medical School in the world to-day owes much to his imagination and his work. He has been called the family physician of three nations, and no man in his time did as much to unite the hearts and minds of that Trinity of Nations which means more to us than any other, Canada, Britain, and the United States of America. In many far places he always carried with him something of the neighbourly kindliness of the Canadian frontier, something of the healing strength and warmth of the Canadian sun, something of the clean freshness of the Canadian air that sweeps and sweetens the dusty and the musty places.

William Osler was born in what was then the little Ontario village of Bondhead. Perhaps the wonderful heroism of the last war, in which this School played so noble a part, served to remind us that there are always somebodies in the streets where the nobodies live. And no one knows from what community or household a great man will come. Certainly Bondhead should be a proud little town. And for this, among other reasons. The two Canadians whose names are most honoured and famous throughout the world for the precious gifts which they brought to the comfort and healing of suffering mankind are Dr. William Osler and Dr. Frederick Banting. Banting's father was also born in Bondhead, in the same month and the same year as Osler. Truly, July, 1849, was a great month for Bondhead, for Canada, and, I think, for the world.

I have not time to tell you of Osler's father and mother and their family. It is sufficient to say that the house of the Rev. Featherstone Lake Osler and his wife, Ellen, was a home of Christian piety, of simple joys, of some hardships, of laughter and of good talk, and of those deep unspoken certainties which join men in love to one another and in adoration and obedience before the ways and laws of God's Providence.

One of Osler's nephews told me the other day how his own mother had brought from that household two lessons which he was never allowed to forget. One was, as his mother constantly reminded him, "If you cannot speak good of any one, keep silent and never speak evil;" the other, "If you are feeling depressed or ill, do not allow your depression or ill-health to spoil the happiness and enjoyment of others."

It is not easy to gaze through the shadows and to see what sort of a boy came to this School nearly eighty-four years ago. When you are older you will find that it is not easy even to remember much of your own boyhood. Does not the greatest of school songs picture those who sing, looking back forty years after and forgetfully wondering what they were like in their work and their play?

Because Osler's mother and father were Cornish, he was always described as one of those dark Celts who are usually found in Cornwall or the Western parts of Wales or Ireland or Scotland. He was short in stature and had a swarthy complexion. His eyes (which somebody once called the windows of the soul) were full of fire and brightness and seemed to dance in his head. He was very lithe and brisk and moved very quickly. One of his nieces said that he always came down the street with a swinging pace, with a spring on the ball of his foot — a habit of walking he kept to his last days. As a boy, and even as a man, he was full of pleasant mischief and fond of harmless pranks. As a matter of fact, he left his school at Dundas at the request of the management. When he was at school at Barrie he was known somewhat playfully as one of "Barrie's bad boys". And even when he was at this School he once spent a few hours in what is called the custody of the law, because of some merriment carried a little too far. I expect that during the time he was at school he was most famous amongst his fellows because in his last year he was first in the hurdle race of 200 yards, and of 400 yards; first in the 100 yards "hop" race (whatever that is); first in the mile steeplechase and in throwing the cricket ball. I think he was the sort of boy you would have all liked. At least, he was the sort of boy that people kept on liking for seventy years.

But his boyhood was not all mischief and laughter and the playing of games, although both work and play were to him the best of fun. When he looked back, he always said that three wonderful things came to him while he was a boy at this School. He thought their coming the most important happening in his life. The three things were, a man, an instrument, and a book. The Reverend W. A. Johnson, who was the first warden of this School, was one of those men who had a genius for teaching, especially for teaching the things he liked to the boys he liked. He loved books, and above all was interested in the wonders of the world around him — in the way of a bird in the air, in the beauty of a flower in the woodland, in the delicate tracery of the moss on the stone. He was one of those pilgrims of whom the first great English poet said "gladly would he learn and gladly teach". A glad teacher likes to meet no one so much as a glad learner, and a glad learner welcomes nobody more than a glad teacher. And so Father Johnson became Osler's friend, teacher, and hero. He gave him his first microscope. What Osler saw through that microscope brought near to him many hidden horizons and opened up a wonderland that awaits everyone with eyes to see. Johnson also first introduced Osler to a famous old book, Sir Thomas Browne's, *Religio Medici*, "The Religion of a Doctor". The English in which it is written is almost the most stately music which has ever been fashioned from the words of our tongue. It is a difficult book and a scholar's book. It must have been an extraordinary man who could interest a boy in that book. It must have been an extraordinary boy who was fascinated by its language and its teaching. Nevertheless, that miracle happened in this School, and when Osler left for the University of Toronto, his boyish plan became a man's purpose. He made up his mind to become a scientist, a doctor, and a teacher.

During Osler's time at this School, and after that at Toronto, another great teacher, a visitor to Trinity College School and a **Professor at Trinity College, James Bovell, brought his wonderful** influence to bear upon the moulding of Osler's life. At McGill, Dr. Palmer Howard, the most famous medical teacher of his day, in Canada, possessed the last strong hand that fashioned the pattern of Osler's dedication to the service of mankind.

Throughout his days, Osler continually said and wrote that the purpose of his life, the direction of his toil, and the success of his labours were due to these three noble teachers. When he wrote his own greatest book he dedicated it to them. His speeches and his letters were full of their grateful memory and I am sure that before the last darkness closed his eyes, their faces passed before him in the proud procession of his life's unforgettable love. I can almost hear them saying to Osler, and Osler saying to those whom he taught in his turn, the words that have always lurked unspoken on the lips of those whose high calling it is to prepare the young for their highest destiny:

"My boy, wherever you are, work for your soul's sake,
That all the clay of you
And all the dross of you
May yield to the fire of you.
Till the fire is nothing but light,
Nothing but light."

When Osler left this School he passed through the universities of Toronto and McGill and of Europe, to the work of his life. He came back to North America to teach, to inspire, and to make real in action the things which he had learnt at the feet of his Masters. Osler was a great and a good man. In many respects I think he was the greatest man whom this country has produced. It is difficult to define a great man. We all know, don't we, that many men are often called "great" for reasons which do not appeal to all of us. Those reasons sometimes do not agree either with the judgment of time, for riches and power and military glory, and many other things of the world, fade as the years go by. But I think we can say that that man is a great man who first discovers new truths, who crystalizes old truths and new truths into a great religion or philosophy which guides men towards wisdom and fills their hearts with the sense of the brotherhood of man and the Fatherhood of God, in which alone human progress can find a firm foundation. A great man, too, is one who makes great discoveries or inventions, and thereby enlarges the happiness and comfort of mankind. There is, too, the artist who enriches human life with beauty, with enduring works of music, of literature, of painting. There is another man who by his character, his work and his example, so impresses the men and women of his own time that he lives thereafter in the hearts of mankind as a lasting influence for good. I think Osler was that sort of man. The things which he did and which I have already recited to you are themselves evidence of a life rich in great achievement. His greatness lies in that rare combination of noble thought, noble words, and noble action. He not only thought great things but he got them done. If he taught and preached, he also organized. Every medical school which he entered was changed and made a living thing by his own joy of life and practical sympathy for his fellows. The medical student, the nurse, the patient, all found a new purpose and a new hope in his presence. Malice and envy were silent before him, and although he spoke no evil and thought no evil of his brothers and sisters, he never lacked courage or allowed personalities to bar the road to what he believed was right and good. He was unique also in his day because he had a thorough knowledge of medicine and science, and the scientific method, yet he was able to clothe his thoughts with grace and power.

He spent all his time with magnificence. He was continually surprising his friends by the things he knew and the use he was able to make of the hours which God had given him. He was punctual in his habits and nearly every waking moment was devoted to the great purpose of his life, the relief of human suffering, the pursuit of wisdom, and the teaching of the young doctor and nurse.

He had a passion for work, and in one of his most famous addresses he called Work the master word of his profession. He

Sir William Osler

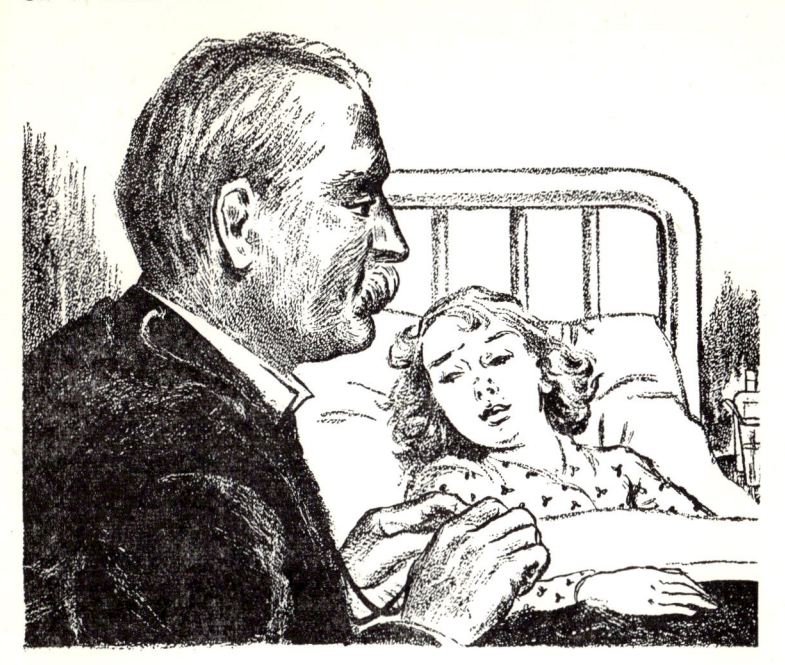

knew, as most great men before him and after him, that labour is the price which the gods have placed upon everything that is precious. I have often thought too that in many ways the two best educated men of their times were Thomas Huxley of England, and William Osler of Canada. They both combined a deep knowledge of the theory and the practice of scientific truth with a shining ability to express themselves in clear, simple, and vital language. Last year I was at a meeting in Oxford and listened to famous scholars stating that the greatest need of the age was a liberal education, or the education fit for a free man. Such an education was defined by Huxley and fulfilled by Huxley and Osler. I would like to see the definition inscribed on the walls of every university in the English-speaking world.

"That man, I think, has had a liberal education, who has been so trained in youth that his body is the ready servant of his will, and does with ease and pleasure all the work that, as a mechanism, it is capable of; whose intellect is a clear, cold logic engine with all its parts of equal strength, and in smooth working order; ready, like a steam engine, to be turned to any kind of work, and spin the gossamers as well as forge the anchors of the mind." (You know what is meant by gossamers. They are those little films of thin webs that float in the air or are poised upon the grass in autumn, catching the sheen of the dew-drops and the glint of the sun.) And then the description of the educated man continues, "Whose mind is stored with a knowledge of the great and fundamental truths of Nature and of the laws of her operations; and who, no stunted ascetic, is full of life and fire, but whose passions are trained to come to heel by a vigorous will, the servant of a tender conscience; who has learned to love all beauty, whether of Nature or of Art, to hate all vileness, and to respect others as himself."

Osler was that rare sort of man. He left, too, many lessons for us, all written and spoken in words that deserve to survive the rusts and ravages of time. The philosophy of his which I like best is that which he sets out in his most famous lecture, on The Way of Life. I have already said how full of life he was, of its joys and its purpose. And so, when he talked to the students at Yale University, he begged them to live in the present, to spend their lives doing and hoping. Sufficient to the day is the goodness thereof. Undress your soul at night and feel the joy that you are alive. Study books, but also men. Keep a fair mind and a fair body, be temperate in all things. He bade them always remember, with Carlyle, that our duty is not to see what lies dimly at a distance, but to do what lies clearly at hand. He knew also and practised the humility of the seeker, the painstaking care, the persistence that searches for conclusions and does not jump at them, the wonder and the devotion that have always been the glories of true science. He never believed that Science at last would darken men's eyes and harden men's hearts, but that its mission was to bring healing to mankind and joy and leisure to man's life. He also walked in that fine tradition of

Medicine that has always laid the gifts of its discovery freely and without payment upon the altar of suffering humanity. When he was a young man he promised that he would never enter the temple of Science in the spirit of the money-changer. He never did.

Those are a few of the reasons why I call him Great. But greatness and goodness are not always the same thing. May I tell you, as I bid you farewell, a few of the reasons why he deserves to be called good?

I think one of the mottoes of his life was

"Two things stand like stone;
Kindness in another's trouble,
Courage in one's own."

For everybody who knew Osler or wrote about him or has spoken to me about him, dwells upon the all-prevading sympathy which marked his nature and his work. So many of his deeds were those "unremembered acts of kindness and of love" that mark a good man's life. He knew that that man is the greatest whose heart contains within it the most objects of compassion. He knew, too, the conclusion of Ruskin, that of all the words which men have brought with them from their wanderings in the wilderness, the sweetest is "loyalty". He never forgot his friends and they never forgot him. Everywhere he went he took with him joy and hope. I wish I could read you some of the letters he wrote for little children who were ill, or tell you some of the stories of his bedside talks in the sickroom of the young, of his cheerful whistle as he entered, of the jokes he made to make them laugh. He had an uncanny knowledge of children. Only the other day a friend of mine phoned to me and told me that when his wife was a little girl she was badly scalded. The great Dr. Osler came to see her, told her some fairy stories, and prescribed for her healing — a box of chocolates!

He had, too, a divine sense of humour — by which I do not mean the biting cruelty of the professional wit, or the smart shallowness of the so-called wisecracker — but that wonderful gift which takes the iron from a man's soul and puts a gentle irony in its place — that sense of humour "which turns the tears of life into a rainbow". Servants and humble people all loved him. All humanity saluted him because he was a man and nothing which belonged to mankind was foreign to him. His house and his heart were open to all comers. His residence at Oxford was known by the delightful name of "The Open Arms". In his last year there, he entertained 1,600 men and officers of the American Forces of the First Great War. When his own greatest sorrow came, in the death of a brave only son, he took what he said was the only medicine that could cure him, the medicine of faith and hope and compassion and time.

Always, above the clamour, he heard the still, sad music of humanity. "I laugh," he said, "in order that I do not weep." His coming was a comfort to all for he scattered health and joy with abundance in his path.

In one of his great addresses to nurses and students he paid tribute to those who work for small rewards in lonely places, and told them, "your passport will be the blessings of Him in whose footsteps you have trodden, unto whose sick you have ministered, and for whose children you have cared." That surely is his passport to our hearts and to Heaven. Such was your schoolfellow, William Osler.

THE APOLOGY OF SOCRATES

PLATO

Not much time will be gained, O Athenians, in return for the evil name which you will get from the detractors of the city, who will say that you killed Socrates, a wise man; for they will call me wise even although I am not wise when they want to reproach you. If you had waited a little while, your desire would have been fulfilled in the course of nature. For I am far advanced in years, as you may perceive, and not far from death. I am speaking now only to those of you who have condemned me to death. And I have another thing to say to them: You think that I was convicted through deficiency of words — I mean, that if I had thought fit to leave nothing undone, nothing unsaid, I might have gained an acquittal. Not so; the deficiency which led to my conviction was not of words — certainly not. But I had not the boldness or impudence or inclination to address you as you would have liked me to address you, weeping and wailing and lamenting, and saying and doing many things which you have been accustomed to hear from others, and which, as I say, are unworthy of me. But I thought that I ought not to do anything common or mean in the hour of danger: nor do I now repent of the manner of my defence, and I would rather die having spoken after my manner, than speak in your manner and live. For neither in war nor yet at law ought any man to use every way of escaping death. For often in battle there is no doubt that if a man will throw away his arms, and fall on his knees before his pursuers, he may escape death; and in other dangers there are other ways of escaping death, if a man is willing to say and do anything. The difficulty, my friends, is not in avoiding death, but in avoiding unrighteousness; for that runs faster than death. I am old and move slowly, and the slower runner has overtaken me, and my accusers are keen and quick, and the faster runner, who is unrighteousness, has overtaken them. And now I depart hence condemned by you to suffer the penalty of death, and they, too, go their ways condemned by the truth to suffer the penalty of villainy and wrong; and I must abide by my award — let them abide by theirs. I suppose that these things may be regarded as fated, — and I think that they are well.

And now, O men who have condemned me, I would fain prophesy to you; for I am about to die, and that is the hour in which men are gifted with prophetic power. And I prophesy to you who are my murderers, that immediately after my death punishment far heavier than you have inflicted on me will surely await you. Me you have killed because you wanted to escape the accuser, and not to give an account of your lives. But that will not be as you suppose: far otherwise. For I say that there will be more accusers of you than there are now, accusers whom hitherto I have restrained: and as they are younger they will be more severe with you, and you will be more offended at them. For if you think that by killing men you can avoid the accuser censuring your lives, you are mistaken; that is not a way of escape which is either possible or honourable; the easiest and noblest way is not to be crushing others, but to be improving yourselves. This is the prophecy which I utter before my departure to the judges who have condemned me.

Friends, who would have acquitted me, I would like also to talk with you about this thing which has happened, while the magistrates are busy, and before I go to the place at which I must die. Stay then awhile, for we may as well talk with one another while there is time. You are my friends, and I should like to show you the meaning of this event which has happened to me. O my judges—for you I may truly call judges—I should like to tell you of a wonderful circumstance. Hitherto the familiar oracle within me has constantly been in the habit of opposing me even about trifles, if I was going to make a slip or error about anything; and now as you see there has come upon me that which may be thought, and is generally believed to be, the last and worst evil. But the oracle made no sign of opposition, either as I was leaving my house and going out in the morning, or when I was going up into this court, or while I was speaking, at anything which I was going to say; and yet I have often been stopped in the middle of a speech, but now in nothing I either said or did touching this matter has the oracle opposed me. What do I take to be the explanation of this? I will tell you. I regard this as a proof that what has happened to me is a good, and that those of us who think that death is an evil are in error. This is a great proof to me of what I am saying, for the customary sign would surely have opposed me had I been going to evil and not to good.

Let us reflect in another way, and we shall see that there is great reason to hope that death is a good, for one of two things: — either death is a state of nothingness and utter unconsciousness, or, as men say, there is a change and migration of the soul from this world to another. Now if you suppose that there is no consciousness, but a sleep like the sleep of him who is undisturbed even by the sight of dreams, death will be an unspeakable gain. For if a person were to select the night in which his sleep was undisturbed even by dreams, and were to compare with this the other days and nights of his life, and then were to tell us how many days and nights he had passed in the course of his life better and more pleasantly than this one, I think that any man, I will not say a private man, but even the great king will not find many such days or nights, when compared with the others. Now if death is like this, I say that to die is gain; for eternity is then only a single night. But if death is the journey to another place, and there, as men say, all the dead are, what good, O my friends and judges, can be greater than this? If indeed when the pilgrim arrives in the world below, he is delivered from the professors of justice in this world, and finds the true judges who are said to give judgment there, Minos and Rhadamanthus and Aeacus and Triptolemus, and other sons of God who were righteous in their own life, that pilgrimage will be worth making. What would not a man give if he might converse with Orpheus and Musaeus and Hesiod and Homer? Nay, if this be true, let me die again and again. I, too, shall have a wonderful interest in a place where I can converse with Palamedes, and Ajax the son of Telamon, and other heroes of old, who have suffered death through an unjust judgment; and there will be no small pleasure, as I think, in comparing my own sufferings with theirs. Above all, I shall be able to continue my search into true and false knowledge; as in this world, so also in that; I shall find out who is wise, and who pretends to be wise, and is not. What would not a man give, O judges, to be able to examine the leader of the great Trojan expedition; or Odysseus or Sisyphus, or numberless others, men and women too. What infinite delight would there be in conversing with them and asking them questions! For in that world they do not put a man to death for this; certainly not. For besides being happier in that world than in this, they will be immortal, if what is said is true.

Wherefore, O judges, be of good cheer about death, and know this of a truth — that no evil can happen to a good man, either in life or after death. He and his are not neglected by the gods; nor has my own approaching end happened by mere chance. But I see clearly that to die and be released was better for me; and therefore the oracle gave no sign. For which reason, also, I am not angry with my accusers or my condemners; they have done me no harm, although neither of them meant to do me any good; and for this I may gently blame them.

Still I have a favour to ask of them. When my sons are grown up, I would ask you, O my friends, to punish them; and I would have you trouble them, as I have troubled you, if they seem to care about riches, or anything, more than about virtue; or if they pretend to be something when they are really nothing — then reprove them, as I have reproved you, for not caring about that for which they ought to care, and thinking that they are something when they are really nothing. And if you do this, I and my sons will have received justice at your hands.

The hour of departure has arrived, and we go our ways — I to die, and you to live. Which is better God only knows.

Translated by BENJAMIN JOWETT

MEN AT WORK

DUELLISTS OF THE DEEP

EDNA STAEBLER

On the sea beside Cape Breton's Cabot Trail, silhouetted by glitter and far from shore, was a little boat with a figure swaying at the top of her mast. Suddenly a man ran out to the end of her bowsprit. For a moment he was suspended; he lunged forward from the waist, poised with an arm extended, recovered, paused an instant, then dashed back to obscurity in the hull. A dory was lowered from the stern and a man jumped into it to play the swordfish that had been stabbed.

Bleached, windswept, and beautiful, Neil's Harbour is almost surrounded by the blue of the North Atlantic. The jagged rims of its cliffs curve round to a rocky point where a red-capped white lighthouse rises against the sky. Scattered over the slopes of a treeless hill, the gables of a hundred little houses point to the sea where the fishing boats come in.

I went down a winding lane past silver shingle stages to a wooden dock. There perhaps twenty children, three dogs, and fifteen men chattered in the salty dialect of the Newfoundlanders who had crossed the Cabot Straight and cleared the shallow earth around the Harbour eighty years ago.

The children, tanned scalps showing through sun-blonde hair, were dynamos in well-washed overalls or starched calico dresses; the great dogs appeared to be undiluted Newfoundlands; the ruddy-faced men, like broad-billed birds in their strange caps with curved peaks six inches long, wore rubber boots, thick trousers, flannel shirts over grey woollen underwear on a day that was warm enough for me to wear shorts and for the children to go barefooted. Shyly conscious of the presence of a stranger, they turned away with a half smile when their curious glances met mine.

Duellists of the Deep

"Here comes the *Robin B*," someone shouted. "Gotta fish."

Passing a longer wharf that was nearer the open sea, came a vessel like the one I'd seen from the Trail. Projecting from her bow was a runway that looked like a diving board ending in a metal hip-high pulpit. As she scraped gently against the dock, a rope through a pulley at the top of a post was tossed to the men aboard. They did something with it that I couldn't see, then three men on the wharf heaved ho. A leviathan was stretched from the deck to the top of the fifteen-foot pole. I was seeing my first swordfish. It was stupendous. The body was round; the skin, dark purple-grey, rough one way, smooth the other, like a cat's tongue; the horny, black fins stood out like scimitars, the tail like the handle bars of a giant bicycle; but the strangest thing was the straight, flat, pointed, sharp-sided sword which was an extension of the head, like a horny upper lip more than three feet long. Slowly releasing the rope, the men guided the creature down to the dock.

A little boy knelt near the head; with a rusty hook he ripped open the glazed membrane of the huge round eye that was uppermost; out of the cavity ran clear, slurpy liquid reminiscent of the kind hairdressers use to set pin-curls. With a shudder I watched the child put his hand into the socket and pull something out of it. He looked up at me.

"Want te heyeball?" he asked.

He opened his hand and I saw a perfect sphere about an inch and a quarter in diameter, clear as glass, reflecting colours like a soap bubble; it was beautiful.

"Take it," he said.

"You mean you're giving it to me?"

"Yes." (Not "Yeah".)

I didn't want to touch the fishy thing but I couldn't spurn a gift; reluctantly I held out my hand. The boy placed the crystal gently on my palm: It felt cool and tender as a piece of firm jelly or a gumdrop that has had the sugar licked off.

"What should I do with it?"

"Take it home and put it in sun and it'll turn roight 'ard. Be careful not to break un."

I held it almost reverently. It didn't even smell like fish.

"How much would the fish weigh?" I asked anyone who could hear me.

"Ower seven hunert pounds, I guess," someone answered. "'E's some beeg."

"What does it taste like?"

"Don't know, never et 'em," said a fisherman.

"Haven't you even tasted them?"

"No, we just ketches 'em and sells 'em fer folk down in States," he said. "Oi don't fancy to try any of the beeg ugly things meself but some round 'ere cut off a bit near the head and taked it 'ome and cooked it; they say hit's got a roight noice flavour to it, loike pork, not strong at all. Americans must loike 'em or they wouldn't pay us fifty cents a pound fer 'em, and take nearly all the Cape Breton catch — a million and a half pounds a year."

With a saw in his hand he knelt beside the fish.

"Want sword?" he asked me.

"Oh, yes, don't you use it?"

He laughed. "No, we just throws 'em overboard."

"I'd like it for a souvenir. What shall I pay you?"

Bending over his work he said, "We don't take money fer what ain't worth nothin'."

The fibrous sword was heavy and felt like bone. The cut end showed soft bloody marrow that was the essence of fishiness.

"Stick in ant heap and ants'll clean un out for you," the fisherman said.

He next sawed off the head, then the fins, the broad black tail, and the fan-shaped crimson gill plates. As each piece came off, the youngsters threw it into the water where white birds darted at it before it sank to the shadowy creatures hovering in beds of waving kelp.

The carcass, washed with salt water, was rolled on a carrier and taken by four men to the scales. Everyone gathered round to learn the weight — six hundred and thirty-four pounds — marked with indelible pencil near the tail.

Next morning I ran down to the shore. I wanted to go swordfishing. All the men gathered in little groups around the stages stopped talking to stare at me as I came along.

"Is it going to be a good day?" I heard myself asking timidly.

After a hopeless pause, somebody answered, "Yis, moight be."

The rest just stared — at me, through me, past me. I wanted to run, but I stayed where I was.

"Would anyone please take me out?"

The men exchanged glances; one of them said, "Well, I'll tell you, miss, ye'd be better off in a boat wi' fo'c'sle. Ye see, we don't have much room in them small ones, if she blows ye'd git terrible wet and you moight be seasick. You wait round till skipper o' one o' them snapper boats comes down."

I sat on a post for half an hour till three men sauntered onto the dock.

"Woman aboard's bad luck," one said.

"I'm good luck. You'll see, I'll bring you good luck."

They looked at each other.

"We been swordfishin' fer two months and ain't got but three . . ."

"Ever been seasick?"

"No," I answered firmly.

"Come on, then."

They helped me into the dory and rowed over to the snapper boat they had made themselves. It was called the *Devil Diver*. Forty feet long and ten feet wide with a Buick engine in the middle, it had a dory in the stern, a high sail-less mast from which the vessel was controlled, a fo'c'sle, foredeck, and removable swordfish rig. This rig consisted of a twelve-foot plank projecting from the stem and, at the end of the plank, a pulpit to which the long pole of the harpoon was fastened. A detachable, double-barbed dart of bronze was socketed in the end of the pole by keeping taught along it the thin strong line that ran to a great coil in a box amidships. A red keg or buoy tied at the end of the hundreds of feet of line could be thrown into the water to mark and retard a wounded fish.

We started without delay. That they might spy a fish even below the surface of the water, two of the men, Jossie and Sam, had climbed the mast where they sat on swings hung short from a cross-piece. The other man, Jack, sat on the wooden door that covered the roaring motor; he was the engineer and the "sticker" who, when a fish was sighted, would run out to the pulpit, untie the harpoon and make the fatal lunge. I sat on the only seat in the boat, a little bench near the motor.

Soon we were out on the open sea, climbing the hill of water that rose to the horizon. I sat very still, very straight, very stiff. Though the water didn't look wild, the boat seemed to heave. The fumes of the engine were strong; I remembered that someone had told me they always made people seasick. I thought I'd better move away from them, but there seemed to be no place for me to go. I clung to the bench and looked at the village, now just a tiny clearing against the great dark hills. Jack, relaxed in front of me, kept his eyes on the water.

"What do you look for?" I shouted.

"Just loike two black sticks, 'bout so high," he held up his hands eight inches apart, "and so," he stretched his arms as wide as they would go.

I tried watching the water for two black sticks — two black sticks — two black sticks — gasoline fumes — no, two black sticks — two black gasoline — I stood up, but there was nothing to hang onto so I sat down again.

"Ye moight be more easy atop the fo'c'sle," Jack said, swinging himself onto the roof of the tiny cabin and sitting on its front edge.

I shuffled to the rail of the boat. To get on top of the fo'c'sle, which was higher than I am, I had to climb up its side from the narrow rail, avoiding the ropes that ran from the mast to the engine. The water was whizzing by and very close. I was scared skinny. I don't know how many times I missed but I know that one time I didn't. I slumped against the mast and breathed the fresh salt air.

Then I felt dizzy. I thought, THIS IS IT. But nothing happened, I waited, I felt no nausea, I realized I never had felt any.

What the heck — I wasn't seasick — I was just unbalanced. It was time I started looking for swordfish.

How could I know when I really saw two black sticks among the billion sharp points of water that raised themselves capriciously round us? Dozens of impish little wavelets deliberately deceived me as they danced up from the surface, imitated the curving fins, posed long enough to give me a thrill, then mercifully disappeared before I could shout what I thought I had discovered.

We were perhaps six miles from land and by simply turning my head I could see the forty miles from the misty purple form of Smokey in the south to fainter, farther Money Point marking the northern tip of Cape Breton Island.

The smaller fishing boats, weaving back and forth inshore, shone white, red, green, and grey with the sun against them in the deep blue water; the larger vessels were silhouetted in the burnished gleam between us and the horizon. There were schooners and jacks, ketches and smacks, snapper boats and skiffs; from Port au Basque, St. John's, Glace Bay, Louisburg and Yarmouth, from all the coast of Newfoundland and all of Nova Scotia they had come to find, and to kill, the wary, wondrous swordfish which from July to September mystifies and provokes the rugged men of the rocky northern seaboard.

Loving the sport, the gamble, the hope of fabulous luck, like men obsessed, they had piled up their lobster traps, hauled in their herring nets, coiled their codfish trawls and become rivals in pursuit of the monstrous creatures that bask in the summer sunshine off the shores of Cape Breton.

In July the search for the precious prey is made near Glace

Bay and Louisburg. When the middle of August comes, the men on the masts follow the broadbilled fish to the fertile grounds between Ingonish and Dingwall where the long swords slash and the toothless mouths gobble the defenceless mackerel and herring. By the end of September the roving gladiators have disappeared from the North Atlantic to go no one knows where.

The capture of the swordfish is as uncertain as the weather that controls it. The smaller vessels with only two men aboard are lucky to catch even three a season; the larger craft with as many as five watchers on a mast, searching many miles from land, may bring in a dozen fish a day — or none.

When a boat came near us, I held my breath as I saw the men aloft sway four feet to the right, four feet to the left, to and fro, to and fro like an inverted pendulum. They shouted something that sounded like "Got arn?"

Jack shook his head, yelling, unmistakably, "Narn."

I asked him what it meant.

"'Ave we got any and we ain't," he said.

There were no clouds in the sky, the sun was warm but the breeze was becoming a wind, our boat leapt and fell in the swells, a wonderful proud thing to feel. And all the time we kept watching for the precious stick-like fins. We saw several sharks, we saw dolphins, we saw a blackfish blow.

Then Jossie on the mast yelled, "FISH!"

"I see 'im," Jack cried, running nimbly to the end of the rigging.

I couldn't see anything but those points of water. Risking my life, I stood up. I saw the fins, those two black sticks, eight inches high.

Jack unfastened the harpoon, leaned against the iron hoop. The engine was switched off. We were close. Jack was poised to strike.

"Aw — a trick!" he called and we all saw that the two black fins were fastened to a piece of board. The men laughed about it but I didn't think it was funny.

"Anyway, now you know what the fins looks loike when they's out of the water."

We settled down again after that, and even I didn't stop watching those little waves forming and disappearing. Sometimes the boat went toward the south, then straight towards the horizon, then north-east, due north, south again, always moving, her men and I watching, waiting, hoping. The same anxiety was in three hundred vessels that searched the sea as we did.

After lunch we saw a boat that had stopped. Almost alongside was its dory with two men, one standing was pulling in a line, the other, crouched over, was baling.

"Must ha' been struck," Jack shouted, pointing. "Swordfish be quiet, restin' fish," he told me; "wouldn't hurt nobody if they's left alone. Swords be made fer slashin' not stabbin', but when a fish is hit near the 'ead 'e sometimes goes crazy loike and turns on boat or dory, can ram 'is whole sword clear through a three-inch plank — and a man too if 'e's settin' in the way. Sword always breaks off and fish dies quick after that, but a man dies quick, too, if sword goes through 'im or 'e gits hisself tangled in a line and dragged down."

The wind was growing stronger and the water rougher, the waves were splashing over the fo'c'sle; I buttoned my jacket over my sweater and tucked my green cotton legs under me. At half past five the boat was turned toward the village. Tired, and feeling as people always do who have fished all day and caught no fish, I leaned against the mast and idly looked at the sea.

Suddenly I was pointing and shrieking, "Look, look, a fish, a fish, a fish."

"By Jimminy, it is! A fish, a fish!" Jack yelled and ran out the rig.

Jossie steered straight towards it. The motor stopped. We were quiet. Tense. We were close. Jack held the harpoon in his hand. The fish was almost alongside.

"Oh, get 'im, get 'im," I prayed.

Jack lunged.

The fish was gone. The pole fell slack in the water, Jack jerked it back to the pulpit. Sam came down from the mast with Jossie tumbling after.

"Ye got 'im right behind front fin," Jossie shouted, then rushed to the stern to shove the dory into the water. Sam was paying out the rope that was coiled in the box. Jack ran back to help with the dory; as soon as it hit the water, Jossie jumped into it; the box of rapidly uncoiling rope and the keg were tossed to him. Standing, he tautened the rope in his hands and was soon pulled away from us by the swimming swordfish.

Without the steadying drive of the motor, the *Devil Diver* was seesawing sideways with the velocity of a machine. I clung to the mast. Jack grinned at me as he passed on his way to the pulpit. Sam started the motor and we were moving again.

"Worst swell I ever were out in," Jack said, sitting beside me.

"What are we going to do now?"

THE END OF WINTER   —James Henderson

Reproduced by permission of the National Gallery, Ottawa.

JAMES HENDERSON, LL.D.
(1871 - 1951)

James Henderson was born in Glasgow, Scotland, in 1871. He attended the Glasgow School of Art, and later studied in London. After graduation he was apprenticed to a firm of lithographers and became an accomplished engraver.

In 1910 Henderson came to Canada, working first in Winnipeg, where he attracted attention by his colour designs for *The Trail*. The following year he moved to Regina, Saskatchewan, and was soon busy on portrait commissions. In 1916 he moved to Fort Qu'Appelle and set up a studio. For many years he was known chiefly for his portraits of Indians. He was admitted as a Chief to the Sioux tribe, who gave him the name Wici-Teo-Wafi Wi-Casa, which means, "The Man Who Paints Old Men".

Henderson exhibited his paintings at Wembley, in Glasgow, Toronto, Montreal, and Ottawa. It was late in life that Henderson began painting landscapes, and is particularly well known for his paintings of the Qu'Appelle Valley.

In 1929, when the Saskatchewan Art Association was formed, Henderson was elected its first Fellow; and in 1950 he was given an honorary degree of Doctor of Laws by the University of Saskatchewan.

End of Winter, one of his canvasses of the Qu'Appelle Valley, hangs in the National Gallery, Ottawa.

"Look fer another fish till that un gits played out."

But he didn't watch the water, he kept turning anxious glances toward the yellow dory.

"Sometimes we loses a fish," he said.

"Sometimes a fish will turn on a dory."

"Sometimes it takes a couple of hours to tire out a swordfish."

We didn't go far from Jossie; we always kept him in sight. He stood in the little dory pulling in line and letting it out as the swordfish tried to escape him by riding him round in the sea.

For over an hour we circled; all the other fishing boats were going in one direction, all going toward a harbour. We were soon left alone on the ocean with the little yellow dory.

"Looks loike 'e moight be a big one; never had a fish take so long," Jack said again and again.

For another hour we waited, then Jossie raised his arm. We rushed to the yellow dory. Jossie was smiling broadly, the water around him was red, the great curved tail of the swordfish was securely tied to the gunwale, its gills stabbed by a long-poled lance.

Jossie clambered aboard the snapper boat. Pulling on the rope, the tail, and the fins, the men hauled in the heavy streamlined body; it stretched across the full width of the boat with its sword running up the side.

"Not the bigges' one I ever seen," was the first comment Jack made, "Only six hunnerd pounds." He thumped Jossie's shoulder with joy.

"'E was a dirty one, though," Jossie said. "Wouldn't go up er down, kep' hittin' the rope with 'is tail." He was grinning. Jack was grinning too and so were Sam and I.

They hauled in the yellow dory, the men climbed up the mast, Jack sat on the engine door, I sat on the little bench.

"Guess you brought us luck like ye said ye would," Jack said to me.

Through darkening waves the *Devil Diver* leaped towards the Harbour and home.

THE SHARK

E. J. PRATT

He seemed to know the harbour,
So leisurely he swam;
His fin,
Like a piece of sheet-iron,
Three-cornered,
And with knife-edge,
Stirred not a bubble
As it moved
With its base-line on the water.

His body was tubular
And tapered
And smoke-blue,
And as he passed the wharf
He turned,
And snapped at a flat-fish
That was dead and floating.
And I saw the flash of a white throat,
And a double row of white teeth,
And eyes of metallic grey,
Hard and narrow and slit.

Then out of the harbour,
With that three-cornered fin
Shearing without a bubble the water,
Lithely,
Leisurely,
He swam —
That strange fish,
Tubular, tapered, smoke-blue,
Part vulture, part wolf,
Part neither — for his blood was cold.

THE LONG TRADITION
WALTER HAVIGHURST

Through the Duluth channel piers Captain Carling took his big steel freighter *Algonquin*, with twelve thousand tons of iron ore beneath her hatches. Beyond the entrance, Lake Superior was a mass of drift ice, packed in solid by the northeast wind. In that white waste, like flies on a vast fly paper, a fleet of steamers struggled slowly. Farther out, under stiff black plumes of smoke, a knot of tugboats were battering a channel.

Captain Carling's voice made sharp jets in the raw March air. "Call Mr. Stearns and Mr. Heffernan. We'll need all hands till we're out of this pack."

The watchman ran stiffly down the ladder to the mates' passageway.

Captain Carling grasped a stanchion as the ship shuddered with the impact of solid ice. Smoke poured out of the red and black stack astern, beyond the long clear cargo deck. The big steel stem drove on, slowly, and the ice sheared up, with a steady, crashing roar, in broken wedges. Through six hundred feet of framing came the rhythmic labour of the engines. The ship was barely moving.

Captain Carling opened the door of the pilot-house. "Line your steer-pole on that tugboat. Don't let her swing off. Ask the engineer for more steam, Mr. Paisley. We've got to keep moving."

The wheelsman gave her a few spokes and Mr. Paisley, First Mate, called the engine room. Then he lifted his patient face to his young captain. "If we don't," he said, "we'll have company."

The captain swept an impatient eye over the fleet scattered in that ice-field — eleven Iron Range vessels that had fought with winter and had entered Duluth harbour before the end of March. They had loaded the earliest cargoes in the history of the Lakes, to begin a season that must be the biggest, fastest, most efficient in all the seasons of the trade.

"I don't want company," Captain Carling declared. "I want to be the first ship through this ice."

While Mr. Paisley stared over the desolate flats he finished Tom Carling's thoughts in his own mind — *and the first ship through the Soo, and the first ship down the rivers, bringing the first cargo to Hamilton's docks.*

He turned his lined face, weathered by forty seasons on the Lakes, to watch the tall scowling figure on the bridge wing. Tom Carling was the youngest captain in the fleets, making his first trip as master. But that wasn't enough for him. He wanted to begin his command with triumph. He wanted to hang up a record on his first trip, to lead the parade down the sea lanes and hear the whistles roaring to him as he took the first ship through the rivers. Mr. Paisley watched him — the restless dark eyes under the visored cap, the aggressive thrust of his shoulders, the stubborn mouth, the staight hard line of his jaw. And he thought, *He'll probably do it, too.*

With her engines groaning and smoke pouring over her counter, the *Algonquin* laboured on. Slowly she closed the gap that separated her from a tugboat smashing at the drift. But on her starboard beam another big ship crept in, fighting to gain a position in the tugboat's wake. Captain Carling didn't need to puzzle over the name *Ottawa*, half obscured in the ice that sheathed her bow. He knew her too well. He smiled grimly, seeing his smoke blowing across that space of ice. He had the wind on his side. Now she was near enough to see the men slipping on her long, ice-coated deck, and the muffled captain, with the frost white on his bearded face, pacing her bridge wing.

As the vessels drew together, the *Ottawa's* captain raised a megaphone, "Out of the way, Mister! Keep off there! When are you going to learn to handle a ship?"

The Long Tradition

Captain Carling's eyes flashed as he strode into the pilot house and grabbed the engine room phone. He called loudly for more steam and jabbed the earpiece down. "Cut in on him!" he said to Mr. Paisley. "Head him off! Push him back!"

Mr. Paisley ordered right wheel and the steer-pole made a slow arc toward the *Ottawa's* looming bow. As the ship swung the long hull gathered up a windrow of broken ice. That piling mash cracked and thudded and pushed sluggishly toward the *Ottawa*. It tightened between the two ships. But the wind was with the *Algonquin,* and her engines were pounding. Slowly the *Ottawa* began to drift.

As Mr. Paisley watched, his grey eyes flickered with admiration. The Old Man, young enough to be his son, had the nerve of a veteran master.

The *Ottawa's* captain stormed above the broken mutter of the ice. He paced his bridge wing like a tiger. He dropped his megaphone and bellowed across. But he was beaten. Easily the *Algonquin* steered into the loose ice at the tugboat's stern.

Captain Carling left Mr. Stearns on the starboard bridge wing on the port, and went into the pilot house. "Called me Mister," he said with a thick smile. He turned to his Mate. "You know him?"

Mr. Paisley nodded. "I sailed with Captain Finch in the *Rutherford*, eighteen years ago."

"And I sailed with him last year," the young captain said. "I was his Mate, and he never called me anything but Mister from the first run till we laid her up — treated me like a deck hand."

Mr. Paisley nodded, remembering the big bearded master with a voice that could roar from the bridge to the engine room. "Bull Finch," he said slowly. "Every man in the *Rutherford* was afraid of him."

"A tyrant to sail with," Captain Carling said.

"But a good seaman, sir. One of the best. He took every man off the *Matthew Black* when she was breaking up in a gale on the Manitou ledges. That was twenty years ago."

"He thinks he runs the Lakes."

"Well," said Mr. Paisley, "he's taken the first ship through the Soo for three years running. I s'pose a man gets to feeling that way."

"He'll feel different this time." Captain Carling stared astern at the *Ottawa's* ice-sheathed stem. "Mister —" he muttered grimly.

Mr. Paisley smiled. He knew how a man could smart under a domineering master. Then it wasn't just pride that itched in his young captain. He was glad of that.

By noon they were out of the ice and throbbing over the pale cold fairway of Lake Superior. It was good to have the deep-loaded rhythm and the familiar ship's routine going on, and it was good to be leading the fleet, with the *Ottawa* a black smoking speck on the grey horizon behind. Captain Carling was determined to keep her there. At the change of every watch he called the engine room, and while his mates relieved each other in their sequence he remained on the bridge. All afternoon he paced the pilot-house and nearly all night. When the grey day broke he was there again.

Before full daylight had come, the wind swung around to northwest, bringing a mist of snow. Captain Carling went aft for breakfast. When he left the dining room the snow was falling faster, storming in a white, noiseless curtain over the long cargo deck. On the bridge again, he looked aft. The shrouded sea was empty.

The morning wore on, with the big ship plodding through the snow. To Captain Carling on the bridge the deep vibration of the engines came with a steady exultation; he was leading the trade across Lake Superior and every turn of those engines carried him nearer to the first passage through the Soo.

Suddenly through the dimness came a deep bass blast. Instinctively Captain Carling looked astern, but the second blast told him the signal was ahead. Then he saw it, in the same

The Long Tradition

instant that the mate at the window saw it—a big, high-riding bow, looming through the swirl of white.

"Left wheel!" the mate snapped, and he reached for the whistle lever.

Captain Carling stepped into the pilot-house and checked the compass course over the wheelsman's shoulder. "He's off his course," he said, watching the dark hull slip past.

"Way off of it."

The Captain stared out at the horizonless sea. "He was afraid of running too close off Keweenaw Point. So he hauled out."

Quickly the upbound ship was swallowed in the white curtain astern. And still the snow fell thicker, until the *Algonquin's* own stack, pouring out its furrow of smoke, was blurred and dim. Reluctantly Captain Carling rang his engine room telegraph down to half speed. There would be more of those ships coming up, and they couldn't be trusted to keep their inshore course. While the snow whitened his shoulders, he paced the bridge wing, scanning the veiled sea.

He stayed there, a muffled, snow-hooded figure, all morning, and he had the porter bring a tray of sandwiches and coffee to the pilot-house at noon.

Aft, at dinner in the dining room, the Chief Engineer cocked his blue eyes around the table. "Looks like we're on a record-breaker," he said with satisfaction. "There's never been a cargo of ore through the Soo in March. Never. And we're just nine-ten hours away."

Mr. Paisley looked up from his soup. "That's just the trouble, Chief."

"What's the trouble?"

"We're nine-ten hours away."

"Well," the Chief grinned and winked at his third assistant, "we can keep the steam on her. All you fellows have to do is handle the steering gear."

"There's blue ice waiting for us," Mr. Paisley said, "in Whitefish Bay."

"We came up through it. We'll get back down."

"Besides, it's going to be night when we reach Whitefish," Mr. Paisley added. "And the lights on the Canadian side aren't working."

"Why not? Why aren't they working?"

"Because we winter our Canadian supply ship in Midland harbour, where the ice never goes out till ten days after the channels are open. When we need those lights most, the keepers are waiting on Georgian Bay for warm weather to free their supply ship."

"Well," said the Chief, dismissing the worries of the bridge with the case of a lifetime in ships' engine rooms, "the American lights are working. Just steer by them."

Up on the bridge Captain Carling wore a deepening line in his brow. But it was not the unmanned Canadian lights that were worrying him; it was the fleet of down-bound ships, racing for the first passage through the canal. Then, quite suddenly, the wind changed and the snow slacked off. With his glasses to his eyes he swept the clearing sea line. Out there, ahead of him, on the port bow, his glasses stopped. Faint and diminishing, a smudge of smoke was trailed across the sky.

Into his mind came the echo of a booming voice. "Out of the way, Mister! When are you going to learn to handle a ship?"

He turned to the Mate. "Ring your engines up. And tell the engineer to watch his gauges. I want every revolution he can deliver."

Mr. Paisley had seen the smudge, too. He stepped to the telegraph, but his hand was idle. "There's ice ahead of us, Captain."

"If Captain Finch can run full speed, I can too. And I'll catch him when he's in the ice." He crossed the narrow room with hungry strides. "A man has to drive hard to come in ahead."

Mr. Paisley looked at him levelly. "I've seen men drive hard aground. They didn't come in at all." Then he added, in another tone, "There's ninety million tons to move this season,"

The Long Tradition

"I said ring your engines up, Mister!"

The Mate's mouth drew tight. "Yes, sir!" The telegraph jangled under his hand.

Captain Carling paced across the bank of windows, a big restless man with youth and authority burning in him. In the choppy sea, ice began to appear, the outlying drift of the pack that was waiting in Whitefish Bay. The ship shook as she plowed into a sluggish berg.

"Mr. Paisley —" there was a slight, apologetic emphasis upon the fullness of the name — "that's a big order, ninety million tons of iron in eight months of navigation. Do you think we can move it?"

The weathered old veteran looked up at him. This was youth, headstrong, willful, yet, underneath all that, deeply, broodingly anxious about the big job.

"Yes," the Mate said slowly, "if we have fair luck with the weather — and if we work together at the job."

"Together?"

Mr. Paisley nodded. "Every fleet and every captain. Every man aboard ship, too. That order is big enough to need us all. It means new records all along the line."

Captain Carling resumed his pacing and his mouth hardened again. "Well, we're going to start with a record. We'll pick up the *Ottawa* in the ice and we'll beat her to the locks."

He went out on the bridge wing, leaving Mr. Paisley with a light of memory in his eyes. He had never had a ship — in forty years. He guessed he wasn't the kind that got ships — too cautious, perhaps, too willing to follow. Maybe that was why they teamed him up with a young captain, with a hunger for difficulty and a driving will. He had served under many captains, some easy-going and some hard, some quiet and some that ruled a ship with their lungs. Already, before the first voyage was made, he knew that Tom Carling was one of the best — alert, watchful, daring, taking nothing for granted, wearing his ship on his mind and on his nerves every minute of every hour. Mr. Paisley had watched him as they came up the St. Mary's, a new captain in the slow, hard battle with winter's ice, the coast guard plane droning over head and the cutter knifing through the floes and the big car ferry battering the tough blue ice that had sealed the channel since December. Night and day young Captain Carling was on the bridge, tireless, giving strength to his men, driving his ship as surely as her engines drove her. Now, after thirty sleepless hours, he was aching to get at that hated stretch of ice in Whitefish Bay. Mr. Paisley looked out at the big muffled figure on the bridge wing. He would take his place in the long tradition — after he learned one lesson more.

At dusk they picked up the flashing blade on Whitefish Point. Slowly it drew near. The light passed abeam before the ice got bad. Then there was a growing mutter as the heavy pack parted beneath the big steel stem.

Somewhere ahead was the dark, lifeless tower of the Canadian light on Ile Parisienne. But that was not what kept the glasses lifted to Captain Carling's eyes. He was searching for the running lights of the *Ottawa*. His eyes bored the horizon, but Whitefish Bay remained a vague and empty waste. He called his men up from their watch below. And he called the engineer. "Keep your gauges up, Chief. We're trying to make the Soo."

Out of the starless dark a thin snow began to fall. There was heavy ice around them now, and even with her engines pounding the *Algonquin* made slow way. Snow had dimmed the flashing light astern. When the ice grew solid, with the engines groaning as the bow bit into piled up windrows, they knew they were abreast of Ile Parisienne.

"Wind seems to be carrying us," the Mate said with narrowing eyes. "That ice is drifting, and we're moving with it."

Captain Carling checked the course over the wheelsman's shoulder. One-forty-one degrees — he was dead on.

"Pull her off ten degrees," he said to the Mate.

While the wheel went over, he stared out at the ghostly, snow-veiled sea. He went out to the bridge wing. Aft, the deck lights were spaced and dim, haloed in that noiseless fall of snow. The lighted bunker hatch was a white blur — and it was less than five hundred feet away. Anxiously he stared ahead, listening to the mutter of the crumpled ice, listening for the sharper, angry note that might tell him of shore ice never broken.

Ile Parisienne was a lonely, desolate arrowhead, lying in a wintry sea, battered by the winds and waves of Lake Superior. He pictured the high hexagonal tower with its far white flashing. He would have given a good deal to see that light sweep through the darkness. But there was only emptiness and the grind of ice along the ship's deep-laden hull. His eyes bored hard into blankness.

Abruptly a deep blast roared out on his port bow.

"Right rudder!" he cried. "Hard over!"

At the same moment, before his ship began to fight her burdened way off, he saw a ship's spaced lights, blurred through the snow. Then a voice bellowed above the churning ice.

"Haul off there, Mister! You're heading straight for Parisienne ledge."

Mr. Paisley was at his captain's side. "The *Ottawa*," he said, as Captain Carling's thoughts were racing. "He's driven aground."

"Man that searchlight!" the captain ordered.

The powerful cone flared out, lighting up the ice-coated hull of the grounded ship. If Captain Finch had not sounded his whistle, the *Algonquin* would at that moment have piled up alongside her.

While he stared through the slanting veil of snow, with his ship already edging away from danger, Captain Carling's thoughts ran in a baffling circle. He turned like a boy to the Mate beside him. "Why did he warn me off, Mr. Paisley?"

"The ore has got to move, sir."

"But that's Captain Finch, of the *Ottawa*."

Mr. Paisley nodded. "Yes. It's Captain Finch."

"Why did he warn me?"

Mr. Paisley repeated, like a schoolmaster drilling a lesson. "The ore has got to move."

From the pilot-house Mr. Stearns called. "Straighten course, sir? We're swinging wide. Bearing two-forty now."

Mr. Paisley rotated his searchlight. It sprayed across the slush ice ahead. "Looks like an open track ahead."

For once Captain Carling was not ready with an order. He stood like a frozen man, with the snow falling around him. Off there, not six hours away, was the Soo, with the canal crews waiting to lock the first ship through in the Lake season. There were the river boats, the mill whistles, the church bells ready to cry out the triumph of the captain who brought the first cargo down. His eyes narrowed, and he looked back through the darkness where the *Ottawa's* lights glowed vaguely. Then he made his decision.

"Left rudder!" he called to the pilot-house. "Ring your engines down to 'Slow Ahead'."

The Long Tradition

He turned to Mr. Paisley. "Fix your searchlight on Captain Finch's ship."

"Yes, sir," said the Mate. In the darkness his eyes were shining deeply.

Slowly the *Algonquin* crunched toward the stranded vessel. The searchlight picked her out again, the ice-coated hull, the snowy decks, the men at the stern rail, staring. Then the voice of Captain Finch blared out again.

"Haul off there, Mister! When are you going to learn to handle a ship? You're heading inshore again."

"I'm standing by!"

There was a silence, while the ice moaned under the *Algonquin's* hull. When the voice came back there was a new note in it. "I'll try to get a cable to you."

Captain Carling raised his megaphone again. "Are you taking any water?"

"No water," Captain Finch roared. "I'm only half aground. But this dumb, devilish ice is hardening around me."

"I'll crack it open," Captain Carling said.

It was a slow, cautious, nerve-wringing job, working alongside the imprisoned ship, crumpling the ice that had sealed her in. It was another job, successful only after many failures, to get a heaving line aboard and haul the heavy cables. They came up dripping, and they quickly rimmed with ice. Hands were numb and backs were aching before that job was done.

When at last they had two lines over the bitts, the snow had ceased. Captain Carling looked up, surprised, at a deep sky breaking open with stars. Across the vague, ice-paved sea, low on the horizon, came the repeated white flash from Point Iroquois, marking the St. Mary's River entrance. Then he saw, out in the channel, the running lights of a freighter plodding on to the Soo.

He stood there for a moment, staring; and what he felt was not disappointment but a silent exultation. All at once the bells and whistles were a hollow noise, an empty, childish celebration;

while the big job went on. One captain could stand on his bridge while the people cheered, but out in the dark channels the fleets were moving, sharing the toil and the danger, bringing the iron down. There was a brief tradition on the Lakes, the rivalry between captains, the records in the books. But suddenly he knew another and deeper one, the long tradition of men pooling their strength against wind and sea, uniting their purpose to get the big job done.

Mr. Paisley saw those running lights out in the channel. "There she goes," he said.

"Who?" said Captain Carling, coming back from his brief reverie.

Mr. Paisley pointed. "The record-breaker. She'll be at the Soo by midnight."

Captain Carling barked at him. "Don't stand there talking about records, Mister. We've got a ship to release before she's damaged."

"Yes, sir," the Mate said quickly.

Captain Carling raised his megaphone. "Stand by on the *Ottawa!* We're taking a strain on your cables."

And Captain Finch boomed back: "All ready, Captain."

TRAIN AT NIGHT

ARTHUR S. BOURINOT

Sometimes at night
I hear a train
Far off
Shunting in the yards,
And half asleep, half awake,
Dreaming,
I see a great giant
Striding the mountains,

Shuffling his huge feet
Along the valleys,
Puffing wearily,
Tired from a long day's hunt,
Whistling eerily
As he trudges,
Shuffles
Home.

THE GREEN KEY TO SUN POWER

GEORGE H. WALTZ, JR.

You ate the sun to-day. Whatever your meal, it was made of stored sunlight. Your breakfast cornflakes gave you the same solar energy that once shone on waving green fields on a bright summer's day; the milk you drank and the meat you ate came from animals who themselves fed on the energy of the sun; like you, they, too, ate the sunlight stored by green plants growing in its rays.

Your 98.4 degrees of bodily warmth all came from the sun. Stored sunlight was burnt in your body as food to heat you to that temperature. And stored sunlight in the form of your clothing helped hold that temperature. All the fibres that made your garments were made by plants from the sun — whether you are wearing cotton and linens that come from the plant at first hand, or leather and wool that came from the plant at second hand, or chemical fabrics like rayon and nylon that came from the plant by way of the chemist's laboratory.

The radiators in your classroom are warmed with the energy of the sun, as is the fireplace in your living room. The logs you burn there give heat because green plants stored away that energy. The coal and oil stored in your basement are sunshine hoarded by plants of prehistoric ages.

How do plants store sunlight? The answer is one of nature's most closely guarded secrets. It is close to the secret of life itself. Without solar energy there could be no life on the face of this earth. Not only would we be without food and warmth; it is likely that we would even be without oxygen to breathe. We would be like goldfish in a bowl without green aquatic plants in the water. Without these green plants, goldfish would soon suffocate. The green plants replenish the goldfish's bowl as they replenish our air with oxygen; in each case the oxygen is a by-product as they store away the sun's energy. Without green plants, our atmosphere, like the water in the fishbowl, would become used up — and we should drown in the open air.

Scientists have a name for this process by which green plants store up the energy of the sun. They call it photosynthesis, which means the building up of chemical compounds by means of light. Inside each green leaf there are mazes of little tunnels. Each tunnel is lined with tiny thin-walled blocks, called cells. Each cell is full of colourless jelly called protoplasm. Inside the protoplasm are tiny green bodies called chloroplasts, from the Greek word for green. Each of these tiny chloroplasts is a factory, running on the energy of the sun. Each of them has raw materials coming into it — moisture and traces of minerals seeping up from the roots, and carbon-dioxide gas coming in from the air through the leaf pores. Each little factory ships out a finished product — plant sugar.

Only the tiny green chloroplasts can make this plant sugar. And, as we have seen, all the energy with which we feed and warm our bodies comes from it.

But what is the actual process? Just what is this green magic which converts carbon-dioxide gas, water, and sunshine into foods and fuels? For more than three hundred years scientists have been striving for the answer. Not long ago, Charles Kettering, the great industrial scientist, was asked what he considered the most important research problem in the world. He answered, "To find out why grass is green." Once science has solved this riddle, we shall have unlocked the storehouse of nature's energy.

When we have discovered artificial photosynthesis, we shall be able to make fuel without the aid of green leaves; we shall even be able, if we wish it, to make foods in laboratories. Few scientists, however, think that nature's way of producing cauliflowers and roses, bacon and milk, will ever be entirely replaced. Without the trace of elements of minerals and vitamins which the soil now supplies, few of us would enjoy a synthetic (chemically produced) beefsteak or a dish of strawberries and cream concentrated into the size of an aspirin tablet. Nevertheless if we knew how the green magic worked, it certainly would help us to get more foods, and perhaps better foods, from each acre of farmland. At its best Nature's green leaf is able to use only two per cent of the sunlight that falls upon it. If man could add only another few per cent he could double the world's production of food, and banish starvation, and the wars which result from it, from the face of the earth.

But it is not so much in producing foods as in producing fuels that artificial photosynthesis would bring its greatest gift to man. Then we could capture and store the sun's energy just as the tree does now. We could put it into man-made substitutes for wood, and coal, and oil. It took Nature millions of years to produce oil and coal from the green plants that first stored it. Perhaps we could run our cars and trucks and furnaces and dynamos from stored sunlight synthesized only a few days before in a laboratory.

How far off is such a discovery? It is difficult to say. It might come next month, next year, or perhaps not for centuries. All research is a slow and painstaking affair; no great discovery is ever the brainchild of one man. All scientists reach a little closer towards the answer which dangles above them because they themselves stand on the shoulders of those who have gone before them. In dozens of laboratories all over the world patient men are working towards the solving of one little part of the big problem. In order to contribute their answer to one phase of it, they must know what every other scientist in every other corner of the world is doing towards solving his little phase. That is one reason, incidentally, why science can progress only in a world of free speech.

In the seventeenth century an inquisitive Dutchman by the name of Van Helmont began man's long search for the "green key". Until then everyone had accepted, without question, an idea that went back to the ancient Greek, Aristotle, an idea that plants got all their needs for life and growth from the soil. Van Helmont planted a five-pound willow twig in a box containing exactly two hundred pounds of soil from which he carefully eliminated every trace of moisture. To avoid other sources of extra weight, he shielded his giant flowerpot carefully from dust, and watered it with natural rain water. Then he placed it in full sun and watered it carefully for five years.

At the end of that time Van Helmont weighed his tree again, and also the soil which he had dried once more. The five-pound twig had become a 169-pound tree. The dry soil, on the other hand, had lost only two ounces.

Where had the tree's additional 163 pounds and 14 ounces come from? Van Helmont reasoned that it must have come from the daily doses of rain water. He was partly right, of course, but he had missed the important thing that sunpower did when it combined water with part of the air to make a new substance. It took a long line of scientists who came after him, including Britain's Priestley and Switzerland's Senebier, to discover the role that the green colouring matter plays. As we have said before, water is just one of the raw materials; the carbon-dioxide gas in air is the other; the green chloroplasts are the factory; and sunlight is the power that runs the factory. Sugar, the product of the factory, has locked within it the energy of that sun power. Each smallest particle, or molecule, of sugar is made of six molecules of hydrogen from the water, six molecules of carbon-dioxide from the air. Six molecules of oxygen are given off by the plant as a waste product from the water; this waste product,

The Green Key to Sun Power

useless to plants, keeps the air supplied with oxygen for animals and man to breathe. Grandma was wrong when she used to take the plants out of the sick room at night, because, as she said, they took the "good" out of the air!

Charles Kettering, who invented the self-starter and no-knock ethyl gasoline, became interested in the '20's in the greatest problem of science to-day. Always a man to seek the answers to his own questions, he had a green-house built near his home at Dayton, Ohio. In 1929 he built a large, modern science building for Antioch College, gathered about him a group of top-notch chemists, physicists, and plant experts, and set up the Kettering Foundation for the study of Chlorophyll and Photosynthesis. These scientists became known as "the green grass boys".

The search for the answer to Kettering's famous question is taking three directions at Antioch.

One is the head-on attack by Dr. Eyester, the laboratory's plant physiologist. A physiologist seeks to investigate the normal ways that a living thing's organs operate. Dr. Eyester uses complicated machines to grind, filter, and wash bushels of green leaves. At the end of this operation he extracts a teaspoonful of nature's mystery package. This is chlorophyll, the green colouring matter of leaves, made up of chloroplasts and the colourless life jelly or protoplasm in which they are embedded. Then Dr. Eyester tries patiently to make the chlorophyll do the same sugar-making job in his test tubes that it did in the green leaves from which it came.

Not long ago Dr. Eyester came one step nearer to success. He dissolved chlorophyll in acetone — the smelly solvent used in transparent household cements — and got a vivid green liquid. When he soaked this liquid in ordinary talcum powder, he was able to get it to do some of the things that chlorophyll did in the leaf.

But he has one long step ahead of him still — to get the chlorophyll mixture to absorb carbon-dioxide and to combine it with the hydrogen from water.

Down the hall from Dr. Eyester is a microchemist, Dr. Rothemund. A microchemist works with doll-size flasks and tubes and microscopic specks of rare chemicals. Dr. Rothemund is trying to synthesize chlorophyll, that is, to make it artificially by chemical combination. So far he has been unable to penetrate Nature's secret. He has been unable to combine the elements carbon, hydrogen, oxygen, nitrogen, and magnesium in precisely the right way. But he has been able to synthesize a part-way step in the process. Some day he, or one of the devoted workers in another corner of the world, who reads of Dr. Rothemund's trials and his failures in the scientific journals, will happen upon the green key.

In a roof-top above these laboratories works Dr. Knoor, the director of the whole laboratory. He uses a by-product of the atomic bomb, a by-product called "tagged atoms". Small quantities of chemicals are put into an atomic pile, like the one we have at Chalk River in Canada. After a time they are withdrawn; they are then radio-active. With mechanical detectives such as photographic film or Geiger counters, scientists can then track these "hot" chemicals through all the compounds into which they enter. In this way an instrument of death is being made to serve the cause of human progress. Dr. Knoor feeds plants with chemicals that have been "tagged", and then spies on them as they wander through the plant's roots, stem, leaves, and fruit. At present he is growing plants in an atmosphere of radio-active carbon-dioxide gas. He hopes in this way to see just what happens to carbon inside the leaves to change it into sugar.

Another scientist Dr. Calvin, at the University of California, maintains a complete radio-active farm, composed of tiny barley shoots and green water slime, or algae. Algae are the simplest form of plant life, and would seem therefore to give the easiest solution of this difficult search for the "green key". The fields of this scientist's farm are glass dishes and test tubes. Dr. Calvin also plays detective with radio-active carbon-dioxide gas. Recently Dr. Calvin found out that photosynthesis continues a short time

The Green Key to Sun Power

after dark. The green leaf would seem to be able to store up a small extra quantity of energy for use after the sun disappears for the night.

The green key is a gigantic jigsaw puzzle of which most of the pieces are still missing. So far science has discovered only a few of the missing parts. Some of these pieces fit together; others still depend upon finding their neighbour pieces before they themselves are of any significance. But that is the way modern science works — bit by bit, from patient research workers all over the world. Science knows no national flags and no frontiers; science cannot flourish behind iron curtains.

When somebody finally puts in the last missing piece of the gigantic jigsaw puzzle, we shall have at the disposal of mankind a source of energy as unfailing and unlimited as the sun itself. To imagine the power, just consider that the normal sunlight falling on an acre of farm field every hour has the same heat value as three-quarters of a ton of coal. In a twelve-hour day, the sun's energy trapped by all the plants of the earth is twelve times as great as the heat energy of all the coal mined on the earth during the same period.

And yet Nature is only two per cent efficient. Just suppose that man could teach the stubborn old lady some of his own industrial efficiency. Then, when that day comes and the green key to sunpower has finally been found, a man-made photosynthesis machine on the roof of a factory will supply all the fuel and power needed to keep that factory running. It is even possible that a smaller sunshine factory on the roof of our family garage will relieve us forever of the need for stopping at a service station for gasoline.

— Adapted.

GRAIN ELEVATORS

JAMES STERLING AYARS

They're ugly, some folks call them — hard and bare
  And stark against the lifted prairie sky.
  And some folks all their lives can live close by
And never seem to know that they are there.

Somehow, they always are a part of me.
  I can no more put them away, I find,
  Than I can put the black land out of mind,
Or from the prairie reaches set me free.

If handsome is as handsome does, then they
  Are beautiful. Without the brittle shell
  Of false pretending, they do very well
The job that they were built to do, I say.

I do not think them alien or forlorn
  In prairie roadside towns where life is toil.
  I find them native as the fertile soil
And growing out of it like wheat or corn.

OPERATION SUBWAY

ALAN M. THOMAS, JR.

Can you imagine what a task it would be to operate upon a living giant the size of the city of Toronto, particularly if the operation had to be performed without putting the patient to sleep or even making him lie down? Yet just such an operation had to be performed by the Toronto Transportation Commission, and it had to be done while the patient went about his daily

Operation Subway

tasks. After twenty years of diagnosis and six years of preparation, the Commission decided to graft upon the patient a supplementary system of veins and arteries to help carry the life blood to and from the heart of the city.

An operation is generally prescribed only when no alternative is possible; such was the condition of the city of Toronto in the years following World War II. In a ten year period the population of the city had nearly doubled, until almost 100,000 people were employed in downtown Toronto. Most of them lived on the edges of the city, a considerable distance from their places of occupation. Every morning this vast army of workers had to be transported to work, and every evening they had to be transported home again. Though the numbers had increased so very much, the surface transportation facilities had increased little, for the simple reason that *there was no more room on the streets*. The number of private cars had increased after the war so that at rush hours the main streets were a tangled network of street cars, automobiles, and people.

The city was in a desperate plight, and the Transportation Commission decided to operate upon the ailing patient.

It was decided that an underground railway should be built to move the army of workers into the city and out of it without interference from surface traffic. Since there was no more room on top of the ground, the new artery had to tunnel under ground. This operation had to be performed with a minimum of inconvenience to the patient. A few arteries could be rerouted, a few even cut off, but it was realized that the more the patient's activities were curtailed, the more loudly he would complain. It was a tremendous challenge to the traffic doctors who had taken on the case.

It meant consulting other authorities throughout the world — London, New York, and Paris, all patients that have survived such an operation. Their advice would be invaluable. Workmen, many of them New Canadians, came from India, South America, Poland, England, Central Europe, Italy — half the countries of

the world. Materials were carefully estimated and purchased:
steel from Ontario, England, United States, and Luxembourg;
concrete from Eastern Canada; timber from British Columbia,
and stone from quarries all across the country. Every resource
of the vast and many-sided construction industry of Canada was
enlisted, for skills of every imaginable sort were involved.
Excavations, tunnels, bridges, houses, railways, communications
— all were necessary, and the right men were made available
before the work started. Huge, ungainly machines: steam
shovels, piledrivers, back-hoes, clam-grabs, derricks, rollers,
pneumatic drills, and squadrons of powerful, slow-moving trucks,
were gathered and organized before a pick fell, or a yellow "No
Thoroughfare" sign was shoved into place.

II

In September, 1949, the first excavation was made. For the
first mile and a half the construction was carried from Front
Street right up Yonge Street, the main artery of the city. This
was a delicate process and required careful probing. Just as a
surgeon must exercise great care that he severs no vital nerve, so
the subway builders had to keep unbroken all the sewage pipes,
gas mains, and communication lines that compose the central
nervous system of the city. Each one was carefully unearthed,
supported while men dug around it, and finally replaced by
alternative services or specially disposed of. As the hole grew
deeper, a piledriver planted forty-foot steel posts along the
side of the street to provide support for the main excavation.
Each of the buildings lining Yonge Street, mile upon mile, was
examined, and, if necessary, provided with special reinforcing.
At the corner of Front and Yonge streets, engineers dug right
under the basement of an ornate old building, the Bank of
Montreal, close enough to see into the basement, while
maintaining special supports and facilities for the Bank to
continue its daily business. Enough foundation was provided

to allow for a new skyscraper on the same site, if and when the Bank should come to build it, directly over the subway.

With the public utilities arranged, and the foundations of buildings made secure, the excavations were covered over. Steel beams, laid across the posts, supported huge 12"x12" beams of British Columbia Fir. Street car tracks were replaced and the street re-opened to traffic, while the builders continued their work underground. Steam shovels, cranes, and trucks were driven into the covered trench to prepare it for the concrete forms that constitute the shell of the subway. An endless tube, the tunnel was pushed northwards, while overhead the pulse of the city beat strongly; street cars thundered over the wooden platform, and trucks, cars, and people pursued their uninterrupted affairs.

Further north, at Alexander Street, the construction engineers, with a sigh of relief, turned off the main street. For approximately three miles north, except at the crossing just above St. Clair Avenue, the subway follows its own right of way. To make this possible in the middle of a crowded city, property had to be purchased, houses and buildings bought and destroyed, and other arrangements made at a cost of close to five and a half million dollars. Here construction was faster and easier. The excavation, carried out in much the same way, did not need to be covered over until the shell was complete. In this way most of the troublesome public utilities were avoided. Even where it was not to remain an open trench, men and machinery could remain in the sunlight and fresh air. However, bridges were necessary over pits that interrupted side streets, and there must be extensive protection for the unwary passer-by.

To see such an operation in progress is an interesting sight, as might have been surmised by the number of people who stood beside the excavations watching the men and machines at work. Indeed, as the work progressed the Toronto Transportation Commission issued two pamphlets, which they humorously entitled "The Sidewalk Superintendent's Handbooks".

III

Let us put ourselves in the places of these spectators and see what is going on.

Everywhere crawl lines of muddy trucks, like huge soldier ants; everywhere piles of materials grow larger and larger. Enough sand is used to fill a railroad train 150 miles long; enough steel, concrete, and timber for a train sixty-seven miles long; enough clay and mud removed for a train four hundred miles long; and the daily army of men grows to more than thirteen hundred. And still the city functions almost normally, despite the numbers of curious citizens who hang on the railings during the day, attracted by the pounding hammers and the shrill chatter of drills.

Beneath the street, tunnels and stations take shape out of the intricate tangle of reinforcing wire, and the endless mud and water. Concrete clatters down metal funnels from the street above, to be stirred free of air bubbles and pressed into shape in colossal steel moulds. Trucks roar and whine through mud and planks, waiting on steam shovels or bringing supplies. And gradually the finished shell emerges, foot by foot, section by section.

It consists of two tunnels, side by side, about three times the width of a country road and two-thirds as high as it is wide. At the stations appear, on each side of the tracks, platforms five hundred feet long and twelve feet wide. At Queen Street there are two stations, one under the other, one of these to serve a line running east and west through the city at some time in the future. As each group of workers moves on up the tunnel, it is quickly followed by another. The departure of the excavators and the concrete-workers is marked by the arrival of the men who lay the tracks, by the heating engineers, the electricians, and the plumbers. After the track is laid, signals are installed with miles and miles of electrical wiring for operational safety devices. Moving stairs, doors, lights, turnstiles, ventilators, and a host of other fixtures and devices fall into place, bringing each section nearer to completion. Each station receives a different colour of paint, for the benefit of travellers who cannot remember the name, but may remember the colour.

The tunnel pushes on farther north. The sides of the open cut are planted with a special shrub to protect them from erosion by snow and water. Special consultants are summoned to deal with a new problem — sound. North of St. Clair Avenue the tunnel crosses Yonge Street just beneath two movie theatres, and their auditoriums must be protected from the rumble of the passing trains. In this area, stations are constructed above ground with adjoining bus terminals to provide connections for the hordes of people who will arrive and depart during the day.

Everywhere the gaunt skeletons of piles, the torn and scarred earth, the forlorn foundations of houses, the scattered piles of equipment, and above all the look of aimless untidiness give way to an emerging design, to a neatly finished arrangement of concrete, rails, modern buildings, and high metal fences that maintain an appearance of confident efficiency.

Above the turmoil, the confusion, and the apparent aimlessness is the ever watchful eye of the engineering office. Turning from estimates of traffic flow, and the planning boards over which they have worked for six years, they maintain an unending vigilance and precise control. No truck moves, and no shovel bites into the earth that has not been planned and co-ordinated with a thousand other operations. Engineers, contractors, draughtsmen, accountants, and publicity experts plot every move and plan every step. Contractors are hired and directed, specifications are checked and rechecked, finished work is examined and plans are amended, schedules are set and maintained as nearly as possible, and citizens are kept informed of each development. A large wall chart with a green line for finished piling, black for decking or covering over, orange for excavating, and blue for concrete poured, records the progress square by square, day by day. Every piece of information, every statistic and fragment of advice gathered from around the world is examined, sorted, and applied to the undertaking.

IV

With the interior completed, the holes refilled, and the streets repaved, the subway is ready for the first train. It is equipped to move a quarter of a million people a day, about fourteen hundred every two minutes at rush hours, and the time from Front Street to Eglinton Avenue is cut in half. Trains rush forty-thousand people an hour through the many-coloured stations from one end of the city to the other. Made up of two, four, six, eight, or ten cars, each train is reversible, with the driver and conductor changing places and jobs at either end of the line. Built as close to the surface as possible, to make necessary a minimum of climbing up and down, the subway is a main artery, a new and vital addition to a great city's circulatory system. Underneath the lines of automobiles and hurrying people, half the population will dart to work and home again without adding to the clutter of the streets. It is a tremendous achievement in transportation, a miraculous operation that the patient has soon forgotten.

THE MACHINE

MARY ELIZABETH COLMAN

I am the machine!
Born of a poet and a mathematician
Mine is the beauty of precision,
The rhythm of motion
Exquisitely spaced for accurate performance,
The grace of balance
So that each of my parts
Moves in exact harmony with every other part.
I am thought made steel;

I am a dream come to life
    in pistons and cogwheels,
    in turbines and transformers.
I am a slave to serve you,
    obedient, docile;
But when I am master
    I kill.
There is no compassion in me;
Who worships me
I destroy.
Pity and hate are alike unknown to me —
I am the machine!

A THUNDERSTORM

ARCHIBALD LAMPMAN

A moment the wild swallows, like a flight
  Of withered gust-caught leaves, serenely high,
  Toss in the wind-rack up the muttering sky.
The leaves hang still. Above the weird twilight,
The hurrying centres of the storm unite
  And spreading with huge trunk and rolling fringe,
  Each wheeled upon its own tremendous hinge,
Tower darkening on. And now from heaven's height,

With the long roar of elm-trees swept and swayed,
  And pelted waters, on the vanished plain
    Plunges the blast. Behind the wild white flash
    That splits abroad the pealing thunder-crash,
Over bleared fields and gardens disarrayed,
  Column on column comes the drenching rain.

FOREST FIRE

EDNA DAVIS ROMIG

Whispers of little winds low in the leaves,
Rustle of warm winds through tall green trees,
A full resinous fragrance, rich, warm, sweet,
A sharp acrid odour, a hint of heat,
Snap, hiss, crackle, a faint blue smoke,
A whirl of black swept by tawny flame —
Deep in the forest the wild wind broke;
Fast in the wild wake the fire-wind came,
A soughing of branches swept sudden and strong
Like the rush and crash when the storm winds meet;
Crimson streams of fire flowed quickly along
The tall, grey grasses and the spruce needles deep;
Red tongues of fire licked the tall pine trees,
Gray twigs fell as though shrivelled by disease;
Broad orange streamers floated everywhere
And bulging puffs of copper smoke filled the molten air.
A pitiable squeaking came from little furry creatures,
Chipmunks and marmots, as they scurried helter-skelter;
Mountain sheep and mountain goats leaping to some shelter,
Warned by their instincts — grim, sure teachers —
And the suffocating stenches from the red, relentless thing;
Like a plummet dropped a blue-jay with a burning broken wing;
The eagles screamed in anger from the smoke-beclouded skies;
A sudden rush of slender deer, dumb fright in liquid eyes . . .
Now burning brands seem missiles sent,
Projectiles hurled through space,
Now and then a chuckle, like mirth malevolent,
A sweeping beauty sinister, a dread and treacherous grace;
And conflagration with the sound of thunder
Has pulled a thousand tall trees under.

But men have come in purpose bent
To halt the fire's fierce race.
They fell great trees and dig deep lanes,
They smother out small flames;
With tools and chemicals and wit
At last they curb, they conquer it.
But fire that raged for half a day
Has burned a hundred years away.

THE TAMING OF No. 3

BLAIR FRASER

Driller Bill Murray and his crew of four had the graveyard shift, midnight to 8 A.M., at Atlantic Oil Company's No. 3 well. It was March 8, 1948 — a clear cold night. Leduc oil field, twenty miles south-west of Edmonton, was under two feet of snow. The evening shift had added twenty-two feet to the well, already a mile deep.

Murray's crew worked four hours, made another eighteen feet. Then they heard a rumbling underfoot, and the derrick platform shivered. Seconds later, a great column of gas and liquid mud blew up in their faces.

Murray yelled, "Cut the lights." The gas was explosive; let a stray pebble smash a light bulb and they might all be burned to death. Somebody threw the master switch. For a minute the crew fumbled around in the dark, then they ran for the boilerhouse and sat down to wait for daylight and a chance to look at No. 3 on its rampage.

It was a spectacle, all right — one that ran for six months and a day, and cost nearly a million dollars. Wild No. 3 brought up not only one and a quarter million barrels of oil in that time — as much as all other Leduc wells produced in the first seventeen months of operation — but also several billion cubic feet of natural gas. It churned twenty-five acres of rich farm land into an evil-looking swamp of black stinking mud which may never bear grain again. By God's mercy, not a man was hurt in the whole long job of killing No. 3, but it kept fifty men working in continual danger. Before it was finally and permanently killed on September 9, it exploded into the most spectacular fire ever seen in Canada, a pillar of flame sometimes 800 feet high and visible for forty miles.

Even on that first March morning, it was a sight to see. The reddish-brown plume of gas and oil and mud reached higher than the 136-foot derrick. The rotary table at the centre of the derrick platform was blown out. The great bushings that held the drill in place were 300-pound cubes of steel — two men could not lift one of them. No. 3 was tossing them around like dice.

Murray sent a man over to camp to telephone Edmonton, and let the management know that No. 3 was blowing wild. No one at the field needed any notice — they could hear it.

Farmer John Rebus, on whose land Atlantic was drilling, was awakened by it in his bedroom a quarter of a mile away; he wondered, not for the last time, whether the $200,000 and twelve-and-a-half per cent royalty he'd got for his mineral rights were enough to compensate for the trouble the wild well would cause him. In the cookhouse next door, where "Ma" Ferguson was fixing breakfast for the day shift, a man couldn't speak to his neighbour without shouting. The steady, high-pitched roar of No. 3 filled the room like something solid.

At daylight the task of killing the well began. The drill pipe was still in the hole and still connected. The plan was to pump heavy mud into the well and choke the flow of oil long enough to get a patented "blow-out preventor" into the casing at the well-head.

They pumped in mud for thirty-eight hours before the great plume died down — thirty-eight hours in which oil spray fell over everything in a blinding rain, and men came in for their meals "so black," Mrs. Ferguson said, "that you couldn't tell

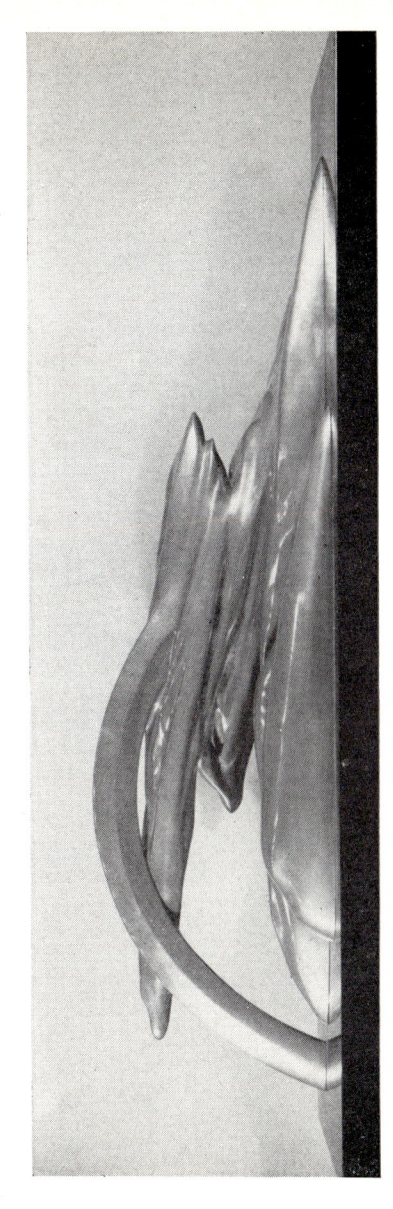

REEF AND RAINBOW — *Elizabeth Wyn Wood*

Reproduced by permission of the Art Gallery of Toronto.

ELIZABETH WYN WOOD, R.C.A., S.S.C.
(1903 -   )

Elizabeth Wyn Wood was born in Orillia, Ontario, in 1903. She studied sculpture in the Ontario College of Art, Toronto, and at the Art Students League, New York. Miss Wood came into prominence by introducing the landscape motif into sculpture. This motif is well illustrated by *Reef and Rainbow*. She has done many figure and portrait pieces, some of which are in private collections, but her work may be seen publicly in her monumental and architectural sculpture. Works of hers include, the Welland-Crowland Memorial, fountains and other installations at Niagara Falls and at Niagara-on-the-Lake. She has work also in the National Gallery, Ottawa, the Vancouver Art Gallery, the Winnipeg Art Gallery, the Library of the University of British Columbia, and the Orillia Public Library.

Miss Wood has been prominent in Art organization in Canada, having been one of the founders of the Canadian Arts Council. She represented Canada at the First General Conference of Unesco, 1946.

Reef and Rainbow, cast in tin, is in the Art Gallery of Toronto. In viewing this unusual piece of sculpture, notice the low-lying reef and the background of cirro-stratus clouds against which the rainbow is seen.

The Taming of No. 3

one from the other." But the plume did sink at last. The well was killed for seventeen minutes, long enough for two men to ram the sealing device into the gap between the drill pipe and the surface casing.

No. 3 was under control — for the moment. Two or three days later the really serious trouble started. Gas began to bubble out of the ground around the derrick.

In a completed oil well, a casing of steel pipe is forced all the way down to the producing zone, which at Leduc is a mile deep. Then cement is pumped down the pipe and forced back up around the sides of the casing, welding it firmly to the surrounding earth. The pressure of oil and gas in the formation (which at Leduc is about 1,850 pounds per square inch) is held down by 5,000 feet of solid ground. It has no escape except through the pipe where it can be controlled.

No. 3 was not a completed well. Only surface casing for the top 300 feet of the hole had been set and cemented. Below that there was nothing to stop the great pressure of gas and oil in the drill hole from pushing its way through relatively loose materials to the surface.

At first it didn't look like much — just a few bubbles spluttering out of the half-frozen mud. But as time went on and the ground thawed, the whole twenty-five-acre field became a swamp of live oil dotted with active craters. Sometimes it oozed up quietly, sometimes it came up in geysers twenty to fifty feet high, but always it kept on coming. The whole field bubbled and quaked like a pot of boiling porridge, and the oil ran down open ditches to collect in great pools in the sump pits below the drilling rig.

For two months they tried to kill No. 3 by working through the original well-head. They planned to lower charges of explosive to set off a blast 2,000 or 3,000 feet below ground that would cave in the hole and seal it. But the drill pipe was clogged and they could not get it clear enough to put their bombs down. They pumped in fantastic quantities of packing material, hoping to plug it — 10,000 bags of cement on one April day, another time about 100 tons of oats, sawdust, redwood shavings, cottonseed hulls and half a dozen patented sealing materials. Nothing happened. All their contrivances just disappeared into the vast formation of the Leduc oil field.

Meanwhile, danger was growing every day. Explosive quantities of natural gas were puffing out of the open craters every few minutes. About 70,000 barrels of oil had collected in the sump pits, ready to be ignited by a gas fire and more of it lay in shallow puddles or trickled down collection ditches all over the field.

By May 14, Atlantic No. 3 was formally recognized as a public menace. The Alberta Government, through its Petroleum and Natural Gas Conservation Board, took over the well and assumed control of an area of four square miles around it. All work ceased at the well-head itself. All other wells in the Leduc area were shut down for three weeks, so that Imperial Oil's pipe line to the railway could be used exclusively for draining away the open pits of inflammable oil that lay around Atlantic No. 3. Roads leading past the wild well were blocked a mile away, and no one was admitted without a Government pass. Work began on an entirely different method of killing No. 3.

To boss the job the Conservation Board borrowed Vincent John Moroney, Imperial Oil's chief of operations, and for the next four months "Tip" Moroney spent all his waking hours, and a good many others, at the field. He carried a sleeping bag in his car, so he wouldn't have to bother going back to Edmonton on a busy night; quite often he considered himself lucky if he had time to unroll it.

Imperial gave Moroney authority to call on all facilities and personnel that he needed, and he recruited a group of their best men, notably Charles Visser, the Company's drilling superintendent and "the best drilling man in Canada," according to one colleague. They also got full and constant co-operation from the other companies in the field, raided them for equipment, advice,

The Taming of No. 3

and men, and putting their operations under numerous handicaps and restrictions which were cheerfully accepted.

Moroney's plan was to drill two relief wells, starting each of them about 700 feet away from the No. 3 hole. They were to be drilled straight down for half a mile. Then each would be bent at an angle toward No. 3 and drilled another half mile. The idea was that the relief wells should meet Atlantic No. 3 at, or near, the point where it entered the oil-bearing formation. Then material could be pumped down the relief holes to seal up No. 3.

It was about as simple as finding a needle in a haystack with a pair of tongs, in the dark.

"Directional" drilling — bending the well at an angle — is simple enough in principle. When the drillers reach the point where they want deflection to begin, they send down a tool called a whipstock, which is a piece of steel shaped like a stick of celery. The whipstock turns the bit in the desired direction, and that's all there is to it — except that the ordinary difficulties of drilling are approximately tripled. Things go wrong about three times as often; the drill gets stuck, or comes apart, and it is necessary to spend days or weeks fishing for the loose end of it.

Atlantic No. 3 was drilled in six weeks. To bring the two relief wells to precisely the same depth took just under four months.

But the real problem was not *how*, it was *where* to drill the relief wells. Nobody knew exactly where the bottom of Atlantic No. 3 was located — no directional survey had been taken. In theory, any ordinary oil well goes straight down; in practice, most of them twist off at a slight angle. The bottom of Atlantic No. 3 might be anywhere in a twenty-five to fifty-foot radius around the plumb line from the well-head.

Moroney got all the data from surrounding wells. There are a dozen derricks within sight of No. 3 — Imperial's own No. 48 is only 300 yards away — and on a good many of these wells careful directional surveys had been taken. Looking at the results in the neighbourhood, Moroney estimated that Atlantic No. 3's deflection would run a few feet northeast.

Then he had to figure the probable deflection of his two relief wells. A drilling bit rotates from left to right; in a directional well, it tends to "walk" a bit to the right as it works its way down. So they started one relief well a little north of due west of Atlantic No. 3 and the other a little west of due south.

Four months later, while gas and oil still bubbled from the field around No. 3, the west relief well struck the oil formation directly under Atlantic's well-head. The south relief well, with even more astonishing accuracy, pierced the Atlantic hole itself about 150 feet above the formation.

All through that four months, danger never ceased. They cut some of the fire hazard by pumping the 70,000 gallons of oil out of the sump pits. They cut it a little more by connecting an outlet to the top of the drill pipe in Atlantic No. 3 and taking off part of No. 3's oil in the normal way. But the place was still highly inflammable, as one roughneck — as the oilman calls his helper — had found out in April.

Smoking was forbidden anywhere within a quarter of a mile of the wild well, but this roughneck thought it would be safe enough to light a cigarette in a small shack. He struck a match, and the shack blew up. The roughneck was blown right through the door, landing spreadeagled in the mud. He picked himself up and ran for his life — witnesses swear he covered the next 100 yards in less than ten seconds.

Luckily the fire didn't spread, and they got it out in a few minutes. But this was in April, before the flow of oil became really bad; it was mostly gas that was escaping from the well at that time. If there had been oil all over the place, as there was a few weeks earlier, the whole field would have gone up in flames. You can imagine, therefore, the problem of keeping boilers hot all summer in the two relief wells.

The sites had been carefully chosen to take advantage of prevailing winds, and wind socks were set up all round the field.

The Taming of No. 3

Any time it looked as if gas or oil spray might be blown across either of the drilling rigs, the fires were cut immediately and the furnaces flooded with steam. This was another thing that slowed up drilling. Sometimes the crew would be held up for days at a stretch.

Still oftener, John Rebus and his wife would take a look at the wind socks and know they should cook no meals that day. They'd get into the car and drive in to town. They kept on doing that until the wind shifted. The camp and cookhouse, originally next door to the Rebus farm, was moved another quarter of a mile back, out of danger.

All these precautions broke down at the end of August. Until then, the "cratering" had been mostly out in the field; the derrick and drilling rig at No. 3 stood quietly in the middle of it, looking exactly like all the other 150 derricks in the Leduc field. But during the first week in September, oil and gas began to break out around the No. 3 hole, undermining the derrick itself. Rocks as big as a man's head were being thrown up right around the hole; if they struck a spark off any of the metal lying about, the whole field would take fire.

Labour Day week end, the derrick began to lean. It leaned southward at first, and a gang of a dozen men went into the blocked-off area to try to jack it up. The whole crew knew that if the derrick fell, fire was almost a certainty — all that metal churning around in the crater would be sure to spark. The jacking project was probably the most dangerous single job of the whole summer. If the spark had come while they were at work, at least ten men would have burned to death.

They hoisted the derrick back to vertical and got out as fast as they could. Within an hour, it was leaning again — northward, this time. It was obviously going to fall. Moroney sent word to the Rebus family that they'd better not sleep at home that night.

The derrick fell at one o'clock Labour Day morning, but still no fire. When dawn came, there was nothing to be seen of the contractor's drilling rig. The whole 136 feet of it had disappeared down the crater, all except a few feet of metal that had broken off the upper part of the derrick. The well was throwing up oil, rocks, and shale like a small volcano, building a mound about fifteen feet high around the central crater. From time to time it would throw up some of the twelve-by-twelve timbers on which the derrick had stood, tossing them around like matches.

That lasted all day Monday. At a quarter past six in the evening, Charlie Smith, a big Texan who had been brought up in June as an expert in directional drilling, thought he'd like to get a picture of the crater. There was a little shack just beside it; from the roof, you could look over the edge of the mound of shale into the boiling, bubbling crater itself. Smith and a companion, Hic Kern, started to walk down the boardwalk toward the hole.

They were about 100 feet away and Smith had stopped to adjust his camera, when Kern yelled, "Look!" Over the crater hung a ball of fire; "about as big as this room," Smith said afterward in the living room of the overnight cabin where he and his wife lived all summer.

"It just hung there quite still, for what seemed a long time," he said. "Actually I suppose it was about a tenth of a second. Then there was a big whoosh and up she went."

Smith and Kern ran as fast as they could, but Smith turned and pointed his camera over his shoulder for the first picture of the blaze — distance about 200 feet. The fire was already about 700 feet high, a great roaring pillar of flame with a plume of dense black smoke.

To the onlooker it seemed a disaster — $50,000 worth of oil burning each day, the most spectacular blaze ever seen in Canada. To oil men, it was a blessed relief.

One oil executive said, "When I heard that Atlantic had finally caught fire and nobody was hurt, I felt better than I had for months. Now we could breathe again."

For the real danger was over now. There was not the danger of gas explosion killing half a dozen men, for all the gas was

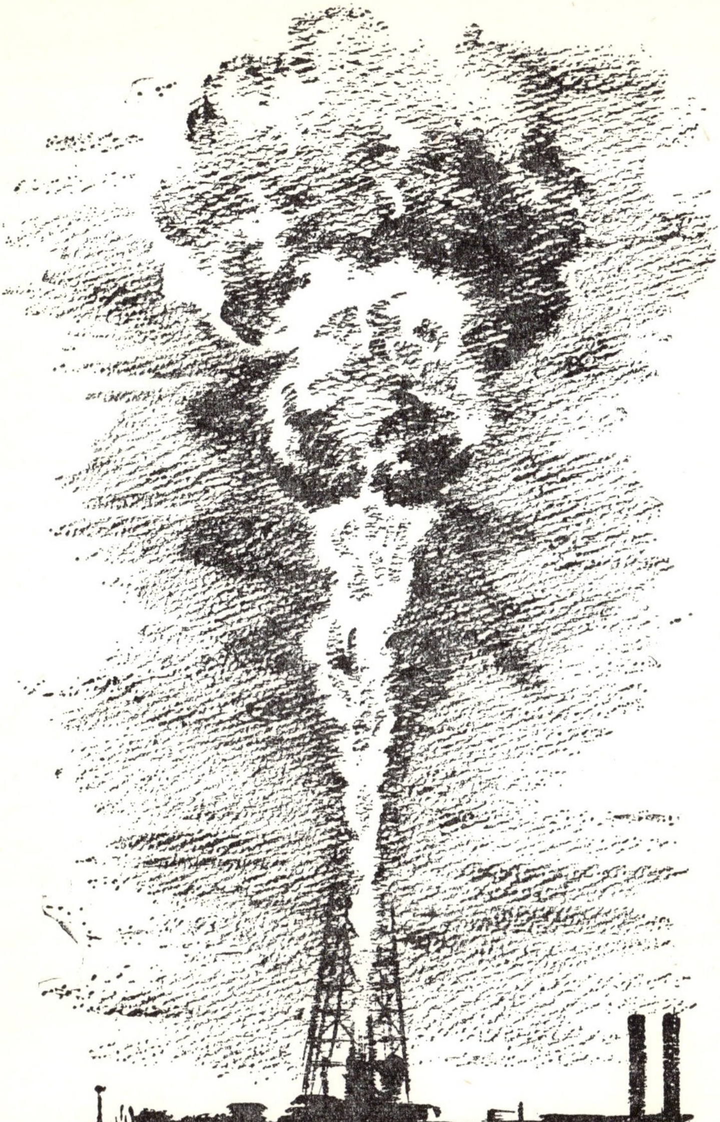

being burned as it left the ground. There was some possibility of the fire spreading. John Rebus moved all his furniture out of the farmhouse and loaded it on his truck, then spent the night on his tractor, plowing up fire guards around the house and buildings. A dozen other tractors and bulldozers circled the blazing field, rolling up dikes to keep the fire contained in an area around the central crater, about 150 feet square.

By morning the danger was past; Rebus put his furniture back in the house, without having had to move it out of his front yard. Meanwhile, workmen were about ready to strike the death blow to No. 3, a mile underground.

When the fire broke out, the west relief well was within a few feet of the oil formation. On the Tuesday, 2,000 gallons of acid were shot down, to increase the porousness of the rock and clear the path for enough water to choke off the oil and kill the fire. Wednesday, another 3,000 gallons of acid went down. That did the trick. The well started taking water at the rate of 1,500 barrels an hour, and the same afternoon steam began to show in the burning well. By 10 P.M. it was evident the flow of oil had been cut; there was no more black smoke in the fire, just pure orange flame from burning gas, and steam from the injected water. The last bits of flame died at 4.45 Thursday morning. Nothing was left of the fire except a blackened field, a few bits of twisted metal, and the dead crater, now an ugly puddle of greenish-grey mud, with a thin layer of water across the top.

Atlantic No. 3 was dead, but not yet buried. The west relief well was still pumping water into the formation; it was not in a position to inject the cement cap that would seal off Atlantic No. 3 for good and all. But just a week later, the south relief well came through.

That started the engineers on the last lap. They pumped in thousands of bags of cement and other packing material—first to seal the bottom 150 feet of the Atlantic well; then after that hardened, to force a column of cement down the south relief

The Taming of No. 3

hole and up the Atlantic hole, until it would show at the surface. It was still a tricky job, unfinished for weeks after the fire had been killed, but the indications were that in the end man would defeat nature.

One interesting question remained: Why did Atlantic No. 3, of all the 150 wells in the Leduc field, alone blow wild?

Back in mid-February, they "lost circulation" at Atlantic No. 3 — the mud they were pumping down the drill pipe to clear the bit and carry up the debris, was no longer coming back up to the surface around the pipe as it should do. Instead it was leaking away into the porous limestone at the bottom, faster than it could be pumped in from the top.

Loss of circulation is a danger signal. Once the driller penetrates the formation, he has only one thing to hold down the enormous pressure of gas and oil. That one thing is the column of mud, with the weight that can be put behind it. If the mud leaks away in the hole, there's nothing to pit against the uprush of oil and gas when the well comes in.

When circulation is lost, the usual practice is to stop drilling until circulation is restored. They tried several times to restore it at No. 3, but nothing seemed to work. Then they tried a method that has been used successfully in the Middle East — drilling without circulation. The new method was not successful at No. 3.

However, there was not much reason, after all, wrangling about whose fault it was, or who should pay whom. Wild No. 3 cost a million dollars or more, from beginning to end, but the million didn't come directly out of anybody's pocket. No. 3 was a natural disaster that paid for itself as it went along. Or perhaps it was posterity that footed the bill — in the form of depleted natural resources.

Of the one and a quarter million barrels of oil produced there during the spring and summer, 250,000 were pumped back into the ground through Atlantic's No. 2 well nearby. The other million barrels were sold by the Conservation Board for nearly three million dollars.

Even the fire, which burned about $150,000 worth of oil in three days, wasn't a total loss. A Toronto stockbroker, at lunch one day with an Edmonton friend, said, "I don't care what it cost, it was worth it three times over. Here in Alberta you've got one of the great oil fields of North America, a tremendous pool of natural wealth just discovered. Up to Labour Day, even Canadians didn't know it was here — now everybody's heard of it from here to Mexico. That fire certainly put Alberta oil on the map."

ON THE GRASSHOPPER AND CRICKET

JOHN KEATS

The Poetry of earth is never dead:
   When all the birds are faint with the hot sun,
   And hide in cooling trees, a voice will run
From hedge to hedge about the new-mown mead;
That is the Grasshopper's — he takes the lead
     In summer luxury, — he has never done
     With his delights; for when tired out with fun
He rests at ease beneath some pleasant weed.
The poetry of earth is ceasing never;
     On a lone winter evening, when the frost
        Has wrought a silence, from the stove there shrills
The Cricket's song, in warmth increasing ever,
     And seems to one in drowsiness half lost,
        The Grasshopper's among some grassy hills.

LONG, LONG AGO

PYGMALION AND GALATEA

RANNIE B. BAKER

Once upon a time in Cyprus there lived a young sculptor whose name was Pygmalion. In early life he found so much to blame in women that he disliked them all, and determined never to marry, but to spend his life among ivory and marble carvings, devoting himself to his art.

In the course of time, ingeniously, and with wondrous skill, he carved from snow-white ivory, a statue of a maiden and gave it the beauty of a real maiden whom one might easily suppose to be alive and desirous to move. Day by day the sculptor wrought, patiently giving to his work all the beauty of his dreams, presenting in it his highest ideal. So well was his art concealed by his skill, that the result seemed the workmanship of nature, far too lovely to remain inanimate. Strangely enough, when the model was completed, the artist felt bound to it, was, indeed, powerless to leave it. This attachment grew like enchantment upon him until he loved the silent beautiful maiden more than anything else in the world. He named her Galatea and bestowed upon her gorgeous raiment and all other gifts suitable for living maidens. Her beads were the amber tears of the Heliades; her necklace was of costly pearls; her garlands were flowers of a thousand tints. From her delicate ears he hung smooth pendants, and he adorned her head with a band of jewels. His house, too, was made beautiful and fit for such a presence; and Galatea, resting upon a rich covering of royal purple, was acclaimed the queen of his home.

Just at this time a festival of Venus, much celebrated throughout all Cyprus, was at hand; and Pygmalion, with all others who loved beauty, joined the worshippers. The odour of burnt offering filled the air; heifers with snow-white necks and spreading horns tipped with gold were slain for sacrifice:

Pygmalion and Galatea

frankincense smoked within the temple. Pygmalion stood before the altar and fearfully made known his request to Venus: "Goddess, who can grant all things, give me, I pray, a wife fair and pure as my Galatea." His ideal was noble as his love was sincere, and Venus blessed him. Thrice the flame from the incense shot a fiery point in air, signifying to the worshipper that the golden goddess had heard his prayer.

When Pygmalion reached home he found his loved statue as he had left her, standing in silence and gazing down upon him. But as he drew nearer, a gentle warmth seemed to radiate from the chill air about her. Was it the sunset that shed a soft flush of light upon her whiteness, making the frozen marble glow? In amazement the sculptor beheld her; then speechless, and struck with a strange thrill of hope, he drew closer. A splendour of gold was upon her hair, faint colour flushed her cheeks, and a new light shone in her eyes. As Pygmalion touched the marble hand, which yielded to his fingers, the chiselled lips softened to a smile, and a clear voice spoke his name. The statue had awakened; and Galatea, miracle of love and beauty, stepped down from her pedestal into the arms of her creator, a living, breathing woman! The artist had worshipped his ideal and it had become real; he had dreamed of beauty, and his dream had come true.

SAUL AND DAVID

THE BIBLE

Arranged by MONA SWANN

SCENE I

IN THE TENT OF SAUL

CHORUS, or TWO NARRATORS.
SAUL, king of Israel.
DAVID.
TWO SERVANTS.

FIRST SEMI-CHORUS. The Lord is my light and my salvation: whom shall I fear?

SECOND SEMI-CHORUS. The Lord is the strength of my life: of whom shall I be afraid?

FIRST SEMI-CHORUS. One thing have I desired of the Lord, that will I seek after; that I may dwell in the house of the Lord all the days of my life, to behold the beauty of the Lord.

SECOND SEMI-CHORUS. For in the time of trouble he shall hide me in his pavilion: in the secret of his tabernacle shall he hide me; he hath set me upon a rock.

FIRST AND SECOND SEMI-CHORUS. Wait on the Lord: be of good courage, and he shall strengthen thine heart: wait, I say, on the Lord.

(The leaders open the curtains again, and the groups move to the sides as before. SAUL *is seated under a canopy held by four attendants; his* TWO SERVANTS *crouch at his feet.)*

FIRST GROUP. But the Spirit of the Lord departed from Saul, and an evil spirit troubled him; and he sat in his house with a javelin in his hand.

Saul and David

FIRST SERVANT. Behold now, an evil spirit troubleth thee. Let our lord now command thy servants to seek out a man who is a cunning player on an harp; and it shall come to pass, when the evil spirit is upon thee, that he shall play with his hand, and thou shalt be well.

SAUL. Provide me now a man that can play well, and bring him to me.

SECOND SERVANT. Behold, I have seen a son of Jesse the Bethlehemite, one David, a shepherd lad, that is cunning in playing, and a mighty valiant man, and a man of war, and prudent in matters, and a comely person, and the Lord is with him.

SAUL. Go unto Jesse and say, Send me David thy son, who keepeth the sheep.

(A SERVANT *goes.* SAUL *sits brooding.)*

SECOND GROUP. And Jesse took an ass laden with bread, and a bottle of wine, and a kid, and sent them by David his son unto Saul. And David came to Saul.

*(*DAVID *has entered. He prostrates before* SAUL.*)*

SAUL. Stand thou before me. *(He gazes at* DAVID.*)* Lo, thou has found favour in my sight. Take thou thy harp, and play with thine hand.

*(*DAVID *takes his harp and seems to play.)*

DAVID. The Lord is my shepherd: I shall not want.
He maketh me to lie down in green pastures; he leadeth me beside the still waters.
He restoreth my soul: he leadeth me in the paths of righteousness for his name's sake.

*(*SAUL *has risen; he lifts his javelin, and throws it at* DAVID; *it misses him.* DAVID *continues unmoved.)*

Yea, though I walk through the valley of the shadow of death, I will fear no evil: for thou art with me; thy rod and thy staff they comfort me.

Thou preparest a table before me in the presence of mine

enemies; thou anointest my head with oil; my cup runneth over.

Surely goodness and mercy shall follow me all the days of my life: and I will dwell in the house of the Lord for ever.

(SAUL *has relaxed, and sunk back upon his stool; he lifts his head, and looks at* DAVID *in wonder.*)

SAUL. Whose son art thou, thou young man?

DAVID. I am David, the son of thy servant Jesse the Beth-lehemite.

SAUL. Blessed be thou of the Lord, O David: for lo, I am refreshed and well, and the evil spirit is departed from me. Wherefore the Lord reward thee good for that thou hast done unto me this day.

FIRST AND SECOND GROUPS. And Saul loved David greatly; and he became his armour-bearer. But he went and returned from Saul to feed his father's sheep in Bethlehem.

(SAUL *has laid his hand on* DAVID'S *head in blessing. The group leaders close the curtains; the* CHORUS *re-forms the line before them.*)

SCENE II

THE CHAMPION OF ISRAEL.

SAUL, king of Israel
JONATHAN, his son.
ABNER, captain of the host.
ELIAB,
ABINADAB, }elder sons of Jesse.
SHAMMAH,
DAVID.
THE VOICE OF GOLIATH.
WARRIORS, etc.

FIRST SEMI-CHORUS. The earth is the Lord's and the fulness thereof; the world and they that dwell therein.

SECOND SEMI-CHORUS. For he hath founded it upon the seas, and established it upon the floods.

FIRST SEMI-CHORUS. Who shall ascend into the hill of the Lord? or who shall dwell in his holy place?

SECOND SEMI-CHORUS. He that hath clean hands and a pure heart; who hath not lifted up his soul unto vanity, nor sworn deceitfully.

He shall receive the blessing from the Lord, and righteousness from the God of our salvation.

FIRST AND SECOND SEMI-CHORUS. This is the generation of them that seek him, that seek thy face, O Jacob.

FIRST SEMI-CHORUS. Lift up your heads, O ye gates; and be ye lift up, ye everlasting doors; and the King of glory shall come in.

SECOND SEMI-CHORUS. Who is this King of glory?

FIRST SEMI-CHORUS. The Lord strong and mighty, the Lord mighty in battle.

SECOND SEMI-CHORUS. Lift up your heads, O ye gates; even lift them up ye everlasting doors; and the King of glory shall come in.

FIRST SEMI-CHORUS. Who is this King of glory?

FIRST AND SECOND SEMI-CHORUS. The Lord of hosts, he is the King of glory.

(The leaders stand ready to draw back the curtains; the groups move L. and R. before them.)

FIRST GROUP. Now the Philistines gathered together their armies, and Saul and the men of Israel set the battle in array against them. And the Philistines stood on a mountain on the one side, and Israel stood on a mountain on the other side, and there was a valley between them. *(The curtains are drawn back. The stage is filled with warriors. The sons of Jesse are among them.* SAUL *is seated on a stool (R. front);* ABNER *and* JONATHAN *are with him.)* And the three eldest sons of Jesse followed Saul to the battle.

SECOND GROUP. And David, his youngest son, kept his father's sheep; and he rose up early in the morning, and left the sheep with a keeper, and took loaves and cheeses as Jesse had commanded him; and he came to the trench as the host was going forth to fight.

FIRST AND SECOND GROUP. For Israel and the Philistines had set the battle in array, army against army.

SECOND GROUP. And David ran into the army, and came, and saluted his brethren.

(*He has run in (L. front), found his brethren, and greeted them.*)

SHAMMAH. Have ye seen this man that is come up? Lo, there went a champion out of the camp of the Philistines, named Goliath, of Gath, whose height is six cubits and a span!

ABINADAB. And he has a helmet of brass upon his head, and he is armed with a coat of mail . . .

ANOTHER WARRIOR. And the weight of the coat is five thousand shekels of brass . . .

ABINADAB. And he has greaves of brass upon his legs, and a target of brass between his shoulders . . .

SHAMMAH. And the staff of his spear is like a weaver's beam; and his spear's head weigheth six hundred shekels of iron; and one bearing a spear goeth before him . . .

ABINADAB. Surely to defy Israel is he come up . . .

(*The voice of* GOLIATH *is suddenly heard off-scene, L. back.*)

VOICE OF GOLIATH. Why are ye come out to set your battle in array? Am not I a Philistine, and ye the servants of Saul? Choose you a man for you, and let him come down to me. If he be able to fight with me, and to kill me, then will we be your servants: but if I prevail against him, and kill him, then shall ye be our servants, and serve us. I defy the armies of Israel this day; give me a man, that we may fight together.

(*The crowd, angry or fearful, has gathered below the platform; some now mount it to see the giant; David alone stands quietly apart, centre-front, and does not look toward the voice.*)

Saul and David

DAVID. *(to a* WARRIOR*).* What shall be done to the man that killeth this Philistine, and taketh away the reproach from Israel? For who is this Philistine, that he should defy the armies of the living God?

FIRST WARRIOR. Lo, it shall be, that the man who killeth him, the king will enrich him with great riches, and will give him his daughter, and make his father's house free in Israel.

(His brother ELIAB *has suddenly seen* DAVID, *and pushes through the crowd to him.)*

ELIAB. Why camest thou down hither? And with whom hast thou left those few sheep in the wilderness? I know thy pride, and the naughtiness of thine heart; for thou art come down that thou mightest see the battle.

DAVID. What have I done? Is there not a cause? for did I not bring loaves and cheeses as Jesse my father commanded me?

SECOND GROUP. And when the words were heard which David spake, they rehearsed them before Saul.

*(*JONATHAN *has heard* DAVID's *words; he goes to tell* SAUL.*)*

JONATHAN. Behold, the shepherd lad, David, whom thou hast made thine armour-bearer, come to the trench with loaves and cheeses, and to look how his brethren fared. And he spoke, saying, What shall be done unto the man that slayeth this Philistine, and taketh away the reproach from Israel? Who is this uncircumcised Philistine, that he should defy the armies of the living God?

SAUL. Let the stripling stand before me.

*(*ABNER *goes to* DAVID.*)*

ABNER. Come up after me. My lord the king would speak with thee.

*(*DAVID *comes to* SAUL, *and kneels before him.)*

DAVID. O king, let no man's heart fail because of him; thy servant will go and fight with this Philistine.

SAUL. Thou art not able to go against this Philistine to fight with him: for thou art but a youth, and he a man of war from his youth.

DAVID. Thy servant kept his father's sheep, and there came a lion, and a bear, and took a lamb out of the flock: and I went after him, and smote him, and delivered it out of his mouth: and when he arose against me, I caught him by the beard, and smote him, and slew him. And behold, therefore, the Lord that delivered me out of the paw of the lion, and out of the paw of the bear, he will deliver me out of the hands of this Philistine.

SAUL. Go, and the Lord be with thee.

JONATHAN (*goes forward and takes his hands*). Be strong, and of a good courage; be not afraid, neither be thou dismayed: for the Lord thy God is with thee whithersoever thou goest.

(DAVID *makes obeisance, and goes towards the steps to the platform; there he stoops to gather stones, while the choric groups speak.*)

SECOND GROUP. And David chose him five smooth stones out of the brook, and put them in a shepherd's bag which he had, even in a scrip; and his sling was in his hand: and he drew near to the Philistine.

FIRST GROUP. And the Philistine came on and drew near unto David; and the man that bare the shield went before him. And when the Philistine looked about, and saw David, he disdained him; for he was but a youth, and of a fair countenance.

(DAVID *has mounted the platform, and stands facing* L. SAUL *and his soldiers have drawn to the* R.)

VOICE OF GOLIATH. Am I a dog, that thou comest to me thus? Come to me, and I will give thy flesh unto the fowls of the air, and the beasts of the field.

DAVID. Thou comest to me with a sword, and with a spear, and with a shield: but I come to thee in the name of the Lord of hosts; that all the earth may know that there is a God in Israel. And all this assembly shall know that the Lord saveth not with sword and spear.

SECOND GROUP. And David put his hand in his bag and took thence a stone and slung it. . . .

(*The army of Israel has been waiting below the platform, watching in tense silence. Now they break into shouts or praise and thanksgiving, as David runs forward, following the stone that he slung.*)

JONATHAN. Lo, he hath smitten the Philistine in the forehead!

ABNER. Goliath hath fallen upon his face to the earth! The battle is the Lord's, and he hath given him into our hands!

SAUL. O men of Israel, arise, and pursue the Philistines, until ye come to the valley, and to the gates of Ekron.

(*He leads the warriors out (L. platform). As they go, their voices are heard.*)

SAUL. O give thanks unto the Lord, for he is good. . . .

ALL. For his mercy endureth for ever!

ABNER. O give thanks unto the God of gods. . . .

ALL. For his mercy endureth for ever!

JONATHAN. O give thanks unto the Lord of lords. . . .

ALL. For his mercy endureth for ever!

(*The voices fade into the distance; the stage is emptied.*)

FIRST AND SECOND GROUPS. So David prevailed over the Philistine with a sling and with a stone but there was no sword in the hand of David.

(*The leaders close the curtain as before.*)

SCENE III

The Covenant of Friendship.

chorus, or two narrators.
saul, king of Israel.
jonathan, his son.
david.
abner, captain of the host.
a little lad.
women dancers.

first semi-chorus. If it had not been the Lord who was on our side, now may Israel say;
If it had not been the Lord who was on our side, when men rose up against us:
Then the waters had overwhelmed us, the stream had gone over our soul:
Then the proud waters had gone over our soul.
second semi-chorus. Blessed be the Lord, who hath not given us as a prey to their teeth.
Our soul is escaped as a bird out of the snare of the fowler: the snare is broken, and we are escaped.
first and second semi-chorus. Our help is in the name of the Lord, who made heaven and earth.

(The leaders draw back the curtains; the chorus *forms two groups as before.)*

(The traverse curtain is partly drawn across the back platform, above the steps, to suggest the entrance to saul's *dwelling. There is the sound of cymbal and tambourine, and as the group speaks* women *enter, dancing. The light suggests sunset time.)*

first group. It came to pass, when David was returned from the slaughter of the Philistine, that the women came out of all

Saul and David

the cities of Israel, singing and dancing, to meet King Saul, with tabrets, with joy, and with instruments of music.

(The dancing women take their places to speak this psalm; it is accompanied with the tambourine, and at each "praise" there is clash of cymbals and a change of posture.)

WOMEN. Praise ye the Lord!
SOME WOMEN. Praise God in his sanctuary. . . .
OTHERS. Praise him in the firmament of his power!
SOME. Praise him for his mighty acts! . . .
OTHERS. Praise him according to his excellent greatness!
SOME. Praise him with the sound of trumpet. . . .
OTHERS. Praise him with the psaltery and harp!
SOME. Praise him with the timbrel and dance. . . .
OTHERS. Praise him with stringed instruments and organs!
SOME. Praise him with the loud cymbals. . . .
OTHERS. Praise him with the high-sounding cymbals!
ALL. Let everything that hath breath praise the Lord! Praise ye the Lord!

(SAUL, JONATHAN, and attendants have entered R. front. The WOMEN see them, and bow low before them.)

WOMEN. Saul hath slain his thousands, and David has slain his ten thousands. . . .
SAUL. *(in great anger)*. Arise; be gone.

(The women disperse in terror, going off L. and R.)

SAUL *(to JONATHAN)*. Behold, they have ascribed unto David ten thousands, and to me they have ascribed but thousands: and what can he have more but the kingdom? Lo, when Abner hath brought him before me, I will smite him even to the wall with my javelin.

(He lifts the javelin; Jonathan seizes his hand.)

JONATHAN. Let not the king sin against his servant, against David; because he hath not sinned against thee, and because his works have been to thee-ward very good; for he did put his life in his hand, and slew the Philistine, and the Lord wrought a great salvation for all Israel: thou sawest it, and didst rejoice: wherefore then wilt thou sin against innocent blood, to slay David without a cause?

SAUL. As the Lord liveth, he shall not be slain.

(SAUL *passes through the traverse curtains to his dwelling;* JONATHAN *awaits* DAVID, *while the stage gradually darkens into nightfall.*)

JONATHAN. Lo, my soul is knit with the soul of David, and I love him as my own soul, and my life is bound up in his life. Lord, remember David: make the way straight before his face!

(DAVID *enters with* ABNER)

JONATHAN (*to* ABNER). Go thou in, and stand beside my father; for the evil spirit is come upon him. (ABNER *goes into the dwelling-place.*)

JONATHAN (*to* DAVID). O David, Saul my father seeketh to kill thee: now therefore, I pray thee, take heed to thyself, and abide in a secret place, and hide thyself.

DAVID. What have I done? what is mine iniquity? and what is my sin before thy father, that he seeketh my life?

JONATHAN. God forbid: thou shalt not die: behold, my father will do nothing either great or small, but that he will show it me: and whatsoever thy soul desireth, I will do it for thee.

DAVID. Behold, it is the new moon, and I should not fail to sit with the king at meat: but let me go, that I may hide myself. If thy father at all miss me, then say, David earnestly asked leave of me that he might run to Beth-lehem his city. If he say thus, It is well; then thy servant shall have peace: but if he be wroth, then be sure that evil is determined by him.

JONATHAN. Lo, I will make a covenant with thee, O David: for I love thee as I love my own soul. (*He raises his hand.*) O Lord God of Israel, when I have sounded my father, behold if there be good towards David, and I then send not to thee, and show thee; the Lord do so and much more to Jonathan:

but if it pleases my father to do thee evil, then I will show it thee, and send thee away, that thou mayest go in peace: and the Lord be with thee, as he hath been with my father. And thou shalt not only while yet I live show me the kindness of the Lord, that I die not: but also thou shalt not cut off thy kindness from my house for ever: no, not when the Lord hath cut off the enemies of David every one from the face of the earth.

DAVID. O Jonathan, I do swear it. Let the Lord even require it at the hand of mine enemies.

JONATHAN. Behold now, hide thyself; and in the morning come to this place, and remain by the stone that showeth the way. And I will shoot three arrows on the side thereof, as though I shot at a mark. And, behold, I will send a boy, saying, Go, find the arrows. If I expressly say unto the lad, Behold, the arrows are on this side of thee, take them; then come thou: for there is peace to thee, and no hurt, as the Lord liveth. But if I say, Behold, the arrows are beyond thee, go thy way: for the Lord hath sent thee away. And as touching the matter which thou and I have spoken of, behold, the Lord is between thee and me for ever.

DAVID. The Lord bless thee, O Jonathan; the Lord shall open to thee his good treasure, and shall bless all the work of thine hand.

(*They embrace.* DAVID *goes out L.;* JONATHAN *watches him go, then enters the dwelling-place. Two attendants come out, and open wide the traverse curtains.* SAUL *is seen, seated before a table, with* ABNER *beside him. The dwelling-place is lit as with torches. The main stage is dark.*)

SAUL (*to* JONATHAN). Wherefore cometh not David, the son of Jesse, to meat?

JONATHAN. David earnestly asked leave of me to go to Bethlehem: and he said, Let me go, I pray thee: for our family hath a sacrifice in the city; and my brother, he hath commanded me to be there. Therefore he cometh not to the king's table.

SAUL. *(rising from his stool in his wrath.)* Thou son of the perverse and rebellious woman, do I not know that thou has chosen the son of Jesse to thine own confusion? For as long as the son of Jesse liveth upon the ground, thou shalt not be established, nor thy kingdom. Wherefore now send and fetch him unto me, for he shall surely die.

JONATHAN. Wherefore shall he be slain? What hath he done?

FIRST GROUP. And Saul took a javelin to smite Jonathan: whereby Jonathan knew that it was determined of his father to slay David.

(While the GROUP *speaks,* SAUL *has taken his javelin as if to cast it at* JONATHAN. ABNER *stays his hand, and* JONATHAN *departs from* SAUL *as he came. He descends the steps and goes out L. The attendants close the traverse curtains once more.)*

(The light increases on the main stage, as the coming of dawn.)

So Jonathan arose in fierce anger: for he was grieved for David, because his father had done him shame.

SECOND GROUP. And it came to pass in the morning that Jonathan went out into the field, and a little lad with him.

*(*JONATHAN *re-enters L. with his bow, followed by the little* LAD.*)*

JONATHAN. Run, find out now the arrows which I shot. Is not the arrow beyond thee? Make speed, haste, stay not.

FIRST GROUP. And Jonathan's lad gathered up the arrows, and came to his master. But the lad knew not anything: only Jonathan and David knew the matter.

JONATHAN. *(giving his bow to the* LAD*).* Go, carry them to the city.

(The LAD *goes.)*

SECOND GROUP. And as soon as the lad was gone, David arose out of a place toward the south, and he and Jonathan kissed one another, and wept one with another.

(DAVID *comes from his hiding-place; he and* JONATHAN *embrace.*)

JONATHAN. Go in peace, forasmuch as we have sworn both of us in the name of the Lord, saying, The Lord be between me and thee, and between my seed and thy seed for ever.

(*He goes R. front.* JONATHAN *watches his going. The leaders close the curtains, as before.*)

SCENE IV

THE CAVE OF EN-GEDI

CHORUS, or TWO NARRATORS.
DAVID.
AHIMELECH THE HITTITE, } captains under David.
ABISHAI,
SAUL, king of Israel.
ABNER, captain of the host.
CAPTAINS under David.
SERVANTS and WARRIORS of Saul.

FIRST SEMI-CHORUS. I will lift up mine eyes unto the hills; from whence cometh my help?
SECOND SEMI-CHORUS. My help cometh from the Lord, which made heaven and earth.
FIRST SEMI-CHORUS. He will not suffer thy foot to be moved: he that keepeth thee will not slumber.

FIRST AND SECOND SEMI-CHORUSES. Behold, he that keepeth Israel shall neither slumber nor sleep.
SECOND SEMI-CHORUS. The Lord is thy keeper. . . .
FIRST SEMI-CHORUS. The Lord is thy shade upon thy right hand.
SECOND SEMI-CHORUS. The sun shall not smite thee by day. . . .
FIRST SEMI-CHORUS. Nor the moon by night.
SECOND SEMI-CHORUS. The Lord shall preserve thee from all evil. . . .
FIRST SEMI-CHORUS. He shall preserve thy soul.
FIRST AND SECOND SEMI-CHORUS. The Lord shall preserve thy going out and thy coming in from this time forth, and even for evermore.

(The line forms into two groups as before; the leaders stand ready to open the curtain.)

FIRST GROUP. And David knew that Saul secretly practised mischief against him: therefore he departed thence, and escaped, and dwelt in strongholds in En-gedi.
SECOND GROUP. And every one that was in distress and every one that was in debt, and every one that was discontented, gathered themselves unto him; and he became a captain over them.

(The leaders draw back the curtain. The scene is dim. The traverse curtains are almost open, and there is a sentry posted on the platform. DAVID stands on the main stage with his captains about him. He raises his arms in prayer.)

DAVID. Be merciful unto me, O God, be merciful unto me: for my soul trusteth in thee: yea, in the shadow of thy wings will I make my refuge, until these calamities be overpast.
AHIMELECH THE HITTITE. I will cry unto God most high; unto God that performeth all things for me.
ABISHAI. He shall send from heaven, and save me from the reproach of him that would swallow me up.
DAVID. My heart is fixed, O God, my heart is fixed. Awake up, my glory; awake psaltery and harp: I myself will awake early.

Saul and David

SOME OF THE CAPTAINS WITH DAVID. For thy mercy is great unto the heavens, and thy truth unto the clouds.

ALL. Be thou exalted, O God, above the heavens: let thy glory be above all the earth. . . .

(The SENTRY *cries out.)*

SENTRY. O David, Saul is come after us with three thousand men to seek us, and lo, he is upon the rocks of the wild goats, and he cometh to the sheep-cotes by the way.

DAVID *(to his captains).* Remain ye in the sides of the cave.

*(*DAVID *and his* CAPTAINS *hide in the shadows.)*

FIRST GROUP. And Saul went into the cave, and his people round about him.

*(*SAUL, ABNER, *and his men enter by the platform; the men set a bolster for* SAUL, *and a cruse of water.)*

A FOLLOWER OF SAUL. Doth not David hide himself in these strongholds? Now, therefore, O king, our part shall be to deliver him into thy hand.

SAUL. Blessed be ye of the Lord; for ye have compassion on me. Go, I pray you, prepare yet, and know and see his place where his haunt is, and who hath seen him there: and come ye again to me, and I will go with you. And it shall come to pass, if he be in the land, that I will search him out through all the thousands of Judah.

(They go. SAUL *lies on the ground, with a few of his followers around him. His spear is stuck upright in the earth at his head.)*

FIRST GROUP. And they rose, and went to seek David; and behold Saul, lay sleeping within the cave, and his spear stuck in the ground at his bolster. And Abner, the captain of the host, lay beside him.

(When they are quietly asleep, DAVID *and his men emerge from the sides of the cave.)*

AHIMELECH. O David, behold the day of which the Lord said unto thee, Lo, I will deliver thine enemy into thine hand, that thou mayest do to him as it shall seem good unto thee.

ABISHAI. Now therefore let me smite him, I pray thee, with the spear even to the earth at once, and I will not smite him the second time.

DAVID. Destroy him not: the Lord forbid that I should stretch forth my hand against my master, the Lord's anointed. But I pray thee, take thou now the spear that is at his bolster, and the cruse of water, and let us go.

(AHIMELECH *takes the spear and* ABISHAI *the cruse, and they, with* DAVID, *disappear in the shadows once more.*)

SECOND GROUP. So David took the spear and the cruse of water from Saul's bolster; and no man saw it, neither awaked: because a deep sleep from the Lord was fallen upon them.

(The light increases at the entrance of the cave (platform).)

FIRST GROUP. And when morning was come, Saul rose up out of the cave, and went on his way. David also arose afterward, and went, and cried after Saul.

(SAUL *and his men have risen and gone forth.* DAVID *follows them, and stands on the platform, looking after them,* R.)

DAVID *(in a loud voice)*. My lord the king!

SECOND GROUP. And when Saul looked behind him, David stooped with his face to the earth, and bowed himself.

(ABNER *runs back;* SAUL *slowly follows.*)

ABNER. Who art thou that cries to the king?

DAVID *(with bowed head, so that his face is hid from* ABNER*)*. Art thou not a valiant man? and who is like to thee in Israel? wherefore then hast thou not kept thy lord the king? For there came one of the people in to destroy the king thy lord. This thing is not good that thou has done. As the Lord liveth, ye are worthy to die, because ye have not kept your master, the

Lord's anointed. And now see where the king's spear is, and the cruse of water that was at his bolster.

(AHIMELECH *and* ABISHAI *appear behind* DAVID *on either side; one holds aloft the spear, and the other the cruse.)*

SAUL. *(amazed).* Is this thy voice, my son David?

DAVID. It is my voice, my lord, O king. (SAUL *bows his face in his hands.)* Wherefore doth my lord thus pursue after his servant? for what have I done? and wherefore hearest thou men's words, saying, Behold, David seeketh thy heart. Behold, this day thine eyes have seen how that the Lord delivered thee this day into mine hand in the cave: and some bade me kill thee: but I said, I will not put forth mine hand against my lord. Yet thou huntest my soul to take it. The Lord therefore be judge, and see, and plead my cause, and deliver me out of thine hand.

SAUL. I have sinned . . . I have sinned . . . Thou art more righteous than I: for thou hast rewarded me good, whereas I have rewarded thee evil. Return, my son David; for I will no more do thee harm, because my soul was precious in thine eyes this day: lo, I have played the fool, and have erred exceedingly.

DAVID *(kneeling before* SAUL*).* Behold the king's spear! *(He hands it to* ABNER.*)* O my lord the king, he that ruleth over men must be just. And he shall be as the light of the morning, when the sun riseth, even a morning without clouds. And, behold, as thy life was much set by this day in mine eyes, so let my life be much set by in the eyes of the Lord, and let him deliver me out of all tribulation.

SAUL. *(raising* DAVID *from the ground).* Blessed be thou, my son David; thou shalt do great things, and also shalt still prevail.

FIRST AND SECOND GROUPS. So David went on his way, and Saul returned to his place.

(The leaders close the curtains as before, and the choric groups re-form.)

Arranged from the Authorized Version of the Bible.

A DISSERTATION ON ROAST PIG

CHARLES LAMB

Mankind, says a Chinese manuscript which friend M. was obliging enough to read and explain to me, for the first seventy thousand ages ate their meat raw, clawing or biting it from the living animal, just as they do in Abyssinia to this day. This period is not obscurely hinted at by their great Confucius in the second chapter of his *Mundane Mutations,* where he designates a kind of golden age by the term of *Chofang,* literally the Cook's holiday. The manuscript goes on to say that the art of roasting, or rather broiling (which I take to be the elder brother), was accidentally discovered in the manner following. The swineherd, Ho-ti, having gone out into the woods one morning, as his manner was, to collect mast for his hogs, left his cottage in the care of his eldest son Bo-bo, a great lubberly boy, who, being fond of playing with fire, as younkers of his age commonly are, let some sparks escape into a bundle of straw which, kindling quickly, spread the conflagration over every part of their poor mansion till it was reduced to ashes. Together with the cottage (a sorry antediluvian makeshift of a building, you may think it), what was of much more importance, a fine litter of new-farrowed pigs, no less than nine in number, perished. China pigs have been esteemed a luxury all over the East from the remotest periods that we read of. Bo-bo was in the utmost consternation, as you may think, not so much for the sake of the tenement, which his father and he could easily build up again with a few dry branches and the labour of an hour or two, at any time, as for the loss of the pigs. While he was thinking what he should say to his father and wringing his hands over the smoking remnants of one of those untimely sufferers, an odour assailed his nostrils, unlike any scent which he had before experienced. What could it proceed from? — not from the burnt cottage — he had smelt that

A Dissertation on Roast Pig

smell before — indeed this was by no means the first accident of the kind which had occurred through the negligence of this unlucky firebrand. Much less did it resemble that of any known herb, weed, or flower. A premonitory moistening at the same time overflowed his nether lip. He knew not what to think. He next stooped down to feel the pig, if there were any signs of life in it. He burnt his fingers, and to cool them he applied them in his booby fashion to his mouth. Some of the crumbs of the scorched skin had come away with his fingers, and for the first time in his life (in the world's life, indeed, for before him no man had known it) he tasted — *crackling!* Again he felt and fumbled at the pig. It did not burn him so much now, still he licked his fingers from a sort of habit. The truth at length broke into his slow understanding, that it was the pig that smelt so, and the pig that tasted so delicious; and, surrendering himself up to the new-born pleasure, he fell to tearing up whole handfuls of the scorched skin with the flesh next it, and was cramming it down his throat in his beastly fashion, when his sire entered amid the smoking rafters, armed with retributory cudgel, and finding how affairs stood began to rain blows upon the young rogue's shoulders, as thick as hailstones, which Bo-bo heeded not any more than if they had been flies. The tickling pleasure, which he experienced in his lower regions, had rendered him quite callous to any inconveniences he might feel in those remote quarters. His father might lay on, but he could not beat him from his pig till he had fairly made an end of it, when, becoming a little more sensible of his situation, something like the following dialogue ensued:

"You graceless whelp, what have you got there devouring? Is it not enough that you have burnt me down three houses with your dog's tricks, and be hanged to you, but you must be eating fire, and I know not what — what have you got there, I say?"

"O Father, the pig, the pig, do come and taste how nice the burnt pig eats."

The ears of Ho-ti tingled with horror. He cursed his son, and he cursed himself that he should beget a son that should eat burnt pig.

Bo-bo whose scent was wonderfully sharpened since morning, soon raked out another pig, and fairly rending it asunder, thrust the lesser half by main force into the fists of Ho-ti, still shouting, "Eat, eat, eat the burnt pig, Father, only taste —" with such-like barbarous ejaculations, cramming all the while as if he would choke.

Ho-ti trembled in every joint while grasping the abominable thing, wavering whether he should not put his son to death for an unnatural young monster, when the crackling scorched his fingers, as it had done his son's, and applying the same remedy to them, he in his turn tasted some of its flavour, which, make what sour mouths he would for a pretense, proved not altogether displeasing to him. In conclusion (for the manuscript here is a little tedious) both father and son fairly sat down to the mess, and never left off till they had despatched all that remained of the litter.

Bo-bo was strictly enjoined not to let the secret escape, for the neighbours would certainly have stoned them for a couple of abominable wretches, who could think of improving upon the good meat which God had sent them. Nevertheless, strange stories got about. It was observed that Ho-ti's cottage was burned down now more frequently than ever. Nothing but fires from this time forward. Some would break out in broad day, others in the night time. As often as the sow farrowed, so sure was the house of Ho-ti to be in a blaze, and Ho-ti himself, which was the more remarkable, instead of chastising his son, seemed to grow more indulgent to him than ever. At length they were watched, the terrible mystery discovered, and father and son summoned to take their trial at Pekin, then an inconsiderable assize town. Evidence was given, the obnoxious food itself produced in court, and verdict about to be pronounced, when the foreman of the jury begged that some of the burnt pig, of which the culprits stood accused, might be handed into the box. He handled it, and they all handled it, burning their fingers, as Bo-bo and his father had done before them, and nature prompting to each of them the same remedy, against the face of all the facts, and the clearest charge which judge had ever given — to the surprise of the whole court, townsfolk, strangers, reporters, and all present — without leaving the box, or any manner of consultation whatever, they brought in a simultaneous verdict of Not Guilty.

The judge, who was a shrewd fellow, winked at the manifest iniquity of the decision; and, when the court was dismissed, went privily, and bought up all the pigs that could be had for love or money. In a few days his Lordship's town house was observed to be on fire. The thing took wing, and now there was nothing to be seen but fires in every direction. Fuel and pigs grew enormously dear all over the district. The insurance offices one and all shut up shop. People built slighter and slighter every day, until it was feared that the very science of architecture would in no long time be lost to the world. Thus this custom of firing houses continued, till in process of time, says the manuscript, a sage arose who made a discovery, that the flesh of swine, or indeed of any animal, might be cooked (*burnt,* as they called it) without the necessity of consuming a whole house to dress it. Then first began the rude form of gridiron. Roasting by the string, or spit, came in a century or two later, I forget in whose dynasty. By such slow degrees, concludes the manuscript, do the most useful, and seemingly the most obvious arts, make their way among mankind.

Without placing too implicit faith in the account above given, it must be agreed that if a worthy pretext for so dangerous an experiment as setting houses on fire (especially in these days) could be assigned in favour of any culinary object, that pretext and excuse might be found in ROAST PIG.

THE BALLAD OF EAST AND WEST

RUDYARD KIPLING

Oh, East is East and West is West, and never the twain shall meet.
Till Earth and Sky stand presently at God's great Judgment Seat;
But there is neither East nor West, Border, nor Breed nor Birth,
When two strong men stand face to face, tho' they come from the ends of the earth!

Kamal is out with twenty men to raise the Border side,
And he has lifted the Colonel's mare that is the Colonel's pride:
He has lifted her out of the stable-door between the dawn and the day,
And turned the calkins upon her feet, and ridden her far away.
Then up and spoke the Colonel's son that led a troop of the Guides:
"Is there never a man of all my men can say where Kamal hides?"
Then up and spoke Mahommed Khan, the son of the Ressaldar,
"If ye know the track of the morning-mist, ye know where his pickets are.
"At dusk he harries the Abazai — at dawn he is into Bonair,
"But he must go by Fort Bukloh to his own place to fare,
"So if ye gallop to Fort Bukloh as fast as a bird can fly,
"By the favour of God ye may cut him off ere he win to the Tongue of Jagai,
"But if he be passed the Tongue of Jagai, right swiftly turn ye then,
"For the length and the breadth of that grisly plain is sown with Kamal's men.
"There is rock to the left, and rock to the right, and low lean thorn between,
"And ye may hear a breech-bolt snick where never a man is seen."

The Ballad of East and West

The Colonel's son has taken a horse, and a raw rough dun was he,
With the mouth of a bell and the heart of Hell, and the head of the gallows-tree.
The Colonel's son to the Fort has won, they bid him stay to eat —
Who rides at the tail of a Border thief, he sits not long at his meat.
He's up and away from Fort Bukloh as fast as he can fly,
Till he was aware of his father's mare in the gut of the Tongue of Jagai,
Till he was aware of his father's mare with Kamal upon her back,
And when he could spy the white of her eye, he made the pistol crack.
He has fired once, he has fired twice, but the whistling ball went wide.
"Ye shoot like a soldier," Kamal said. "Show now if ye can ride."
It's up and over the Tongue of Jagai, as blown dust-devils go,
The dun he fled like a stag of ten, but the mare like a barren doe.
The dun he leaned against the bit and slugged his head above.
But the red mare played with the snaffle bars, as a maiden plays with a glove.
There was rock to the left and rock to the right, and low lean thorn between,
And thrice he heard a breech-bolt snick tho' never a man was seen.
They have ridden the low moon out of the sky, their hoofs drum up the dawn,
The dun he went like a wounded bull, but the mare like a new-roused fawn.
The dun he fell at a water-course — in a woeful heap fell he,
And Kamal has turned the red mare back, and pulled the rider free.
He has knocked the pistol out of his hand — small room was there to strive,
"'Twas only by favour of mine," quoth he, "ye rode so long alive:

"There was not a rock for twenty mile, there was not a clump of tree,
"But covered a man of my own men with his rifle cocked on his knee.
"If I had raised my bridle-hand, as I have held it low,
"The little jackals that flee so fast were feasting all in a row:
"If I had bowed my head on my breast, as I have held it high,
"The kite that whistles above us now were gorged till she could not fly."
Lightly answered the Colonel's son: — "Do good to bird and beast,
"But count who come for the broken meats before thou makest a feast.
"If there should follow a thousand swords to carry my bones away,
"Belike the price of a jackal's meal were more than a thief could pay.
"They will feed their horse on the standing crop, their men on the garnered grain,
"The thatch of the byres will serve their fires when all the cattle are slain.
"But if thou thinkest the price be fair, — thy brethren wait to sup,
"The hound is kin to the jackal-spawn, — howl, dog, and call them up!
"And if thou thinkest the price be high, in steer and gear and stack,
"Give me my father's mare again, and I'll fight my own way back!"
Kamal has gripped him by the hand and set him upon his feet.
"No talk shall be of dogs," said he, "when wolf and grey wolf meet.
"May I eat dirt if thou hast hurt of me in deed or breath;
"What dam of lances brought thee forth to jest at the dawn with Death?"

The Ballad of East and West

Lightly answered the Colonel's son: "I hold by the blood of my clan:
"Take up the mare for my father's gift — by God, she has carried a man!"
The red mare ran to the Colonel's son, and nuzzled against his breast,
"We be two strong men," said Kamal then, "but she loveth the younger best.
"So she shall go with a lifter's dower, my turquoise-studded rein,
"My broidered saddle and saddle-cloth, and silver stirrups twain."
The Colonel's son a pistol drew and held it muzzle-end,
"Ye have taken the one from a foe," said he; "will ye take the mate from a friend?"
"A gift for a gift," said Kamal straight; "a limb for the risk of a limb.
"Thy father has sent his son to me, I'll send my son to him!"
With that he whistled his only son, that dropped from a mountain-crest —
He trod the ling like a buck in spring, and he looked like a lance in rest.
"Now here is thy master," Kamal said, "who leads a troop of the Guides,
"And thou must ride at his left side as shield on shoulder rides.
"Till Death or I cut loose the tie, at camp and board and bed,
"Thy life is his — thy fate it is to guard him with thy head.
"So thou must eat the White Queen's meat, and all her foes are thine,
"And thou must harry thy father's hold for the peace of the Border-line,
"And thou must make a trooper tough and hack thy way to power —
"Belike they will raise thee to Ressaldar when I am hanged in Peshawur."

They have looked each other between the eyes, and there they
    found no fault,
They have taken the Oath of the Brother-in-Blood on leavened
    bread and salt:
They have taken the Oath of the Brother-in-Blood on fire and
    fresh-cut sod,
On the hilt and the haft of the Khyber knife, and the Wondrous
    Names of God.
The Colonel's son he rides the mare and Kamal's boy the dun,
And two have come back to Fort Bukloh where there went
    forth but one.
And when they drew to the Quarter-Guard, full twenty swords
    flew clear —
There was not a man but carried his feud with the blood of
    the mountaineer.
"Ha' done! ha' done!" said the Colonel's son.
    "Put up the steel at your sides!
"Last night ye had struck at a Border thief — to-night
    'tis a man of the Guides!"

*Oh, East is East and West is West, and never the twain shall
    meet,*
*Till Earth and Sky stand presently at God's great Judgment
    Seat;*
*But there is neither East nor West, Border, nor Breed, nor
    Birth,*
*When two strong men stand face to face, tho' they come from
    the ends of the earth.*

GULLIVER COMES TO GIANTLAND

JONATHAN SWIFT

One of the reapers, approaching within ten yards of the ridge where I lay, made me realize that with the next step I should be squashed to death under his foot, or cut in two with his reaping hook. And therefore, when he was again about to move, I screamed as loud as fear could make me. Whereupon the huge creature trod short, and looking round about under him for some time, at last saw me as I lay on the ground.

He considered awhile, with the caution of one who endeavours to lay hold on a small dangerous animal in such a manner that it shall not be able either to scratch or bite him, as I myself have sometimes done with a weasel in England. At length he ventured to take me behind by the middle, between his forefinger and thumb, and brought me within three yards of his eyes, that he might behold my shape more perfectly. I guessed his meaning, and my good fortune gave me so much presence of mind that I resolved not to struggle in the least as he held me in the air about sixty feet from the ground, although he grievously pinched my sides, for fear I should slip through his fingers. All I ventured was to raise my eyes toward the sun and place my hands together in a supplicating posture, and to speak some words in a humble melancholy tone, suitable to the condition I then was in: for I feared every moment that he would dash me against the ground as we usually do any little hateful animal which we have a mind to destroy. But my good star would have it that he appeared pleased with my voice and gestures, and began to look upon me as a curiosity, much wondering to hear me pronounce articulate words, although he could not understand them. In the meantime I was not able to forbear groaning and shedding tears and turning my head towards my sides; letting him know, as well as I could, how cruelly I was hurt by the pressure of his thumb and finger. He seemed to understand my meaning; for lifting up the lappet of his coat, he put me gently into it and immediately ran along with me to his master, who was a substantial farmer and the first man I had seen in the field.

The farmer having (as I supposed by their talk) received such an account of me as his servant could give him, took a piece of a small straw about the size of a walking staff and therewith lifted up the lappets of my coat, which, it seems, he thought to be some kind of covering that nature had given me. He blew my hair aside to take a better view of my face. He called his farm hands about him, and asked them, as I afterwards learned, whether they had ever seen in the fields any little creature that resembled me. He then placed me softly on the ground on my hands and knees, but I immediately got up and walked slowly backwards and forwards to let those people see I had no intent to run away. They all sat down in a circle about me, the better to observe my motions. I pulled off my hat and made a low bow towards the farmer. I fell on my knees and lifted up my hands and eyes and spoke several words as loud as I could. I took a purse of gold out of my pocket and humbly presented it to him. He received it on the palm of his hand and then applied it close to his eye to see what it was. Afterwards he turned it several times with the point of a pin (which he took out of his sleeve), but could make nothing of it. Whereupon I made a sign that he should place his hand on the ground. I then took the purse, and opening it, poured all the gold into his palm. There were six Spanish pieces of four pistoles each, besides twenty or thirty smaller coins. I saw him wet the tip of his little finger upon his tongue and take up one of my largest pieces and then another; but he seemed to be wholly ignorant of what they were. He made me a sign to put them again into my purse and the purse again into my pocket, which, after offering it to him several times, I thought it best to do.

The farmer, by this time, was convinced I must be a rational creature. He spoke often to me, but the sound of his voice pierced my ears like that of a water mill, yet his words were articulate enough. I answered as loud as I could in several languages, and he often laid his ear within two yards of me; but all in vain, for we were wholly unintelligible to each other. He then sent his servants to their work, and taking his handkerchief out of his pocket, he doubled and spread it on his left hand, which he placed flat on the ground with the palm upward, making me a sign to step into it, as I could easily do, for it was not above a foot in thickness. I thought it my part to obey. For fear of falling, I laid myself full length upon the handkerchief, with the remainder of which he lapped me up to the head for further security. In this manner, he carried me home to his house. There he called his wife and showed me to her; but she screamed and ran back as women in England do at the sight of a toad or a spider. However, when she had awhile seen my behaviour and how well I observed the signs her husband made, she was soon reconciled and by degrees grew extremely kind to me.

II

It was about twelve at noon and a servant brought in dinner. It was only one substantial dish of meat, fit for the plain condition of a husbandman, in a dish of about four-and-twenty feet diameter. The company were the farmer and his wife, three children, and an old grandmother. When they were sat down, the farmer placed me at some distance from him on the table, which was thirty feet high from the floor. I was in a terrible fright and kept as far as I could from the edge for fear of falling. The wife minced a bit of meat, then crumbled some bread on a wooden plate, and placed it before me. I made her a low bow, took out my knife and fork, and fell to eat, which gave them exceeding delight. The mistress sent her maid for a small wine cup, which held about two gallons, and filled it with drink. I took up the vessel with much difficulty in both hands, and in a most respectful manner drank to her ladyship's health, expressing the words as loud as I could in English, which made the company laugh so heartily that I was almost deafened with the noise. This liquor tasted like a weak cider and was not unpleasant.

Then the master made me a sign to come to his side. But as I walked on the table, being at great surprise all the time, as the reader will understand, I happened to stumble against a crust and fell flat on my face, but received no hurt. I got up immediately, and observing the good people to be in much concern, I took my hat (which I held under my arm out of good manners), and waving it over my head, shouted three huzzas to show I had got no harm by my fall. But advancing forward towards my master (as I shall henceforth call him), his youngest son, who sat next to him, a lively boy of about ten years old, took me up by the legs and held me so high in the air that I trembled in every limb; but his father snatched me from him and at the same time gave him such a box on the left ear as would have felled a European troop of horse to the earth, ordering him to be taken from the table. But being afraid the boy might owe me a spite, and well remembering how mischievous all children among us naturally are to sparrows, rabbits, young kittens, and puppy dogs, I fell on my knees, and pointing to the boy, made my master to understand as well as I could that I desired his son might be pardoned. The father complied and the lad took his seat again, whereupon I went to him and kissed his hand, which my master took, and made him stroke me gently with it.

In the midst of dinner my mistress's favourite cat leaped into her lap. I heard a noise behind me like that of a dozen stocking weavers at work; and turning my head, I found it proceeded from the purring of that animal, who seemed to be three times larger than an ox, as I computed by the view of her head and one of her paws while her mistress was feeding and stroking her. The fierceness of this creature's face altogether frightened me, though I stood at the farther end of the table about fifty feet off; and though my mistress held her fast, for fear she might give a spring and seize me in her talons. But it happened there was no danger, for the cat took not the least notice of me when my master placed me within three yards of her. And as I have been always told, and found true by experience in my travels, that fleeing or showing fear before a fierce animal is a certain way to make it pursue or attack you, I resolved in this dangerous crisis to show no manner of concern. I walked fearlessly five or six times before the very head of the cat, and came within half a yard of her; whereupon she drew herself back as if she were more afraid of me. I had less apprehension concerning dogs, whereof three or four came into the room as is usual in farmers' houses. One of these was a mastiff equal in bulk to four elephants, and another, a greyhound somewhat taller than the mastiff but not so large.

When dinner was almost done, the nurse came in with a child of a year old in her arms. He immediately spied me and began to squall. The mother took me up and put me towards the child, who presently seized me by the middle and got my head into his mouth, where I roared so loud that the urchin was frightened and let me drop. I should infallibly have broken my neck if the mother had not held her apron under me. The nurse, to quiet her babe, made use of a rattle, which was a kind of hollow vessel filled with great stones and fastened by a cable to the child's waist.

When dinner was done, my master went out to his laborers, and as I could discover by his voice and gesture, gave his wife a strict charge to take care of me. I was very much tired and disposed to sleep. My mistress, perceiving this, put me on her own bed, and covered me with a clean white handkerchief, but larger and coarser than the mainsail of a man-of-war.

I slept about two hours and dreamt I was at home with my wife and children, which increased my sorrows when I awaked and found myself alone in a vast room, between two and three hundred feet wide and more than two hundred high, lying in a bed twenty yards wide. My mistress was gone about her household affairs and had locked me in. The bed was eight yards from the floor. I dared not presume to call; and if I had, it would have been in vain, with such a voice as mine, at so great a distance as from the room where I lay to the kitchen where the family stayed. While I was under these circumstances, two rats crept up the curtains and ran smelling backwards and forwards on the bed. One of them came up almost to my face, whereupon I rose in a fright and drew out my sword to defend myself. These horrible animals had the boldness to attack me on both sides, and one of them held his forefeet at my collar; but I had the good fortune to rip up his belly before he could do me any mischief. He fell down at my feet; and the other, seeing the fate of his comrade, made his escape, but not without one good wound on the back, which I gave him as he fled, and made the blood run trickling from him. After this exploit, I walked gently to and fro on the bed to recover my breath and loss of spirits. These creatures were of the size of a large mastiff, but infinitely more nimble and fierce; so that if I had taken off my belt before I went to sleep, I must have infallibly been torn to pieces and devoured. I measured the tail of the dead rat and found it to be two yards long, lacking an inch; but it went against my stomach to draw the carcass off the bed, where it lay still bleeding. I observed it had yet some life, but with a strong slash across the neck, I thoroughly dispatched it.

Soon after, my mistress came into the room, who, seeing me all bloody, ran and took me up in her hand. I pointed to the dead rat, smiling and making other signs to show I was not hurt; whereat she was extremely rejoiced, calling the maid to take up the dead rat with a pair of tongs, and throw it out of the window.

III

Following the advice of a friend, my master carried me in a box the next market day to the neighbouring town, and took

along with him his little daughter, my nurse. The box was closed on every side, with a little door for me to go in and out and a few gimlet holes to let in air. The girl had been so careful as to put the quilt of her baby's bed into it, for me to lie down on. However, I was terribly shaken and discomposed in this journey, though it were but of half an hour; for the horse went about forty feet at every step, and trotted so high that the agitation was equal to the rising and falling of a ship in a great storm, but much more frequent. My master alighted at an inn which he used to frequent. After consulting awhile with the innkeeper and making some necessary preparations, he hired the *grultrud,* or crier, to give notice through the town of a strange creature to be seen at the sign of the Green Eagle, not so big as a *splacnuck* (an animal in that country very finely shaped, about six feet long), and in every part of the body resembling a human creature, who could speak several words, and perform a hundred diverting tricks.

I was placed upon a table in the largest room of the inn, which might be near three hundred feet square. My little nurse stood on a low stool close to the table, to take care of me and direct what I should do. My master, to avoid a crowd, would allow only thirty people at a time to see me. I walked about on the table as the girl commanded. She asked me questions, as far as she knew my understanding of the language reached, and I answered them as loud as I could. I turned about several times to the company, paid my humble respects, said they were welcome, and used some other speeches I had been taught. I took up a thimble filled with liquor, which Glumdalclitch, my master's daughter, had given me for a cup, and drank their health. I drew out my sword and flourished with it after the manner of fencers in England. My nurse gave me a part of a straw, which I exercised as a pike, having learned the art in my youth. I was that day shown to twelve sets of company, and as often forced to act over again the same fopperies, till I was half dead with weariness and vexation; for those who had seen me made such wonderful reports that the people were ready to break down the doors to come in. My master, for his own interest, would not permit anyone to touch me except my nurse; and to prevent danger, benches were set round the table at such a distance as to put me out of everybody's reach. However, an unlucky schoolboy aimed a hazelnut directly at my head, which very narrowly missed me; otherwise it came with so much violence that it would have infallibly knocked out my brains, for it was almost as large as a small pumpkin; but I had the satisfaction to see the young rogue well beaten and turned out of the room.

ROBINSON CRUSOE MEETS HIS MAN FRIDAY

DANIEL DEFOE

For twenty-five years Robinson Crusoe has dwelt alone on his desert island. Sole survivor of a shipwreck, he has salvaged much of value, has built himself a summer home and a "castle", has tamed flocks and raised crops. In all these years he has never heard the sound of another human voice, nor seen a sign of another human being. Then one fine day he experiences a great shock.

It happened one day about noon that on going toward my boat I was exceedingly surprised with the print of a man's naked foot on the shore. I stood like one thunderstruck, or as if I had seen an apparition. I listened, I looked round me, but I could hear nothing nor see anything. I went up to a rising mount to look farther; I went up and down the shore, but it was all one: I could see no other impression but that one. I went to it again to see if there were any more and to observe if it might not be my fancy. But there was no room for that, for there was the very print of a foot.

How came it thither I knew not nor could I in the least imagine; but, like a man perfectly confused and out of myself, not feeling, as we say, the ground I went on, I came home to my fortification, terrified to the last degree, looking behind me at every two or three steps, mistaking every bush and tree, and fancying every stump at a distance to be a man. Nor is it possible to describe in how many various shapes my affrighted imagination represented things to me, how many wild ideas were found every moment in my fancy, and what strange, unaccountable whims came into my thoughts by the way.

When I came to my castle (for so I think I called my habitation ever after this), I fled into it like one pursued. Whether I went over by the ladder or went in at the hole in the rock, which I had called a door, I cannot remember. For never frightened hare fled to cover or fox to earth with more terror of mind than I to this retreat.

I slept none that night; the farther I was from the occasion of my fright, the greater my apprehensions were. I presently concluded that it must be some of the savages of the mainland opposite, who had wandered out to sea in their canoes and, either driven by the currents or by contrary winds, had made the island, but were gone away again to sea, being as loath, perhaps, to have stayed in this desolate island as I would have been to have had them.

While these reflections were rolling upon my mind, I was very thankful in my thoughts that I had not been thereabouts at that time, and that they did not see my boat, by which they would have concluded that some inhabitants were in the place, and perhaps would have searched farther for me. Then terrible thoughts racked my imagination about their having found my boat and having suspected that there were people here; and that, if so, I should certainly have them come again in greater numbers and devour me; and that if it should happen that they should not find me, yet they would find my enclosure, destroy all my corn, and carry away all my flock of tame goats, and I should perish at last for mere want.

In the middle of such reflections it came one day into my thoughts that this might be the print of my own foot, when I came on shore from my boat; this cheered me up a little, and I began to persuade myself it was all a delusion; that it was nothing else but my own foot. Why might I not have come that way from the boat? Again I considered also, that I could by no means tell, for certain, where I had trod and where I had not; and that if at last, this was only the print of my own foot, I had played the part of those fools who try to make stories of spectres, and then are frightened at them more than anybody.

Now I began to take courage and to peep abroad again, for I had not stirred out of my castle for three days and nights, so that I began to starve for provisions; for I had little or nothing within doors but some barley cakes and water. Then I knew that my goats needed to be milked too, which usually was my evening diversion. Encouraging myself, therefore, with the belief that this was nothing but the print of one of my own feet and that I might be truly said to start at my own shadow, I began to go abroad again and went to my country house to milk my flock.

But to see with what fear I went forward, how often I looked behind me, how I was ready, every now and then, to lay down my basket and run for my life, would have made anyone think I was haunted with an evil conscience, or that I had been lately most terribly frightened; and so, indeed, I had.

However, as I went down thus two or three days, and having seen nothing, I began to be a little bolder and to think there was really nothing in it but my own imagination. But, I could not persuade myself fully of this till I should go down to the shore again, and see this print of a foot, and measure it by my own, and see if there was any similarity, that I might be assured it was my own foot.

But when I came to the place — first it appeared evident to me that when I laid up my boat, I could not possibly be on shore anywhere thereabouts; secondly, when I came to measure the mark with my own foot, I found my foot not so large by a great deal. Both these things filled my head with new imaginations and made me fearful again to the highest degree. I went home again, filled with the belief that some man or men had been on shore there, or that the island was inhabited, and I might be surprised before I was aware.

I continually made my tour every morning to the top of the hill, which was from my castle about three miles or more, to see if I could observe any boats upon the sea, coming near the island or standing over toward it. But I began to tire of this hard duty after I had for two or three months constantly kept my watch but came always back without any discovery.

I was surprised one morning early by seeing no less than five canoes all on shore together on my side the island, and the people who belonged to them all landed and out of my sight. The number of them broke all my measures; for seeing so many and knowing that they always came four or six or sometimes more in a boat, I could not tell what to think of it or how to attack twenty or thirty men singlehanded; so I lay still in my castle, perplexed and discomforted. However, I put myself into position for an attack, and was ready for action if anything happened.

Having waited a good while, listening to hear if they made any noise, at length, being very impatient, I set my guns at the foot of my ladder and clambered up to the top of the hill, standing so that my head did not appear above the hill and the invaders could not perceive me by any means. Here I observed by the help of my glass that they were no less than thirty in number, that they had a fire kindled, and that they had meat dressed. How they had cooked it I knew not, or what it was; but they were all dancing with barbarous gestures, in their own way, round the fire.

While I was thus looking on them, I perceived by my glass two miserable wretches dragged from the boats for the slaughter. I saw one of them immediately fall, being knocked down, I suppose, with a club or wooden sword, for that was their way, while the other victim was left standing by himself till they should be ready for him. In that very moment this poor wretch, seeing himself a little at liberty and unbound, Nature inspired with hopes of life, and he started away from them and ran with incredible swiftness along the sands directly toward me, or rather toward that part of the coast where my habitation was.

I was dreadfully frightened, I must acknowledge, when I saw him run my way, especially when, as I thought, I saw him pursued by the whole body. However, I kept my station, and my spirits began to recover when I found that there were not above three men that followed him; and still more was I encouraged when I found that he outstripped them exceedingly in

Robinson Crusoe Meets His Man Friday

running and gained ground on them, so that if he could but hold it for half an hour, I saw that he would easily get away from them all.

There was between them and my castle a creek; and this I saw plainly he must necessarily swim over, or the poor wretch would be taken there. But when the escaping savage came thither, he made nothing of it, though the tide was then up; but, plunging in, swam through in about thirty strokes or thereabouts, landed, and ran on with exceeding strength and swiftness.

When the other three savages came to the creek, I found that two of them could swim, but the third could not, and that, standing on the other side, he looked at the others, but went no farther, and soon after went softly back, which, as it happened, was very well for him in the end.

I observed that the two who swam were yet more than twice as long swimming over the creek as the fellow that fled from them. It came very warmly upon my thoughts that now was the time to get me a servant, and perhaps a companion or an assistant, and that I was called plainly by Providence to save this poor creature's life. I immediately ran down the ladders, fetched my two guns, for they were both at the foot of the ladders, and getting up again with haste to the top of the hill, I crossed toward the sea.

Having a very short cut and all down hill, I placed myself in the way between the pursuers and the pursued, hallooing aloud to him that fled, who, looking back, was at first perhaps as much frightened at me as at them. But I beckoned with my hand to him to come back; and in the meantime I slowly advanced toward the two that followed; then rushing at once upon the foremost, I knocked him down with the stock of my piece. I was loath to fire, because I would not have the rest hear. Though, at that distance, it would not have been easily heard, and being out of the sight of the smoke, too, they would not have known what to make of it.

After I had knocked this fellow down, the other, who still pursued, stopped as if he had been frightened, and I advanced toward him; but as I came nearer, I saw he had a bow and arrow and was fitting it to shoot at me. So I was then obliged to shoot at him first, which I did, and killed him at the first shot.

The poor savage who fled was so frightened with the fire and noise of my piece that he stood stock-still, and neither came forward nor went backward, though he seemed rather inclined still to fly than to come on. I hallooed again to him and made signs to come forward, which he easily understood, and came a little way, then stopped again, and then a little farther, and stopped again; and I could then see that he stood trembling as if he had been taken prisoner and thought he was to be killed, as his two enemies had been.

I beckoned to him again to come to me and gave him all the signs of encouragement that I could think of; and he came nearer and nearer, kneeling down every ten or twelve steps, in token of acknowledgement for saving his life. I smiled at him, and looked pleasantly, and beckoned to him to come still nearer. At length he came close to me; and then he kneeled down again, kissed the ground, laid his head upon the ground, and taking me by the foot, set my foot upon his head. This, it seems, was in token of swearing to be my slave forever. I took him up, and made much of him, and encouraged him all I could.

But there was more work to do yet; for I saw the savage whom I had knocked down was not killed but only stunned with the blow and began to come to himself; so I pointed and showed my savage that his enemy was not dead. Upon this he spoke some words to me, and though I could not understand them, yet I thought they were pleasant to hear; for they were the first sound of a man's voice that I had heard, my own excepted, for above twenty-five years.

But there was no time for such reflections now; the savage who was knocked down recovered himself so far as to sit upon the ground, and I saw that my savage began to be afraid; but when I saw that, I presented my other piece at the man, as if I would shoot him. Upon this my savage made a motion to me to lend him my sword, which hung naked in a belt by my side, which I did. He no sooner had it but he ran to his enemy, and at one blow cut off his head so cleverly that no executioner in Europe could have done it sooner or better. I thought this very strange for one who, I had reason to believe, had never seen a sword in his life before, except the native wooden ones. However, it seems, as I learned afterward, the savages make their wooden swords so sharp and so heavy and the wood is so hard, that they will even cut off heads with them, ay, and arms, and that at one blow too.

When my savage had done this, he came laughing to me in sign of triumph and brought me the sword again and, with abundance of gestures which I did not understand, laid it down with the head of the savage that he had just killed before me.

But that which astonished him most was how I killed the other Indian so far off. Pointing to him, he made signs to me to let him go to the fallen savage; and I bade him go, as well as I could. When he came to the body, he stood like one amazed, looking at it, turning it first on one side, and then on the other, and looked at the wound the bullet had made. He took up the savage's bow and arrows and came back; so I turned to go away and beckoned him to follow me, making signs to him that more might come after them.

Upon this he signed to me that he should bury his pursuers with sand, that they might not be seen by the rest if they followed; and so I made signs to him to do so. He fell to work, and in a few minutes he had scraped a hole in the sand with his hands, big enough to bury the first in, and then dragged the body into it and covered it, and did so by the other also.

Then calling him away, I carried him, not to my castle, but quite away to my cave, on the farther part of the island. Here I gave him bread and a bunch of raisins to eat and a draught of water, which I found he was indeed in great distress for from his running. Having refreshed him, I made signs for him to go and lie down to sleep, pointing him to a place where I had laid some rice straw and a blanket, which I used to sleep upon myself sometimes. So the poor creature lay down and went to sleep. He was a comely, handsome fellow, perfectly well made, with straight, strong limbs, not too large, tall and well shaped; and, as I reckon, about twenty-six years of age. He had a good countenance, not a fierce and surly aspect, but seemed to have something very manly in his face; and yet he had all the sweetness and softness of an European in his countenance too, especially when he smiled. His hair was long and black, not curled like wool; his forehead very high and large; and a great vivacity and sparkling sharpness in his eyes. The colour of his skin was not quite black, but very tawny; and yet not an ugly, yellow, nauseous tawny, but of a bright kind of a dun-olive colour, that had in it something very agreeable, though not very easy to describe. His face was round and plump; his nose small, not flat like that of the negroes; a very good mouth, thin lips, and his fine teeth were well set and as white as ivory.

After he had slumbered about half an hour, he awoke again and came out of the cave to me; for I had been milking my goats, which I had in the enclosure just by. When he espied me, he came running to me, laying himself down again upon the ground, with all the possible signs of an humble, thankful disposition, making a great many antic gestures to show it. At last he laid his head flat upon the ground, close to my foot, set my foot upon his head, as he had done before, and after this, made all the signs to me of subjection, servitude, and submission imaginable, to let me know how he would serve me as long as he lived. I understood him in many things and let him know I was very well pleased with him.

In a little time I began to speak to him and teach him to speak to me. First, I made him know his name should be *Friday*, which was the day I saved his life. I called him so for the memory of the time. I likewise taught him to say *Master*, and then let him know that was to be my name. I likewise taught him to say *Yes* and *No*, and to know the meaning of them.

Next, I gave him a pair of linen drawers, which I had out of the poor gunner's chest, which I found in a wreck, and which with a little alteration, fitted him very well. Then I made him a jerkin of goat's skin, as well as my skill would allow, for I was now grown a tolerably good tailor. And I gave him a cap which I made of hare's skin, very convenient and fashionable enough; and thus he was clothed, for the present, tolerably well, and was mighty well pleased to see himself almost as well clothed as his master. It is true, he went awkwardly in these clothes at first, but he took to them at length very well.

This was the pleasantest year of all the life I led in this place. Friday began to talk pretty well and understand the names of almost everything I had occasion to call for and of every place I had to send him to, and talked a great deal to me; so that I began now to have some use for my tongue again, which, indeed, I had very little occasion for before. Besides the pleasure of talking to him, I had a singular satisfaction in the fellow himself: his simple, unfeigned honesty appeared to me more and more every day, and I began really to love the creature; and on his side, I believe he loved me more than it was possible for him ever to love anything before.

HOW THEY BROUGHT THE GOOD NEWS FROM GHENT TO AIX

ROBERT BROWNING

I sprang to the stirrup, and Joris, and he;
I galloped, Dirck galloped, we galloped all three;
"Good speed!" cried the watch, as the gate-bolts undrew;
"Speed!" echoed the wall to us galloping through;

Behind shut the postern, the lights sank to rest,
And into the midnight we galloped abreast.

Not a word to each other; we kept the great pace
Neck by neck, stride by stride, never changing our place;
I turned in my saddle and made its girths tight,
Then shortened each stirrup, and set the pique right,
Rebuckled the cheek-strap, chained slacker the bit,
Nor galloped less steadily Roland a whit.

'Twas moonset at starting; but while we drew near
Lokeren, the cocks crew and twilight dawned clear;
At Boom, a great yellow star came out to see;
At Düffeld, 'twas morning as plain as could be;
And from Mecheln church-steeple we heard the half-chime,
So Joris broke silence with, "Yet there is time!"

At Aershot, up leaped of a sudden the sun,
And against him the cattle stood black every one,
To stare through the mist at us galloping past,
And I saw my stout galloper Roland at last
With resolute shoulders, each butting away
The haze, as some bluff river headland its spray:

And his low head and crest, just one sharp ear bent back
For my voice, and the other pricked out on his track;
And one eye's black intelligence, — ever that glance
O'er its white edge at me, his own master, askance!
And the thick heavy spume-flakes which aye and anon
His fierce lips shook upwards in galloping on.

By Hasselt, Dirck groaned; and cried Joris "Stay spur!
Your Roos galloped bravely, the fault's not in her,
We'll remember at Aix" — for one heard the quick wheeze
Of her chest, saw the stretched neck and staggering knees,
And sunk tail, and horrible heave of the flank,
As down on her haunches she shuddered and sank.

So, we were left galloping, Joris and I,
Past Looz and past Tongres, no cloud in the sky;
The broad sun above laughed a pitiless laugh,
'Neath our feet broke the brittle bright stubble like chaff;
Till over by Dalhem a dome-spire sprang white,
And "Gallop," gasped Joris, "for Aix is in sight!

"How they'll greet us!" — and all in a moment his roan
Rolled neck and croup over, lay dead as a stone;
And there was my Roland to bear the whole weight
Of the news which alone could save Aix from her fate,
With his nostrils like pits full of blood to the brim,
And the circles of red for his eye-sockets' rim.

Then I cast loose my buffcoat, each holster let fall.
Shook off both my jack-boots, let go belt and all
Stood up in the stirrup, leaned, patted his ear,
Called my Roland his pet-name, my horse without peer;
Clapped my hands, laughed and sang, any noise, bad or good,
Till at length into Aix Roland galloped and stood.

And all I remember is, — friends flocking round
As I sat with his head 'twixt my knees on the ground;
And no voice but was praising this Roland of mine,
As I poured down his throat our last measure of wine,
Which (the burgesses voted by common consent)
Was no more than his due who brought good news from Ghent.

MOSES GOES TO THE FAIR

OLIVER GOLDSMITH

As we were now to hold up our heads a little higher in the world, my wife suggested that it would be proper to sell the colt, which was grown old, at a neighbouring fair, and buy us a horse that would carry single or double upon an occasion, and make a pretty appearance at church or upon a visit. This at first I opposed stoutly; but it was as stoutly defended. However, as I weakened, my antagonist gained strength, till at last we agreed to part with him.

As the fair happened on the following day, I had intentions of going myself; but my wife persuaded me that I had got a cold, and nothing could prevail upon her to permit me from home. "No, my dear," said she, "our son Moses is a discreet boy, and can buy and sell to very good advantage. You know all our great bargains are of his purchasing. He always stands out and higgles, and actually tires them till he gets a bargain."

As I had some opinion of my son's prudence, I was willing enough to intrust him with this commission; and the next morning I perceived his sisters very busy in fitting out Moses for the fair,—trimming his hair, brushing his buckles, and cocking his hat with pins. The business of the toilet being over, we had at last the satisfaction of seeing him mounted upon the colt, with a deal box before him to bring home groceries in.

He had on a coat made of that cloth they call thunder and lightning, which, though grown too short, was much too good to be thrown away. His waistcoat was of gosling-green, and his sisters had tied his hair with a broad black ribbon. We all followed him several paces from the door, bawling after him, "Good luck! good luck!" till we could see him no longer.

When it was almost nightfall, I began to wonder what could keep our son so long at the fair. "Never mind our son," cried my wife; "depend upon it, he knows what he is about. I'll warrant we'll never see him sell his hen on a rainy day. I have seen him buy such bargains as would amaze one. I'll tell you a good story about that, that will make you split your sides with laughing—. But, as I live, yonder comes Moses without a horse, and the box at his back."

As she spoke, Moses came slowly on foot, and sweating under the deal box, which he had strapped round his shoulders like a pedler.

Moses Goes to the Fair

"Welcome, welcome, Moses! Well, my boy, what have you brought us from the fair?"

"I have brought you myself," said Moses, with a sly look, and resting the box on the dresser.

"Ay, Moses," cried my wife, "that we know; but where is the horse?"

"I have sold him," replied Moses, "for three pounds five shillings and twopence."

"Well done, my good boy," returned she; "I knew you would touch them off. Between ourselves, three pounds five shillings and twopence is no bad day's work. Come, let us have it, then."

"I have brought back no money," cried Moses, again; "I have laid it all out in a bargain — and here it is," pulling out a bundle from his breast; "here they are, — a gross of green spectacles, with silver rims and shagreen cases."

"A gross of green spectacles!" repeated my wife, in a faint voice. "And you have parted with the colt, and brought us back nothing but a gross of green paltry spectacles!"

"Dear mother," cried the boy, "why don't you listen to reason? I had them a dead bargain, or I should not have bought them. The silver rims alone will sell for double the money."

"A fig for the silver rims!" cried my wife, in a passion; "I dare swear they won't sell for above half the money at the rate of broken silver, five shillings an ounce."

"You need be under no uneasiness," said I, "about selling the rims, for they are not worth sixpence; for I perceive they are only copper varnished over."

"What!" cried my wife; "not silver! the rims not silver!"

"No," cried I; "no more silver than your saucepan."

"And so," returned she, "we have parted with the colt, and have got only a gross of green spectacles, with copper rims and shagreen cases? A murrain take such trumpery! The blockhead has been imposed upon, and should have known his company better."

"There, my dear," cried I, "you are wrong; he should not have known them at all."

"To bring me such stuff!" returned she; "if I had them, I would throw them into the fire."

"There again you are wrong, my dear," said I; "for though they are copper, we shall keep them by us, as copper spectacles, you know, are better than nothing."

By this time the unfortunate Moses was undeceived. He now saw that he had been imposed upon by a prowling sharper, who, observing his figure, had marked him for an easy prey. I therefore asked the circumstances of his deception. He sold the horse, it seems, and walked the fair in search of another. A reverend-looking man brought him to a tent, under pretence of having one to sell.

"Here," continued Moses, "we met another man, very well dressed, who desired to borrow twenty pounds upon these, saying that he wanted money, and would dispose of them for a third of the value. The first gentleman whispered me to buy them, and cautioned me not to let so good an offer pass. I sent to Mr. Flamborough, and they talked him up as finely as they did me; and so at last we were persuaded to buy the two gross between us."

Our family had now made several vain attempts to be fine. "You see, my children," said I, "how little is to be got by attempts to impose upon the world. Those that are poor and will associate with none but the rich are hated by those they avoid, and despised by those they follow."

THE PIED PIPER OF HAMELIN

ROBERT BROWNING

Hamelin town's in Brunswick,
By famous Hanover city;
The river Weser, deep and wide,

The Pied Piper of Hamelin

Washes its wall on the southern side;
A pleasanter spot you never spied;
  But, when begins my ditty —
Almost five hundred years ago —
To see the townsfolk suffer so
  From vermin, was a pity.

  Rats!
They fought the dogs, and killed the cats,
And bit the babies in the cradles,
And ate the cheeses out of the vats,
And licked the soup from cooks' own ladles;
Split open the kegs of salted sprats,
Made nests inside men's Sunday hats,
And even spoiled the women's chats
By drowning their speaking
With shrieking and squeaking
In fifty different sharps and flats.

At last the people in a body
To the Town Hall came flocking:
"'Tis clear!" cried they, "our Mayor's a noddy;
And as for our Corporation — shocking!
To think we buy gowns lined with ermine
For dolts that can't or won't determine
What's best to rid us of our vermin!
You hope, because you're old and obese,
To find in the furry civic robe ease?
Rouse up, Sirs! Give your brains a racking
To find the remedy we're lacking,
Or, sure as fate, we'll send you packing!"
At this the Mayor and Corporation
Quaked with a mighty consternation.

  An hour they sat in council,
    At length the Mayor broke silence:

"For a guilder I'd my ermine gown sell;
  I wish I were a mile hence!
It's easy to bid one rack one's brain —
I'm sure my poor head aches again,
I've scratched it so, and all in vain.
Oh for a trap, a trap, a trap!"
Just as he said this, what should hap
At the chamber door but a gentle tap?
"Bless us," cried the Mayor, "what's that?
(With the Corporation as he sat,
Looking little though wondrous fat;
Nor brighter was his eye, nor moister
Than a too-long-opened oyster,
Save when at noon his paunch grew mutinous
For a plate of turtle green and glutinous)
Only a scraping of shoes on the mat?
Anything like the sound of a rat
Makes my heart go pit-a-pat!"

"Come in!" — the Mayor cried, looking bigger;
And in did come the strangest figure!
His queer long coat from heel to head
Was half of yellow and half of red;
And he himself was tall and thin,
With sharp blue eyes, each like a pin,
And light loose hair, yet swarthy skin,
No tuft on cheek nor beard on chin,
But lips where smiles went out and in —
There was no guessing his kith and kin!
And nobody could enough admire
The tall man and his quaint attire:
Quoth one: "It's as my great-grandsire,
Starting up at the Trump of Doom's tone,
Had walked this way from his painted tombstone."

The Pied Piper of Hamelin

He advanced to the council-table:
And, "Please your honours," quoth he, "I'm able,
  By means of a secret charm, to draw
  All creatures living beneath the sun
  That creep, or swim, or fly, or run,
After me so as you never saw!
  And I chiefly use my charm
  On creatures that do people harm,
  The mole, and toad, the newt, and viper,
  And people call me the Pied Piper."
(And here they noticed round his neck
A scarf of red and yellow stripe,
To match with his coat of the self-same check,
And at the scarf's end hung a pipe;
And his fingers, they noticed, were ever straying
As if impatient to be playing
Upon this pipe, as low it dangled
Over his vesture so old-fangled.)
  "Yet," said he, "poor Piper as I am,
  In Tartary I freed the Cham,
  Last June, from his huge swarms of gnats;
  I eased in Asia the Nizam
  Of a monstrous brood of vampire bats;
  And, as for what your brain bewilders,
  If I can rid your town of rats
  Will you give me a thousand guilders?"
"One? — fifty thousand!" was the exclamation
Of the astonished Mayor and Corporation.

Into the street the Piper stept,
Smiling first a little smile,
As if he knew what magic slept
In his quiet pipe the while;
Then like a musical adept,
To blow the pipe his lips he wrinkled,

And green and blue his sharp eyes twinkled,
Like a candle flame where salt is sprinkled;
And ere three shrill notes the pipe uttered,
You heard as if an army muttered;
And the muttering grew to a grumbling;
And the grumbling grew to a mighty rumbling;
And out of the houses the rats came tumbling!
Great rats, small rats, lean rats, brawny rats,
Brown rats, black rats, grey rats, tawny rats,
Grave old plodders, gay young friskers,
    Fathers, mothers, uncles, cousins,
Cocking tails and pricking whiskers,
    Families by tens and dozens,
Brothers, sisters, husbands, wives —
Followed the Piper for their lives.
From street to street he piped advancing,
And step for step they followed dancing,
Until they came to the river Weser,
Wherein all plunged and perished!
— Save one, who, stout as Julius Caesar,
Swam across and lived to carry
(As he the manuscript he cherished)
To Rat-land home his commentary:
Which was, "At the first shrill notes of the pipe,
I heard a sound as of scraping tripe,
And putting apples, wondrous ripe,
Into a cider-press's gripe:
And a moving away of pickle-tub-boards,
And a leaving ajar of conserve-cupboards,
And a drawing the corks of train-oil flasks,
And a breaking the hoops of butter-casks;
And it seemed as if a voice
(Sweeter far than by harp or by psaltery
Is breathed) called out, 'Oh rats, rejoice!
The world is grown to one vast dry-saltery!

The Pied Piper of Hamelin

So, munch on, crunch on, take your nuncheon,
Breakfast, supper, dinner, luncheon!'
And just as a bulky sugar-puncheon,
All ready staved, like a great sun shone
Glorious, scarce an inch before me,
Just as methought it said, 'Come, bore me!'
— I found the Weser rolling o'er me."

You should have heard the Hamelin people
Ringing the bells till they rocked the steeple.
"Go," cried the Mayor, "and get long poles!
Consult with carpenters and builders,
And leave in our town not even a trace
Of the rats!" — when suddenly, up the face
Of the Piper perked in the market-place,
With a, "First, if you please, my thousand guilders!"

A thousand guilders! The Mayor looked blue;
So did the Corporation too.
For council dinners made rare havoc
With Claret, Moselle, Vin-de-Grave, Hock;
And half the money would replenish
Their cellar's biggest butt with Rhenish.
To pay this sum to a wandering fellow
With a gipsy coat of red and yellow!
"Beside," quoth the Mayor with a knowing wink,
"Our business was done at the river's brink;
We saw with our own eyes the vermin sink,
And what's dead can't come to life, I think.
So, friend, we're not the folks to shrink
From the duty of giving you something for drink,
And a matter of money to put in your poke;
But, as for the guilders, what we spoke
Of them, as you very well know, was in joke.

Beside, our losses have made us thrifty;
A thousand guilders! Come, take fifty!"

The Piper's face fell, and he cried,
"No trifling! I can't wait; beside,
I've promised to visit by dinner-time
Bagdad, and accept the prime
Of the head cook's pottage, all he's rich in,
For having left, in the Caliph's kitchen,
Of a nest of scorpions no survivor, —
With him I proved no bargain driver,
With you, don't think I'll bate a stiver!
And folks who put me in a passion
May find me pipe to another fashion!"
"How?" cried the Mayor, "d'ye think I'll brook
Being worse treated than a cook?
Insulted by a lazy ribald,
With idle pipe and vesture piebald?
You threaten us, fellow? Do your worst:
Blow your pipe there till you burst!"

Once more he stept into the street,
And to his lips again
Laid his long pipe of smooth, straight cane;
And ere he blew three notes (such sweet,
Soft notes as yet musician's cunning
Never gave the enraptured air),
There was a rustling that seemed like a bustling
Of merry crowds justling at pitching and hustling;
Small feet were pattering, wooden shoes clattering,
Little hands clapping, and little tongues chattering,
And, like fowls in a farmyard when barley is scattering,
Out came the children running.
All the little boys and girls,
With rosy cheeks and flaxen curls,

The Pied Piper of Hamelin

And sparkling eyes and teeth like pearls,
Tripping and skipping, ran merrily after
The wonderful music with shouting and laughter.
The Mayor was dumb, and the Council stood
As if they were changed to blocks of wood,
Unable to move a step, or cry
To the children merrily skipping by —
And could only follow with the eye
That joyous crowd at the Piper's back.
But how the Mayor was on the rack,
And the wretched Council's bosoms beat,
As the Piper turned from the High Street
To where the Weser rolled its waters
Right in the way of their sons and daughters!
However, he turned from South to West,
And to Koppelberg Hill his steps addressed
And after him the children pressed.
Great was the joy in every breast:
"He never can cross that mighty top!
He's forced to let the piping drop,
And we shall see our children stop!"
When lo! as they reached the mountain's side,
A wondrous portal opened wide,
As if a cavern was suddenly hollowed;
And the Piper advanced and the children followed;
And when all were in to the very last,
The door in the mountain-side shut fast.
Did I say, all? No! One was lame,
And could not dance the whole of the way;
And in after years, if you would blame
His sadness, he was used to say —
"It's dull in our town since my playmates left;
I can't forget that I'm bereft
Of all the pleasant sights they see,
Which the Piper also promised me:

For he led us, he said, to a joyous land,
Joining the town and just at hand,
Where waters gushed and fruit-trees grew,
And flowers put forth a fairer hue,
And everything was strange and new;
The sparrows were brighter than peacocks here,
And their dogs outran our fallow deer,
And honey bees had lost their stings,
And horses were born with eagles' wings;
And just as I became assured
My lame foot would be speedily cured,
The music stopped, and I stood still,
And found myself outside the Hill,
Left alone against my will,
To go now limping as before,
And never hear of that country more!"

Alas, alas for Hamelin!
   There came into many a burgher's pate
   A text which says that heaven's gate
   Opes to the rich at as easy rate
As the needle's eye takes a camel in!
The Mayor sent East, West, North, and South,
To offer the Piper, by word of mouth,
   Wherever it was men's lot to find him,
Silver and gold to his heart's content,
If he'd only return the way he went,
   And bring the children behind him.
But when they saw 'twas a lost endeavour,
And Piper and dancers were gone for ever,
They made a decree that lawyers never
   Should think their records dated duly
If, after the date of the month and year,
These words did not as well appear,

The Pied Piper of Hamelin

"And so long after what happened here
On the twenty-second of July,
Thirteen hundred and seventy-six."
And the better in memory to fix
The place of the children's last retreat,
They called it, the Pied Piper's Street —
Where any one playing on pipe or tabor,
Was sure for the future to lose his labour.
Nor suffered they hostelry or tavern
To shock with mirth a street so solemn;
But opposite the place of the cavern
They wrote the story on a column,
And on the great church-window painted
The same, to make the world acquainted
How their children were stolen away;
And there it stands to this very day.
And I must not omit to say
That in Transylvania there's a tribe
Of alien people that ascribe
The outlandish ways and dress
On which their neighbours lay such stress,
To their fathers and mothers having risen
Out of some subterraneous prison
Into which they were trepanned
Long time ago in a mighty band
Out of Hamelin town in Brunswick land,
But how or why, they don't understand.

WHAT I HEARD IN THE APPLE BARREL

ROBERT LOUIS STEVENSON

Mutiny on the high seas! Young Jim Hawkins is sailing on board the *Hispaniola* with Squire Trelawney and Doctor Livesey who have chartered the ship under Captain Smollet. They are in search of treasure buried on a desert island by Flint, the notorious pirate. Jim has been made much of by Long John Silver, who, unknown to Jim and the squire and the doctor, is one of the greatest rascals unhanged. Many of the other seamen are also rogues who had sailed with Flint. This story tells how Jim discovers the traitors' plans to take over the *Hispaniola*.

Now, just after sundown, when all my work was over, and I was on my way to my berth, it occurred to me that I should like an apple. I ran on deck. The watch was all forward looking out for the island. The man at the helm was watching the luff on the sail and whistling away gently to himself; and that was the only sound excepting the swish of the sea against the bows and around the sides of the ship.

In I got bodily into the apple barrel and found there was scarce an apple left; but, sitting down there in the dark, what with the sound of the waters and the rocking movement of the ship, I had either fallen asleep or was on the point of doing so, when a heavy man sat down with rather a clash close by. The barrel shook as he leaned his shoulders against it, and I was just about to jump up when the man began to speak. It was Silver's voice, and before I had heard a dozen words, I would not have shown myself for all the world, but lay there, trembling and listening in the extreme of fear and curiosity; for from these dozen words I understood that the lives of all the honest men aboard depended upon me alone.

"No, not I." said Silver. "Flint was cap'n; I was quartermaster, along of my timber leg. The same broadside I lost my leg, old

What I Heard in the Apple Barrel

Pew lost his deadlights. It was a master surgeon, him that ampytated me — out of college and all — Latin by the bucket, and what not; but he was hanged like a dog, and sun-dried like the rest, at Corso Castle. That was Roberts' men, that was, and comed of changing names to their ships — *Royal Fortune* and so on. Now, what a ship was christened, so let her stay, I says. So it was with the *Cassandra*, as brought us all safe home from Malabar, after England took the *Viceroy of the Indies;* so it was with the old *Walrus*, Flint's old ship, as I have seen amuck with the red blood and fit to sink with gold."

"Ah!" cried another voice, that of the youngest hand on board and evidently full of admiration, "he was the flower of the flock, was Flint!"

"Davis was a man, too, by all accounts," said Silver. "I never sailed along of him; first with England, then with Flint — that's my story; and now here on my own account, in a manner of speaking. I laid by nine hundred safe, from England, and two thousand after Flint. That ain't bad for a man before the mast — all safe in bank. 'Tain't earning, now; it's saving does it, you may lay to that. Where's all England's men now? I dunno. Where's Flint? Why, most on 'em aboard here, and glad to get the duff — been begging before that, some on 'em. Old Pew, as had lost his sight and might have thought shame, spends twelve hundred pound in a year, like a lord in Parliament. Where is he now? Well, he's dead now and under hatches; but for two years before that, shiver my timbers! the man was starving. He begged, and he stole, and he cut throats, and starved at that, by the Powers!"

"Well, it ain't much use, after all," said the young seaman.

"'Tain't much use for fools, you may lay to it — that, nor nothing," cried Silver. "But now, you look here; you're young, you are, but you're smart as paint. I see that when I set my eyes on you, and I'll talk to you like a man."

You may imagine how I felt when I heard this abominable old rogue addressing another in the very same words of flattery as he had used to myself. I think, if I had been able, that I would have killed him through the barrel. Meantime, he ran on, little supposing he was overheard.

"Here it is about gentlemen of fortune. They lives rough, and they risk swinging, but they eat and drink like fighting cocks, and when a cruise is done, why, it's hundreds of pounds instead of hundreds of farthings in their pockets. Now, the most goes for rum and a good fling, and to sea again in their shirts. But that's not the course I lay. I puts it all away, some here, some there, and none too much anywheres, by reason of suspicion. I'm fifty, mark you; once back from this cruise, I set up gentleman in earnest. Time enough, too, says you. Ah, but I've lived easy in the meantime; never denied myself o' nothing heart desires, and slep' soft and ate dainty all my days, but when at sea. And how did I begin? Before the mast, like you!"

"Well," said the other, "but all the other money's gone now, ain't it? You daren't show face in Bristol after this."

"Why, where might you suppose it was?" asked Silver derisively.

"At Bristol, in banks and places," answered his companion.

"It were," said the cook; "it were when we weighed anchor. But my old missus has it all by now. And the 'Spyglass' is sold, lease and good will and rigging; and the old girl's off to meet me. I would tell you where, for I trust you; but it 'ud make jealousy among the mates."

"And can you trust your missis?" asked the other.

"Gentlemen of fortune," returned the cook, "usually trusts little among themselves, and right they are, you may lay to it. But I have a way with me, I have. When a mate brings a slip on his cable — one as knows me, I mean — it won't be in the same world with old John. There was some that was feared of Pew, and some that was feared of Flint; but Flint his own self was feared of me. Feared he was, and proud. They was the roughest crew afloat, was Flint's; the devil himself would have

What I Heard in the Apple Barrel

been feared to go to sea with them. Well, now, I tell you, I'm not a boasting man, and you seen yourself how easy I keep company; but when I was quartermaster, *lambs* wasn't the word for Flint's old buccaneers. Ah, you may be sure of yourself in old John's ship."

"Well, I tell you now," replied the lad, "I didn't half a quarter like the job till I had this talk with you, John; but there's my hand on it now."

"And a brave lad you were, and smart, too," answered Silver, shaking hands so heartily that all the barrel shook, "and a finer figurehead for a gentleman of fortune I never clapped my eyes on."

By this time I had begun to understand the meaning of their terms. By a "gentleman of fortune" they plainly meant neither more nor less than a common pirate, and the little scene that I had overheard the last act in the corruption of one of the honest hands — perhaps of the last one left aboard. But on this point I was soon to be relieved, for Silver giving a little whistle, a third man strolled up and sat down by the party.

"Dick's square," said Silver.

"Oh, I know'd Dick was square," returned the voice of the coxswain, Israel Hands. "He's no fool, is Dick." And he turned his quid and spat. "But, look here," he went on, "here's what I want to know, Barbecue: how long are we a-going to stand off and on like a blessed bumboat? I've had a'most enough o' Cap'n Smollet; he's hazed me long enough, by thunder! I want to go into that cabin, I do. I want their pickles and wines, and that."

"Israel," said Silver, "your head ain't much account, nor ever was. But you're able to hear, I reckon; leastaways, your ears is big enough. Now, here's what I say; you'll berth forward, and you'll live hard, and you'll speak soft, and you'll keep sober, till I give the word; and you may lay to that, my son."

"Well, I don't say no, do I?" growled the coxswain. "What I say is, when? That's what I say."

"When! by the Powers!" cried Silver. "Well, now, if you

want to know, I'll tell you when. The last moment I can manage; and that's when. Here's a first-rate seaman, Cap'n Smollett, sails the blessed ship for us. Here's this squire and doctor with a map and such — I don't know where it is, do I? No more do you, says you. Well, then, I mean this squire and doctor shall find the stuff, and help us to get it aboard, by the Powers. Then we'll see. If I was sure of you all, sons of double Dutchmen, I'd have Cap'n Smollett navigate us halfway back again before I struck."

"Why, we're all seamen aboard here, I should think," said the lad Dick.

"We're all foc's'le hands, you mean," snapped Silver. "We can steer a course, but who's to set one? That's what all you gentlemen split on, first and last. If I had my way, I'd have Cap'n Smollett work us back into the trades at least; then we'd have no blessed miscalculations and a spoonful of water a day. But I know the sort you are. I'll finish with 'em at the island, as soon's the blunt's on board, and a pity it is. But you're never happy till you're drunk. Split my sides, I've a sick heart to sail with the likes of you!"

"Easy all, Long John," cried Israel. "Who's a-crossin' of you?"

"Why, how many tall ships, think ye, now, have I seen laid aboard? and how many brisk lads drying in the sun at Execution Dock?" cried Silver, "and all for this same hurry and hurry and hurry. You hear me? I seen a thing or two at sea, I have. If you would on'y lay your course, and a p'int to windward, you would ride in carriages, you would. But not you! I know you. You'll have your mouthful of rum to-morrow and go hang."

"Everybody know'd you was a kind of a chapling, John; but there's others as could hand and steer as well as you," said Israel. "They liked a bit o' fun, they did. They wasn't so high and dry, nohow, but took their fling, like jolly companions every one."

"So?" says Silver. "Well, and where are they now? Pew was that sort, and he died a beggarman. Flint was, and he died of rum at Savannah. Ah, they was a sweet crew, they was! on'y, where are they?"

What I Heard in the Apple Barrel

"But," asked Dick, "when do we lay 'em athwart, what are we to do with 'em, anyhow?"

"There's the man for me!" cried the cook admiringly. "That's what I call business. Well, what would you think? Put 'em ashore like maroons? That would have been England's way. Or cut 'em down like that much pork? That would have been Flint's or Billy Bones's."

"Billy was the man for that," said Israel. "'Dead men don't bite,' says he. Well, he's dead now hisself; he knows the long and short on it now; and if ever a rough hand come to port, it was Billy."

"Right you are," said Silver, "rough and ready. But mark you here: I'm an easy man— I'm quite the gentleman, says you; but this time it's serious. Dooty is dooty, mates. I give my vote —death. When I'm in Parlyment and riding in my coach, I don't want none of these sea-lawyers in the cabin a-coming home, unlooked for, like the devil at prayers. Wait is what I say; but when the time comes, why let her rip!"

"John," cries the coxswain, "you're a man!"

"You'll say so, Israel, when you see," said Silver. "Only one thing I claim—I claim Trelawney. I'll wring his calf's head off his body with these hands. Dick!" he added, breaking off, "you just jump up, like a sweet lad, and get me an apple, to wet my pipe like."

You may fancy the terror I was in! I should have leaped out and run for it, if I had found the strength; but my limbs and heart alike misgave me. I heard Dick begin to rise, and then someone seemingly stopped him, and the voice of Hands exclaimed:

"Oh, stow that! Don't you get sucking of that bilge, John. Let's have a go of the rum."

"Dick," said Silver, "I trust you. I've a gauge on the keg, mind. There's the key; you fill a pannikin and bring it up."

Dick was gone but a little while, and during his absence Israel spoke straight on in the cook's ear. It was but a word or two that I could catch, and yet I gathered some important news; for, besides other scraps that tended to the same purpose, this whole clause was audible: "Not another man of them'll jine." Hence there were still faithful men on board.

When Dick returned, one after another of the trio took the pannikin and drank—one "To luck"; another with a "Here's to old Flint"; and Silver himself saying, in a kind of song, "Here's to ourselves, and hold your luff, plenty of prizes and plenty of duff."

Just then a sort of brightness fell upon me in the barrel, and, looking up, I found the moon had risen, and was silvering the mizzentop and shining white on the luff of the foresail; and almost at the same time the voice of the lookout shouted "Land ho!"

THE REVENGE

ALFRED, LORD TENNYSON

1

At Flores in the Azores Sir Richard Grenville lay,
And a pinnace, like a flutter'd bird, came flying from far away:
"Spanish ships of war at sea! we have sighted fifty-three!"
Then sware Lord Thomas Howard: "'Fore God I am no coward;
But I cannot meet them here, for my ships are out of gear,
And the half my men are sick. I must fly, but follow quick.
We are six ships of the line; can we fight with fifty-three?"

2

Then spake Sir Richard Grenville: "I know you are no coward;
You fly them for a moment to fight with them again.
But I've ninety men and more that are lying sick ashore.
I should count myself the coward if I left them, my Lord Howard,
To these Inquisition dogs and the devildoms of Spain."

So Lord Howard passed away with five ships of war that day,
Till he melted like a cloud in the silent summer heaven;
But Sir Richard bore in hand all his sick men from the land
Very carefully and slow,
Men of Bideford in Devon,
And we laid them on the ballast down below;
For we brought them all aboard,
And they blest him in their pain, that they were not left to Spain,
To the thumbscrew and the stake, for the glory of the Lord.

4

He had only a hundred seamen to work the ship and to fight,
And he sailed away from Flores till the Spaniard came in sight,
With his huge sea-castles heaving upon the weather bow.
"Shall we fight or shall we fly?
Good Sir Richard, tell us now,
For to fight is but to die!
There'll be little of us left by the time this sun be set."
And Sir Richard said again: "We be all good English men.
Let us bang these dogs of Seville, the children of the devil,
For I never turn'd my back upon Don or Devil yet."

5

Sir Richard spoke and he laugh'd, and we roar'd a hurrah, and so
The little *Revenge* ran on sheer into the heart of the foe,
With her hundred fighters on deck, and her ninety sick below;
For half of their fleet to the right and half to the left were seen,
And the little *Revenge* ran on thro' the long sea-lane between.

6

Thousands of their soldiers look'd down from their decks and laugh'd,
Thousands of their seamen made mock at the mad little craft
Running on and on, till delay'd

By their mountain-like *San Philip* that, of fifteen hundred tons,
And up-shadowing high above us with her yawning tiers of guns,
Took the breath from our sails, and we stay'd.

7
And while now the great *San Philip* hung above us like a cloud
Whence the thunderbolt will fall
Long and loud,
Four galleons drew away
From the Spanish fleet that day,
And two upon the larboard and two upon the starboard lay,
And the battle-thunder broke from them all.

8
But anon the great *San Philip,* she bethought herself and went,
Having that within her womb that had left her ill content;
And the rest they came aboard us, and they fought us hand
    to hand,
For a dozen times they came with their pikes and musqueteers,
And a dozen times we shook 'em off as a dog that shakes his ears
When he leaps from the water to the land.

9
And the sun went down, and the stars came out far over the
    summer sea,
But never a moment ceased the fight of the one and the
    fifty-three.
Ship after ship, the whole night long, their high-built galleons
    came,
Ship after ship, the whole night long, with her battle-thunder
    and flame;
Ship after ship, the whole night long, drew back with her dead
    and her shame.
For some were sunk and many were shatter'd, and so could
    fight us no more —
God of battles, was ever a battle like this in the world before?

10

For he said "Fight on! fight on!"
Tho' his vessel was all but a wreck;
And it chanced that, when half of the short summer night was gone,
With a grisly wound to be drest he had left the deck,
But a bullet struck him that was dressing it suddenly dead,
And himself he was wounded again in the side and the head,
And he said "Fight on! fight on!"

11

And the night went down, and the sun smiled out far over the summer sea,
And the Spanish fleet with broken sides lay round us all in a ring;
But they dared not touch us again, for they fear'd that we still could sting,
So they watch'd what the end would be.
And we had not fought them in vain,
But in perilous plight were we,
Seeing forty of our poor hundred were slain,
And half of the rest of us maim'd for life
In the crash of the cannonades and the desperate strife;
And the sick men down in the hold were most of them stark and cold,
And the pikes were all broken or bent, and the powder was all of it spent;
And the masts and the rigging were lying over the side;
But Sir Richard cried in his English pride,
"We have fought such a fight for a day and a night
As may never be fought again!
We have won great glory, my men!
And a day less or more
At sea or ashore,
We die — does it matter when?
Sink me the ship, Master Gunner — sink her, split her in twain!

Fall into the hands of God, not into the hands of Spain!"

12

And the gunner said "Ay, ay," but the seamen made reply:
"We have children, we have wives,
And the Lord hath spared our lives.
We will make the Spaniard promise, if we yield, to let us go:
We shall live to fight again and to strike another blow."
And the lion there lay dying, and they yielded to the foe.

13

And the stately Spanish men to their flagship bore him then,
Where they laid him by the mast, old Sir Richard caught at last,
And they praised him to his face with their courtly foreign grace;
But he rose upon their decks, and he cried:
"I have fought for Queen and Faith like a valiant man and true;
I have only done my duty as a man is bound to do:
With a joyful spirit I Sir Richard Grenville die!"
And he fell upon their decks, and he died.

14

And they stared at the dead that had been so valiant and true,
And had holden the power and glory of Spain so cheap
That he dared her with one little ship and his English few;
Was he devil or man? He was devil for aught they knew,
But they sank his body with honour down into the deep,
And they mann'd the *Revenge* with a swarthier alien crew,
And away she sail'd with her loss and long'd for her own;
When a wind from the lands they had ruin'd awoke from sleep,
And the water began to heave and the weather to moan,
And or ever that evening ended a great gale blew,
And a wave like the wave that is raised by an earthquake grew,
Till it smote on their hulls and their sails and their masts and their flags,
And the whole sea plunged and fell on the shot-shatter'd navy of Spain,
And the little *Revenge* herself went down by the island crags
To be lost evermore in the main.

GLOSSARY

A light stroke (´) indicates lightly accented syllables, a heavy stroke (ʹ), strongly accented syllables. Key to pronunciation is as follows: a, pat; ā, hate; ã, hare; ä, car; e, pet; ē, evil; ė, term; i, hit; ī, nice; o, dot; ō, omen; ô, organ; oi, coil; ou, lout; u, hut; ú, put; ü, rule; ū, hue; th, think; ᴛʜ, than; ə represents *a* in abide, *e* in woven, *i* in stencil, *o* in collect, *u* in focus.

A

ab sorp tion (ab sôrpʹ shən or ab zôrpʹ shən) great interest (p. 121)

ac ces si ble (ak sesʹ i bəl) easy to get at (p. 156)

ac claim (ə klāmʹ) welcoming applause (p. 31)

A con ca gua (äʹ kōn käʹ gwə) a mountain in the Andes—the highest mountain in the Western Hemisphere (p. 173)

ac rid (akʹ rid) bitter (p. 418)

a do be (ə dōʹ bi) made of sun-dried mud brick (p. 161)

adzed (adzd) hewn with a tool something like an ax (p. 216)

Af ghans (afʹ ganz) natives of a mountain country N.W. of India (p. 73)

Aire dale (ārʹ dāl) large dog, terrier breed, that has a rough, brown, or tan coat with black markings on it (p. 79)

al ien (ālʹ y ən *or* āʹ li ən) out of place (p. 410)

An de an (an dēʹ ən *or* anʹ di ən) of the Andes Mountains of South America (p. 173)

a non y mous (ə nonʹ i məs) nameless; without anything to identify one (p. 36)

Ant arc ti ca (ant ärkʹ ti kə) continent lying around the South Pole (p. 214)

A pach e é (ə pashʹ i) fierce tribe of Indians once living in the S.W. deserts of U.S.A. (p. 219)

ap pend age (ə penʹ dij) external part of an animal, like arms or legs (p. 34)

ap prais ing ly (ə prāzʹ ing li) as if to set a value upon someone or something (p. 29)

ap pre hen sion (apʹ ri henʹ shən) fear (p. 467)

ar du ous (ärʹ jü əs *or* arʹ dū əs) requiring much effort and energy (p. 87)

ar ro gant (arʹ ə gənt) haughty or overbearing (p. 20)

ar tic u late (är tikʹ ū lit) spoken distinctly (p. 465)

as cribe (əs krībʹ) attribute (p. 445)

as sail ed (ə sāldʹ) attacked (p. 454)

a thwart (ə thwôrtʹ) across (p. 59)

at ta ché (atʹə shāʹ) official on the staff of an embassy (see embassy) (p. 161)

aus tere (ôs tērʹ) harsh, stern (p. 350)

aux il ia ry (ôg zilʹ ya ri) assisting, helping (p. 226)

B

Ba ha mas (bə häʹ məz) group of British islands S.E. of Florida (p. 218)

bank rupt cy (bangkʹ rupt si) condition of no longer being able to pay one's debts (p. 216)

505

barque (bärk) three-masted ship with first two masts square-rigged and last mast fore-and-aft rigged (p. 224)
be reft (bi reft′) deprived (p. 491)
bil let (bil′ it) thick stick of wood (p. 196)
bin na cle (bin′ ə kəl) brass stand containing ship's compass near helm of ship (p. 220)
bi noc u lars (bī nok′ ū lərz) field glasses (p. 60)
bitt (bit) strong post on a ship's deck to which ropes are fastened (p. 401)
bol ster (bōl′ stər) long bed pillow (p. 452)
bo nan za (bō nan′ zə) rich mine of gold (p. 219)
bra ces (brā′ cəz) ropes used to set sails of ships at desired angle (compare to halliards) (p. 214)
brack en (brak′ ən) large ferns (p. 83)
breech - bolt (brēch′ bōlt) part of a breech-loading rifle which is moved back and forth along the rifle to open and close the bore and usually rotated to lock it in position (p. 458)
brig an tine (brig′ ən tēn or brig′ ən tin) two masted ship. The foremast is square-rigged; the mainmast is fore-and-aft rigged (p. 267)
brin dled (brin′ dəld) gray, tan, or tawny with darker stripes and spots (p. 310)
buc ca neer (buk′ ə nēr′) pirate (p. 497)
buck o (buk′ ō) a bullying, domineering fellow (p. 274)
buoy an cy (boi′ ən si) power to keep things afloat (p. 217)

burgh er (bėr′ gər) a citizen (p. 329)
byre (bīr) cow barn (p. 460)

C

Cad bor o saur us (kad′ bor ə sor′ əs) a mythical sea serpent which is supposed to lurk in the waters of B. C. (p. 97)
cal kin (kal′ kin) a sharp-pointed piece of iron or steel, projecting downward on the shoe of a horse, to prevent slipping (p. 458)
can did (kan′ did) frank (p. 192)
can is ter (kan′ is tər) can filled with bullets that is fired from a cannon (p. 204)
cant dogs (kant dôgs *or* dogs) movable iron spikes at the end of cant hook (used to grip and turn over logs) (p. 283)
cap stan (kap′ stən) an upright machine for lifting or pulling. Sailors use a capstan for hoisting the anchor (p. 152)
cas sock (kas′ ək) long black robe worn by priests (p. 115)
Celt (selt or kelt) member of a people to which belong the Highland Scottish, Irish, Welsh, and Bretons (p. 365)
Chan cel lor of the Ex cheq uer (chan′ sə lər of the eks chek′ ər) highest official of the treasury in Great Britain (p. 326)
Chim bo ra zo (chim′ bō rä′ zō) volcano of the Andes Mountains of South America (p. 104)
chim ney (chim′ ni) a wide crack in a cliff. Mountain climbers often scale cliffs by squeezing themselves up chimneys (p. 71)

Chinook   darnel

Chi nook (shi nük′) warm westerly winds which blow from the Rockies into Alberta (p. 99)

ci pher ing (sī′ fər ing) figuring, meaning arithmetic (p. 51)

clam or ous (klam′ ər əs) demanding noisily (p. 31)

col leen (kol′ ēn or ko lēn′) girl (Irish) (p. 193)

col lier ies (kol′ yər iz) coal mines (p. 149)

col umn (kol′ əm) part of a newspaper written by a special writer (p. 17)

come ly (kum′ li) having a pleasant appearance (p. 437)

com pen sa tion (kom′ pən sā′ shən) some other thing that helps to make up for a loss or injury (p. 34)

com pro mise (kom′ prə mīz) to put in danger: put under suspicion (p. 330)

con de scen sion (kon′ di sen′ shən) pleasantness to those in lesser positions (p. 247)

con dor (kon′ dər) large vulture with bare head and neck found on lofty mountains in California and South America (p. 173)

con fla gra tion (kon′ flə grā′ shən) big fire (p. 418)

con ger eel (kong′ gər ēl) large ocean eel (long slippery fish shaped like a snake) caught for food along coasts of Europe (p. 152)

con ser va tion (kon′ sər vā′ shən) saving, protecting from being used up (p. 424)

con stit u ents (kən stit′ ū ənts) voters in a politician's riding (p. 27)

con tem pla tive ly (kən tem′ plə tiv li or kon′ təm pla′ tiv li) thoughtfully (p. 88)

con ten tious (kən ten′ shəs) fond of arguing (p. 220)

con tour lines (kon′ tür līnz) lines on topographical maps joining places which are at an equal height above sea level (see also topographical) (p. 70)

co-op er a tive (kō op′ ər ā tiv) an organization in which the members share the profits and losses (p. 216)

cope (kōp) deal successfully (with) (p. 261)

cor mo rant (kôr′ mə rənt) a very large greedy sea bird that has a pouch under the beak for holding the fish it catches (p. 105)

Cor nish (kôr′ nish) people from Cornwall, a county in south-west England (p. 365)

Co to pax i (kō′ tō pak′ si) volcano in the Andes Mountains of South America (p. 104)

cou gar (kü′ gər) a large brownish yellow American wild cat, a mountain lion (p. 75)

cove (kōv) fellow (slang) (p. 319)

cov e nant (kuv′ ə nənt) solemn agreement between two people (p. 444)

cow ered (kou′ ərd) crouched in fear (p. 75)

cruse (krüz or krüs) jug made of earthenware (p. 452)

cu li nar y (kū′ li när′ i) having to do with food (p. 457)

D

dar nel (där′ nəl) weed with poisonous seeds that looks somewhat like rye (p. 238)

507

deal (dēl) heavy board of pine or fir wood, usually more than 7 inches wide and 6 feet long (p. 268)

def er en tial ly (def′ ər en′ shəl li) respectfully (p. 243)

de mor al iz ing (di mor′ əl īz ing) discouraging, confusing (p. 39)

de plet ed (di plēt′ əd) exhausted, used up (p. 431)

dep re da tion (dep′ ri dā′ shən) inroad (p. 332)

de ride (di rīd′) make fun of; laugh at in scorn (p. 286)

deuce-score (dūs - scor) in tennis, where score is tied at five games each, the set must go on till one player has beaten the other by two games (p. 39)

dis in te grate (dis in′ ti grāt) break up (p. 125)

doc ile (dos′ il *or* dō′ sīl) easily manages (p. 417)

dog ged (dôg′ id or dog′ id) stubborn; persistent (p. 263)

do mes tic i ty (dō′ mes tis′ i ti) tame, or family, life (p. 65)

dry - salt er y (drī′ solt′ ər i) places where foods or hides are treated by salting and drying (p. 488)

E

ea sel (ē′ zəl) stand for holding an artist's drawing board (p. 14)

ec stat i cal ly (ek stat′ i kəl i) with great joy (p. 246)

ee rie (ēr′ i) strange, weird (p. 187)

ei kon (ī′ kon) picture of a holy person in Greek Catholic church (p. 109)

e jac u la tion (i jak′ ū lā′ shən) exclamation (p. 456)

em bas sy (em′ bə si) the office of an ambassador in a foreign land (p. 161)

er rant (er′ ənt) wandering, roving (p. 286)

es tu ar ies (es′ tū ãr′ iz) mouths of rivers made wide by the tides (p. 226)

e vade (ė vād′) avoided by cleverness (p. 83)

ex hi bi tion ist (ek′ si bish′ ən ist) someone who shows off what he ought to keep concealed (p. 33)

ex hil a rat ed (eg zil′ ə rāt əd) high spirited (p. 245)

ex ult ing (eg zult′ ing) rejoicing greatly (p. 362)

ey rie (âr′ i or ī′ ri) nest of bird of prey in a high place (p. 71)

F

fac tion (fak′ shən) a group of people representing one side of a political opinion (p. 30)

fal low deer (fal′ ō dēr) small European deer with a yellowish coat that is spotted with white in summer (p. 492)

fath om (faᴛʜ′ əm) to understand fully (p. 357)

fault zone (fôlt zōn) a part in a vein of rock where a part is broken and pushed up or down (p. 71)

feu de joie (fuh də jwah′) a firing of guns as an expression of joy (p. 337)

fis sure (fish′ ər) a long narrow crack in a rock (p. 72)

flo til la (flō til′ ə) group of small ships or boats sailing together (p. 185)

foaled (fōld) born (p. 238)

for bear (fôr bãr′) hold back (p. 463)

fra ter ni ty (frə tėr′ ni ti) brotherhood (p. 176)
frus trat ing (frus′ trāt ing) defeating (p. 35)
fur tive ly (fėr′ tiv li) stealthily (p. 206)
fu tile ly (fū′ til li) uselessly (p. 73)

G

Gal a te a (gal′ ə tē′ ə) ivory statue made by Pygmalion and given life by Aphrodite (p. 434)
ge o log ic (jē′ ə loj′ ik) concerned with geology, that science which deals with the structure and history of the earth's crust (p. 258)
ge o log i cal sur vey map (jē′ ə loj′ i kəl sėr′ vā map) map showing types of stone and heights of an area (p. 70)
ghast ly (gast′ li *or* gäst′ li) horrible (p. 175)
girth (gėrth) strap that keeps a saddle in place (p. 480)
glum ly (glum′ li) gloomily (p. 21)
glu ti nous (glü′ ti nəs) sticky (p. 486)
grape shot (grāp shot) cluster of small iron balls used as a charge for cannon (p. 204)
greave (grēv) armour for the leg below the knee (p. 440)
griev ous ly (grēv′ əs li) causing great pain (p. 463)
gris ly (griz′ li) frightful (p. 458)
gua no (gwä′ nō) manure of sea birds (p. 120)
Guay a quil (gwī′ ä kēl′) port of E. Ecuador (p. 155)
gue ril las (gə ril′ əz) independent bands of warriors who are not soldiers in uniform (p. 107)

guil der (gil′ dər) silver coin of the Netherlands (p. 486)
guil le mot (gil′ i mot) a narrow-billed diving bird (p. 120)
gump tion (gump′ shən) common sense, good judgment (p. 238)
gut (gut) narrow passage (p. 459)

H

hal liards (hal′ yərdz) ropes used to raise and lower sails on a ship (p. 214)
har assed (har′ əst) worried (p. 20)
haz ard ous (haz′ ər dəs) dangerous (p. 34)
hex ag o nal (heks ag′ ə nəl) six-sided (p. 399)
hu mil i ty (hū mil′ i ti) humbleness of mind (p. 370)

I

i lex (ī′ leks) an evergreen oak of S. Europe with leaves like holly (p. 110)
im plic it (im plis′ it) unquestioning, complete (p. 457)
in ad e quate (in ad′ ə kwit) not good enough (p. 36)
in an i mate (in an′ i mit) lifeless (p. 434)
in cred u lous (in kred′ ū ləs) not believing (p. 40)
in ev i ta bly (in ev′ i tȧ bli) cannot be avoided (p. 225)
in gra ti at ing (in grā′ shi āt ing) in a manner to bring oneself into favour (p. 241)
in iq ui ty (in ik′ wi ti) very great injustice (p. 457)

509

In qui si tion (in′ kwi zish′ ən) court appointed by the Roman Catholic Church to discover and suppress heresy and to punish heretics (p. 500)

in sist ence (in sis′ təns) act of continuing to make a strong, firm statement of a position (p. 234)

in tan gi ble (in tan′ ji bəl) not capable of being touched (p. 260)

in ten sive ly (in ten′ siv li) thoroughly (p. 84)

in ter cept (in′ tər sept′) cut off, obstruct (p. 58)

in tol er a ble (in tol′ ər ə bəl) unbearable (p. 154)

in var i a bly (in vär′ i ə bli) without exception (p. 36)

i ro ny (ī′ rə ni) event contrary to what one would normally expect (p. 37)

J

jave lin (jav′ lin) light spear thrown by hand (p. 437)

jibed (jībd) changed course, as a ship does by shifting its sails (p. 74)

K

Kaf fir (kaf′ ər) South African negro (p. 326)

Kash mir (kash mēr′) a mountain state in northern India (p. 68)

kite (kīt) hawk with long, pointed wings (p. 460)

kraal (kräl) village of South African natives (p. 326)

L

lab y rinth (lab′ i rinth) a maze, or confusing network of passageways (p. 160)

lan yard (lan′ yərd) short rope or cord used on ships to fasten rigging (p. 277)

leav end (lev′ ənd) made with yeast (p. 462)

lee (lē) side of a ship sheltered from the wind (p. 214)

leers (lērs) sly, evil, sidelong glance (p. 310)

li a na (li ä′ nə) tough jungle vines (p. 170)

Lloyd's (loidz) association of insurance men in London, England, which specializes in ship insurance (p. 225)

log ic (loj′ ik) reasoning (p. 370)

loo'ard = leeward (lü′ ərd or lē′ wərd) in the direction toward which the wind is blowing (p. 278)

luff (luf) forward edge of a sail (p. 494)

lure (lūr) a bait, or decoy (p. 70)

lu rid (lū′ rid) sensational or startling (p. 220)

M

Ma dras (mə dras′) seaport of S.E. India (p. 217)

mael strom (māl′ strəm) great or violent whirlpool of water (p. 186)

maimed (māmd) disabled (p. 56)

ma lev o lent (mə lev′ ə lənt) spiteful, wishing evil on others (p. 310)

man i fest (man′ i fest) clear (p. 457)

man za ni ta (man′ zə nē′ tə) a kind of evergreen desert shrub (p. 68)

mar mot (mär′ mət) gnawing animal with a thick body and bushy tail. Woodchucks and prairie dogs are marmots (p. 321)

Mar ti nique (mär′ ti nēk′) French island in West Indies (p. 276)

mas tiff (mas′ tif) large dog with drooping ears and hanging lips (p. 467)

mead (mēd) meadow (p. 432)

met al lur gy (met′ əl ėr′ ji) science of separating metals from their ores, and refining them for use (p. 235)

mis sile (mis′ il) object that is thrown or shot, like an arrow, or bullet (p. 418)

mo men tum (mō men′ təm) force resulting from movement (p. 34)

N

Nas sau (nas′ ô) capital of the Bahamas (p. 218)

Nav i ga tion Acts (nav′ i gā′ shən akts) laws passed by British Parliament in seventeenth and eighteenth centuries. These were designed to keep trade in British ships (p. 215)

non cha lant (non′ shə lənt) cool and unconcerned (p. 170)

O

o bei sance (ō bā′ səns or ō bē′ səns) deep bow of respect (p. 442)

o bese (ō bēs′) extremely fat (p. 485)

ob nox ious (əb nok′ shəs) very disagreeable (p. 456)

off watch (off woch) the part of a ship's crew which is off duty at any given time. Usually a watch spends four hours off duty and four hours on (p. 214)

Ol i vet (ol′ i vet) the Mount of Olives—small ridge of hills to the east of Jerusalem where Jesus talked with His disciples (p. 174)

o ver - com pen sate (ō′vər com′- pən sāt) over-doing things to make up for a weakness one feels (p. 35)

P

pa lo mi no (pa lə mē′ nō) a beautiful silver-and-gold Western show horse (p. 94)

pan ni kin (pan′ i kin) metal cup (p. 499)

Pap pas (pop′ əs) (Greek) priest in Greek Catholic church (p. 109)

par o dy (par′ ə di) humorous imitation (p. 286)

Paw nees (pô nēz′) an American Indian tribe that lived near the forks of the Platte River (p. 227)

pe des tri an ism (pi des′ tri ən izm) walking (p. 34)

pem mi can (pem′ i kən) dried meat pounded into a paste with melted fat (p. 184)

pen i tence (pen′ i təns) sorrow for wrong doing, repentance (p. 85)

pen ny - dread ful (pen′ i - dred′ fəl) a cheap paper or magazine containing stories of wild and improbable adventures (p. 152)

per e grine (per′ i grin) a kind of large falcon (p. 67)

per emp to ry (pər emp′ tə ri) imperious, urgent (p. 196)

Per se us (pėr′ si əs) an ancient Greek hero (p. 112)

pet rel ((pet′ rəl) small black-and-white sea bird with long pointed wings, flies far out to sea and braves the storms (p. 202)

pet rol (pet′ rəl) British name for gasoline (p. 161)

pha lanx (fal′ angks) number of animals or persons, grouped closely so as to protect each other (p. 63)

511

pie bald (pī′ bôld′) spotted in two colours (p. 490)

pike (pīk) spear (p. 502)

pin ions (pin′ yənz) stiff flying feathers on a bird's wings (p. 69)

pin nace (pin′ is) ship's boat (p. 500)

pique (pēk) pommel of the saddle (p. 480)

piqued (pēkt) caused a feeling of wounded pride (p. 252)

plum met (plum′ it) a weight fastened to a line to test plumbness in building (p. 69)

pom pous ly (pom′ pəs li) in a self-important way (p. 38)

Po po ca ta petl (pō pō′ kä tä′ pet əl) volcano in South Mexico near Mexico City. The rhythm of the poem suggests that the poet pronounced the word with the accent on the third syllable (p. 104)

po rous ness (pō′ rəs nis) quality of being full of tiny holes allowing the passage of water (p. 430)

pos tern (pōs′ tərn) gate (p. 480)

Pre fect (prē′ fect) a monitor at a school (p. 363)

pre mon i tory (prē mon′ i tō′ ri) giving warning beforehand (p. 455)

pres tige (pres tēzh′ or pres′ tij) reputation; distinction based on what is known of one's abilities, achievements, etc. (p. 93)

pre text (prē′ tekst) excuse (p. 457)

pri ma don na (prē′ mə don′ ə) a temperamental star in an opera (p. 22)

pri me val (prī mē′ vəl) pertaining to the first ages of the world (p. 310)

pri mor di al (prī môr′ de əl) existing at the very beginning; primitive (p. 258)

pri va teer (prī′ və tēr′) an armed ship given the right in time of war to capture enemy ships for profit (p. 218)

priv i ly (priv′i li) secretly (p. 457)

pros e cu tor (pros′ i kū′ tər) attorney in charge of the government's side of a case against the person who has been accused; prosecuting attorney (p. 353)

pros trate (pros′ trāt) lie down flat (p. 437)

pro to zo a (prō′ tə zō′ ə) a tiny one-celled animal that can be seen through a microscope (p. 50)

psal ter y (sôl′ tər i) ancient musical instrument played by plucking the strings (p. 445)

Psy che (sī′ kè) the human soul or spirit pictured as a beautiful girl with butterfly wings (Greek and Roman Myth) (p. 208)

pun cheon (pun′ chən) large barrel (p. 489)

Pyg ma li on (pig mā′ li ən) a sculptor who fell in love with a statue he had made (p. 434)

Q

quar ry (kwor′ i) animal pursued in a hunt (p. 69)

quay (kē) a solid landing place where ships load and unload (p. 151)

quest ing (kwest′ ing) searching (p. 64)

quid (kwid) one pound, or 20 shillings (slang) (p. 321)

R

ra tion al (rash′ ən əl) sensible (p. 464)

realm (relm) kingdom (p. 175)

rep ar tee (rep′ är tē′) witty replies (p. 38)
re prov ing (ri prüv′ ing) finding fault with, blaming (p. 265)
res o lute (rez′ ə lūt) determined (p. 480)
res o lu tion (rez′ ə lū′ shən) determination (p. 356)
re trib u to ry (ri trib′ u tō′ ri) inflicting punishment in return for a wrong (p. 455)
Rhen ish (ren′ ish) wine from the River Rhine or regions near it (p. 489)
roy al ty (roi′ əl ti) payment for the use of any of various rights (p. 420)
ru di ment (rü′ di mənt) part to be learned first; beginning (p. 181)
rue ful ly (rü′ fəl i) sorrowfully (p. 92)
ruse (rüz) a tricky scheme (p. 40)

S

Sam Browne (sam′ broun′) polished leather belt having a supporting piece passing over the right shoulder, worn by British officers in World World I (p. 264)
sap phire (saf′ īr) a bright-blue precious stone (p. 59)
sar don i cal ly (sär don′ i kəl i) in a bitter, sarcastic manner (p. 206)
scourge (skėrj) to whip; to punish (p. 286)
scru ti nized (skrü′ ti nīzed) examined closely and carefully (p. 358)
sex tant (seks′ tənt) an instrument used by sailors to measure the altitude of the sun, or a star, etc. in order to determine their position (p. 267)

sha green (shə grēn′) a kind of untanned leather with a granular surface, made from the skins of horses, etc. (p. 483)
skep tic (skep′ tik) one who questions or doubts beliefs which other people accept (p. 224)
slav er (slav′ ər) drool, or let saliva run out of mouth (p. 62)
snaf fle (snaf′ əl) a thin, jointed bit on a horse's bridle (p. 459)
sough ing (suf′ ing *or* sou′ ing) rustling (p. 418)
sparse (spärs) thinly scattered (p. 61)
spec u la tive (spek′ ū lā′ tiv) thoughtful (p. 261)
spiel (spēl) speech, talk (slang) (p. 323)
spruce (sprüs) neat or trim (p. 220)
so journ er (sō′ jėrn ər) one who stays for a brief time (p. 209)
so lic i tude (sə lis′ i tūd) anxiety (p. 34)
sti ver (stī′ vər) Dutch coin worth about two cents (p. 490)
sub sid′ ing (səb sīd′ ing) growing less, dying down (p. 250)
suede (swād) a soft leather with a velvety finish (p. 4)
sun ders (sun′ dərs) separates, parts, severs (p. 249)
su per fi cial (sü′ pər fish′ əl or sū′ pər fish′əl) on the surface (p. 76)
sup pli ca ting (sup′ li kā′ ting) begging humbly (p. 463)
swarth y (swôr′ ᴛнi or swôr′thi) having a dark skin (p. 365)

T

tat ter de mal ion (tat′ ər di māl′ yən or tat′ ər di mal′ yən) tattered, ragged (p. 197)

taut (tôt) stretched tight (p. 214)

te nac i ty (ti nas′ i ti) "stick-to-it-iveness" (p. 38)

the o ret i cal ly (thē′ ə ret′ i kəl i) according to thought or fancy rather than to actual practice or fact (p. 80)

thonged (thôngd *or* thongd) fastened with narrow strips of leather (p. 264)

Ti err a del Fu e go (ti er′ə del fū ā′ gō) island off south coast of South America (p. 214)

tim ber - drog er (tim′ br drō′ gėr) a man who drives logs down the river (p. 270)

tim brel (tim′ brəl) a small drum with metal disks (p. 445)

toad ies (tōd′ iz) fawning flatterers (p. 204)

top o graph i cal map (top′ə graf′ i kəl map) a kind of map showing in detail the surface features of a region (see also *contour lines*) (p. 70)

trav erse (trav′ ərs) crosswise (p. 448)

trib u la tion (trib′ ū lā′ shən) great trouble (p. 453)

trib une (trib′ ūn) defender of the people (p. 202)

tro phy (trō′ fi) a prize for victory, such as a silver cup (p. 12)

tur bine (tėr′ bin *or* tėr′ bīn) an engine or motor in which a wheel with vanes is made to revolve by force of water, steam or air (p. 417)

tur quoise (tėr′ koiz *or* tėr′ kwoiz) greenish-blue precious stone (p. 461)

twain (twān) two (p. 461)

U

u nan i mous ly (ū nan′ i məs li) without a single opposing vote (p. 31)

un - cowed (un′ koud) unafraid, not frightened (p. 56)

un dis cord ant (un′ dis kôr′ dənt) in harmony (p. 176)

u ni ped (ū′ ni ped) one-legged creature (p. 34)

V

Val pa rai so (val′ pə rī′ zō) seaport of Chile on Pacific (p. 217)

vig il (vij′ əl) anxious watching (p. 35)

vig i lance (vij′ iləns) watchfulness (p. 65)

W

wan ton (won′ tən) playful, unrestrained (p. 58)

whim si cal (hwim′ zi kəl) having many odd or capricious notions or fancies; fanciful (p. 91)

wind lass (wind′ ləs) machine for pulling and lifting things, turned by a crank (p. 272)

wind row (wind′ rō′) row of piled up ice (p. 393)

withe (wiᴛH) tough willow twig (p. 44)

ACKNOWLEDGMENTS

ACKNOWLEDGMENTS

Grateful acknowledgment is made to the following publishers and authors for permission to use copyright material.

George Allen & Unwin Ltd. — "The Child is Father to the Man" from *Memoirs of Childhood and Youth* by Albert Schweitzer; "Balsa for Kon-Tiki" from *The Kon-Tiki Expedition* by Thor Heyerdahl.

Appleton-Century-Crofts, Inc. — "How Abe Lincoln Paid for His Stockings" from *The Graysons* by Edward Eggleston; "The Flower-Fed Buffaloes" from *Going to the Stars* by Vachel Lindsay. Copyright, 1926.

James Sterling Ayars and *Classmate* — "Grain Elevators".

Louise Baker and McGraw-Hill Book Company, Inc. — "Out on a Limb", from *Out on a Limb*, copyright, 1946.

Rannie B. Baker and Row, Peterson & Company — "Pygmalion and Galatea" from *In the Light of Myth*, Copyright, 1925.

Leslie Gordon Barnard and *This Week Magazine* — "Four Men and a Box".

A. C. Benson and John Lane, The Bodley Head Limited — "The Hawk".

Nathaniel A. Benson — "The Patriot". Permission must be obtained from the author or from The Copp Clark Co. Limited, for performances where admission is charged.

Arthur S. Bourinot — "Train at Night" from *Collected Poems of Arthur S. Bourinot*.

Brandt & Brandt — "Nancy Hanks" by Rosemary Benét from *A Book of Americans*, published by Rinehart and Company, Inc. Copyright, 1933.

Leonard W. Brockington — "Sir William Osler".

Winston S. Churchill and Odhams Press Ltd. — "Escape" from *My Early Life*. Copyright, 1930.

The Clarendon Press, Oxford — "I love all beauteous things" by Robert Bridges from the *Shorter Poems of Robert Bridges*.

Mary Elizabeth Colman — "The Machine", first published in the *Canadian Poetry Magazine*.

Constable & Company Limited — "To Iron-Founders and Others" by Gordon Bottomley.

Willis G. Craig — "Black Pirate of the Peaks", reprinted from *The Open Road for Boys*.

Grace Noll Crowell — "The Palomino".

Mrs. W. H. Davies and Jonathan Cape Limited — "Leisure" from *The Collected Poems of W. H. Davies*.

Walter de la Mare and Messrs. Faber & Faber — "Nicholas Nye", "The Listeners".

Mazo de la Roche — "Tiny Tim".

J. M. Dent & Sons (Canada) Limited, Toronto and Vancouver — "The Donkey" by G. K. Chesterton.

Dorrance & Company, Inc., Philadelphia — "Forest Fire" from *Blue Hills* by Edna Davis Romig.

Doubleday & Company, Inc. — "The Tom-Cat" from *Awakening and Other Poems*, by Don Marquis; "O Captain! My Captain!" from *Leaves of Grass* by Walt Whitman; "Out of Bounds" from *Windy Island* by Theodore Acland Harper. Copyright, 1931.

His Royal Highness, The Duke of Edinburgh — "Canadian Achievement".

Blair Fraser — "The Taming of No. 3" from *Maclean's Magazine*, November 1, 1948.

Elsie Park Gowan and the Canadian Broadcasting Corporation — "The Hunting Trail of the Great Spirit".

Roderick Haig-Brown and *Maclean's Magazine* — "Ghost Cat".

Walter Havighurst — 'The Long Tradition".

Henry Holt and Company, Inc. — "The Death of the Hired Man" from *The Complete Poems of Robert Frost*. Copyright, 1930, 1949.

Herbert Jenkins Ltd. — "The Homecoming of the Sheep" from *The Complete Poems of Francis Ledwidge*.

Thelma Knoles and *The American Girl* — "Double Play". Reprinted by permission of *The American Girl*, a magazine for all girls published by the Girl Scouts of the U. S. A.

Alfred A. Knopf Inc. — "The Blue Flower" by Josephine Blackstock from *Youth Replies, I Can*: Stories of Resistance, edited by May Lamberton Becker.

Longmans, Green & Company — "Canadian Winter and Spring" from *The Unkown Country* by Bruce Hutchison; and "He Was Seldom Surprised by His Horses" from *Father on the Farm* by Kenneth C. Cragg.

The Macmillan Company of Canada, Limited — "The Shark" from *The Collected Poems of E. J. Pratt*; Mrs. Bambridge, The Macmillan Company of Canada, Limited, and A. P. Watt & Son for "The Ballad of East and West" from *Barrack Room Ballads* by Rudyard Kipling, and "The Children's Song" from *Puck of Pook's Hill* by Rudyard Kipling.

The Macmillan Company (New York) and the authors — "The Axe Has Cut the Forest Down" from *Away Goes Sally* by Elizabeth Coatsworth; and "On Strike" from *How Green Was My Valley* by Richard Llewellyn. Copyright, 1940.

Macmillan & Co. Ltd. and the authors — "The Ice-Cart" by Wilfred Gibson, and "Stupidity Street" by Ralph Hodgson.

McClelland and Stewart Ltd. — "At the Cedars" and "Off Rivière du Loup" by Duncan Campbell Scott; "The Sinking of the *Mariposa Belle*" from *Sunshine Sketches of a Little Town* by Stephen Leacock; "Dream River" by Marjorie L. C. Pickthall; "A Petticoat for Linda" from *Tambour and Other Stories* by Thomas Raddall.

Thoreau MacDonald — "Maple Bloom" by J. E. H. MacDonald.

Harold Matson — "Kid Brother" by Norman Katkov, first published in the *Saturday Evening Post*. Copyright, 1951 by the Curtis Publishing Company.

The Musson Book Company Ltd., Toronto — "White Water" from *Lake of Gold* by John Buchan.

Alfred Noyes, Messrs. Blackwood & Sons Ltd., and A. P. Watt & Son — "Old Grey Squirrel" from the *Collected Poems of Alfred Noyes*.

Oxford University Press and A. T. A. Dobson — "The Song of the Sea Wind" from *The Poetical Works of Austin Dobson*.

Remington Putnam Book Company, Baltimore — "A Little Song of Life" by Lizette Woodworth Reese.

The Ryerson Press — "Lucille" from *The Complete Poems of Robert W. Service*; "Lone Wolf" from *Kings in Exile* by Sir Charles G. D. Roberts; "A Thunderstorm" and "Heat" from *The Selected Poems of Archibald Lampman*.

The Family of Frederick George Scott — "The Unnamed Lake" by Frederick George Scott.

Charles Scribner's Sons — "Mending the Clock" by Sir James Matthew Barrie.

Sidgwick and Jackson Limited — "Romance" by W. J. Turner.

Sir John C. Squire — "To a Bull-Dog".

Edna Staebler — "Duellists of the Deep" from *Maclean's Magazine*, July 15, 1948.

Mrs. James Stephens and Macmillan & Co. Ltd. — "The Snare" by James Stephens, from the *Collected Poems* of James Stephens.

Jesse Stuart — "Split Cherry Tree", first published in *Esquire*.

Miss Mona Swann — "Saul and David". Permission to perform this play must be secured in advance from Messrs. Samuel French (Canada) Ltd., 480 University Avenue, Toronto. Rate for amateurs $10.00 per performance.

Willis Kingsley Wing — "The Green Key to Sun Power" by George H. Waltz, Jr. Copyright, 1948 by the author; published in *Maclean's Magazine*, February 1, 1948.

Kerry Wood and The Copp Clark Co. Limited — "Runaway Bull" from *Cowboy Yarns for Young Folk*. Copyright, 1951.

Young America Magazines — "Rabble Rouser" by Rolland Upland.

It will be noticed that numerous copyright selections are contained in this text. Care has been exercised to locate ownership of copyright material. The publishers will be glad to receive information that will enable them to rectify any reference or credit in subsequent editions.